The Police Manager

The Police Manager
Seventh Edition

Egan K. Green

Ronald G. Lynch

Scott R. Lynch

ELSEVIER

AMSTERDAM • BOSTON • HEIDELBERG • LONDON
NEW YORK • OXFORD • PARIS • SAN DIEGO
SAN FRANCISCO • SINGAPORE • SYDNEY • TOKYO
Anderson Publishing is an imprint of Elsevier

Acquiring Editor: Pamela Chester
Development Editor: Ellen Boyne
Project Manager: A. B. McGee
Designer: Kristen Davis

Anderson Publishing is an imprint of Elsevier
225 Wyman Street, Waltham, MA 02451, USA

Library of Congress Control Number: 2012943711

British Library Cataloguing-in-Publication Data
A catalogue record for this book is available from the British Library.

ISBN: 978-1-4557-3047-6

For information on all Anderson publications visit our website at http://store.elsevier.com

Printed in the United States of America
12 13 14 15 16   10 9 8 7 6 5 4 3 2 1

Dedication

This book is dedicated to my parents, Daisy and Lewis,
who saw potential where others saw detachment.

Contents

Part 1   Introductory Concepts of Police Management

Part 2   Behavioral Aspects of Police Management

Part 4   Modern Police Management: Major Issues

Online Instructor and Student Resources

Thank you for selecting Anderson Publishing's *The Police Manager*. To complement the learning experience, we have provided a number of online tools to accompany this edition. Two distinct packages of interactive resources are available: one for instructors and one for students.

Please consult your local sales representative with any additional questions. You may also e-mail the Academic Sales Team at textbook@elsevier.com.

1   For the Instructor

1.1   Qualified adopters and instructors can access valuable material for free by registering at: http://textbooks.elsevier.com/web/manuals. aspx?isbn= 9781455730476

- **Test Bank** Compose, customize, and deliver exams using an online assessment package in a free Windows-based authoring tool that makes it easy to build tests using the unique multiple choice and true or false questions created for *The Police Manager*. What's more, this authoring tool allows you to export customized exams directly to Blackboard, WebCT, eCollege, Angel, and other leading systems. Test bank files are also offered in Word format.
- **PowerPoint Lecture Slides** Reinforce key topics with focused PowerPoints, which provide a perfect visual outline with which to augment your lecture. Each individual book chapter has its own dedicated slide show.
- **Lesson Plans** Design your course around customized lesson plans. Each individual lesson plan acts as a separate syllabus containing content synopses, key terms, and more open-ended critical thinking questions designed to spur class discussion. These lesson plans also delineate and connect chapter-based learning objectives to specific teaching resources, making it easy to catalogue the resources at your disposal.

2   For the Student

2.1   Students can access all the resources below by simply following this link: http://www.elsevierdirect.com/companion.jsp? ISBN=9781455730476

- **Self-Assessment Question Bank** Enhance review and study sessions with the help of this online self-quizzing asset. Each question is presented in an interactive format that allows for immediate feedback.

- **Case Studies** Apply what is on the page to the world beyond with the help of topic-specific case studies, each designed to turn theory into practice and followed by interactive scenario-based questions that allow for immediate feedback.

Preface

I considered it quite an honor to build on the fine text that Ronald Lynch and Scott Lynch had put together in previous editions of *The Police Manager*. The baseline material for guiding police managers was so comprehensive and well explained that I tried to keep the core of this book intact. I have streamlined and combined some of the material to even chapter lengths to a degree, with the hope that this will assist classroom instructors. I have also incorporated pedagogical materials that should prove helpful for instructors to use to stimulate class discussions. For example, several chapters now have learning exercise scenarios that can activate student thought processes about the specific circumstances and conundrums that police managers often face. Furthermore, case studies and "Evolving Role of Technology" boxes have been added to many chapters to highlight technological advances that should prove helpful for police managers. Hopefully, these additions to the work that Ronald Lynch and Scott Lynch have already written in previous editions of this book will help up-and-coming police managers carry out their responsibilities. This book is not a complete source of information on the subject of police management, but reading it along with the other excellent books on this topic can help make a manager more effective, efficient, and productive.

It is quite possible that there is too much material for an instructor to complete in a regular semester or quarter. However, I hope instructors will find that the material is structured in a way that they can select specific chapters that may be helpful for their particular classes. For example, instructors in rural areas may be inclined to exclude some chapters in an effort to ensure that they cover Chapter 20: *Leading Small and Medium-Sized Law Enforcement Agencies*. This book is structured in such a way to let the instructor use his or her discretion in determining the most appropriate material to cover.

Any projects this big require thanks to a multitude of people. Special gratitude goes to contributors to previous editions of this book:

S.B. Billbrough, Regional Director, DEA—Retired (deceased)
George Murphy, Mobil Corp.—Retired, New York
John Vermilye, Former Director, Department of Public Safety, Lakewood, Colorado (deceased)
Mike Swanson, Institute of Government, University of Georgia
Dick McMahon of the Institute of Government, University of North Carolina
G. Patrick Gallagher, Director of the Institute for Liability Management, Vienna, Virginia
Dr. James P. Morgan

Chief Jay Leffert
Chief Larry Hesser, Chief of Police, Georgetown, Texas
Colonel Ed Werder, Chief of Police, Cooper City, Florida
Dr. Robert Lacey, Director, Criminal Justice Institute, Broward County, Florida—Retired
Sheriff Kevin Beary of Orange County

I owe a debt of gratitude to Officer Jason Arant of the Martin Police Department in Martin, Tennessee, and Chief Don Goodman of the Radford Police Department in Radford, Virginia. Their assistance and expertise on the material was helpful for the revisions to this edition. I also owe Mickey Braswell another thanks.

Egan K. Green

Introductory Concepts of Police Management

For new or veteran police managers, understanding the basic ideals and tenets of management styles can serve to improve relations between police agencies and their communities, as well as police managers and their subordinates, and make the managers' tasks easier. Part One of this book provides a historical overview of management and provides examples of issues that lay the groundwork for understanding approaches to management and supervisory positions.

Chapter 1 provides a history of management research and implemented ideas. Much of this background literature comes from industry instead of public service, but the lessons this research provides about the nature of interactions between supervisors and subordinates, as well as the interactions between fellow subordinates, can be applied to law enforcement management. Understanding the balance between productivity and subordinate considerations should help all police managers.

Chapter 2 explores the motivations that police officers have to become police managers, including a discussion of the potential drawbacks that officers should consider. It also explains the relationships between philosophy, values, beliefs, principles, and behavior. Understanding these concepts should prove beneficial to police managers in their daily work routines. Because they will affect an entire police department, the policies and procedures as well as the outcomes of the concepts are also discussed.

Because a great deal of a law enforcement agency's internal interaction, and its interactions with the public, are the result of the department's culture, Chapter 3 discusses the role of culture. This can be helpful to police managers who wish to change a culture that has developed in a department. It can also be helpful for understanding how departmental policies can impact the culture within a police agency. Wilson's groundbreaking research on policing styles is used as an example of how officer discretion is influenced by a police department's culture and how the agency head influences that culture.

Part One of this book should provide a solid foundation of background material for understanding the more specific aspects of police management that are covered throughout the text. The chapters provide examples and learning exercises that should help the potential or current police manager be better prepared for the challenges of supervising criminal justice personnel.

1

A History and Philosophy of Police Management

LEARNING OBJECTIVES

1. The student will gain knowledge of the background and principles that make up today's police management.
2. The student will become aware of the integration of technical, behavioral, and functional factors with the purpose of achieving stated objectives.
3. The student will learn the four levels of organization and why they must work together toward stated objectives in order to justify the trust and respect of the community's citizens.
4. The student will recognize his or her role in achieving goals of the organization through the most effective and efficient use of assigned resources—people, money, time, and equipment.
5. The student will become familiar with the three philosophies of management and how they are employed by police managers today.

Are the problems that confront **police managers** on a day-to-day basis very different from the problems that confront managers in industry and government? Are they different from those occurring in schools, hospitals, or churches? If we examine materials geared specifically toward industry or government, the answer is a resounding *no*. The problems facing police managers are similar to those that concern business executives, social leaders, and university personnel. The purpose of the organization may differ greatly from agency to agency, but the management process is quite similar.

What, then, distinguishes the successful and effective police organization from one that is poorly run and under constant pressure due to its ineffectiveness? What is it that causes one police department to be exciting, interesting, and challenging, whereas another is dull, suffers from high turnover rates, and is losing its battle against crime?

The major difference between the effective and the ineffective can usually be traced to the management of the organization and, more specifically, to a difference in the **philosophies of management**. The differences can be seen in the organizational structure and in the amount of decision-making power granted to captains, lieutenants, and sergeants. The difference is clearly reflected in the attitudes and managerial philosophies of top management personnel.

The Police Manager's Role

What do police managers do? They listen, talk, read, write, confer, think, and decide—about people, money, materials, methods, and facilities—in order to plan, organize, direct, coordinate, and control their research service, production, public relations, employee relations, and all other activities so that they may more effectively serve the citizens to whom they are responsible. Police managers, therefore, must be skilled in listening, talking, reading, writing, conferring, thinking, and deciding. They must know how to use their personnel, money, materials, and facilities so as to reach whatever stated objectives are important to their organizations.

A study conducted by Harvard Business School identifies three elements common to all successful managers in government and industry: (1) the will to power, (2) the will to manage, and (3) empathy.

This study defines the **will to power** as the manager's ability to deal in a competitive environment in an honest and ethical manner and, once this power is obtained, to use it to accomplish the goals of the organization. The **will to manage** is described as the pleasure the manager receives in seeing these objectives accomplished by the people within the organization. It is important to note that the third quality, **empathy**, does not stress the manager's technical ability, but rather the ability to relate to other people and determine how they can best be helped to develop their full potential.

The police manager's responsibility is to unify his or her organization. There are commonly four levels to an organization: (1) the **system**—the total organization and its environment; (2) the **subsystem**—the major divisions or bureaus; (3) the **event**—a series of individual activities of similar type (normally a patrol watch or detective unit); and (4) the **element**—the incidents from which service to the community is measured. These four levels of the police department should coordinate in order for the police to reach stated objectives and justify the trust and respect placed in their hands by the citizens of their community.

Many police departments today have more than these four levels of organization. As a result, there is often an overlap of the different levels, and lines of authority and responsibility become unclear. A common problem might exist where a division is commanded by a captain, who is assisted by a lieutenant. The assistant chief in the organization might not be clear on his or her specific role within the division and might make decisions that actually belong to the captain and the lieutenant. As a result of this interference, the lieutenant might begin to make decisions that belong to the sergeant. The sergeant, in turn, might make line operation decisions that should be made by the police officer. The result is that very little decision making is left to the individual police officer at the element, or bottom, level of the department. (See Figure 1-1.)

Community-oriented policing (COP) helps to maintain a balance among the four major levels within the police department. In agencies in which COP has been successful, usually the only ranks required at the working level are the police officer, the investigator, or the special police officer, all of whom are members of the element level of the department. In a typical COP scenario, at the first-line supervisory level, the sergeant is designated as the individual responsible for coordinating the team's activities. She is a **first-line supervisor**, making decisions at the event level, but assisting at the element level. At the subsystem or team level, the lieutenant is designated as the commander. He

Level	Organizational Unit	Primary Responsibility
System	Department	Chief, Assistant Chiefs
Subsystem	Bureau or Division	Majors, Captains
Event	Division, Section, Watch	Captain, Lieutenant
Element	Squad	Lieutenant, Sergeant, Police Officer

FIGURE 1-1 Organizational levels.

is responsible for individual team achievements, but leaves the choice of method to the sergeants and officers involved. At the system level is the chief of police and a key assistant, who is called the captain or assistant chief.

Police departments are beginning to reorganize with a stronger emphasis on the reduction of levels between the top of the department (the chief of police) and the bottom of the department (the police officer). The typical pyramid hierarchy that has been prevalent in the past is slowly beginning to flatten, and this trend seems likely to continue in the immediate future.

COMMUNITY POLICING

Policing was very different in the 1960s than in modern times. Police had become socially isolated from the communities they were protecting. Technological advances like the automobile and the radio had assisted law enforcement in many ways, but had taken their toll by weakening police relations with citizens. As a result of these technological advances, community members rarely interacted with the police in any way other than calls for service. As these problems became more evident, police managers saw the need to return their focus to the community.

Variations of community policing vary widely by jurisdictions. Some agencies reinstituted foot patrol where it was feasible, while other agencies have made simple changes such as having their officers' name tags include first and last names. Yet despite the enormous differences in implementation, the underlying philosophy of community policing remains the same: to ease interaction between the community and the police. Community-oriented policing (COP) is a form of this. Under this program, police alter their organizations so that reducing fear of crime and order-maintenance through citizen cooperation become central goals. Officers and citizens work together through mutually agreed-upon strategies for accomplishing these goals. However, it is vital that all involved personnel understand that the agency's central mission cannot be compromised with this plan.

Typically agencies collect information from a particular community about which criminal-justice−related issues are a concern and they jointly develop strategies for addressing them. Officers will be permanently assigned to that beat to help develop relations with the community members and ease communication about community problems and proposed solutions. Obviously, this gives lots of decision-making power to lower-level officers who are working most closely with citizens. COP programs also give the community the opportunity to evaluate the officers, including managers, who are involved in addressing their needs and hopefully create more community satisfaction.

The Management Process

Effectiveness in reaching the objectives of the organization depends on the management process. That process is composed of three major areas: (1) **technical factors**, (2) **behavioral (psychological) factors**, and (3) **functional factors**.

The technical factors comprise skills that are common to all police agencies. They include the ability to investigate crimes and accidents, as well as to perform preventive patrol and execute other routine procedures. These skills are not a subject of this text.

In any organization, the behavioral factors involve the circular flow of verbal and nonverbal communication that is part of everyday operations. These factors deal with human interaction and are essential skills in a law-enforcement organization.

The functional factors are those involved in producing desired results. They are designed to assist the police manager in controlling the organization. These factors include planning, organizing, decision making, problem solving, and managing by objectives.

The management process is the integration of all these factors, with the purpose of achieving stated objectives. Police managers must utilize both theory and tools so that they may more effectively use the functional factors and behavioral factors in unison with the technical factors, thereby raising the overall level of service provided to the community. (See Figure 1-2.)

Technical Factors	Behavioral Factors	Functional Factors
Investigation	Leadership	Planning
Preventive patrol	Values	Organizing
Fingerprinting	Conflict resolution	Decisionmaking
Calls for service	Change process	Problem solving
Property management	Communication	Managing by
Record keeping		objectives
Personnel allocation		
Traffic control		

Results

FIGURE 1-2 Integration through management.

History of Management

The history of management can be divided into three broad philosophical approaches and overlapping periods:

1. scientific management (1900–1940)
2. human relations management (1930–1970)
3. systems management (1965–present)

The scientific management theory dominated the period from the beginning of the twentieth century to about 1940. Frederick Taylor, the "father of scientific management," emphasized time and motion studies. His study (1911) of determining how pig iron should be lifted and carried is one of the classics of the scientific management approach. His recommendations for faster and better methods of production, in this case in the shoveling of pig iron, stress the importance of efficiency of operation through a high degree of specialization. The "best method" for each job was determined, and the employees were expected to conform to the recommended procedures. Employees were seen as economic tools. They were expected to behave rationally and held to be motivated by the wish to satisfy basic needs.

Taylor theorized that any organization could best accomplish its assigned tasks through definite work assignments, standardized rules and regulations, clear-cut authority relationships, close supervision, and strict controls. Emphasis was placed entirely on the formal administrative structure, and such terms as *authority, chain of command, span of control,* and *division of labor* were generated during this time.

In 1935, Luther Gulick formulated the now famous **POSDCORB**. This acronym—*p*lanning, *o*rganizing, *s*taffing, *d*irecting, *co*ordinating, *r*eporting, and *b*udgeting—has been emphasized in police management for many years.

Gulick emphasized the technical and engineering side of management, virtually disregarding the human side. Any changes in management during this period were designed to improve efficiency; little or no thought was given to the effect that the change process would have on the officer.

The major criticisms of the scientific management theory as it relates to law enforcement are:

1. Officers were considered to be passive instruments; their personal feelings were completely disregarded. Any differences, especially with regard to motivation, were ignored. All employees were basically treated alike.
2. The employee was considered to be an "economic man" who could be motivated through wage-incentive plans or through the fear of job loss.
3. The focus was on technical efficiency and not on the effectiveness of the organization.
4. The efficiency of operation was to be obtained only through:
   a. the division of labor—breaking down the police task into its smallest components.
   b. the specialization of police activities, resulting in vertical and horizontal groupings that were each headed by a single supervisor.
   c. the orderly arrangement of administrative units into a simple but rigid structure of line and staff departments.
   d. the use of a small span of control whereby the managers supervised only a few subordinates.

Beginning in 1930, the negative features of the scientific approach began to outweigh many of the established principles and practices. Strong criticism was brought against the failure of police management personnel to recognize the necessity for instilling dignity and pride in their employees. The impetus for the human relations management approach came from studies conducted by Harvard scholar Elton Mayo in the Hawthorne plant of the Western Electric Company (1933). The studies were initially designed to improve the existing physical facilities that affected work output. These studies focused on finding ways to bring about changes in production by changing working conditions, such as the number of hours, the number of breaks per day, and the physical environment.

One of the first studies involved the effect of lighting on the output of each worker. A research group and a control group were established, with the research group being introduced to varying levels of light. It was first believed that the stronger the light, the greater would be the output of the employee. As the researchers increased the light intensity, output did go up. However, as they lowered the intensity of light below the original base level, output continued to rise. It was this startling fact that led the researchers to more carefully examine the causes for the increased output.

The researchers then began initiating smaller research groups, and they worked very closely with the employees in revamping working hours, rest periods, and complaint procedures. They invited creative comments on the part of employees. The researchers soon realized that the organization had more than just the formal organizational structure. The **informal organizational structure**—consisting of the rumor process, cliques, and informal status systems—was soon recognized as being an important factor in the increase or decrease of productivity. The individual employees involved in the study began to feel a sense of belonging and felt that they were being treated as more than just tools to be used in the completion of a task.

In the 1940s and 1950s, police departments began to recognize the strong effect of the informal structure on the organization. Police agencies began to use such techniques as job enlargement and job enrichment at all levels to generate a greater interest in law enforcement as a profession.

Police departments began to realize that the classical concepts of the formal structure, with strong separation of staff and line operations, were not adequately meeting the goals of law enforcement. The trend began to change, allowing staff personnel to have direct authority over some line functions, and community relations units were created within the administrative function of the department.

The communication process within police agencies became a major problem for the police manager. The span of control originally established as an aid to effective police operations soon became a large problem. Levels that developed within the organization thwarted effective communication between the police manager at the top of the organization and the police officer at the bottom.

During this period, industry recognized the difficulties created by the scientific management approach and began to deemphasize the tall organizational structure. Sears Roebuck, for example, developed the **flat organizational structure**, which provided for fewer levels of supervision. This type of structure required delegation of responsibilities and emphasized careful selection, training, and placement of new employees.

During the 1950s, the management structure began to shift toward the more democratic or **participatory management** that is familiar in law enforcement today. Studies indicated that the supervisor who was "employee-centered" was usually more effective than the one who was "production-centered." The behavioral sciences became a source of information for police managers.

The human relations management approach also had its limitations. With the emphasis placed on the employee, the role of the organizational structure and its importance became secondary. The primary goal seemed to be social rewards, and little attention was given to the necessity for completion of tasks. Many police managers saw this structure as unrealistic. Douglas McGregor pointed out in his studies that the "soft" approach to management led, in many instances, to an abdication of management authority. Employees began to expect more and give less in return.

Management professionals in all fields of government and industry soon recognized the need for developing a third management approach that would encompass the positive features of both the scientific management and human relations structures.

In the mid-1960s, the features of the human relations and scientific management approaches were brought together in the **systems management** approach. This approach fused the individual and the organization; it was designed to help managers use their employees in the most effective way, while reaching desired production goals.

The systems management approach emphasized the organization as a unit, rather than concentrating on one element, such as employees or organizational structure. The importance of the elements within any organization was not minimized, but the total system came to be seen in terms of definitive levels such as system, subsystem, event, and element.

The systems management approach recognized that: (1) it was still necessary to have some hierarchical arrangement to bring about cooperation and coordination; (2) authority and responsibility were essential; and (3) overall organization was required. This approach went still further by recognizing that an organization can reach its stated objectives and goals only through the interrelationship of its parts. In 1950, Abraham Maslow developed his *hierarchy of needs,* in which he classified the needs of people at different levels. Studies by Frederick Herzberg reinforced Maslow's theories concerning the motivation practices that produce the most effective results in any organization.

Further studies by Douglas McGregor in the 1950s stressed the general theory of human motivation as developed by Maslow (1954). McGregor (1960) developed a set of assumptions about human behavior in which he showed how the scientific management approach was based on a specific set of assumptions, which he labeled *Theory X.* McGregor's *Theory Y,* on the other hand, comprised the assumptions of the systems management approach.

In 1964, R.R. Blake and J.S. Mouton emphasized two universal ingredients or concerns that each manager must have. They defined these as the *concern for production* and the *concern for people,* using these as the basis for their *managerial grid.* They identified, for example, the manager who was heavily production-oriented and minimally people-oriented as a "9, 1 manager." The reverse, the manager who had low concern for production and a very high concern for people was a "1, 9 manager." As the theories developed by McGregor, Blake and Mouton, and others are carefully examined, it becomes obvious that under the systems management approach, the concern for reaching objectives and performing assigned tasks requires more than an emphasis on control or autocratic behavior patterns. The police manager, in order to be effective, must have a sense of interdependence with others and the ability to recognize and deal with conflict and change.

The police manager must develop meaningful tools and methods to implement the latest theoretical approaches to the field of management. Tools are designed to assist the police manager to be effective and efficient in performing daily tasks. This means that the manager must possess more than simple knowledge of technical management skills. The ability to handle people is also a necessary part of the manager's day-to-day operation. Stated simply, it is the police manager's role to achieve the goals of the organization through the most effective and efficient use of the available resources—people, money, time, and equipment. The goals of the organization can only be reached through team cooperation, not by an individual. Police managers can best obtain these organizational goals through the police officers who work with them on a day-to-day basis.

How procedures will change course in the future is hard to predict. One direction, however, seems fairly obvious. Law enforcement personnel of both lower and upper levels will be more qualified to do their respective jobs in the future, and they will be increasingly rewarded for their abilities and production. These rewards will come not only in the form of pay increases and the upgrading of fringe benefits, but also by virtue of the manner in which the agency itself is run. The people within the agency will have an opportunity to develop pride, to increase their skills, and to feel that they are achieving success while working for a specific police department within the police profession as a whole.

WHY IT'S IMPORTANT

New managers in many fields sometimes struggle with how to assert their authority. Some think that it's enough to just be in charge and that subordinates must willingly fall in line with the new supervisor's wishes/orders. When subordinates are unresponsive to their new manager, the reaction may be to force action with threat of reprimand or even dismissal. However, it is important for managers to understand that there is often more to the issue than he or she is seeing. Treating a subordinate as nothing more than an employee who should follow orders ignores the human side of that officer. As Chapter 1 demonstrates, the scientific management theory worked under these assumptions and created many of these problems.

Understanding the different management philosophies may help a manager to understand which philosophical model is most useful for supervising officers. Subordinate officers may have excellent ideas for addressing a community crime issue and might wish for the opportunity to have their voices heard. For example, if a community is suffering from a series of vandalisms, a new manager may mandate more patrols in the areas that are most often victimized, whereas the officers who have been working the beat for a while may feel they can more effectively address the problem by spending their time questioning some informants they have known. They may even have a suspect who is often unsupervised in the evenings because his only parent is working. These officers may have ideas about directing the youth toward more constructive activities that might keep him from becoming an adult criminal. If these ideas are dismissed because a new manager simply wants someone caught and arrested, the youth may suffer a completely different fate than if the officers had been allowed to intervene. Additionally, the subordinate officers might resent this outcome. Therefore, the systems management approach may be more beneficial for all the involved parties. It can be beneficial for police managers to understand the different management philosophies, including their benefits and drawbacks.

References

Blake, R. R., & Mouton, J. S. (1964). *The Managerial Grid*. Houston, TX: Gulf Publishing Company.

Maslow, A. H. (1954). *Motivation and Personality*. New York: Harper & Row, Publishers.

Mayo, E. (1933). *The Human Problems of an Industrial Civilization*. New York: The Macmillan Company.

McGregor, D. (1960). *The Human Side of Enterprise*. New York: McGraw-Hill Book Company.

Taylor, F. W. (1911). *The Principles of Scientific Management*. New York: Harper and Brothers.

Discussion Questions

1. In reference to the police manager's role, which is the most difficult for him or her to develop: the will to power, the will to manage, or empathy?
2. Among the four levels of an organization (system, subsystem, event, element), where, in your opinion, are most operational decisions made by police commanders in the average police agency?
3. In team policing, what is an effective method of bringing together the four major levels within a police department?
4. How does one go about developing technical, behavioral, and functional skills?
5. Where do most police departments seem to be in terms of philosophy—scientific management approach, human relations management approach, or systems management approach?
6. What do you think it will take to be an effective police officer and police manager in the future? What factors do you think might influence future police management philosophies?

From Philosophy to Outcomes

LEARNING OBJECTIVES

1. The student will become familiar with the experiences of a chief of police.
2. The student will understand some of the stress placed upon the chief of police.
3. The student will understand the terms *philosophy, value, belief*, and *principle.*
4. The student will identify his or her important values and beliefs that relate to the role of a police manager.
5. The student will understand the relationship of principles to behavior to outcomes.

Introduction

This chapter deals with translating intentions into success. It begins with a discussion of the motivations for becoming a police manager. It then presents a simple model in which the police manager's philosophy—his or her values and beliefs—can be expressed in stated principles that guide behavior through decisions, routine activities, standards, policies, and procedures. Figure 2-1 shows a diagram of the model, the components of which are discussed in turn.

Motivation

James P. Morgan suggests that the things that motivate those who aspire to achieve high management levels, up to and including the top position in a law enforcement agency, can be grouped under two general headings: personal and professional (see the box titled "Motivators for Going to the 'Top of the Hill'").

MOTIVATORS FOR GOING TO THE "TOP OF THE HILL"

PERSONAL MOTIVATORS

Salaries for the heads of law enforcement agencies are affected by the size of the community and, to a degree, by its affluence; the salary of the previous chief; the salaries of neighboring chiefs; and "market" conditions. Money, however, should not be the primary motivator behind a person's drive to become a high-ranking law enforcement official. If so, one might not be prepared to admit that money is not everything. One chief was approached and asked to apply for a particular chief's vacancy. His answer was "You could not pay me enough to take that job." Such an answer, however, could only be voiced by those who have experienced life at the "top of the hill."

For example, say that the job and the money are right and you decide to go for the brass ring. Do you realize that you are entering a position that offers less stability and protection than that enjoyed by the rank and file?

As a patrol officer, there is the union to defend you if you are under administrative attack. Become a chief and you are on your own, and subject to attack by politicians, the press, and the public. Speak out to explain your side of the story, and at best you will be labeled "too defensive," and at worst "insubordinate." This can be very taxing mentally because you are ultimately responsible for the actions of subordinates (defended by their unions) and have to answer for hiring them in the first place, their training, and their supervision. In addition to personnel problems, you are, of course, responsible for all rules, policies, and procedures. There even appear to be no statutes of limitation when it involves your responsibility for the actions of subordinates.

Physical protection for street officers has improved significantly in the past decade, and for that we often say "thank God." As lifetime members of the International Association of Chiefs of Police (IACP), chiefs receive complimentary issues of *Police Chief* magazine. An advertisement in the magazine once began with: "Dress for Stress." It was a company advertising its line of personal protection gear, saying that it can "help you withstand the stress and strain of whatever is thrown at you." The ad was talking about helmets, body armor, and protective shields that protect one physically. If, unfortunately, the protection breaks down, there is always workers' compensation for line-of-duty injuries. But what about the line-of-duty hazards faced by a top-level law enforcement official? In most cases, top-level officials are not in the line of deadly force or dangerous projectiles. They are, however, subject to mental stress and strain for which there is no protective gear.

Chiefs are aware of what individuals in general, and police officials in particular, can do to relieve the effects of the arrows shot by the **three Ps**—politicians, the public, and the press. However, when everything fails, what recourse does the chief have? Workers' compensation? Disability? Not a chance.

Some chiefs experience a breakdown as a result of the stress and strain of the job. They can be a lawsuit waiting to happen if rehired by another agency. When inquiring as to their rights as sworn officers to disability pension because of being unable to perform their duties, they would not be eligible for consideration, because there was no specific incident such as being shot or being in a car accident. Even documentation of cumulative incidents could not be entertained on their behalf.

Police officers under the same pension plan, if injured to the point where they could no longer perform their duties, would receive at least three-quarters of their salary. When viewed in this light, the high salaries received by top officials in reality become quite unattractive.

PROFESSIONAL MOTIVATORS

While attending professional conferences and interacting with peers in "corridor conferences," it becomes quite clear, even though "off the record," that top law enforcement officials often do not have the power of persuasion or the courage of their convictions. If you want to keep your job, be a good manager, but forget about being a strong leader. Mind you, it is not all bad to learn how to negotiate, especially on budget matters. Although it is acceptable behavior to compromise one's convictions, one should not compromise one's integrity. The thin line between the two becomes blurry at times and requires constant refocusing. Going to automatic weapons might have to be postponed because a council member likes revolvers. The real reason for your concession, however, was to obtain council acceptance of take-home patrol cars. The problem arises when the city manager or mayor asks you to overlook specific criminal activity in the community in return for getting the council member to drop his or her objection to automatic weapons—that is unacceptable.

The bottom line is that the top person in a law enforcement agency really does not have the power to make all the changes he or she feels are necessary.

Is it a big deal to be invited to a prestigious community event? What do you do if someone insults you or, even worse, your spouse? The top law enforcement official becomes a target and must expect the worst with no opportunity for recourse. When a patrol officer is at a gathering, if the same thing takes place, he or she could respond with a verbal "equalizer" or, in a serious case, an arrest. When was the last time a chief of police arrested a loud and disorderly drunken citizen?

The more professional a chief is as a result of education and training, the more frustration this lack of control of the agency can cause, and the more intense the mental strain. This frustration reaches beyond the bounds of the individual agency and is intensified by issues such as the "confusion" surrounding the evaluation of many national programs aimed at criminal justice programs in general.

Lawrence W. Sherman (1997) reported that some popular crime prevention programs had been evaluated and found to be ineffective by the Law Enforcement Assistance Administration (LEAA), yet their funding continued. Sherman and others bring this type of information to the table of public opinion, thus raising interest and concern.

Philosophy

When a person's ambition and career goals cause him or her to decide that pursuing a police manager's position is worth the challenges and difficulties, the person can then focus on how this ambition translates into **management philosophy**. A philosophy may be defined as the sum total of a person's values, beliefs, and principles. Values are a person's assumptions about ends worth striving for, whereas beliefs are a person's assumptions about what is true. Values and beliefs together can be developed into principles that can serve as standards or guidelines for how those in the police department should behave.

Values

Values are defined as the assumptions about ends worth striving to obtain. Values combined with beliefs can be developed into principles that can serve as standards for others concerning what is important in individual police agencies.

We can speak of three types of values—intrinsic values, extrinsic values, and values that are relevant to how the police department should operate. **Intrinsic values** are those

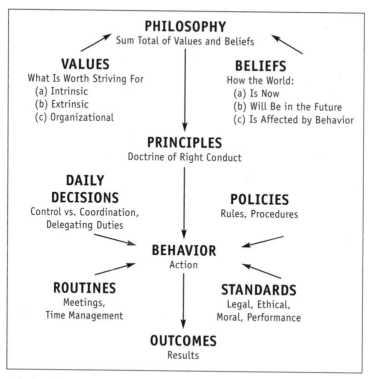

FIGURE 2-1 Philosophy to outcomes.

that guide an individual's actions, such as honesty, commitment, dedication, and sensitivity to others. **Extrinsic values** are the values pertaining to what the individual seeks to achieve for himself or herself. For example, a person's motivations in his or her career and personal life may be related to values such as commitment to family, need for financial security, and desire for recognition. Figure 2-2 gives examples of intrinsic and extrinsic values.

Values influence police departments in two ways—first, through the values of the individuals, and second, through the values adopted by the department. A leader's personal values may influence the actions of all people in the department, because a person's values will be inferred from his or her actions. For example, a police manager who is courteous to everyone demonstrates that he or she sincerely respects all people. Those serving under this manager will see that they, too, are expected to show courtesy and regard for everyone. On the other hand, a chief who treats employees with less than full respect, or one who makes unkind remarks about individuals or groups, implicitly gives license to those serving under him or her to also use such behavior.

The success of a police department depends in part on the nature of the values that the department adopts, either formally or informally. Successful police departments are

Intrinsic	Extrinsic
Honesty	Comfortable retirement
Loyalty	Exciting life
Commitment	Sense of accomplishment
Sensitivity	World at peace
Trust	Financial security
Creative	Success
Loving	Recognition
Forgiving	Self-respect
Patience	Freedom
Cheerful	Friendship
Ambitious	Wisdom

FIGURE 2-2 Values.

usually values-driven. Examples of values that may be formally adopted in the policy manual include:

Honesty—truthful, sincere, forthright, straightforward
Integrity—principled, courageous, honorable
Commitment—reliable, law-abiding, involved
Justice—equitable, open-minded, admits errors, tolerant
Sensitivity—caring, kind, compassionate, helping, sharing
Excellence—maintains high degree of competence, informed, prepared, industrious
Accountable—accepts responsibility for actions, leads by example, safeguards reputation of department and profession

A police agency may value openness or detailed reports or sharp dress. These values are often rooted in tradition and may or may not be found in policies or procedures. They are usually emphasized in training programs and in the personal instruction of field training officers.

Beliefs

Whereas values are assumptions about ends worth striving for, **beliefs** are assumptions about what is true, or opinions formed from observation and experience. Values tend to be fundamental and unchanging, whereas beliefs change, depending on facts, circumstances, and situations.

There are three different types of beliefs that concern us here. First, there are beliefs regarding the world as it exists. For example, the police manager may believe, based on observation and experience, that the department's employees are competent, dedicated, and honest. The second type of belief includes beliefs about the future (e.g., the next three to five years). For example, the manager may believe that, given the fiscal problems the city government faces, the department will have to meet increased demands without being able to hire additional personnel. The third kind of belief is called **management belief**. These beliefs include the belief that if people are involved in the decision-making process, they will have a greater commitment to implementing decisions.

The policy manual of the North Carolina State Bureau of Investigation (SBI) provides examples of the beliefs adopted by one law enforcement agency:

We believe that:

1. Bureau employees are committed to making the world a better place to live and to pursuing excellence in all they do, unselfishly serving the public.
2. Employees develop a commitment to excellence when they participate in decisions about the management of their areas of responsibility.
3. The best way to provide efficient and effective service to the citizens of North Carolina is to hire talented people and then give them the opportunities for training and education they need to develop their talents and initiative to the fullest.
4. In fostering an environment that promotes creativity and encourages possibility thinking throughout the Bureau that employees are effective. We plan Bureau work to be satisfying, productive, and challenging, and encourage intelligent risk-taking without fear of failure.
5. Victims of crime and their families need special consideration after experiencing the trauma of losing a loved one, suffering a violation of their personal rights, or losing property.
6. The Bureau is responsible for treating victims of crime and their families in a manner that assures their dignity, self-esteem, and constitutional rights.

Executives of the SBI, in making their decisions or evaluating those made by subordinates, compare the decisions against the criteria of the stated values and beliefs. As a result, major decisions made at the executive level consistently reflect the values and beliefs of the SBI and the principles developed from them.

Principles

A **principle** is a rule or code of conduct that policies, decisions, practices, and procedures should follow. Principles are developed by combining values and beliefs. Police department principles must be stated clearly so that the behavior of all people in the department can be consistent with them. If the chief wants to build a cohesive, consistent, and committed police department, he or she must ensure that everyone understands the principles that should guide behavior.

Principles are best stated in a policy manual. It can be helpful to divide the principles into categories. For example, principles dealing with leadership might state that: (1) we shall advise personnel what is expected of them, or (2) we shall share expectations—our expectations of ourselves and expectations of others.

A few general principles are better than a long list of detailed principles because people can more easily understand and adhere to a few. The development of many principles may create conflict between principles or uncertain definitions as to how one principle might fit with the others.

The North Carolina State Bureau of Investigation (1992) has developed principles derived from its values and beliefs:

We shall:

1. Do everything within our power and authority to prevent criminal behavior.
2. Promote an open and trusting flow of information within our organization.
3. Make decisions consistent with legal and ethical standards to guarantee justice for all.
4. Protect the constitutional rights of all persons.
5. Treat all persons with dignity, respect, courtesy, and compassion.
6. Always tell the truth.
7. Neither shirk from our assigned power nor use such power for personal gain.
8. Hold all persons accountable for the reasonable consequences of their behavior.
9. Sustain an organizational climate in which our people can succeed.

Examples of the relationship of principles developed from beliefs are shown in Figure 2-3.

Behavior

It is insufficient for a police manager to state the principles that follow from his or her values and beliefs. If they are to be successfully translated into results, principles must be reflected in actions and behavior, above all in the actions and behavior of the chief. Here we discuss four examples of how values, beliefs, and principles can be reflected in actions and behavior: daily decision making, routine activities, standards, and policies and procedures.

Daily Decisions

The police leader's values and beliefs—and his or her commitment to the organization's values, beliefs, and principles—will be evaluated according to how he or she makes decisions. Do the daily decisions reflect a commitment to openness and trust, or do they reflect a desire to keep control tightly in the police leader's own hands? Does the leader demonstrate a commitment to the principle that personnel will operate as team members by insisting that decisions are made only after consultation with everyone involved? Does the manager truly believe that people are competent, allowing them to act on their own judgment, or does the manager insist that every action be approved by a supervisor? If new weapons are to be selected, does the chief make the decision alone, or does he or she delegate responsibility to those who will carry and use the weapons? How a manager makes decisions, whether they are major decisions or the many minor decisions that must be made daily, will tell personnel much about the manager's values and beliefs and commitment to the principles that the organization has elected to follow. For example, assume that the police manager wants to examine the issue of shift schedules. If the

Beliefs:

- Valid and relevant information enables people to make free and informed choices, which increases the likelihood that they will be committed to those choices.

- People support what they help to create.

- Taking risks and understanding failure is necessary for originating effectiveness and professional growth.

- We can't change other people's behavior directly; we may change it by changing our behavior in a way that others can respond to.

- All people have values and beliefs; everything they do stems from those values and beliefs. People ultimately infer your values and beliefs through what you do; consistency and congruence between stated values and beliefs and behavior are necessary for effectiveness, because that is one way people judge us.

- Trust is essential to organizational effectiveness; trust results when people make themselves vulnerable and ultimately experience positive consequences from it.

- Discounting our own or others' capabilities leads to the wrong person taking responsibility for actions; in so doing, learning is sacrificed and the effectiveness of the organization is diminished.

Principles—We Shall:

- Share all relevant information.

- Involve people in decisions that affect them.

- Support people in taking risks to achieve desired outcomes.
- Use mistakes to learn, not to burn.
- Take risks to achieve desired outcomes.

- Control our own behavior; manage others.
- Behave in a way that lets others make choices about their behavior.

- We should state our values and beliefs.
- We should behave consistently with our stated values and beliefs.
- We should continually check for consistency/congruence between our stated values and beliefs and our behavior.

- Take personal risks.
- Follow all other principles.

- Value people's capabilities and allow everyone to be acountable for his or her actions.

FIGURE 2-3 From belief to principle. *Adapted from "From belief to principle" by Schwarz, R., McMahon, D., Carlson, P., Jenne, K., & Lynch, R.,1992, Management Group, Institute of Government, University of North Carolina at Chapel Hill.*

manager makes decisions without input or assistance from other personnel, then he or she may appear to mistrust people or to think people in the department do not have adequate decision-making skills. On the other hand, the manager who delegates the decision-making responsibility to a special task force, gives them guidance, and listens to their feedback demonstrates an approach that was formulated from a different set of values and beliefs.

Decisions that emphasize coordination as opposed to control and delegation or centralized decision making give a clear message to all police department personnel that they are competent and trusted—that openness is an important value.

Routine Activities

The police leader will also be judged by how he or she conducts himself or herself in routine activities. When holding or attending meetings, does the chief dominate the meeting or allow others to participate and contribute? Does the chief have an open-door policy—approachable and accessible to everyone—or does he or she stay in the office and summon others as needed? How a chief conducts the daily routine and deals with people on a daily basis tells much about his or her values, beliefs, and commitment to principle.

Think of the police manager who says that it is important to be involved with the community—one who attends community meetings, is open to the press, and joins civic groups. An opposite example is the manager who states that agency personnel should share relevant information but refuses to attend roll call, only shares information with immediate commanders, and rarely answers memos from officers and clerks.

Standards

Standards are criteria imposed by an authority or adopted by consent that serve as the basis for evaluating actions or performance. There are four types of standards that concern us: legal, ethical, moral, and performance.

Legal standards are established by law. Because law enforcement officers are sworn to uphold the law, in an ideal world there would be no need to question the requirement that police departments adhere to legal standards. In practice, of course, whether police officers adhere to legal standards depends on the quality of training, the effectiveness of law enforcement officers, and the application of good judgment and just practices when police officers enforce the law. So, inevitably, how a police department fulfills its responsibility to meet legal standards depends on the values, beliefs, and principles that guide the actions and behavior of individuals.

Ethical standards govern professional conduct. Ethical standards for law enforcement have been developed by the International Association of Chiefs of Police; however, a state or local law enforcement agency may also develop its own ethical standards.

Moral standards pertain to right or wrong behavior as prescribed by the individual. These actions may be generally accepted standards such as "keep your promises," or they may be specific to individuals—whether we should pay for college education of our children or should assist them in paying for their first home. Moral standards in the police department may be whether one should accept the take-home car and, if so, to what extent one would be allowed to conduct personal business in the car, assuming that there are no legal standards (rules and regulations) or ethical standards (agreements made between the police chief and his or her employees). Moral standards in many instances cannot be forced on subordinates by the chief of police. As a result, the chief must guard against attempting to control moral behavior through written policies, but must be able to deal with behavioral standards under a different category such as legal, ethical, or performance standards for the police agency.

Performance standards are used to judge professional behavior. For example, there are standards for filing reports or for testifying in court, and most police departments have a set of performance standards used for recruitment and promotion. These standards are usually found in the procedure manual.

Policies and Procedures

A **policy** is a stated or written guide for action intended to encourage uniform and consistent action. Policies are especially important because they permit the chief to influence the department's direction in many different matters. Except for instances in which, for example, retaining legal standards calls for precise, detailed procedures, procedures can also be used to ensure that day-to-day conduct conforms to the principles adopted by the department.

Policies should reflect the principles adopted by the department. Consider, for example, a principle that "we shall have an open and trusting flow of information." This principle can be directly reflected in policies regarding how information is shared, as when security levels are set for intelligence and internal affairs documents.

An ideal **policy statement** should involve three main features. First, it should state the purpose of the policy. Second, it should establish a general standard of conduct or behavior that can be applied to day-to-day decisions and conduct. Third, it should indicate how, and under what circumstances, discretion is left to the individual.

A procedure prescribes the actions that should be taken in a given situation. While no police department can operate without rules and procedures, police managers must understand that using procedures has both advantages and disadvantages—the key element being flexibility. Whenever exact compliance is required and situations can be foreseen, instruction in standard procedures and regulations saves both time and thought. Lack of flexibility, however, removes the opportunity for individual discretion, initiative, and judgment.

Written policies and procedures should be easily accessible to all. For example, a police department may have one relatively short policy manual, which contains policies covering constitutional rights, personnel resources, fiscal management, training and education, and news media relations. It may then develop several procedure manuals. One manual may cover behavior and administrative practices applicable to all department personnel regardless of their assignment, whereas other manuals may be created for each division of the department containing procedures that apply specifically to those departments (e.g., Division of Criminal Information, Division of Laboratory Services, and the Field Operations Division).

Outcomes

Leading based on a strong philosophy is a complex issue that incorporates numerous values, beliefs, principles, and behavior patterns. The following example is oversimplified and does not capture the different and often conflicting values and beliefs that can guide a chief's behavior. But this example can give some understanding of how the chief's philosophy affects the final **outcome**.

This scenario involves two police chiefs. Chief A says that the values that are important for him are to see to it that people are committed, dedicated, trustworthy, and honest. His belief about the agency is that most of the personnel in this agency do not become involved in the use of drugs. The principle developed might state, "It is my responsibility to see to it that members of this police department are able to work in a drug-free environment."

As a result of this principle, based on values and beliefs, the chief implements this principle through behavior. In speeches praising personnel, the chief emphasizes that he trusts his officers and states how serious the drug problem could be, but that in his police agency there are committed professionals who never become involved in using drugs. In meetings, the chief emphasizes to his key executives that they should spread this message throughout the agency and the community. The chief then develops a written policy that says "Police officers shall be drug tested only if there is some reasonable suspicion that an officer may be using drugs. Such testing shall adhere to legal and ethical standards."

Chief B has the same stated values as Chief A. However, she believes that a few police officers, perhaps only five percent, are using drugs during off-duty time. The chief states the same principle as Chief A: "It is the responsibility of the chief to create and to maintain a drug-free work environment." This chief uses stronger control, seeing to it that personnel do not take excessive leave time. In routine meetings, the chief emphasizes the need for drug testing and sees to it that the department develops appreciation for a drug-free police agency. Again, this police chief, like the first, adheres to the legal, ethical, and moral standards of the agency. This chief, however, develops a different policy, which says "This agency shall have random drug testing of all police officers."

As police officers from each department get together to discuss their respective drug testing policies, an officer from Department A might say that her police chief is easy to work for because the chief trusts the officers. She uses as an example of this trust the policy concerning drug testing only upon reasonable suspicion. A second officer, from Department B, might agree that his chief also trusts officers but obviously not as much as the first chief. The second officer might go on to state that his chief does not praise them enough and, in fact, is somewhat suspicious of the officers in the department because of the random drug testing policy.

The outcomes might also be different. For example, in Department A, because of the emphasis on trust and the beliefs that such trust can and will be practiced in the department, that agency might develop team management practices more easily, may become involved in workgroups and, perhaps, together as a team, may have open communication including exposure and feedback. Members of that agency may be willing to discuss successes and failures.

The outcome in Department B may be one of a conservative approach to management. Department B may require a taller organizational structure, further development between two ranks that work with each other, such as officer to sergeant and sergeant to lieutenant, but not necessarily between all ranks of the agency. The outcome might involve more centralized decision making, slower involvement of personnel, and less respect and commitment to the directions and visions created by Chief B.

As this example shows, there can be numerous outcomes stemming from values, beliefs, principles, and behavior. Some of these outcomes may be planned, but some may be totally unexpected.

Conclusion

Abraham Maslow has told us that we all aspire to self-fulfillment. Because the law enforcement field would seem to allow participants to achieve all the other levels in his hierarchy of needs, only the top level remains to be achieved. Candidates for positions at the "top of the hill" must be aware of the obstacles and frustrations they will face on their way there and when they arrive.

While developing principles, police leaders should obtain input from all department personnel. This can be accomplished through the use of special task forces, through meetings with department personnel, through formal contacts with members of the department, and through daily informal contacts, some of which may carry a greater weight than any of the other aforementioned methods.

The police manager can guarantee success if he or she develops a policy statement that clearly delineates the values and beliefs that are most important. Then employees can have an understanding of the direction being endorsed by the manager. The police manager can establish eight to ten principles that can guide the behavior of all personnel. Each person can then call on the principles to guide his or her growth.

The police manager can use different techniques to implement values, beliefs, and principles. The first is to put them in writing and distribute to all personnel, sworn and nonsworn. The leader then must act consistently with these principles, administering praise for behavior that reflects them and dealing quickly with behavior that is inconsistent.

The leader can take advantage of everyday situations to give guidance and understanding. Reiteration of the principles at roll calls and staff meetings emphasizes their importance. The manner in which the leader spends his or her time also reflects the importance of the principles. By being available and responding in a sincere and honest manner, the police manager will go far to solidify an open flow of information within the police agency.

References

North Carolina State Bureau of Investigation. (1992). *Policy Manual.* Raleigh, NC: North Carolina State Bureau of Investigation.

Schwarz, R., McMahon, D., Carlson, P., Jenne, K., & Lynch, R. (1992). *From belief to principle (figure).* Chapel Hill, NC: Developed by Management Group, Institute of Government, University of North Carolina at Chapel Hill.

Sherman, L. W. (1997, August 6). Crime prevention's bottom line. *The Wall Street Journal,* p. A15.

Discussion Questions

1. Discuss what you see as the pros and cons of becoming a chief of police.
2. What qualities must a person possess to be an effective chief of police?
3. Identify your intrinsic and extrinsic values.
4. Develop one management belief and one principle consistent with that belief.
5. Develop an effective set of management beliefs and principles for a police department.
6. Select an established police agency policy and procedure manual and define the principle behind the policy.
7. The North Carolina SBI policy manual refers to hiring talented people. How can an agency focus on hiring people with intrinsic values? Is it preferable to try to train those values?

Learning Exercise

Write a policy statement explaining how patrol officers should use their patrol vehicles. Decide whether the vehicles are to be taken home by the officers, whether they may be used for personal use, and whether passengers can be transported in them. Also include any other issues that you think are relevant to the policy. Be sure to include the three features discussed in the chapter.

Here is a list of possible issues to consider while drafting your policy.

- If the patrol car is take-home, can the officer stop at the store on the way home from work?
- Do you require officers to live in the jurisdiction where they work? If not, how do you determine how to pay for the gas for the out-of-jurisdiction driving?
- If cars are not take-home vehicles, where are the cars garaged when the officer is off duty?

3

Organizational Culture

LEARNING OBJECTIVES

1. The student will understand why culture is important in a police department.
2. The student will understand how culture is developed.
3. The student will learn ways to identify the culture of a police department.

Introduction

Culture is a formal force that controls the behavior of department personnel. It is a combination of our assumptions, values, beliefs, traditions, and the role modeling of others we follow. Although the **organizational culture** of the individual police department is rarely, if ever, found in its writings, it is easy to observe from the actions of the department personnel who actually determine what is right or wrong for the individual police department.

There is a strong emphasis on establishing an organizational culture through **role modeling** the behavior patterns of its police executives. For example, the police manager who maintains that honesty is extremely important but will not answer inquiries from subordinates about incidents that may be going on within his or her area of responsibility creates a culture that is inconsistent with the values he or she has stated.

Why Culture Is Important

Police departments react to calls for service. Some are major calls, such as homicides, robberies, or injuries, and some are minor, such as theft of hubcaps, a loud party, or traffic problems in the community. The way in which the individual officer deals with each of these incidents is controlled by his or her perception of the culture of the respective police department.

When there is a conflict between a sergeant and an officer, or between a supervisor and his or her subordinates, they each rely on the culture of the department to make the right decision as to how such a conflict should be resolved. If the organizational culture is that conflict is not confronted directly, then the sergeant or supervisor may back down. However, if the sergeant and supervisor realize that they will be supported in their reasonable decisions, then they may take a completely different course of action in dealing with a conflict between themselves and a subordinate.

Organizational culture can be positive, and it can allow personnel to maintain high ethical standards with the need for only a few specific rules. On the other hand, the

27

culture can be very negative, requiring multiple rules, close supervision, and eventually a police department in which trust is not considered an important part of the culture.

In this context, culture is defined as a set of assumptions that sworn and non-sworn members of a police agency hold in common concerning the way that police department operates.

The culture of the police department shapes how decisions will be made. It limits and encourages certain behaviors, is used as a key to solving difficult problems and, in many ways, is the way in which police leaders shape the meaning of events in order to achieve the police mission and create the vision that they have for their individual police departments.

How Culture Is Developed

The police manager will make a decision based on his or her values, beliefs, and principles. Members of the department—sworn and non-sworn—observe the police manager's actions. They then begin to interpret his or her beliefs, values, and principles. They can either accept or reject the police manager's beliefs, thereby forming a culture for the police department.

Culture can be developed through statements of values, beliefs, and principles. Once these are in writing, actions will be interpreted by personnel within the agency concerning whether the manager acts consistently with the stated values, beliefs, and principles.

When a chief or police manager has an open door, talks to subordinates, and keeps personnel advised of pending actions as well as current activities, he or she becomes more open to the public. If the officers disagree and act inconsistently with that **openness**, yet receive no consequences from the police manager, the manager's beliefs fail to become the agency's culture. If the officers are disciplined, the culture of openness is enforced.

Another force in the development of culture is to reward the openness. Allow officers and personnel within the police department to share the flow of information and they will be honored for their behavior. It is important for the chief and other police managers to understand the values and beliefs so that there can be consistency in implementation of these principles.

Culture is developed from observing the actions of fellow officers in addition to the managers. The role of the training officer and the emphasis of a sergeant at a roll call also tend to develop and strengthen the department's culture.

Which beliefs, values, and principles become part of a culture depends on the perception of the members of the police department, especially the way in which they perceive the chief's response to those values, beliefs, and culture. This is one reason it is very important for police managers to be consistent with their actions and their principles.

The Police Subculture

All occupations develop subcultures. The same is true of hobbyists and even students. When people share similar values, concerns, interests, beliefs, experiences and, in this case, occupations, they form a subculture within society. The police culture is one of these. Each agency develops its own specific culture, but an overview of the police culture may help managers understand their subordinates' concerns. Although managers promoted from within their agencies will likely have an understanding of their department's culture, newly hired managers or newly promoted managers should benefit from a broad view of the culture of American police.

Quite a bit of research has been done on the police culture and a number of consistencies have been found. For example, police tend to share an "**us versus them**" mentality. As Gaines and Kappeler (2011) state, "Police officers tend to see the world as being composed of cops and others. If a person is not a police officer, he or she tends to be considered an outsider who is viewed with some level of suspicion." This mentality may affect the type of interaction that officers have with the public. Furthermore, first-line officers may shift this attitude toward administrators within their own departments if they believe the decision makers are creating policies that do not reflect the realities and dangers of street-level work. This can obviously create tensions between officers and their managers.

Concerns over the dangerous nature of their work also influence police thought and interactions. This ever-present concern helps officers to bond and makes looking out for each other a priority in their work. The police culture therefore encourages loyalty to fellow officers as a priority because it also means assisting fellow officers who may be in danger. This concern over danger also allows officers to observe and note the bravery that their work requires. For example, Herbert (1998) points out that police officers encourage each other to be brave. Those opportunities may occur while they are alone or in assistance of other officers. The front-line officer's ability to cope with danger contributes to his or her acceptance among fellow officers or even training officers. Young police are often excluded from total acceptance among more seasoned officers until they prove their valor in the line of duty. It is vital that police managers recognize this concern among police and make it clear that administrative decisions are not intended to increase the danger that officers face.

While the danger officers deal with in their work bonds them and gives them a sense of **solidarity**, it is important to note that a great deal of research notes the tendency of police officers to associate with other officers when outside of work and associate with civilians with diminishing frequency as time on the force increases (Sherman, 1982; Manning, 2006). This may help create solidarity among the officers, but it may inhibit officers' abilities to distinguish some civilians from the criminals the officers see so often. There are no policies that a police manager can put in place to address this issue, and it should not necessarily be interpreted as a negative tendency. It is simply something a police manager should be aware of, particularly if community concerns about police interaction arise.

Cynicism, or a negative world view, is another common characteristic of the police culture. Furthermore, this attitude increases with time on the force; the longer people work as police officers, the more cynical they tend to become. Given the nature of their work, this is somewhat understandable. On a regular basis they deal with hardened criminals who are often lying to them, causing them to put more effort into figuring out what happened at a crime scene. Because they are constantly filtering conversations for inconsistencies and discovering lies on a regular basis, it is easy for officers to become distrustful of civilians. They also see the worst sides of human personalities on a regular basis. Acts that may shock many civilians are commonplace for officers on the street. As a result, they see the world with a jaded viewpoint on human behavior. Again, there is no policy that an agency can put in place to restrict this naturally occurring attitude. However, being aware of this inclination, police managers can watch for indications that some officers' attitudes are so negative that they may perhaps benefit from alternative assignments for a while to prevent burnout.

The police manager should be aware of these characteristics and use this understanding to guide decision making and interactions with subordinate officers. For example, because research indicates that cynicism and alcohol use among police officers increase with time on the force, a manager should be aware of these tendencies if his or her department is, generally speaking, an older department. Of course, this would not mean that all the officers are too cynical to work well with the public or that they all have drinking problems, but it may be among the things a manager considers when making hiring decisions. Likewise, the manager can benefit from understanding how a departmental culture can influence individual discretionary decisions that officers make.

Policing Styles

Wilson (1968) conducted pioneering work on uniformed police officer discretion, referred to as policing styles. He collected data from a number of communities ranging from very urban areas such as Oakland to smaller cities and suburban areas from the states of New York and Illinois. His work led him to conclude that uniformed patrol officers develop trends in how to use their discretion in responding to potential crimes. He called these trends *policing styles* and he identified three of them: the legalistic style, the service style and the watchman style.

In explaining the **legalistic style**, Wilson (1968, p.188) states:

> *Because the legalistic police style encourages patrolmen to take a law enforcement view of the situations they encounter, it also encourages them to take as their standard of justice one which assumes that the function of the law is to punish, on the basis of individual culpability, those who depart from the behavior required by the law.*

The legalistic-style officers differentiate between very serious and minor offenses, but they still view the law as a clear guide for acceptable behavior. Consequently, they are prone to enforce the law in close accordance with the law. This style obviously requires officers to use very little discretion. By referring to the guidelines provided by the law, the officers can determine how to respond to citizen behavior.

Service style officers approach all calls professionally and seriously; however, they differ from their legalistic counterparts in the way in which they intervene in situations. These officers are less likely to impose official interventions such as arrest. These types of officers are typically found in middle-class communities that have a strong sense of agreed-upon norms. Therefore, the officers will intervene frequently for calls for service, but their intervention does not tend to be formal because the neighborhood characteristics limit or control the behavior to a large degree.

The **watchman style** of policing tends to occur in communities that lack serious criminal events. As a result, these officers mainly act in an order-maintenance capacity. It is true that all officers act in accordance with the watchman-style principles in much of their work; however, the homogenous nature of the communities where this style is most prevalent engrains this style into the patrol officers' regular discretionary use. Furthermore, the watchman mentality extends beyond preferring order over law enforcement duties; it also influences judgment about the seriousness of offenses. How the law judges the seriousness of a potential intervention is less important to these officers than the consequences of the group affected by the offender's behavior.

All these styles are important for police managers to understand because manager preferences influence the use of discretion of first-line officers. Wilson (1968, p.140) states, "What is the defining characteristic of the patrolman's role...becomes the style of strategy of the department as a whole because it is reinforced by the attitudes and policies of the police administrator." Obviously, managers cannot supervise every discretionary situation that their officers handle. However, managers and upper-level administrators can shape the culture of a department based on policies and actions that demonstrate the preferences of the agency's brass. Therefore, a chief who demands that his or her officers provide service to the jurisdiction's citizenry will shape his or her agency's culture toward a service orientation. The orientation can certainly be influenced by community factors such as crime problems and enforcement preferences, but agency priorities communicated to subordinates about how to approach their duties can be transmitted from an agency's command structure. There will still be officers whose personal preferences for legalistic or watchman styles might be displeased by the agency's focus, but some of their discretionary situations will still be influenced the culture created by the chief's preferences.

The same can be said for a department's cultural acceptance of corruption. As is discussed in Chapter 17, an agency that does not send an explicit message throughout its culture that corruption will not be tolerated risks cultural acceptance of unethical activities.

Identifying Your Police Department's Culture

The task of the newly appointed police manager, especially when coming from outside the agency, is to learn, understand, and work with the organizational culture. He or she must also make decisions about which part of the culture, if any, is to be changed.

When the new chief or the new manager comes from within the police department, he or she should be familiar with the organizational culture. However, when being promoted from a mid-manager's position to an **executive position** in the police department, he or she may not be familiar with the values and beliefs of the chief. Only through daily personal contact and conversation about the police organization's culture can the culture be easily identified by the new police manager.

If the manager comes from another state, then his or her responsibility is to learn the culture of the police department, and the culture of the surrounding area. Think about a police chief who might come from another part of the country. Perhaps where he or she came from, the use of guns was something that was frowned on by the community. However, in the new community, there are many hunters and others who strongly believe in the right to legally carry guns. If the chief were to attempt to convince the city council to pass ordinances concerning control of weapons, he or she might be attempting to change the culture of the entire community—which might bring about dismissal.

To identify the culture, the new police manager can play the role of a good investigator. He or she can start with a review of the policies, rules, and procedures, and then use task forces to analyze these procedures to determine whether they are still effective or acceptable. The manager would then examine many of the physical surroundings—for example, the condition of the uniforms, the condition of the rooms in which people work, and the condition of vehicles. He or she can further evaluate the educational level of personnel and can examine the culture of openness by looking at who is authorized to discuss what happens within the police department with the media.

WHY IT'S IMPORTANT

A police manager's influence extends beyond just supervising immediate subordinates. Wilson (1968) noted that street-level patrol officers develop "styles" of policing that greatly influenced their use of discretion. While officers' styles are partly a result of personality, background, and experiences, Wilson noted that officers' judgments about the appropriate manner in which to handle discretionary situations are largely affected by an overarching departmental philosophy. Much of this philosophy is communicated to subordinates through departmental policies. Talarico and Swanson (1978) concluded that departmental strategy guides officers' use of discretion.

If a police chief is not very concerned about casual marijuana users, but is determined to reduce drunk driving in his or her jurisdiction, subordinate officers are likely to reflect these philosophies. The officers are not bound by the chief's wishes. If they find casual marijuana users, they can still enforce those laws. However, departmental points of emphasis encourage officers to reflect their supervisors' views when deciding how to use discretion. A good police manager is able to effectively communicate departmental goals or points of emphasis.

Further examination should include department rituals, such as always saluting a senior officer or special privileges for high-ranking officials. Then the new manager can identify the culture. Probably one of the most effective ways is by socializing in an informal atmosphere with members of the police agency and listening to "**war stories**" concerning past endeavors. These give good clues about the organizational culture of the police department.

There is a series of questions that the new police manager can ask in order to identify the culture. The first issue is reputation. The new police manager can check with sources external to the police department to answer this question. For example, a discussion with local merchants may disclose that the police department is viewed more as a night watch service or a service police organization rather than a crime-fighting department. The **external reputation** of the department can also be examined through prior newspaper articles.

The second issue addressed is **status**, and this is an issue that deals with internal operations of the department. For example, is a detective held in higher esteem than a patrol officer, even though both positions may be of equal rank? Are any special considerations given to age? For example, are the older police officers viewed not only as more experienced, but also as those who can really assist you in finding ways to be effective? Another internal issue might be that although there is no specific rule, emphasis on college-educated officers is shown by the fact that in the last five years, only officers with a college education have been promoted above the rank of sergeant. As a result, the culture of this police agency is such that people joining the department who have not completed a college education strive to achieve this goal, fully recognizing that in a matter of a few years, the agency may only be selecting college graduates for the position of sergeant.

A police manager can then look at the management style of his or her fellow leaders. Does the management style rely on control? Does the department perceive itself as a problem-solving organization? Does it see itself emphasizing coordination activities so that the department's goals are reached, or does it predominantly compromise any issue that may arise? How are decisions reached? Unilaterally? In small teams? Are they reached by delegation alone, or is there very little delegation?

The next area to look at examines the policies of the police department itself. A good examination of the written policies can give the new manager an idea of the department's culture. However, many of the **unwritten policies**, norms, or customs also provide an excellent analysis of the police department's culture. If the police agency does not have anything written concerning a dress code for non-uniformed personnel, but all the investigators and non-sworn personnel you find working the building are wearing jackets and ties or dresses, a dress code is probably being enforced.

There are some questions that, if answered, can help a new police manager identify his or her unit's culture. How are the unit's common areas furnished and decorated? How about the work area's furnishings and decorations? Are only certificates and plaques allowed on the walls, or are employees allowed to hang items of a personal nature? If this police department had a T-shirt, what would the motto be? Are there special interest groups that this agency pays more attention to than others, such as Mothers Against

Drunk Driving, the local news media, or the Chamber of Commerce? During recruit school, what stories about the history of the department are told? Are there mistakes in this department and, if so, are they forgiven or carried forever? Where do people spend their time? If the leaders say that the personnel are extremely important, do they take the time to meet with them at roll call or visit the offices of the non-sworn personnel? Once the police manager has answered these questions, he or she can evaluate whether the values, beliefs, and principles on which these factors depend are consistent with those of the new police manager. Many times the answers to some of these questions bring about what are called the *artifacts*. The artifacts are products of the police department's past and can provide the basis for a quick analysis of what their present culture may hold as the current standard. Discussions about the developed artifacts can determine the strength of parts of the police agency's culture. Such discussions will show the weight between honesty and loyalty.

A strong culture may be a great help to the police manager if he or she agrees with that culture, but it also can be an obstacle to change. The issue that the new manager must resolve is that of effectiveness and being trusted by the personnel of the department.

The police manager will find that there are cultures in other agencies within city government that are different from the police culture. With an issue of conflict, the personnel department may be less prone to deal directly with conflict and the city attorney's office may be prone to compromise, whereas a chief may believe that a conflict should be dealt with directly.

Trying to identify a police department's culture is difficult. The shared beliefs and the organizational values and how they are arrived at by officers sometimes can give different interpretations to the artifacts. Questionnaires are not always valuable, and sometimes listening to espoused values and beliefs can be misleading. The best way to determine the organizational culture is to observe the behavior of the personnel of the department. Consider the police chief whose stated belief is that female officers are just as important to the police department as male officers and should not be treated any differently, but when assignments are observed, female officers are not assigned to some of the more critical areas of investigation or patrol.

Changing the Culture

To change the police department's culture, a police manager must behave consistently with his or her own values and beliefs.

One way to begin to develop a new culture is to change the artifacts, or signs, of the old culture. If the patrol cars are old, purchase new ones; allow for take-home vehicles if possible; and use a different design. If promotions in the past have been based predominantly on seniority, strive for an assessment center approach, thereby creating a more open and trusting promotional system. A new police manager may have to maintain some signs of the old culture, but change the way that they are interpreted. Staff meetings may be important, but the new manager can change those from including only a select few to opening them to more subordinates. Roll calls, though necessary, may now be attended by executives, creating a more open flow of information.

Some of the direct methods that the police manager may use in changing the culture include identifying and discussing the operating beliefs and values of the police agency. The new police manager can then modify, remove, increase, or decrease the strength of these values, or change the priority of such values when necessary.

A police manager can explain to others how to make sense of individual actions and situations. The manager can role-model and explain what he or she is modeling so it is clearly understood. Finally, the manager can make use of situations that arise in day-to-day operations to explain how he or she would deal with similar issues in the future.

There are some indirect methods also. Police managers must allocate their time consistently with what they perceive to be important. They must ask for and share information on things that are important. They should measure and reward what they really believe in and what they really consider to be true values. They must recruit, select, promote, and, when needed, dismiss people based on a set of professional standards: legal, ethical, moral, and performance.

If they have the authority, they can structure the police department in a way that is consistent with their beliefs. For example, a flat organizational structure may emphasize coordination on the role of all executives, whereas a tall organizational structure may emphasize control.

The new police manager must act consistently, especially in moments of truth. For example, when there is pressure from a political body and outside sources to discipline a police officer for alleged misconduct, yet the police manager believes that the officer's conduct was reasonable, this becomes a moment of truth. Does the chief bend to the pressures of city council, the press, and citizens' groups? Or does the chief stand behind the officer, even at the risk of losing his or her position?

An example of changing culture may be how the new police manager deals with the issue of conflict. Before his or her assignment, conflict may have been considered negative and was avoided. The new manager then discusses the reasons he or she believes in the value of openness and believes that conflict brings about growth and does not hamper overall operations. He or she develops a new principle—"we shall face all issues"—and then does not play referee, but allows personnel to resolve their conflicts. Assume that patrol and records have a problem concerning the time limits of information being analyzed and returned to the patrol force. Instead of the new manager ordering a certain solution to the problem, he or she plays the role of facilitator and allows them to join together.

The new police manager, once realizing that this new culture is beginning to develop, could then follow through with a conflict training program and finally issue general policies and procedures that may assist in dealing with conflict throughout the police department.

This appears to be time-consuming and frustrating to many people, and it will be. But in the long run it will be effective. Establishing a new or improved culture takes about

12 to 18 months; however, it will affect the level of behavior of police personnel for many years into the future.

Consider the new chief who takes over a corrupt, closed police department, then opens communication, relies on trust, and prosecutes those who act illegally. After a few years, the department becomes a model and the values of trust, openness, and honesty are practiced long after the chief leaves or retires.

Conclusion

Culture comprises many values, beliefs, and principles. An effective culture that is developed by the police manager will allow that manager to be viewed as a strong leader and successful in almost all facets of his or her behavior.

On the other hand, an ineffective culture will make the police manager appear weak, out of control, unable to communicate, and unable to coordinate activities. Police managers who either instill or retain an ineffective culture will most likely fail.

References

Gaines, L. K., & Kappeler, V. E. (2011). *Policing in America* (7th ed.). Waltham, MA: Elsevier.

Herbert, S. (1998). Police subculture reconsidered. *Criminology, 36*(2), 408–432.

Manning, P. K. (2006). The police: Mandate, strategies and appearances. In V. Kappeler (Ed.), *The police and society: Touchstone readings* (3rd ed.). (pp. 94–122). Prospect Heights, IL: Waveland Press.

Sherman, L. (1982). Learning police ethics. *Criminal Justice Ethics, 1*(1), 10–19.

Talarico, S. M., & Swanson, C. R. (1978). Styles of policing: A preliminary mapping. *Policy Studies Journal, 7*, 398–406, http://dx.doi.org/10.1111/j.1541-0072.1978.tb01784.x.

Wilson, J. Q. (1968). *Varieties of police behavior: The management of law and order in eight communities.* Cambridge, MA: Harvard University Press.

Discussion Questions

1. Visit a local police department and identify five activities that define its culture.
2. What do you believe is your style of policing?
3. Assume you are a new police chief. How would you develop your culture for the police department?
4. List three techniques that you believe would be effective in changing a police agency's culture.

Behavioral Aspects of Police Management

The police manager's role demands knowledge and understanding of the psychological aspects of management—an awareness of the effect that operations have on the people within the police department.

Part Two deals with the organizational environment facing the police manager. A discussion of the various theories about people in organizations, including police departments, is included.

Chapter 4 discusses leadership behavior styles and shows the various styles available to a police manager. This chapter also considers the qualities necessary to be a successful police manager and places strong emphasis on use of the managerial grid. This section provides criteria that may be used in helping police managers decide which style of leadership is best for them within their own environments.

Chapter 5 deals with the skills and techniques needed to develop sergeants. The chapter includes discussions concerning supervisory liability and shows how to implement a system to achieve peak performance. It further discusses the need for a field training program.

Chapter 6 discusses ways to provide for an orderly succession when key people are scheduled for transfer or retirement or because of a death on the staff. It discusses the need for diversity and civilianization of positions. Ways in which to prepare personnel, including mentoring and promotions, are also discussed.

Chapter 7 discusses the principles of motivation by expanding on the earlier discussion of Maslow's hierarchy of needs, and explains Herzberg's motivation-hygiene theory, and the relationship between these two theories and Douglas McGregor's Theory X and Theory Y. This material can help police managers make their subordinates more productive and satisfied.

Chapter 8 deals with the latest techniques available to management concerning the issue of human behavior. The materials on transactional analysis will not only help police managers analyze their personal behavior, but will also give them tools with which to gain insight into the behavior of others. Through the implementation of some of the techniques mentioned in this chapter, police managers will eventually gain a greater insight into themselves and will thus be in a better position to help bring about changes in their departments.

Chapter 9 deals with another human behavior model that can help the police chief to understand department personnel. Such understanding can, of course, allow for smoother operations and easier implementation of policies and goals.

In short, the psychological aspects of management discussed in this section provide a base on which police managers can build specific procedures and techniques to be implemented within their own agencies.

4

Leadership Behavior Styles

LEARNING OBJECTIVES

1. The student will become aware of the numerous styles of leadership.
2. The student will understand how choosing a leadership style will help the police manager become aware of departmental goals and purposes of the organization.
3. The student will understand the principles underlying the "learning" police department.
4. The student will understand the five disciplines that help create an innovative learning agency.

The qualities of leaders and the processes of leadership have long been considered important areas of inquiry. Early speculation about the personality traits and qualities of a successful leader has given way to the study of leadership behavior and analysis of situational factors such as the type of group and the nature of the group's task.

Several scholars have studied leadership behavior and have sought to classify the different approaches to leadership and the different ways of exercising the leadership role. The style of leadership chosen by a manager largely depends on what he or she intends to accomplish.

Police managers must understand that their subordinates will follow their leadership for one or a combination of four reasons:

1. Fear of their authority and the manner in which they control, direct, and plan.
2. Personal liking.
3. Personal respect, based on the manager's actions, values, and consistent manner in dealing with subordinates.
4. Trust, based on the manager's professional competence and proven ability to make decisions and manage conflict and change.

Trust is a result of numerous personal contacts between the manager and the people he or she supervises directly. This kind of leadership is the most lasting and the most effective.

Qualities of a Successful Police Manager

Managers need to exhibit certain qualities in order to be successful, regardless of the management style they use. The following qualities, when exhibited by managers, help the individual to reach success in day-to-day operations.

1. Patience—managers must be calm and steadfast, despite opposition to their beliefs, opinions, and attitudes.

2. Wisdom—managers must have the ability to fairly and equitably judge the behaviors and actions of subordinates.
3. Virtue—managers must show moral excellence, not only speaking it, but also by everyday actions in dealing with departmental problems and personal issues.
4. Empathy—managers must learn to accept and understand the feelings of their subordinates, always being prepared to see others in a positive light.
5. Kindness—managers must try to be kind and gentle in all their dealings with others.
6. Trust—managers must develop confidence in subordinates, not just respecting their position or knowledge, but also allowing them to achieve their personal goals as well as those of the organization.
7. Knowledge—managers must constantly attempt to upgrade their knowledge of technical matters, the management theories being developed and implemented in government and industry, and facts as they occur within their own departments.
8. Self-control—managers must be able to restrain their emotions.

Police managers can develop these qualities by:

1. Showing a high frustration tolerance.
2. Encouraging full participation of subordinates.
3. Emphasizing the subordinate's right to express another point of view.
4. Understanding the rules and acts of ethical competitive warfare.
5. Expressing hostility tactfully.
6. Accepting victory with controlled emotions.
7. Never permitting setbacks to defeat them.
8. Knowing how to "be his or her own boss."
9. Continually seeking success.
10. Being experts in their fields.

Styles of Leadership

Leadership can be defined as the role of the manager in influencing subordinates to work willingly to achieve the stated objectives of the organization. In essence, leadership involves accomplishing stated **departmental objectives** through other people in the department. Therefore, leaders have two major concerns: they must be concerned with *purpose* and they must show *concern for people.*

Many writers have attempted to define styles of leadership. Writers emphasizing the scientific management approach of the 1920s argued that the primary function of the leader was to set up and enforce performance criteria to meet the goals and objectives of the agencies (Taylor, 1911). The manager's main concern was for purpose or production, with very little concern for the needs of the employees within the agency.

With the human relations movement initiated by Elton Mayo (1945), the function of the leader was to focus on the individual needs of employees and not on those of the organization itself.

In essence, the scientific management movement emphasized concern for purpose or task and the human relations movement stressed concern for people. Leaders who were primarily concerned with tasks were said to be "task-oriented" or "authoritarian" leaders, whereas those who emphasized concern for interpersonal relationships were said to be "people-oriented" or "democratic" leaders. The style chosen by the leader depended on the assumptions he or she made concerning the members of the department. The police manager who felt and believed in Theory X's assumptions was predominantly an authoritarian leader. The police manager who believed in Theory Y's assumptions was more democratic. In 1958, Robert Tannenbaum and Warren H. Schmidt suggested that leadership varies along a continuum from boss-centered at one extreme to subordinate-centered at the other (Hersey & Blanchard, 1972). Based on this analysis, they defined four styles of leadership—tell, sell, consult, and join.

Under the ***tell* style of leadership**, the manager makes his or her own decisions and announces them to subordinates, expecting them to be carried out without question. An example of this type of leadership would be a police chief who makes all the decisions in the daily operation of his or her agency—establishing schedules, assigning personnel, giving specific orders on how each crime must be investigated, choosing who should attend what training program. After reaching all these decisions, the chief advises his or her immediate subordinates—the middle managers—who, in turn, advise supervisors, who advise the officers. In essence, there has been no input by any member of the department below the chief's level, and the chief has made his or her decisions based on personal experiences.

The manager who chooses the ***sell* style of leadership** makes all the decisions, but rather than simply announcing them to subordinates, attempts to persuade them to accept the decisions. Recognizing the potential for resistance on the part of subordinates, the manager concentrates on selling them ideas.

Under the ***consult* style of leadership**, the manager does not make any decision until the problem has been presented to members of the group and until he or she has listened to their advice and suggestions. The manager still makes the decision, but not until after consulting with members of the staff.

The manager who uses the ***join* style** delegates the authority for making decisions to subordinates. He or she may reserve the right to be part of the decision-making process, but views his or her primary function as one of helping to define the problem and to indicate the limits within which the decisions must be made. After the problem has been freely discussed by the subordinates, either a consensus or majority opinion will bring forth the final decision. There are three major disadvantages to the *join* type of leadership. First, it is time-consuming; second, it is frustrating; and third, it calls for mature subordinates who have the ability and willingness to arbitrate and arrive at some form of agreement.

Leaders who are at the *tell* end of the continuum are primarily concerned with purpose or task; they attempt to influence subordinates by use of the power delegated to them by the organization. Leaders at the other end of the spectrum are more group-oriented and allow a greater amount of freedom to subordinates in accomplishing their assigned tasks. The *join* type of leader must be aware of the fact that it is easy to carry this type of leadership to the point where decisions are not being reached and the members of the department are not gaining any personal satisfaction. In such instances, people are left to rely on their own initiative, and there is no attempt to influence anyone's behavior. This scenario is not included in the leadership continuum because it is really an absence of leadership as opposed to a leadership style. The police manager must constantly be aware of the decision-making process within the department, and not allow his or her personal behavior to be interpreted as an abdication of leadership.

Another method of viewing leadership is the grid model, originally developed by Robert R. Blake and Jane S. Mouton, which represents a two-dimensional view of management behavior (Blake, Mouton, & Ashe, 1991). In the grid, the emphasis is on the two most basic concerns that any manager is believed to have: (1) the concern for production and (2) the concern for people.

The police manager will adopt a fairly specific set of behavior patterns in dealing with these two major concerns, and these behaviors will be considered a specific style of management most prevalent for the individual manager.

Under the managerial grid, five styles of management are suggested (see Figure 4-1). According to the grid concept, the concern for production and concern for people have been rated on a scale of 0 to 9. The five predominant styles have been identified as 9,1— authority compliance; 1,9—country club; 1,1—impoverished; 5,5—middle of the road; and 9,9—team.

The 9,1 (or **authority compliance**) manager believes that efficiency in operations comes from arranging work conditions in such a way that interference by human elements is minimal.

The 1,9 (or **country club**) manager pays thoughtful attention to the needs of people on the theory that satisfying relationships lead to a comfortable, friendly organizational atmosphere and work tempo.

The 1,1 (or **impoverished**) manager exerts the minimum effort to get the required work done and is concerned with people only to the degree that it sustains organizational membership.

The 5,5 (or **middle-of-the-road**) manager believes that adequate organizational performance is possible through balancing the need to accomplish tasks with main-taining a satisfactory level of morale.

The 9,9 (or **team**) manager believes that work is accomplished through the interde-pendence of people who are committed to organizational purposes. This interdepen-dence leads to relationships of trust and respect.

Police managers of the 9,1 type make decisions and expect these decisions to be treated as final. They stand for ideas, opinions, and attitudes, even though this may sometimes appear offensive to other people. When conflict arises, such managers cut it off or allow it to continue only if they feel they are going to win with their position. When operations within the department become confusing, they defend, resist, and counter-argue any kind of change that may threaten their individual positions. These police managers have a tendency to drive themselves and others, thereby creating stress within themselves and sometimes promoting stress and burnout in others.

Managers of the 9,1 type sometimes seem too strong and tend to overwhelm other people within the police department, especially those who do not have the same level of knowledge. When holding meetings, they may attempt to control by monopolizing the conversation and correcting points made within the meeting that they feel are not correct, no matter how trivial such points might be. In most meetings, 9,1 types attempt to structure things so that only "how?" as opposed to "why?" questions are discussed.

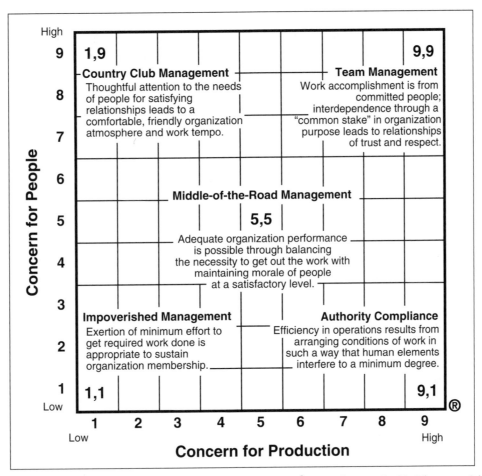

FIGURE 4-1 The Leadership Grid® figure. *Source: The Leadership Grid® Figure from* Leadership Dilemmas—Grid Solutions, *by Robert R. Blake and Anne Adams McCanse (formerly the Managerial Grid Figure by Robert R. Blake and Jane S. Mouton). Houston: Gulf Publishing Company, p. 29. Copyright © 1991, by Scientific Methods, Inc. Reproduced by permission of the owners.*

Managers of the 1,9 type, on the other hand, support decisions that promote good personal relations, embracing the opinions, attitudes, and ideas of others rather than attempting to push their own. They avoid conflict, but when it occurs, they attempt to soothe people's feelings.

Such managers value acceptance and tend to say things they believe others want to hear. They dread the possibility of mentioning information that might be interpreted as negative and are continually striving, in meetings and elsewhere, to please people. The result is that productivity tends to be low or may even come to a halt.

The 1,1 manager is indifferent to others and normally accepts the decisions of both superiors and subordinates. Such managers avoid taking positions and are not likely to reveal their opinions, attitudes, or ideas. They strive for neutrality. Because they remain uninvolved on issues, they rarely show feelings of approval or disapproval and may seem indifferent to the processes within the police department.

In a management sense, such people appear passive. In meetings, they have a tendency to let others lead the conversation. They volunteer little or no information; when asked direct questions, they tend to give short answers and avoid elaborating. In some meetings, they may appear to be bored.

Managers of the 5,5 type search for workable, if not perfect, decisions; they are willing to compromise with people who hold opinions, ideas, and attitudes different from their own. When conflicts arise, they try to negotiate them away.

In meetings, they try to impress others regardless of their status, reputation, or prestige. When they are asked questions, they tend to be tentative; they prefer to avoid giving direct answers until they understand everyone else's position fully. This caution may sometimes look like fear of being wrong, but it is actually a way of testing and probing the positions of others in order to eventually support the majority viewpoint.

A 9,9 manager places a high value on creative decisions that result in understanding and agreement. Such managers listen for and seek out ideas, opinions, and attitudes different from their own. They have strong convictions but are willing to respond to sound ideas and are more than willing to change when such ideas tend to achieve the purpose of the police department and are acceptable to the personnel within the agency. When conflict does arise, the 9,9 manager attempts to identify the reasons for the conflict and seeks to resolve underlying causes, thereby reducing the number of conflicts that may eventually arise within the agency.

In meetings, 9,9 types command the respect of others by their behavior. They seem to enjoy the give-and-take processes within meetings, but are usually geared toward keeping the meeting focused on its original purposes. They listen keenly and are able to distinguish fact from opinion.

In attempting to determine whether his or her management style is affected more by the scores on a managerial grid instrument or those on the Johari window, individual managers place more weight on the grid scores. In reality, subordinates have a tendency to describe the police manager's communication style more accurately; therefore, police managers who are aware of both their managerial grid and Johari scores are more likely to be among those whose style is accurately described by subordinates. This is especially true when the subordinate is at least two levels away from the manager's present position. For example, sergeants identify the styles of captains more quickly and more accurately than they do the styles of higher level managers.

When the managerial and communicative styles are identical, little confusion will arise. However, when managerial style, which might be 9,9, is confused with communication style, which might appear to be closer to 9,1, the manager must be aware of these differences as perceived by subordinates. Only through a more open communication process will subordinates be able to identify both the management and communicative styles accurately. Effective police managers strive for consistency in these areas.

The Learning Police Agency

According to Peter Senge (1990), organizations that place an emphasis on learning are sometimes referred to as **double-loop learning organizations**. Leaders in these organizations demonstrate behaviors of openness, systematic thinking, creativity, self-confidence, and empathy. By contrast, adaptive, or **single-loop learning**, focuses on solving problems in the present without examining how these problems may affect the entire police department or the effect they may have on the future.

Senge believes that there are five specific disciplines that tend to create a police department that will be an innovative learning agency. According to Senge (p.6), "Though developed separately each will, I believe, prove critical to the others' success just as occurs with any ensemble. Each provides a vital dimension in building organizations that can truly learn, that can continually enhance their capacity to realize their highest aspirations." The five disciplines are *systems thinking, personal mastery, mental models, building a shared vision,* and *team learning.*

Systems Thinking

This discipline recognizes that multiple levels of understanding, explanation, and issues develop in any complex situation. For example, **systems thinking** requires a complete look at all four levels as described in Chapter 1. Explanations at the element level explain "who did what to whom" and dooms the individual police leader to a reactive stance. Examination at the event level, which defines a pattern of behavior, focuses more on seeing some longer-term trends and assesses what effect they would have on the police department. This level begins to be responsive to issues that may be more complex. In systems thinking, the question raised is: "What has caused our pattern of behavior?" As a result, a careful analysis is made of the entire issue. An example of this would be: in a training program, the instructor and a member of the class, such as a patrol officer, have a difference of opinion as to whether the training is appropriate for the job to be performed. An examination at that level would solve the conflict between the instructor and the officer. However, examining the pattern of behavior would begin to evaluate whether other officers either act consistently or inconsistently with the teachings. A systemwide approach would examine whether there is a need to provide this training and how much input has been received from the patrol officers, who may be responsible for implementing the ideas that are presented within the program itself.

Personal Mastery

Personal mastery indicates a special level of ability on the part of the leader. This discipline starts with clarifying the issues that really matter to the police department. The police leader becomes interested in joining together personal learning and organizational learning.

Mental Models

Mental models are deeply ingrained assumptions, values, beliefs, generalizations, and images that have an effect on how we understand our responsibilities in the world around us. This discipline starts with being able to first look inward and then examining "pictures" of what the police department is and whether or not they are accurate. Personal mastery allows members of the police department to feel free to expose their own ideas in a way that allows others to think and learn.

Building a Shared Vision

When a genuine vision for the future exists, the members of the police department will learn and make decisions consistent with that vision. They will support the vision, assuming that the leaders in their individual behaviors also support this vision. **Building a shared vision** is more than just providing a vision statement. It is the opportunity for people to develop this vision and to find ways in which it can be achieved. A police leader with the vision that his or her agency be considered the most progressive in his or her geographical area, and who constantly brings about innovative changes within the department, is attempting to implement practices that are consistent with the vision on a day-to-day basis. When this vision is shared with all members of the department, they, too, may commit to the same vision. By allowing these persons to interact with other agencies and learn that their agency is one of the most professional in the area, they too will assist in building this shared vision.

Team Learning

Team learning means that information is constantly shared between members of the department. It means a dialogue, which is a Greek term for the free flow of meaning through a group. The creation of task forces to deal with all issues within the department leads to consistent team learning. In addition, when these teams spend time developing an answer to the specific issue and a set of guidelines for future behavior, team learning begins to take place.

These five disciplines form a developmental path for the police leader so that he or she can acquire the necessary skills, competencies, and techniques to assist him or her in achieving great personal success as well as assisting the department. A police leader may find that each member of the agency has a different level of innate ability to practice and understand each of the five disciplines. Therefore, the police leader should use people to assist others so that they, too, can develop a skill level in each of the disciplines equal to the best that each has to offer.

The major difference between the five learning disciplines and other management practices is that these disciplines are personal.

Is There a Best Style?

Emphasizing that the police manager has two primary concerns—for people and for production—is there really a best style for effective direction, planning, and control of a police agency?

Research conducted in industry indicates that the manager who is able to balance both concerns is more effective than the manager who deals with only one. Likewise, successful police managers must contribute to the specific objectives of the police department while also helping individuals within the agency to achieve their personal goals.

Rensis Likert (1961) did extensive research in analyzing high-production, as opposed to low-production, managers. His studies indicated that the managers who focused primary attention on the human aspects while building effective teams were more successful than managers who were job-centered. The manager who achieved high production used general rather than close supervision of subordinates.

Even though Likert's studies suggest that the employee-centered, democratic leader is most successful, his findings leave some doubt as to whether a single style of leadership behavior can or should apply to all situations. The recommendation for using a single style of leadership leaves to chance the cultural or traditional differences that may exist and does not provide clear explanations of the effect of education and standard of living on the employees. Therefore, most studies indicate that the effective leader does not use a single style of leadership behavior but instead takes into consideration numerous existing variables.

Adaptive Leadership

Police managers are often trained to seek an ideal leadership behavior pattern that they can employ to maximize the effective operation of their individual agencies. In reality, however, the effective police manager is able to integrate all the available styles and adapt to meet each situation. In essence, police managers who are able to change their style of leadership according to the situation and the needs of their employees are those who will be most effective in attaining both personal and organizational objectives.

In choosing a leadership style, the police manager must consider three major variables:

1. Personal relationships with members of the department.
2. The degree of structure in the task that the agency has been assigned to perform.
3. The authority, power, and responsibility provided by the manager's position within the organization.

The effectiveness of the leadership style chosen by the police manager will depend on the closeness of the relationship between the manager and subordinates, the degree of structure in the task, and the authority of the manager. In essence, the more flexibility given to the manager, the greater the possibility for effective decisions.

For example, the police manager who is assigned the task of eliminating corruption and unethical conduct within an agency will find that a democratic leadership style or an attempt to develop team decision making will be the least effective method of controlling the situation. Under such conditions, the manager who is more autocratic and has a high regard for production will be more successful on a short-term basis. Another example is the police manager who is faced with a riot or emergency condition. His or her success will depend on an immediate response to the issues. He or she may not have time to explain the situation to subordinates and engage in team decision making. Once the crisis is over, however, the manager may find a different leadership style much more effective.

Reality Leadership

Reality leadership focuses on the realities in a given situation. The police manager must develop the best kind of executive behavior for each administrative situation. The most effective manager will advise subordinates ahead of time regarding which conditions will produce which style of leadership. For example, a police chief may employ group decision making in general, while reserving the authority to make all decisions concerning promotions of key personnel.

Police managers must realize that their leadership style must be judged in the light of departmental goals and purposes of the organization. Furthermore, depending on its nature and its location within the agency, a group may need a particular kind of leadership. For example, the police manager may find an open, team style of management most effective in dealing with units composed of intelligent, mature employees. However, in other units, in which the tasks are mundane in nature, such as basic filing, the police manager may find that an autocratic style would be more effective. Police managers must always realize that they, as leaders, are only as effective as their subordinates will allow them to be, and in most group situations the entire group is really responsible for the success or failure of the stated objectives.

Deciding How to Lead

In reaching decisions, police managers are affected by: (1) forces within themselves and (2) forces in the situation.

Police managers, in deciding which style of leadership or management is most appropriate, are affected by their value systems, by the amount of confidence they have in their subordinates, and by their leadership inclinations, which have been brought about by the success that they have already achieved within their organizations. For example, if they have been successful by being heavily autocratic in leadership style, chances are that they will continue this style, regardless of the levels they reach in the bureaucratic structure. In situations that have an element of uncertainty, managers will not jeopardize their own security by delegating too much responsibility and authority to subordinates.

Subordinates usually will receive greater freedom if they clearly demonstrate the need for independence and exhibit a readiness to assume responsibility. In choosing a leadership style, the manager will consider the amount of subordinates' interest in the problem. For example, when the first-line supervisor has the knowledge and experience necessary to deal with the situation, understands the goals of the organization, and has learned to share in the decision-making process, the chances become greater that the style of leadership chosen by the manager will be more democratic.

Different forces in the total situation greatly affect the leadership style employed by the manager. The effectiveness of the group itself in its past decision-making processes gives some indication of how much freedom it should be given in each situation. If the organizational structure is highly bureaucratic in both principle and policy, with numerous levels between top and bottom, the chances of effective group decision making are greatly reduced. The problem itself and the pressure of time also affect the style of leadership that can be employed.

The effective police manager should choose a style of management that attempts to bridge the gap between the management process and actual line operations. The manager must learn to be a "multicrat"—flexible enough to deal with each situation.

Consider the effective police chief who deals with the department's command operations and internal operations by employing techniques that bring about high-quality team decisions. However, in dealing with the political structure of the community, this chief becomes a more compromising manager. Depending on the demands of particular pressure groups, the chief may employ a different style of leadership and be most effective in bringing about peace and tranquility to the community.

Effective Leadership Practices

Police managers can become more effective by searching for opportunities and treating each assignment as a new venture regardless of the status of that assignment. They can constantly question the status quo and design new ways to improve the department. Effective police managers can find something that is broken and fix it. Many police managers find opportunities that add adventure to every responsibility they have and they make this adventure fun.

James Kouzes and Barry Posner (1987) believe that people are willing to both admire and follow leaders who are honest, consistent in word and deed, competent, forward-looking, and inspirational, and who have a sense of direction, concern for the future, and a winning track record—that is, enthusiastic, energetic, and positive. They define five leadership practices that, when followed, would make the police leader an effective manager, thereby creating a more professional police department. These effective leadership practices are: (1) challenging the process, (2) inspiring a shared vision, (3) enabling others to act, (4) modeling the way, and (5) encouraging the heart.

Challenging the Process

Leaders look for ways to alter the status quo, new processes, and ways to change the system operating within the police agency to one that will achieve its goals and objectives. Those who challenge the process initiate change, and the result of this is igniting enthusiasm in themselves as well as others. There are two commitments that leaders under this practice employ: (1) they search out challenging opportunities to change, grow, innovate, and improve, and (2) they experiment and take risks.

Inspiring a Shared Vision

The four attributes of a vision are: (1) having a future orientation, (2) creating an image and actually seeing the future, (3) having a sense of the possibilities, and (4) taking pride in being a different police agency. Therefore, vision means invoking images with a strong future orientation, a standard of excellence, and a quality of uniqueness. The two major commitments of this practice include the ability to envision the future and to enlist others in a shared vision.

Enabling Others to Act

Police leaders must make others feel like owners of the police department—not hired hands. They strive for cooperation as opposed to competition—trying to do a good job and trying to outdo others are two different things. Police department personnel are most likely to cooperate when they know that they will deal with each other again. The two commitments that these practices develop are fostering collaboration and strengthening others.

Police leaders who enable others to act always try to develop integrative solutions. They seek many outputs. They are willing to meet in teams as well as one-on-one. They keep all personnel in the department posted as to the progress being made as well as the direction. They seek specific and broad support. Collaboration has trust at its core. The foundation of trust is believing that the other members of the police department have integrity. This can be demonstrated by meeting commitments and keeping promises. Things that the police manager can do to foster collaboration include always saying "we," creating interactions between members of the department, creating a climate of trust to focus on gains rather than losses, involving people in planning and problem solving, and being a risk-taker when it comes to trusting others.

Modeling the Way

The police manager must have a philosophy—a set of high standards by which the department is measured, a set of values and beliefs about how the employees—sworn and non-sworn—as well as citizens ought to be treated, and a set of strong principles that make the police organization unique and distinctive.

The police leader makes two commitments in modeling the way. The first is to set an example that is positive, and the second is to plan small wins. By setting the example, the police manager asks all members of the department to observe a set of standards—the same standards by which the police leader will live. By planning small wins, the manager is continually involved in the growth process and personnel become committed to the overall goal. Some strategies to help facilitate this process include making a plan, taking one step at a time, reducing the cost of saying "yes," and giving people choices and making these choices highly visible.

Encouraging the Heart

Successful leaders have high expectations of themselves as well as other members of the department. These expectations become very powerful. The police manager gives heart by visibly recognizing the contributions of members of the department to the common vision. They practice two commitments: The first is recognizing these contributions—that is, linking rewards with performances. Ways to recognize such accomplishments include developing tough, measurable performance standards, installing a formal systematic process for rewarding performance, being creative about such rewards, letting others design the nonmonetary compensations to make the recognition public, and finding members of the department who are doing things right. The second commitment includes celebrating accomplishments. One strategy may include schedules of celebrations. The police manager could be a leader and a coach, and employ his or her internal values of trust, honesty, commitment, and above all, love.

Total Quality Management

History

Dr. W. Edwards Deming has been called the father of **Total Quality Management** (TQM). Deming was an engineer who received his master's degrees in mathematics and physics, and a doctorate in physics from Yale University. His training as a statistician helped him develop his theory of management, which was based upon statistics on subtle variations in manufacturing levels used to improve the quality of manufacturing.

TQM was originally introduced in the United States in the mid-1930s and was first accepted by industry. However, despite the strong manufacturing power in post-World War II industry, the United States did not adopt Dr. Deming's management approach.

Japan, however, did implement TQM. And after proving successful in the areas of manufacturing for many years, TQM was embraced by major American industries in the 1980s. Ideas, as proven by the history of management philosophies, originate in the minds of a few, are tested, accepted in the industrial setting, and eventually accepted by the federal government and other government entities. President H.W. Bush, during his tenure, adapted TQM as his approach to running the executive branch of the federal government. Today, TQM, in various forms, has been adopted by many police agencies throughout the country and is beginning to appear more and more in a number of law enforcement journals.

The first issue addressed by TQM is the definition of the term *quality*. Deming defines quality as customer satisfaction. He, therefore, requires constant improvement in order to have true total quality. His definition, however, is not necessarily shared by others defining quality. For example, others define the term as zero defects.

Deming further defined how TQM could be implemented in business by advising that business or industrial settings could implement his "14 points." They are:

1. Constancy of purpose for improvement of product and services.
2. Adopt the new philosophy.
3. Cease dependence on mass inspection (quality comes from improvement of the process).
4. End the practice of awarding business on price tag alone (low bid versus quality).
5. Improve constantly and forever the systems of production and service.
6. Institute training.
7. Institute leadership—Help others to do a better job.
8. Drive out fear—Make people feel secure with the freedom to succeed or fail.
9. Break down barriers between staff areas.
10. Eliminate slogans, exhortations, and targets for the workplace.
11. Eliminate numerical quotas.
12. Remove barriers to pride of workmanship (control, equipment).
13. Institute a vigorous program of education and re-training (teamwork).
14. Take action to accomplish the transformation (plan of action).

From these 14 points, writers have established a series of primary principles. Because TQM was first applied to manufacturing, these principles sometimes refer to products. However, TQM proponents insist that service can be viewed as a product and, therefore, these principles need only minor modifications to be applied to law enforcement.

Uses for Law Enforcement

TQM has been defined as a journey that people take in order to do the right things at the right time. TQM requires thinking long-term actions based on achieving immediate objectives while working toward long-term goals. TQM allows police departments to create quality actions, be more cost-effective, and allow personnel to analyze the positive and negative trade-offs of any decision prior to its implementation.

In reviewing the above mentioned principles, the question arises as to whether all or some can be applied to law enforcement. In many instances, the implementation of each of these principles can be difficult.

The first principle, "the customer is the ultimate determiner of quality," leaves open a very broad question as to who really are the customers of the police. Obviously, customers include citizens of the city or county or those who live in adjoining localities but work daily within a particular jurisdiction. It also includes those who are arrested, and, of course, refers to others served on a daily basis.

The list of "customers," however, includes many more. Other customers served include the courts, as well as other offices of local government, especially the corrections and law enforcement agencies with which the department interacts on a daily basis; the media; and those who come in contact with police even though they may not fall within these groups. An example would be a request for service from other governmental entities throughout the United States.

Orange County, Florida, Sheriff's Office

After much input from the participants in an executive development program, TQM for the Sheriff's Office was defined by using only four primary principles. These include:

1. The customer is the ultimate determiner of quality.
2. Quality will be built into our service early in the development process and will be continually tracked from input to activity, to output.
3. Quality requires continuous improvement of input and process.
4. Quality improvement requires total organizational commitment, command commitment, and strong employee participation.

Ideas were developed and tested for ways of achieving each of the TQM principles adhered to by the agency. The first step was the implementation of the General Order outlining the process. Training played an important role in the implementation of each of the TQM principles.

Surveys of employees and citizens, and follow-up surveys of outside agencies defined customer satisfaction. Quality assurance letters were sent to citizens who had come in contact with the agency. There was supervisory input, as well as employee meetings, and continual measuring of both praise and complaints involving agency personnel.

Three major functions of the Sheriff's Office were relied upon to ensure that TQM was implemented throughout the agency. The accreditation process raised standards and clearly defined TQM as it applied to the agency. The second major function was training. In this broad area, people were prepared to implement the high standards that were recommended by the command staff. The third function, quality assurance, clearly established a review of the quality of service provided by the agency. The functions of inspections and quality control rested not in a separate division in the Sheriff's Office, but were the responsibility of every employee. Guaranteeing high quality was a major responsibility of each supervisor.

Summary of TQM

Regardless of its form, TQM incorporates fresh ideas and stresses longstanding management principles like participatory management and quality circles. TQM represents a new framework that will help rejuvenate management principles as well as be a great advantage to bringing about the implementation of the police department's philosophy—a philosophy that strives for total quality service to the community it serves.

Developing Organizational Teamwork

The police manager can bring about effective teamwork within his or her department by establishing systematic procedures. The manager must determine what is to be done, how it is to be done, who is to do it and, eventually, how effectively it is being accomplished. This process of developing organizational teamwork can also provide a basis for reviewing the progress of change, for helping to identify problems, and for planning individual and group development.

The first step is to clarify the work requirements. The police manager must reach an agreement with subordinates as to the functions and responsibilities that are to be performed, the authority that will be given to the subordinates, and the expected results.

The development of **functions-authority-results** (FARs) is the key to the careful development of organizational teamwork between the manager and his or her subordinates. A simple three-column table, as shown in Figure 4-2, can easily be established. In the first column, both the subordinate and the manager agree on the tasks for which the subordinate is responsible. Next, the police manager must outline the authority he or she is willing to give to the subordinate. Authority may be broken down into three levels: (1) the subordinate may have to report before acting; (2) the subordinate may have the

Functions	Authority	Results
Organizational structure	Act-report	Simplified structure
Budget preparation	Report-act	Prepared line-item budget
Assignment of personnel	Complete	Scheduled by incident
Robbery prevention programs	Complete	5% robbery reduction

FIGURE 4-2 **The Leadership Grid® figure.** *Source: The Leadership Grid® Figure from* Leadership Dilemmas—Grid Solutions, *by Robert R. Blake and Anne Adams McCanse (formerly the Managerial Grid Figure by Robert R. Blake and Jane S. Mouton). Houston: Gulf Publishing Company, p. 29. Copyright © 1991, by Scientific Methods, Inc. Reproduced by permission of the owners.*

authority to act and then report to the manager; and (3) the subordinate may be given complete authority, meaning that he or she is responsible only for the overall results of his or her actions.

The police manager should recognize that the tasks may be quite similar for each subordinate, but the levels of authority can be different. As a subordinate begins to exhibit the ability to accept responsibility, the level of authority can move from report-act to complete authority.

Once this major step has been clarified and agreement has been reached on the FARs, the manager can then divide his or her attention between the management of tasks and the management of subordinates. Under the broad category of management of personnel, the police manager should evaluate the performance of subordinates. This comes under the third column.

The manager also must assess the potential that his or her subordinates have for future development. Working with each subordinate, the police manager should plan a career development program. This program should indicate possible paths or promotions and the acceptance of added responsibilities within the framework of the subordinate's present assignment. The purpose of this process is to guarantee use of the abilities of the subordinate, ensuring growth for both the individual and the department.

In managing tasks, the second responsibility of the manager is to review the work progress and the problems generated in carrying out the FARs. Specific objectives must be set, and they must be carefully evaluated to determine whether they have been reached. It is important that problems be analyzed, that decisions be reached concerning the overcoming of obstacles, and that action be taken by both the manager and the subordinate to solve the problems in bringing about change.

Figure 4-3 indicates the process of organization for the manager. Through this process, the department is strengthened and the abilities of the individual within the department are developed to their fullest.

Approaches to the Organizational Development Process

Approaches to change fall into two broad categories: those oriented toward changing people and those oriented toward changing the structure or system.

People-oriented approaches include attempts to change the philosophies and attitudes of the individuals within the department. Many police agencies send key personnel to specialized schools with the hope that exposure to new information will enable them to perform assigned functions adequately. An agency may also provide consultants for the same purpose. But for the most part, this approach has not proved to be very successful for police departments.

In some instances, it is necessary for police managers to transfer individuals who hold key positions. By transferring personnel on a periodic basis, managers can bring in "new blood" to initiate changes in day-to-day operations. These periodic changes in position

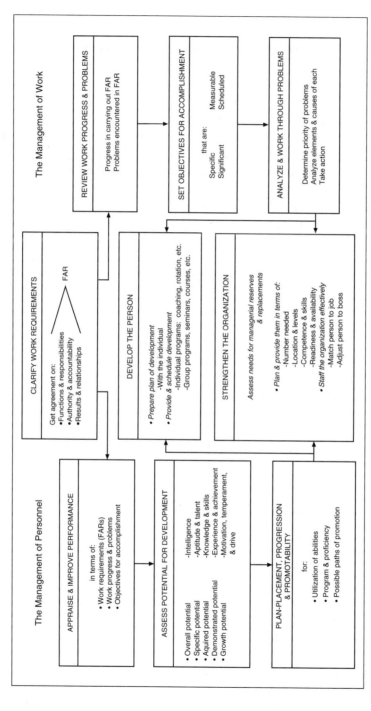

FIGURE 4-3 Functions-Authority-Results (FARs).

can be seen as a challenge and often produce a commitment to implementing new procedures. This approach seems to be more effective than attempting to change the individual who presently holds the position.

Another people-oriented approach to change is **team development**. Starting with the managers at the top level, team training programs can be implemented. Each unit forms a cohesive team that forces evaluation of present practices and instills in the members a commitment to change and upgrade the department. The development of decision-making teams within an agency has proven to be an effective strategy for bringing about change.

Revising the present organizational climate as it relates to personal interactions is another people-oriented strategy for change. Such techniques as projects designed to evaluate the feedback and exposure communicative processes and sensitivity training are examples. Developing a new style of leadership or a new planning process can help to reduce resistance to change in department personnel.

Other people-oriented strategies, such as giving pay raises, creating rewards through an evaluation system, or initiating a strong control system that forces people to change have been the least effective strategies.

Structure-oriented approaches for change might include creating additional units within the department, dissolving present units, or combining them with already established divisions.

Another approach for structural change is instituting new procedures, rules, and regulations. By placing emphasis on enforcing the rules, changes can be implemented. Changes in technology and equipment are also tools for revising the system. The use of computers in decision making has created changes in police agencies throughout the United States.

In deciding which approach to use, the manager should carefully evaluate the conditions in his or her own department. If, for example, the manager feels that the climate for change is positive, then changes that are directed toward people may prove more effective than those directed toward structure. In instances in which resistance to change may be high, the manager may begin the overall process by implementing structural changes such as reorganization, developing computer systems, and purchasing new equipment.

No matter which approach the manager chooses, he or she should avoid becoming defensive about proposed changes and should not consider opposition to them as a personal threat. He or she should also avoid being unrealistic in the goals that he or she sets, the time frames, and the degree of commitment necessary on the part of the personnel under his or her command.

Finally, the police manager should not disregard the consequences of the change process. Whatever approach is employed, the manager must be aware of the major effects that the strategy will have on everyone involved. Initiating changes without any thought as to how these changes will affect the rest of the police department may create serious difficulties in the implementation of programs for upgrading the department.

References

Blake, R. R., Mouton, J., & Ashe, J. (1991). *The managerial grid*. Houston: Gulf Publishing Company.

Hersey, P., & Blanchard, K. H. (1972). *Management of organizational behavior* (2nd ed.). Englewood Cliffs, NJ: Prentice-Hall.

Kouzes, J., & Posner, B. (1987). *The leadership challenge*. San Francisco: Jossey Bass.

Likert, R. (1961). *New patterns of management*. New York: McGraw-Hill Book Company.

Mayo, E. (1945). *The social problems of an industrial civilization*. Boston: Harvard Business School.

Senge, P. M. (1990). *The fifth discipline*. New York: Doubleday.

Taylor, F. W. (1911). *The principles of scientific management*. New York: Harper and Brothers.

Discussion Questions

1. How may a police manager develop the qualities necessary to become an effective leader?
2. What style of management would be most appropriate for leading a police department?
3. If you were to take over a police department that was corrupt, inefficient, and ineffective, what style of management would you attempt to implement and why?
4. How can the five effective leadership practices be implemented?
5. Develop a vision. The questions that can be addressed to clarify this vision include: (a) How would you like to change the world for yourself, your department, or your division? (b) If you could invent the future, what future would you invent for yourself and your department or division? (c) What is your dream about your future as it relates to law enforcement? (d) What is your personal agenda and what do you want to improve?
6. What can a department do that indicates that the leaders are challenging the process, inspiring a shared vision, enabling others to act, modeling the way, and encouraging the heart?

5 ▦

Creating a Breed of Super-sergeants[1]

LEARNING OBJECTIVES

1. The student will understand the importance of the role of the first-line supervisor.
2. The student will be able to recognize important Supreme Court cases that affect supervisors.
3. The student will understand the concept of "Performance Management."

When it comes to the performance of law enforcement officers in the field, there is no one so important as the **first-line supervisor**, who is undoubtedly critical to the delivery of quality police services. While the acknowledgment of this fact is universal, first-line supervisors who meet the demanding standards and expectations of this position are *sui generis,* or in a class by themselves, a rare exception.

As much as we acknowledge their importance, is there a concomitant commitment to their preparation for the demanding tasks they are expected to perform? Agencies often give personnel stripes without pre-promotional training; we expect a lot from them while they wait months or years before they receive any adequate contextual training directly related to the responsibilities of their new positions. Then, from a management perspective, we are critical of their performance and, in many cases, in accepting less than superior accomplishment from them, we allow the organization to operate at less than its best. In fact, we condemn ourselves to mediocrity in our roles as managers.

This situation can only remind us of Charles Garfield's statement in his book, *Peak Performers* (1987, p. 52), when he says: "Peak performers are not ordinary people with something added, but ordinary people with nothing taken away." In our initial selection and hopefully our promotions, we pick the best. But something happens when organizations do not nurture and do not develop the potential in their people.

This attitude comes from our results-oriented society. We confuse process with product. We evaluate the results, find them less than satisfactory, and neglect to look at the process that has undoubtedly brought about those very results. Then two things happen: we either accept the status quo, or we inveigh against the individuals targeted for this criticism, and end up doing nothing to correct the situation.

I want to share my concerns with you about the process while stating emphatically that we as a profession must single-mindedly readjust our goals to concentrate on performance, and excellent performance at that. All the good things that we want from policing—the quality protection and service—will not come about, unless we recognize

---

[1]Chapter 5 is included with the permission of G. Patrick Gallagher.

the critical necessity of lavishing care and attention on the preparation and nurturing of a breed of super-sergeants. Process *and* performance!

The Status Quo

We have arrived at a point where these supervisors do not have enhanced experience and qualifications; they are becoming more hesitant about the real role they should assume as the specter of liability looms even larger. Their questions in training sessions lead me to believe that, for most, the topic of supervisory liability is ever-present and is a driving force behind their actions. Having no clear indication of what they have to do, nor having adequate preparation for what they should do, many tend to withdraw from active supervision because they are out of their comfort zones, despite years of experience on the street. They become **passive supervisors**, or mere observers of the myriad activities swirling around them. Sure, they handle the paperwork smoothly, but not having been nurtured themselves, they find themselves inadequate at nurturing and developing others, who happen to be the next wave of supervisors.

There is a clear causal connection between this failure on the part of the profession to "do the right thing" when it comes to preparing supervisors and the growth and complexity of the liability concerns that we shoulder today. Think of the gap between the expectations that the profession and individual managers have for first-line supervisors and their preparation. Supervisors stand with each foot in a different world: **management** and operations. That role is unique to first-line supervision. Our failure first of all to acknowledge, and then to support, this particular role stymies chief executives, for their ability to reach and affect the **operational world** is limited by the quality of that supervision.

I believe in such an environment that supervisors with the best of intentions have their confidence eroded; they fail to attain their optimum performance capability. Furthermore, even for those with the best of intentions, many lack the necessary support to do the job correctly for they quite frequently (and accurately) say that when they do want to take action to correct the sub-par conduct of an officer, they are discouraged by their supervisors. From lieutenant on up there must be a realization of the importance of the role of these supervisors; support means that all management levels encourage and assist supervisors, and that they cooperate with them; that **mid-level managers** take as their essential goal the improvement and mentoring of the sergeants reporting to them. Most importantly, lieutenants must be held responsible for the sergeants' success. Lieutenants cannot succeed in their positions if the sergeants reporting to them are not more successful through this interaction, if the lieutenants do not mentor the sergeants.

This obviously begs a question: Where do we find these super-lieutenants? That will take a good deal of evaluation of the process that currently develops mid-level managers. For an excellent treatment of this subject, read the Police Executive Research Forum book titled *Managing Innovation in Policing: The Untapped Potential of the Middle Manager* (Swanger & Geller, 1985).

The Burden of Supervisory Liability

Let us first address the question of supervisory liability. In **Doe v. Calumet City**, a supervisor who was hypersensitive to liability failed to do the right thing—i.e., break down a door to rescue the two children of a woman who had escaped from a rapist who had entered her home. (He mistakenly feared that the department would be liable for the damages to the door.) In this case, the supervisor, paralyzed by the fear of liability, ended up incurring far greater supervisory liability than that which he had feared. Thrust into giving direction in a critical incident, only the thought of potential liability came to mind. Directed by this, as a supervisor he froze, neglecting to employ reasonable means of dealing with the woman and rescuing her children. However, in fairness to him, we could ask the question as to whether he was adequately prepared. I would guess that he probably had not been.

In the 1994 case of **Shaw v. Stroud**, a Fourth Circuit Court of Appeals decision dealing with a case of wrongful death, it is interesting to note that the trooper involved in the shooting death, had, over his nine-year tenure in the department, been supervised by two sergeants, one for the first seven years, and the other up to the time of the incident.

Testimony showed that the trooper had an established pattern of allegedly using excessive force. His first supervisor did nothing about it. The appellate court ruled on a motion for qualified immunity that his inaction rose to the level of "deliberate indifference" necessary to find him guilty, if the trooper was guilty, of this wrongful death claim. He could have been held liable "for the excessive force used by the state trooper at the time of the incident, so as not to be entitled to a defense of qualified immunity; the supervisor's **deliberate indifference** to pervasive and unreasonable risk of harm, bore an affirmative link to the harm suffered." Obviously even the court said that he typified the less-than-competent supervisor regarding his oversight of the trooper.

In contrast, the current supervisor had taken several affirmative steps to control the situation: he followed standard operating procedures in response to complaints, made records of complaints, monitored the trooper's actions by riding with him, reported the trooper's actions to his supervisor and followed the lieutenant's direction. The appellate court commented that his conduct merited him **qualified immunity**, because while his supervision might have been "negligent," it did not rise to the level of "deliberate indifference." Neither simple nor gross negligence constitutes the necessary level of proof in federal cases for supervisors. Rather, a higher burden of proof, *deliberate indifference*, must be present to prove supervisory negligence.

But let us debrief this case more thoroughly. If the second supervisor had been an excellent supervisor, what would he have done? That trooper, with his complaint record and his pattern of arrests, accompanied by use of force, certainly would have been the ultimate challenge for the supervisor who should have reviewed all the evaluations and the other material in the file, and who should have looked at his arrest records over time and seen the consistent pattern of force and "resisting arrest" charges—far more than other troopers. He should have engaged in some form of performance management with him, laid out specific goals and regularly monitored the performance plan through weekly meetings and reviews of every single report. That trooper should have experienced a form of supervisory structure and support that he probably had never been exposed to in the past to force him to change. The current sergeant had to be a lot more direct with the trooper, specifying performance standards. He should have regularly ridden along with the trooper, and through it all he should have exemplified the principle that organizational and personal change comes from "gentle pressure, relentlessly applied." Finally, having set up a plan, he should have notified the lieutenant who, ideally, would have suggested other ways to either reform the trooper or, in concert with the sergeant, taken the proper but more drastic step of having him go through a fitness for duty evaluation, and possible termination.

In the actual case, the second supervisor received qualified immunity because his quality of supervision was only "negligent," or "grossly negligent." But the model for peak performance is far above that. How many current supervisors are prepared to take the total approach, to properly handle an officer with a similar record? Or one that shows the early signs of moving in a similar direction? How many, if they took that approach, would receive the direct encouragement and support of their supervisor?

A Statement of the Problem

There is something of a contradiction here. If their role is so important, then why is more not done to set up first-line supervisors for success, given their responsibilities? Why are preparation and training not lavished on them to make sure that they are ready for the situations that they will have to face? Additionally, why is there not more accountability?

In many cases, first-line supervisors are unconsciously set up for failure by management, or at least for performance far below what the profession needs and far below the levels at which the supervisor wants to function. No one really wants to perform at a mediocre level.

We continue to carry the onerous burden resulting from not adequately preparing supervisors for the full range of tasks that their position involves. [Law enforcement executives around the country, when asked in training sessions what is their number one internal problem, list the almost universal problem of the quality of first line supervision.] There is a certain irony here, because the answer has been consistent over time (that question has been asked at executive development sessions for close to 20 years), yet when these same executives have been asked what specific steps they have taken to remedy this problem, there are few who can indicate what they have done.

So they "live with it." Edwards Deming (1986), a quality guru, has given us some insight that might help explain what is happening. He states that we have *process problems* before we have *people problems*. If we ignore reexamining the process employed, we will end with *people who have problems*. Continue to do this and we will undoubtedly *have people problems*.

This applies directly to the plight of supervisors. Every part of the supervisory developmental process should be critiqued before it can rightfully be said that the first-line supervisor is adequately prepared. Following up on Deming's thoughts, in our profession we wonder what to do with the problem of first-line supervisors performing below our expectations, yet fail to scrutinize the process that fosters this situation, and that will guarantee that it continues to exist. By doing this we inevitably leave in place a process that will continue to produce more new supervisors who in time may become "problems," potential liability, and more officers who fail to attain a peak level of performance.

The Birth of a Process

Having presented the preceding, the challenge is to lay out the skeletal framework for a process that will attain our objective, the development of super-sergeants able at once to handle and possibly redeem the "**problem officer**," but also able to maximize the performance of the average, good, and peak performers. Simultaneously they must stand as an example of a leader at the supervisory level, committed to the departmental values and upholding the performance standards of the agency as articulated in the policies. If the process can become accepted and implemented widely enough, then we would not call these people "super-sergeants" but just committed officers doing everything expected of them, doing even the ordinary things extraordinarily well.

I ask you to weigh all these suggestions and incorporate into your process those that you feel will produce the best results.

The components of this process are as follows:

1. The development and implementation of a Field Training Supervisor (FTS) program patterned on the Field Training Officer (FTO) program;
2. The implementation of the process of performance management at all levels within the organization;
3. The establishment of a peak performance-oriented supervisory style;
4. Concentration not only on those whose performance is sub-par, but on protecting and raising the level of performance of every single person without neglecting those who are average or superior;
5. Responsibility and accountability placed on lieutenants measuring their success by the accompanying success of the sergeants reporting to them;
6. Establishment of a basic bias toward the achievement of success by providing support in every form with the provision of a *Supervisor's Field Manual Checklist;*
7. Careful attention to supervisor training in all high-risk/critical task policies before they are expected to enforce them;
8. A recognition that the primary service population of one rank is the rank reporting to him or her, and that discovering subordinates being successful, not failing, is the primary reason for the existence of the higher rank.

We should be open to appreciating the challenges that first-line supervisors face, and their importance in delivering quality services and in restoring credibility for policing. It is important to identify the steps, some of which are outlined above, that could make it easier for them to be peak performers as supervisors.

It is evident that there must be a multi-component process of preparing supervisors and fostering their development by concentrating on performance. Every aspect of this preparation must be focused on developing "super-sergeants," a process that can be called **performance-oriented supervision**.

The following specific components and the accompanying principles of this process must be integrated into initial preparation and training. They must become part of a system of nurturing support for excellent supervision that requires the complete and total commitment of everyone from the law enforcement executives to managers—those who supervise first-line supervisors.

This paradigm shift must come to those who are currently first-line supervisors; it must come if officers are to receive the guidance and example they need; it must come because the next generation of supervisors (today's officers), whom we do not want to be tomorrow's inadequate supervisors, needs their example.

A Misbalanced Emphasis

In many departments, the major emphasis is focused on ferreting out those who are poor performers, breaking the rules, "problem officers," or officers who have problems. These represent only three to five percent of the department, yet in many cases the processes in place center on them to the exclusion of all others, i.e., the good and excellent performers. Policies and discipline are used to deal with these "problems" while the other 95 to 97 percent of the department's complement is overlooked, or even ignored. Their performance most naturally can only go up, stay the same, or go down.

In most cases, performance levels either stay the same, and we lose the potential of even better performance from them, or start to taper off as it is perceived by those officers that no one really cares about their efforts. The Gallagher-Westfall Group has launched a campaign with the slogan: "Catch a cop doin' something right." Its purpose is to highlight the efforts of 95 percent of officers who do a good job, and to encourage them on a daily basis to do an even better job.

With strong commitment on the department's part to widening the focus of supervisors so that their responsibilities are seen on the one hand as correcting those whose performance is sub-par, and on the other as assisting in every way possible to improve the quality of work of everyone else, a revolutionary change will take place that will uplift the quality of work and the environment within which it takes place, and ultimately the larger policing community.

Performance Management

Regardless of the level of supervision, but certainly at the first level, a process of ***performance management*** must be implemented. This process must be taught and implemented at every level, with each higher level of supervision responsible for its consistent and uniform implementation. Few agencies are satisfied with their performance evaluation process. Departments all over the country search for a better form to be utilized. The form is only a means to an end—i.e., raising performance levels. It is part of the process, not the process itself.

Let us look at this process. Who fills out 90 percent of the **performance evaluations** in any agency? The sergeants. We have high hopes for the evaluations, but most departments fail to completely train and assist sergeants in evaluation procedures. Competence in this task requires that sergeants continuously collect data on performance and be trained in distinguishing levels of performance—e.g., "excellent," "above standards," "meets standards," and "below standards." These two functions are not accomplished.

Given the current situation, sergeants may tend to give better evaluations than are deserved. They become hypersensitive to making the tough calls on inadequate performance because they cannot document it sufficiently to withstand challenges. These unmerited and inflated evaluations only serve to demotivate those who are basically good performers. Thus, the organization loses their additional contribution, and the individual is denied the chance to achieve excellence. For the recipients of the inflated evaluations, they are lulled into a sense of satisfaction with the status quo, while remaining mired in mediocrity.

The process of *performance management* is composed of three phases: (1) performance planning; (2) observation, interaction, and adjustments in supervisory styles; and (3) the performance evaluation.

During the performance planning phase, the supervisor meets with the officer, or the lieutenant meets with the sergeant, and jointly they settle on three to five goals that are specific, measurable, attainable, relevant, and trackable. These goals will be different for the rookie officer and the seven-year veteran. They could not be the same for the newly promoted sergeant and the experienced supervisor newly assigned to a particular shift. Together, the supervisor and the subordinate agree on the supervisor's role in helping the subordinate attain these designated goals.

In the second phase, the supervisor (sergeant or lieutenant) meets frequently with the subordinate and reviews the progress being made, while adjusting the goals and timetables, guided constantly by the attainment of success. In the third or evaluative phase, the performance evaluation is completed at the end of the agreed-upon period, which might be different for each of the individual goals. This process is totally performance-based, it is fair, it is informally structured, and it exemplifies a caring form of supervision. The process involves both parties; it is entirely geared to set up the officer for success.

Performance management gives the supervisor a means of facing the biggest challenge, which is dealing with good performers, and motivating them to perform at an even higher level. The person working at 80 percent of his or her ability must be assisted and encouraged to reach 85 percent, and then 90 percent. Performance management does just that.

LEARNING EXERCISE

Develop a performance management plan for a rookie officer. Be sure to include three to five goals and explain how they are measurable, attainable, and relevant. Then create a performance management plan for a five-year veteran. Discuss the differences in these plans with your classmates. How and why are they different? How can they be improved?

The Correct Focus: Liability or Performance?

Overall, too much is made of the liability ogre. The process for avoiding liability is to concentrate on constant improvement of performance. The systems or processes in place for every level of supervision, especially that of the first level, must be the raising of the levels of performance, and the immediate correction of any action that falls short of the department's performance standards—i.e., policies and procedures.

The focus on liability only develops a system that does the minimum amount to avoid it, that has performance stand just one notch away from liability. On the contrary, the focus on performance improvement has the potential to continuously raise the individual officer's and the department's performances. A process based on daily incremental improvement accomplishes far more than just doing enough to avoid liability.

The story is told of the Japanese CEO who was going to be interviewed by an American reporter. He asked the reporter if he wanted to accompany him on his daily rounds of the office. As the CEO met his employees, he greeted them by name, and continuously asked the same question: "Good morning, Joe. What are you doing to improve quality today?" The question never varied, but every employee had to be constantly prepared to mention something that he was doing to contribute to the overall quality of their work. The CEO was selling quality in performance, and incrementally the improvement was substantial. Quality was achieved through consistent efforts at having each person's performance improve each day.

How is this *performance improvement* process implemented? Through the clear messages of the chief executive, every supervisory level commits itself to a form of service leadership. We readily agree that law enforcement exists to "protect and serve." But it must be recognized that the primary service population for the captain is the lieutenant, for the lieutenant it is the sergeant, and for the sergeant it is the officers. This **continuum of service** is founded on the principle that not a day must go by when each level cannot ask itself the question: "Have I done something to improve the performance of my people?" "Have I, by my interaction with all of my subordinates, effected something to help them do the job better?" To achieve superlative performance, the answer must always be an emphatic "Yes!"

When this acknowledgment takes place, then we have to understand that the process of performance improvement has three phases:

Proactive: policy and training in all tasks and all critical policies,
Active: the quality of daily supervision and the supervisor's exemplary conduct,
Reactive: correction, discipline, evaluations, audits, inspections, and most importantly rewards and recognition.

When all components of this process are in place, then the message and the expectation are clear: as an organization the highest level of performance is expected, and the supervisors are truly committed to do everything possible to help subordinates succeed.

Try this form of evaluation: take each of the three phases of performance improvement and grade your department and yourself on their quality and then on their interaction one with another. We usually find that there are inadequacies in certain phases or, as in the Reactive Phase, discipline is overemphasized to the complete exclusion of praise and recognition. We must learn to celebrate success and good performance. We must hold up examples of good performance and say, in effect, that they are living examples of the policies in action. We must concentrate on these goals, and celebrate often!

Credible, Relevant, Contextual Supervisory Training

While possibly ignoring some excellent training programs for supervisors, let us look at the preparation that exists generally around the country. Supervisory training starts the first day that an officer is exposed to a supervisor—i.e., the first day on the job. The officer picks up a **supervisory style** through many different means. At the end of five years' service, for example, the officer is now promoted and, in the absence of extensive support and training for this new position, he or she draws upon his or her experiences with supervisors and the style in which those supervisors handled their responsibilities. The new supervisor is guided by the manner in which he or she was treated or ignored. For this delicate transition, in which the sergeant is now to stand with a foot in both the operational and managerial worlds, the profession does very little.

Second, there may be some supervisory training after a certain period in that position. However, it comes after the new supervisor has already spent some time on the job. With the best of training, the problem is exacerbated when supervisors who start out with a high degree of commitment and possibly some training early on, fail to receive support from *their* supervisors—the lieutenants. Without support, despite their best efforts, they may fall back into the old, more comfortable, non-confrontational pattern. And the profession loses, because the officers, under that supervisor in their most formative years, are denied the model of a real supervisor.

Third, there is little preparation for the highly critical, low- and high-frequency events that really test a supervisor's mettle. The most difficult tasks occur with low frequency, yet they demand the best in supervisors or officers to handle them with professional poise according to the highest standards.

Training for supervisors must build on contextual situations relevant to the exacting demands that will be made on them. Regardless of how good supervisory training is, it will have little impact unless there is a strong, supportive environment from above and necessary interventions by the next level of supervision to expand the sergeant's level of confidence, competence, and experience.

Field Training Supervisor (FTS) Program

High-quality supervisory training is not always available when there are promotions to sergeant. However, to allow the new sergeant to "play it by ear" or incorporate the supervisory ideas picked up over the years only perpetuates the cycle of poor supervision. How can this critical gap be bridged?

Can we identify our best supervisors? Can we admit that we need more sergeants like them? Why is a department not able to identify its three best sergeants, those who represent the most exemplary qualities desired in a supervisor? Why is that soon-to-be promoted sergeant not assigned to a **Field Training Supervisor** (FTS) who, through a semi-structured program, guides the new sergeant through the many stages, making the initiation rite more positive? Then, at monthly intervals through the period of probation, the FTS continues to work with the sergeant, to serve as a mentor over the first year of probation? If the FTS program were in place, and if lieutenants accepted their responsibility to work daily to improve the performance of the new sergeant, would our expectations be more easily realized?

The Field Training Supervisor program would have some degree of structure, evaluations, and required items to be covered by the FTS and the new sergeant. The FTS program would exist to help achieve success and confidence in this demanding role. The FTS process would also legitimize the probationary period for sergeants, because there would be extra support for this developmental period, and the sergeant would move from probation because he or she actually "proved" that he or she could do the job. Probation for this rank would no longer be a meaningless term. There might even be a fair process for indicating that someone did not perform the job satisfactorily, and he or she might lose the promotion. In the end, the process would have been improved, and if that occurs, then performance at the officer and sergeant levels would be elevated. That is what supervision is all about.

Successful Performance

There are always marked differences between the formal or written policy authored by the chief executive, the informal policy released at roll calls with a particular twist that supervisors might place on it, and the operational policy as employed by officers in the field. Practice, usages, and customs develop rapidly, and can be accepted by the courts as official policy—the argument often raised by plaintiff's counsel in lawsuits. As a result of this flawed process, one policy given to 30 supervisors could have 30 applications.

Why does this occur? What is wrong with the process of disseminating policies throughout the department? If policies are important, especially those relating to the high-risk/critical tasks, there must be training in those policies. One rule is:

> Never *ask a supervisor to enforce a high risk/critical task policy unless he or she has first been trained in the application of the policy.*

This training must be based on hypothetical situations, and while "every incident is different," there must be an attempt to have a higher degree of uniform application of the policy, and a greater understanding of the policy's operational requirement. Officers and sergeants are very much task-oriented people; they spend all their time performing tasks. Therefore, when new policies are issued, they may not want them to interfere with their main concern, which is handling the multitude of tasks assigned to them. Therefore, training in the policies, as well as training in new case law, must be presented in terms of hypotheticals, representing the real-world situations that they will face.

Furthermore, to this end, if we accept the principle of annual requalification with weapons, then we should accept the concomitant principle of annual requalification with the policies that govern the use of the weapons, that help supervisors and officers make the best decisions when they employ force, conduct pursuits, handle and transport prisoners, and make arrests. I believe that if the policies are important enough to exist for the high-risk/critical tasks, then we should be absolutely certain that everyone knows his or her contents even if it is necessary to periodically test personnel, as does the Las Vegas Metropolitan Police Department.

Until our leadership makes a strong commitment to training all supervisors extensively in the application of policies, there will be a great deal of disparity between what the chief executive writes and what is practiced in the streets.

The Raison d'Etre for Supervisors

Leadership guru Ken Blanchard remarked that the only reason supervisors exist is to raise the level of performance of those reporting to them. We can accept this statement. But let us examine it more closely, along with some of its implications. It remains quite clear that if a squad is not performing well, if there are objective measures (little work activity, poor performance, sloppy paperwork, quality of service complaints, rudeness, etc.), then, to a certain extent, we can hold the sergeants responsible. That is axiomatic. If chief executives declare that one of the greatest internal problems is the performance of first-line supervisors, to what extent would we hold the next level of supervision—lieutenants—responsible? The answer to this question is usually "not much." At a recent training session for the command staff of a major metropolitan department, a captain, when we discussed the performance expectations for first-line supervisors, disagreed with the rest of the command staff, and stated that lieutenants were the critical problem. "They don't care; they're dinosaurs!"

There are two truths here: one is, if this captain is correct, then the non-performance of the lieutenants only aggravates the problem the department has with the first-line supervisors. Second, because he was not part of the solution himself, he was part of the problem. He was accepting the status of the lieutenants without realizing that he had to redouble his efforts to change their attitudes, that he had to initiate a form of performance management for them because, knowing the problem, he became an accessory, by doing nothing except complaining about their performance. If a problem does exist with first-line supervision, then how can all the lieutenants to whom they report earn high performance evaluations? What specific actions are lieutenants taking to ameliorate the sergeants' poor performance? In retrospect, there appeared in this case to be deficiencies at the first and second levels of supervision, and the management level also. The lieutenants cannot ignore their primary service population—i.e., the sergeants. Nor can the captain ignore his or hers, that of the lieutenants and their performance. Can we expect good performance in keeping with the department's standards in this managerial environment? Probably not.

Values-Oriented Supervision

Unless departments operate on the basis of solid, core values, and unless supervisors at every level from the chief or sheriff on down exemplify those values in every action, then the necessary support will not be present. As a profession we must realize that we cannot develop the process of community-oriented policing, which demands mutual trust between the community and the police, unless the department and its officers have firmly embedded a trusting attitude toward the department and all those in it, in their conduct and their actions.

Values are beliefs that are so strong that they shape the way we act—they assist us in making decisions. They are what we stand for, and therefore they must be threaded through all policies and procedures; they must be part of training and must guide discussions and the manner in which we treat others. I believe that the value statement must become a prominent part of any promotional ceremony, and supervisors must reaffirm their commitment to these values.

Conclusion

The primary method for law enforcement executives and managers to make their job easier, for them to succeed in dramatic fashion, is to have their people perform at their highest levels. The most effective manner in which an executive can reach the operational level is through the exemplary performance of sergeants. Aside from the care and attention placed on the basic academy education, thorough preparation and careful nurturing of first-line supervision is essential. No one wants to perform mediocre work; it is the greatest insult to a person to even accept it. People in any position want to succeed. We have to set them up for success, constantly asking the question: "What can I do to help my people to excel? What can I do to make them look good?" If we are totally committed to this goal, and if we are successful, then the specter of liability vanishes, the department experiences a pattern of great performances, success begets success, and the entire profession of policing is raised to a higher level of performance.

References

Deming, W. E. (1986). *Out of the crisis*. MIT Press.

Garfield, C. (1987). *Peak performers: The new heroes of American business*. William Morrow.

Swanger, G., & Geller, W. A. (1985). *Managing innovation in policing: The untapped potential of the middle manager*. Washington, DC: Police Executive Research Forum.

Discussion Questions

1. Why are sergeants so important to a police agency?
2. Should a person be required to have completed a course on supervision before being promoted to the position of sergeant?
3. What qualities must a person possess to be an effective sergeant?

Learning Exercise

Ryan walked into the police department for his shift. He had been promoted to sergeant a month earlier and he was still learning to handle the challenges of being a front-line supervisor. When he was promoted, he became supervisor to the officers who were his peers. Now he was of the same rank that they had all jointly complained about a few weeks ago. His officers were treating him slightly differently, and he was struggling with the job of supervising them. Ryan had begun to realize that he was no longer the same kind of friend to the officers. He had had corrective discussions with two of his officers and concluded that he was going to have to write a disciplinary report concerning one of the officers' interactions with the public during traffic stops. The officer was older than Ryan and had been a mentor to Ryan when he became a police officer eight years ago. The man also had more time as an officer than Ryan and his lieutenant. This made any kind of corrective action difficult, but it came with the job, so Ryan wanted to talk to Lieutenant Addison about his consternation.

Ryan knocked on the Lieutenant's office door. Lieutenant Addison looked up from his desk. "Hey Ryan, come on in." He held up a finger with his left hand to signify that he would be with Ryan momentarily, looked back down to his desk, and finished writing something before he put down his pen and devoted his attention to Ryan. "So what's happening, Sergeant?"

Ryan explained the situation to his lieutenant and asked his advice. Lieutenant Addison thought for a moment before speaking. Finally, he said, "Well, if you've spoken with him about it a couple of times, we're going to have to correct it. You've given him his chances to correct the problem. If it was just one or two complaints, we might think it was the people he stopped, but we've had these complaints about him over the course of a number of years now." Ryan nodded. Addison continued, "Meet with him and tell him you're going to write him up, so it won't come as a surprise. But I think you also need to tell him that if we keep getting complaints, he's going to stay at home a few days." Ryan sighed, nodded, and said, "It's just awkward because he's been around for a long time."

Addison said, "Yeah, but he knows better. I know he's been doing this job for a long time and everyone likes him, but he has to fix this. This isn't the first time he's screwed up. Remember, there's a reason he's not a sergeant after all these years." Ryan looked at his lieutenant, who smiled the crooked smile of a man who knew more than he was telling.

Ryan nodded. "Okay. I'll talk with him."

As he sat there silently, Lieutenant Addison detected the struggle Ryan was having. "So how are you holding up with the new position?"

Grateful for the opportunity to talk to someone about it, Ryan told the lieutenant he was having a bit of trouble adjusting to his new duties and figuring out how he fit in with the other patrol officers. "I was the guy that complained about departmental policies with them two months ago. Now I think they see me as part of the same system because I'm supervising them." He continued with some of his adjustment frustrations before finishing.

Lieutenant Addison sat silently for a few seconds, then said, "You know, one of the hardest parts of supervising officers is tailoring your management style to each officer differently. Some officers resent orders, so you have to make suggestions to them. But some officers think suggestions are just that and don't believe they have to do what you want because it wasn't an order. So they have to be given orders instead of suggestions, but of course they think you're a jerk because you're always ordering them around. Then you'll have some officers who want you to double-check every decision they make so you're spending all your time with them, while other officers have good judgment and you barely have to manage them. Those guys will be self-sufficient. Figuring out how to individually manage each of your officers is a big challenge, but keep in mind that there are some guys who are never going to be satisfied. No matter how you treat them, they are going to think it should have been handled differently."

1. As a supervisor should Ryan attempt to manage the shift as a whole or should he manage them individually? What are the advantages, if any, and disadvantages, if any, of either style?
2. Should Ryan assume and attempt to maintain the same level of friendship he had with his shift prior to his promotion? Why or why not? Be specific.

3. In this scenario, Ryan took an opportunity with his supervisor to discuss some of the frustrations he was having. Would there ever be a time that a supervisor would discuss those same frustrations with an officer who is below him in rank? Why or why not? Be specific.
4. What indicator was mentioned within the scenario that makes it imperative that Ryan address the older officer concerning the complaints lodged against him?
5. During their conversation Lt. Addison indicated to Ryan why the older officer was never promoted to the rank of sergeant. Should Ryan, when counseling the older officer, inform him that he will never be promoted to the rank of sergeant? Why or why not. Be specific.

6 Succession Planning[1]

LEARNING OBJECTIVES

1. The student will understand the need and purpose of planning for the leaving of key executives.
2. The student will be able to recognize the recent programs for allowing executives to leave the agency.
3. The student will understand the three components of succession planning.

Introduction

It sounds so elementary—when people leave, replace them with competent, capable, and energized people. And yet throughout the United States, and perhaps among public safety agencies around the world, the task is formidable. In many if not most instances, the ability to identify, qualify, assess, process, and hire, and/or promote suitable candidates is arduous, and often lacks the timeliness necessary to provide for the continuity of operations desired by the chief executive.

There are never as many suitable leaders available as an agency needs, or will need. Programs like Deferred Retirement Option Plans (DROP), coupled with rapid growth, contribute to the problem, where managers and leaders are now more in control of *when* they wish to leave as opposed to when the organization unilaterally made those decisions. Thus, voids in leadership can happen at any time or, conversely, they do not happen when the organization might be better served if they had.

For those who are inside that same organization, those who "have been there," why is it that their talents are not always known, particularly if they have been nurtured through career path planning and other development interventions throughout their tenures? If such interventions during the course of their employment have not produced the results or skills necessary for today's contemporary policing, why have they not been directed toward assignments where they can be and are successful? Failure to communicate assessment and development efforts and their results honestly, and in a timely fashion, breeds frustration, anger, and a feeling of futility by all parties. This raises the organizational distractions that make achieving the mission more difficult while at the same time increasing the level of disenfranchisement.

Succession planning is routinely thought of as an exercise in planning for the right personnel to replace command level officers upon their retirement. Recent trends have demonstrated that retirement plans are changing rapidly and our workforce is aging. In addition, the senior officer who met eligibility requirements for retirement 20 years ago, and in some jurisdictions even today, was 62 to 65 years of age and had served 30 to 35

---

[1]This chapter is included with the permission of Edward Werder.

75

years. In many cases he served in the military before joining the field of law enforcement and saw his public service as an extension of military service. Today, entry-level candidates often do not join the organization with the benefit of prior military service, nor are they faced with the same age requirements as some of their predecessors. They therefore start earlier, and younger, and are required to serve a lesser number of years in order to satisfy both **vesting** requirements and the conditions for retirement.

In "younger/serve fewer years/out earlier," vesting in contemporary agencies can take as little as six years rather than what has been the tradition of 10 or even 15 years. Years required for eligibility to retire are 25 years or less today, rather than the previous 30 or 35 years of service. A defined benefit plan now can provide as much as 4 percent per year of credible service for only 20 or 25 years, as opposed to 1.6 percent, 2 percent, or 3 percent, which was, and is still, customary for longer terms of service in many departments.

These factors have made the job of succession planning that much more difficult for a number of reasons, in addition to the ones already mentioned. Among the most salient is that the employee now has more control over when, and how, he or she will separate from employment. In years past, it was the employer, or the legislative statute or ordinance, that determined when, how, and under what conditions an employee would be granted retirement benefits. Some current programs that have been added in recent years are:

- deferred retirement option plans
- buy-back retirement packages
- mergers and bifurcated benefits
- 401As in lieu of defined benefit plans
- management enhancements to existing retirement plans
- health care provisions that maximize at a certain number of years of service
- investment plans versus defined benefit plans
- early buyouts to accelerate retirements

Leaders of law enforcement agencies need to provide additional analysis in succession-planning processes to ensure future leaders and employees are equipped with the necessary knowledge and skills to keep their departments progressive. Succession planning involves looking at the entire **organizational personnel life cycle** and providing tools for employee success at all levels to ensure that managers and leaders are selected and developed throughout their careers in law enforcement.

Is it a "young department," staffed with personnel whose average age is less than 35? Is it an aging department, one with a considerable number of employees in whose hands the future level of achievement of the entire agency is determined by their individual choice to retire, or not? Can employees retire after 20 years as opposed to 35? Are the non-sworn employees eligible to leave the department in the near future due to their age or eligibility for retirement, while the sworn members need many more years to become eligible for retirement? In that scenario, will the administrative "engine" of the department come to a halt earlier than expected due to the lack of an effective transition of **administrative processing capabilities**? Will this happen at the same time that the chief executive is marketing the overall competence of his agency?

Effective succession planning can prevent or at least reduce the complications that arise when the agency fails to diagnose the health of the organization, not only for today, but also throughout the course of employment of its members. There are various strategies that can be utilized to assess the systemic effects that such plans can have. First, however, there must be the commitment to adopt, implement, and utilize succession planning as a complementary tool of **human resource management**.

There are three components of succession planning, only one of which concerns itself with the *end* of an employee's career. They are separation, entry, and career enhancement. The first deals with attrition, the second with hiring, and the third with **workforce development planning**. The specific topics of each include the following:

Employee Separation: Responding to Attrition
- Normal attrition
- Terminations
- Position elimination
- Death
- Disability
- Retirement option programs

Entry: Hiring for the Present and the Future
- Recruitment diversity
- Lateral transfer into the agency
- Citizenship
- Bonus programs
- Service contracts
- Civilianization

Career: Workforce Development Planning
- Workforce planning
- Mentoring
- Educational incentive programs
- Promotions
- Diversity of workforce allocation
- Career development and cross-training
- Re-employment of retired personnel

The lessons learned by utilizing effective succession planning are many and complementary. The aftereffects include, among others, enhanced morale, a reduction in unnecessary and unwarranted professional compliance issues, improved marketing of the agency through word of mouth from appropriately treated former employees, better entry-level employees by virtue of acquiring a higher percentage of the limited supply of qualified candidates, and better-prepared candidates for leadership and other positions.

It is clear that failing to address any one or two of these three components exposes the department to inefficient or ineffective operations, public criticism, and the potential of compromising the public's safety and security.

The essential tool for succession planning is the training of key personnel throughout the agency. It is not singularly the responsibility of human resources staff. The responsibility lies throughout the agency, primarily with **command staff**, in understanding their role even when minor personnel decisions are considered. A keen understanding of the three components of succession planning should stimulate critical thinking throughout the agency. It should (1) identify the multiple reasons employees leave the organization and assess and plan for the impact of those departures; (2) attract and select the most talented and motivated candidates; and (3) enhance, through multiple opportunities, the careers of those who are capable of leadership challenges in the future.

Several foundation blocks drive succession planning. The primary elements of that foundation are political and financial backing. There are associated costs and each has a political impact. The more universal the organization's commitment to succession planning, the more the costs can be absorbed as normal business practices. The retention of personnel due to an effective succession plan can also create cost savings and a more efficient organization, based in part upon the continuity of operations and in part upon the synergism within the leadership that results.

Recent trends suggest that employees are being **multitasked** as their roles become more complex and expanded. Communities demand more, recruits receive greater levels of training, and the legal, social, and environmental conditions within which they work continue to become more complex. A model developed to analyze the impact of replacing staff examines the entry of new personnel, career development of staff, and how employees exit the organization.

Within each component of succession planning one should always consider **budgetary processes** and **political processes**, as they are the foundation blocks that enable positive growth and sound succession planning. Although the **succession model**

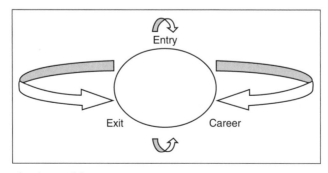

FIGURE 6-1 Succession planning model.

is circular in nature and usually starts at the exit process, it can be used effectively at any starting point (see Figure 6-1). It is important to complete the model's circular cycle regardless of the starting point. It represents an important organizational diagnostic tool. It helps ensure that the organization is in a constant state of readiness when faced with **attrition cycles**.

A brief discussion of each of the cycles follows. It is not meant to be an exhaustive review but rather a source of stimulus for improving the use and replacement of an organization's most expensive resource: its people.

Employee Separation

Organizations generally do a fair job of dealing with attrition; some are better than others. But with the advent of deferred retirement options, often referred to as **DROP**, and other programs, large numbers of employees leaving within days or months of each other have created significant stressors within departments. The specifics of these types of plans vary, but they often benefit an employee by allowing him or her to collect a greater retirement pension in exchange for providing more years of service to their employers. Agencies can benefit because their human resource components have had up to five years to plan for the exodus and provide competent, trained replacements. While not *all* the reasons for not planning effectively can be laid at the feet of human resources, it nonetheless results in a degree of crisis management, vacancies left unfilled, less than prepared people assigned with the same or better performance of their predecessors, and organizational discord. Who was chosen, how were they selected, who did they know, why wasn't "I" selected, and other questions permeate an organization already affected by the loss.

How would an organization perform were it to lose multiple key executives, managers, and employees, such as in the September 11, 2001, terrorist attacks? On a smaller scale, what would happen if a smaller number were lost in a car accident or plane crash? Would there be key people in plentiful supply, and would your organization know who and where they were? What preparation would they have received? What mentoring opportunities and experiential learning would they have received? While such a tragedy hopefully will not occur again, and certainly not to your organization specifically, how "deep" is your bench? If the entire upper management were to leave, perhaps as a result of a "buyout" or the hiring of a new executive, would there be a group of successors ready to take the helm? Finally, would you, your peers, and subordinates want to work for them?

This is not a new problem. In fact, that is part of the problem. Replacing key employees due to attrition has been a long-standing managerial concern. There are usually substantial consequences when key people leave, including decreased productivity, costs of hiring a new employee, and increased training time. Some indirect but nonetheless important consequences can include continuity of operations, employee morale, and the sheer difficulty of replacing *that particular* employee.

Attrition is defined as the turnover of sworn and professional support staff. It is the exit of human capital. The loss of these employees occurs in many ways:

1. Resignation—who is leaving; why are they leaving
2. Termination—fairness (dignity and respect) coupled with consistency
3. Elimination of position—retrenchment management, "bumping," etc.
4. Death—contingency planning
5. Disability—creates a deployable workforce problem
6. Retirement—the most challenging of all areas of attrition

In addition to the attrition categories listed above, special retirement programs can either accelerate or decelerate employee attrition. The smallest change in an employee retirement plan—i.e., 25 to 20 years, increasing the years of service multiplier, **"buying out"** higher salaried employees so that they will leave earlier and be replaced by lower salaried employees—can accelerate retirements, deplete a workforce, and have lasting ramifications. Common "buy out" options can include purchasing service time from prior service with other agencies, purchasing future service time, and early "buy out" by the governmental entity as a retirement incentive. The impact of such changes is often predictable within specific short time frames, solely based upon the elements of the "buy out," or can be clarified by completing employee surveys.

Conversely, programs such as DROP, where employees can "retire" from their current defined benefit retirement plans yet continue working for a defined period, can decelerate the loss of agency personnel. The DROP functions as if the employees ended their employments, with their retirement monthly benefit deposited into a special tax-deferred retirement account for a specified number of years. The plans differ in that some guarantee a specific rate of interest while others have a variable amount or even allow the employees to control their investments within defined categories.

The common term of the DROP is five years, although some plans have only three years. Depending on the employee's final organizational compensation level, those final three to five years, with the impact of compounding interest, can produce a significant nest egg. For that and other reasons, many employees are willing to remain, subsequently deferring the need for their replacements.

Entry

As our workforce ages, community expectations change, the level of diversity requirements change, and our demands change. Recruitment, screening, selection, training, and retention processes become increasingly important. With this in mind, the Succession Planning Model becomes critical in overcoming the challenges brought on by these changes and challenges that confront law enforcement executives. Adaptability, accuracy, legality, fairness, and finding the best talent available, each requires that the agency's recruitment, processing, training, and retention efforts should be aggressive, ongoing, and interrelated.

Financial issues and the impact upon the annual budget make it difficult to maintain the continuity of the entire Entry component, not just the recruiting cycle. It is often "feast or famine," with the feast portion becoming less and less of a recurrence. Retrenchment management has often failed to address the organizational and professional impact that breaking one or more of the cycles can have on overall agency performance. Not only in the short term, but hiring mistakes, either hiring the wrong person or failing to hire the right person, can have a generational impact on the employees, the management-union relationship, the agency, and the community. Other human resource functions are affected as well.

Recruitment

The IACP Police Image and Ethics Committee (2003) has also identified the problem of **minority representation** by noting the importance of addressing the shortage of minorities in policing and how a workforce that resembles the community an agency serves can build public trust. This, in conjunction with identifying the core competencies that an ideal law enforcement and professional staff member should have in the 21st century, mandates that the human resources function within an agency be of utmost importance. Thus, the management and staff assigned to it must be knowledgeable; energized; current in the law, court decisions, and regulatory agencies; and imbued with social interaction skills that make candidates become employees.

How extensive is the recruiting effort? Where is it done? What marketing skills does the organization have or is it willing to employ? Cultivating and maintaining recruiting contacts is the lifeblood of the successful recruiting effort. Colleges and universities, public service announcements, advertising, Internet utilization, and particularly the agency's Web site can be key tools in attracting the very best potential employees and expanding the outreach to minority candidates. With the free use of computers at public libraries, even those who might not have been able to afford a computer can nonetheless have access.

Let us not forget that current employees can be one of the key ingredients in attracting qualified candidates. But are the current employees qualified themselves? Do they represent all the attributes of a key person—a building block, if you will—in the future of a dynamic organization? And so the cyclical impact of making sound decisions today pays dividends in the future if quality drafting is consistent and professional, or debt service if it is periodic and uncertain. An organization can only achieve what its leadership, in concert with qualified, well-prepared, and capable employees, will allow it to achieve.

Diversity

Diversity presents a number of issues to organizations, and particularly to the human resources component. Perhaps the most complex question is "What is diversity?" It tends to shift as new groups assert their identities, immigration policies change or are modified/not adhered to, or existing groups are not proportionately represented. Esty et al.

(1995) define diversity in the workplace as understanding, valuing, accepting, acknowledging and celebrating differences among people in 10 dimensions. These dimensions are: class, ethnicity, age, race, hierarchical status, gender, religion, physical ability/disability, family situation, and sexual orientation. These dimensions obviously encompass a number of abilities, working styles, ethnicities, and cultural backgrounds.

The strides made in law enforcement organizations have been measurable, yet many would say it has been too little, too late. Perhaps an organization has a representative number of a particular group at the entry or even supervisory level. But has a meaningful diversity program been in existence long enough to have proportionality at the middle management, management, and executive levels?

The workforce is becoming increasingly diverse. The organization called Diversity Best Practices (www.diversitybestpractices.com) provides evidence indicating that most of the new workers entering the labor market are women or minorities. Tapia and Spence (2012) point out that females made up more than half of the American workforce in 2010. The British Association of Women Police (2006) has developed a document titled "Gender Agenda 2," outlining five long-term aims. Their vision statement, worthy of consideration by all law enforcement agencies, is to generate a thriving police organization that supports women officers or deputies in achieving their full potential and making a full contribution to policing. Recognizing that diversity is critical to the health of all law enforcement agencies should inspire organizations to establish specific diversity policies and standard operating procedures.

There are a number of other methods to enhance recruitment and retention of sworn personnel. Some may offer flexibility in attracting, or at least considering, candidates that otherwise might not receive further processing. This serves not to recommend but rather to identify some that otherwise might remain unknown:

- lateral transfers
- United States citizenship (those who have applied may continue the process)
- educational bonus
- bilingual bonus
- obligated-service or contractual-service agreement

Civilianization

Adding civilians to the police department workforce is another consideration that is becoming more commonplace in police departments. Kostelac (2008) cites Department of Justice numbers that demonstrate the growth of civilianization in law enforcement agencies over the past several decades. Civilian employees composed 7.5% of all police personnel in 1950. By 1970 that number had increased to nearly 14%. The ratio reached 26.7% in 1990 and by 2006, the number stood at 30.8% of all police employees. In addition to increasing in numbers, civilian employees are also receiving an increasing number of tasks. They are now more likely than in previous eras to carry out duties that have traditionally been reserved for sworn personnel (Bayley & Shearing, 2004), including parking enforcement, taking citizen reports for specified offenses, dealing with minor traffic accidents, and supporting crime victims (Kostelac, 2008).

This trend offers a number of advantages to the police manager who implements it. There is a cost-saving benefit because non-sworn personnel typically cost less to train and equip than uniformed, sworn officers. Non-sworn positions are often lower salaried positions as well, saving the department additional funds. Furthermore, the duties that civilian employees can handle will often free sworn officers to deal with more pressing matters. Given the advantages of this approach and increasingly tight budgets, the civilianization movement in policing is likely to gain momentum.

Workforce Development Planning

The key question: What sort of competencies are needed to fill a position, where does leadership potential lie, and how can the organization assess an individual's specific strengths and weaknesses? Utilizing an approach in which the organization "looks for someone just like Sara" may not necessarily fill the organizational void created when Sara leaves. Sara may have been an excellent employee, but over the years did not maintain the contemporary training and skills to advance the agency. She may have been personable and qualified at the time of assignment, but the years perhaps eroded the core and technological competencies necessary in this fast-paced world. Hiring someone to mirror Sara might therefore shortchange the organization, because Sara was the right person at *that* time, but may not be the right person for *this* or *tomorrow's* time.

Workforce planning is an ongoing process and requires committed involvement from members of the organization at all levels. As leaders, you should: (a) be proactive in identifying competencies needed to meet present and future work demands; (b) provide counseling to employees to determine career interests; (c) develop specific plans for fulfilling those interests; and (d) identify methods to close the gap between what the organization needs and what the existing workforce provides in terms of real competencies.

Opportunities would then, of necessity, have to be merit based. Preparation and participation in training for an individual development plan would not guarantee promotion; it would offer the potential of self-motivated achievement.

A workforce plan has four basic steps. Within those steps are varying degrees of complexity based in part upon how many of these functions are currently being performed by human resources and how many still need to be initiated:

1. Develop or update the organization's strategic plan. If you do not know where you are going, how can you get there?
2. Conduct job analyses to identify core competencies for position classifications, incorporating future needs identified through strategic planning, i.e., Knowledge, Skills, and Abilities (KSA).
3. Assess where employees are today in terms of their skill levels.
4. Plan and communicate methods to close gaps between required competencies and current employee assessments to manage human capital.

As an example of conducting job analyses, the Federal Office of Personnel Management (OPM) prepared a set of five executive core qualifications defining the competencies and characteristics required for entry into the Senior Executive Service. It is used by many agencies in selection, performance management, and leadership development for management and executive positions. The leadership competencies are:

- leading change
- leading people
- results-driven
- business acumen
- building coalitions/communications

Examples of closing the gap between organizational needs and employee abilities can involve leadership training (FBI/SPI/SMIP, etc.), mentoring programs, tuition reimbursement, supervisory training of all types, participation in promotional processes, seeking innovative methods for career development, and managing specialized assignment through temporary placements and other alternatives. Among those alternatives are such concepts as rehiring retirees or civilianization.

EVOLVING ROLE OF TECHNOLOGY

Departmental efforts to select the most appropriate personnel for specific tasks can be made much easier today than in previous generations. For example, training opportunities, promotion testing, and duty assignment opportunities can be sent by e-mail to all members of the department as a mass e-mail or posted on an internal webpage. The specific information can be included in the electronic communication that can serve to free supervisors from having to answer too many specific questions during briefings or other daily work.

In order for an agency to stay abreast of employee special skills, an agency manager can establish a computerized database that categorizes specific types of expertise that officers may have. For example, when first hired, new employees could answer questionnaires on which they can list their special skills and interests. If a second language is listed, that information would be stored in the database. If a suspect is arrested who does not speak English, the database can be checked for employees who might speak the suspect's language. The employees should be reminded of the database so they can have their profiles updated as they develop more skills. Additionally, the database can be developed at no cost to the department if its creation and management is left to interns, who are often comfortable with computer-based work.

The National Institute of Justice also offers numerous opportunities through its website, www.nij.gov, to download training documents. Additionally, the site offers opportunities to sign up for certification courses as well as web-based training on a number of topics, including forensic evidence and crime mapping. The International Association of Chiefs of Police also offers in-service training materials through their website, www.theiacp.org. The Internet allows law enforcement agencies many opportunities to train their officers in areas that can help them replace retiring officers, or bring new skills to their departments.

Mentoring

Mentoring involves encouraging individuals in a coordinated way to utilize personal motivation to promote professional growth. Success can occur in any size agency and the essential elements remain similar. Some of those elements are: (1) that the organization values its employees, (2) it encourages their career, and (3) it promotes upward mobility opportunities (Williams, 2000).

Mentoring also depends on the willingness and quality of those who will become mentors and role models. In addition, the ideal mentor must have the traits of patience, empathy, trust, understanding, caring, and a willingness to put others before oneself. Informal mentoring is commonplace in many agencies, such as when a senior employee takes someone "under his wing." But successfully training mentors is a critical component to the ultimate success of the program. Several major law enforcement organizations (IACP, IPTM, and others) offer two-day training workshops specific to law enforcement mentoring.

In a successful mentoring experience everyone wins—the candidate, the organization, and the person doing the mentoring. Candidates first learn skills, aptitudes, and attitudes necessary to develop in an expedient environment with a greater likelihood of success, without having to learn through their own mistakes. The organization benefits through increased productivity at an earlier time, salary savings due to the mentors doing their job as part of, or in addition to, their regular duties, and enhanced recruitment as the organization becomes more attractive as a place to work. The people doing the mentoring enhance their status in the organization, learn through the eyes of their students, and, through coaching, elevate their own abilities to handle personnel-related issues.

Some tips: Don't oversell the initiative. Understand that there *must* be support from the top of the organization. There must be union support if it involves represented members. Proper planning is the key to success. Volunteerism should be the key in selection of both mentors and those who choose to be mentored.

Supervisory capabilities are often defined by how well the organization has recruited, developed, and retained its human capital. Without conscientious, competent, and well-trained "grassroots" employees, supervisory candidates are limited in number and limited to the scope of their past experience and their capabilities with new ones.

Promotions

A vital component of succession planning is promotions. However, it is the employee who has to play a major role in pursuing promotions. Like motivation, the organization should provide an environment where employees feel that their greatest accomplishments can come only if they play a more pivotal role in their organization. It is often disincentives, however, that reduce the number of qualified candidates who participate in the promotional process or even contemplate that they will.

Whetstone (2001) discusses survey results of a large midwestern police department and the reasons officers or deputies either do, or do not, participate in the promotional process. The explanations for participating in the process were consistent for males and females, white and minority, with only the order of priority for those reasons being somewhat different. "Personal goals" were listed as the highest priority by males and whites, while females and minorities rated career opportunities highest.

Reasons for not participating are the most important findings of the survey, for they can be instrumental in helping an organization adjust the conditions that reinforce upward mobility and avoid policies and practices that self-limit the employees' desire to participate. Again the survey results among those four groups were the same; only the priority assigned to each was somewhat different.

The most common responses for not participating in the promotional process were:

- salary decrease
- not ready for the test
- child care concerns
- family relations

Males, whites, and minorities all rated "salary decrease" as the number one reason, citing the decrease in pay that results from the loss of overtime opportunities and court pay. Females rated "childcare concerns" highest.

Some of the reasons cited for nonparticipation were "professional reasons." Clearly, the reasons cited were positive in terms of current job satisfaction, in that they felt a sense of stability in their current assignment. In all four groups, potentially changing their job satisfaction and loss of stability were the leading reasons for not participating. Loss of shift by virtue of losing their seniority in the promoted role was a strong factor as well.

"Organizational reasons" also came into focus. The perception of promotions as not being merit-based and that hidden agendas exist was reflected in all four groups. Males' and whites' number-one organizational reason for not participating was "unfair test process." For females and minorities, it was "biased administration." Thus, if an organization can address the disincentives in a positive way, it may subsequently expand the pool of viable candidates.

Departments must be willing to market themselves, not only to their citizens, but to their employees as well. Each represents a constituency that must be nurtured and protected. The organization must promote the factors that will be beneficial to its employees, such as the benefits of long-term pay increases, additional advancement opportunities, enhanced specialized training, assuming the image of a role model, and actually shaping the organization's future. If the disincentives to promotion can be addressed, the pool of willing and capable candidates is sure to increase.

Diversity in Promotion

There must be both the recognition and the adoption of defensible and realistic goals in achieving diversity. A workforce evaluation of Equal Employment Opportunity guidelines should be completed. This is a requirement for agencies receiving federal funds. Ideally, the demographics of the agency should mirror those of the community it serves. It should also mirror the gender and ethnic makeup of the available workforce in the agency's jurisdiction.

The agency must have an action plan to include actionable steps that are intended to reduce the imbalance or underutilization of a particular protected class of individuals. This is reflective not just of the entry level but throughout the ranks, to include professional staff positions. It is essential to consider diversity before, during, and after the promotional process, including the assignments of those who are ultimately promoted.

Career Development and Cross-Training

Whether referred to as career pathing or a career development plan, employees should receive objective information as to how they can meet their individual career development goals. It should be recorded so that it can be referred to when gauging whether progress toward their personal or organization goals are on schedule, behind schedule, or perhaps have changed. Then new career-pathing plans are prepared to channel their energies toward constructive goals. Employees so focused are less likely to be rumor-mongers or troublemakers because they are self-directed and on a schedule, with little time for insignificant or unimportant diversions.

Tuition reimbursement, educational incentives, loan repayments, and loan forgiveness may be organizational programs to facilitate employee development. Requiring education attainment prior to certain promotional opportunities may also maintain the focus of energized employees. Investing in people has never been bad policy, and inventing new ways to retain qualified personnel is certainly worth the effort.

Specialized Assignments

By providing opportunities for specialized assignments, executives hope employees will be able to better view the agency as a whole. Short-term training assignments, where practical and available, should be given to all employees within the agency. At the supervisory and executive levels, **inter-agency exchanges** for limited periods provide insight into the strengths and weaknesses of practices in both agencies, allowing for improvements in both. Modifying practices that can be improved upon, adopting practices that enhance the parent agency, or eliminating those in either organization that have limited utility alone justifies the exchange. Measuring the candidate's capacity for upward mobility, both by self-inventory and organizational need assessment, is a bonus that can pay long-lasting dividends.

Temporary exposure to specialized assignments of their choice allows employees to assess whether the duties, skills, responsibilities, and abilities are attainable, as well as what it will take to complete the preparation process. The future decisions the organization makes are matters of cost and the capacity to achieve successful outcomes. Employee placement in positions where there is the greatest chance of success at a reasonable cost is a wise expenditure of the public's dollar.

Involuntary assignments can occur for a number of reasons. Military activations, the short- or long-term illness of an incumbent, ineffective leadership, and retirements can cause a transfer that is not the choice of the person being transferred. The executive staff should use discretion when such organizational needs arise, making sure that such changes are implemented in a fair and impartial manner. Open, face-to-face discussions should be held with the affected employees describing the reasons, duration, and perhaps even why they were chosen. Oftentimes the employees who may have been uprooted from their current assignments will find relief in knowing that their organization believed they had the capacities for new assignments. Awareness of employees' abilities is a powerful tool.

Posting of specialized assignment vacancies can go a long way in minimizing the belief that hidden agendas or organizational bias exists. Fair access is an important step in maintaining or improving morale. Likewise, current command staff should know the aspirations of their subordinates and contact those employees to make sure that they have the opportunity to compete for announced opportunities. This increases morale in the current assignments, because the employees then know that their command is interested in their career as well as improving their organization. This breeds loyalty, respect, and organizational commitment.

Use of Retired Employees

Sometimes the best new tool is the one you already had. That is not to say that all former employees made a substantial contribution to the organization before and can do so again. It means that some retirees took with them part of the "brain trust," and after their departure the organization lost some specialized skills. Perhaps the workforce development planning of their replacements did not achieve what the organization needed, or perhaps the replacement also left or the issues changed and a "utility infielder" is needed once again.

By hiring or contracting with them, the former employees often pick up just where they left off; they feel the sense of pride when "their number was called," and can help again to develop their replacements. They can usually do so at a reduced cost, particularly when they enter into a contract and the organization avoids the cost of mandated benefits required for regular employees. Meanwhile, the organizational need is filled and the executive staff can focus upon more pressing issues and problems.

Thoughts for the Future

In many cases, organizations have addressed both skill-based training and development for entry and first-line supervisory positions. Some administer the process quite well, while others perform some components well but other components are severely challenged. Some organizations have no process at all for any position beyond the entry level. Even when there is a process for the lower organizational positions, those beyond them appear to be measured by the candidates' performance and endurance only. That does not guarantee success for either the candidate or the organization. While performance may be an optimal yardstick for the *current* position, it does not always reveal capabilities necessary for the next for future position. In fact, without specific job task analyses for the various positions that carry with them significant responsibility, and the development criteria to achieve them, placing the right commander in the right position may be nothing short of pure luck or guesswork. What organization can afford to meet the future in so cavalier a fashion?

Employees and their union need to understand the employees' role in self-managing their careers once the environment of fair play has been firmly established. The chief executive needs to cultivate a relationship in which the union hierarchy and the command level of the department are mutually committed to enhancing the organization through the meaningful development of its employees and members. Once that relationship is in place, although it is an ever-evolving one built upon trust and respect, succession planning becomes a tool all can use. Without that dual commitment, they stay their course and we, the organization, stay ours. Who suffers when the relationship is tense, strained or nonexistent? The employee/member of both entities.

While there may be a vast supply of talent at all levels within an organization, do we know who has it, or even where they are? Conversely, do the employees know where the "rungs of the ladder" are that they must climb to achieve personal and organizational success? Are talented and capable people now in place in the organization's leadership positions? Are there enough qualified employees at the lower levels of the organization and are they ready to step up? Are they qualified, competent, and trained in their current positions to breed the level of success we currently desire, notwithstanding their potential consideration for a higher leadership position?

There is never enough qualified leadership in any organization, regardless of its size. We all want more than we have. When leadership is important, the skills we tend to focus on become qualitative rather than exclusively quantitative. It is no longer "how many" or "how much," but rather how good, how successful, how long will it last, and how satisfied was our customer—the citizen. Thus, the eye for detail, the sense of urgency, the desire never to accept less than the optimal solution or performance defines some of the attributes that organizations crave.

It is never too late to begin, to continue, or to finish developing succession planning. It continues to have an impact on the organization generations after it is developed. It influences policy, service, and outcomes by virtue of the caliber of people it develops at all levels. If serving citizens is the nature of the business we are in, we must find better and more cost-effective methods to provide it. Employee continuity can be enhanced through career opportunities and salary enhancements during the process of upward mobility. Employees will develop a sense of pride in knowing that they are more capable of delivering quality public service today than they were yesterday, and will be prepared for the challenges of tomorrow.

LEARNING EXERCISE

Sheriff Bryson is struggling with his attempt to balance recruitment and retention of new officers in his aging department. He has put more of his budget into recruiting at colleges with criminal justice programs. He hopes to bring in more educated people to add special skills to this department, such as the ability to speak foreign languages and use computer technology. However, in the interest of impartiality, he has made all of his newly hired deputies work in the jail for several months before he allows them to work in any other division in the department. "Everyone has to pull their time in the detention center," he would tell them at their orientations. Some of the long-time employees had grown accustomed to working in the jail and seemed content there, but the new hires seemed particularly eager to start working in the patrol division.

Two months ago, the sheriff was able to recruit a young man named Jesse who was just graduating with a master's degree in criminology. Jesse is a confident and direct young man. He has been asking his supervisor at the jail how soon he will be able to transfer to the patrol division. If Sheriff Bryson allows him to transfer too soon, there will grumbling throughout the department. Deputies who have been trying to get to the patrol division for years will be dissatisfied that they have waited so long without a transfer and that the new guy was able to get there in just a few months. However, Jesse had written a master's thesis on the utility of procuring grants to update police patrol technology and techniques; he has expertise that the other deputies do not have. Furthermore, Jesse has more options than the other deputies. He already has a master's degree and if he is not transferred soon, he may seek a job with another agency that will put him on patrol. Failing to transfer Jesse may mean that Sheriff Bryson will lose him as an employee.

- How do you think Sheriff Bryson should weigh Jesse's transfer request with his attempt at impartiality within his department?
- Is it fair to judge Jesse on a different set of criteria than the other deputies in the department?
- Is there enough benefit in giving Jesse his requested transfer to overcome the negative feelings that other deputies may end up having toward the sheriff? Are there any concessions Sheriff Bryson can make to appease Jesse without upsetting other deputies who have been working at the department for years?
- Even if Sheriff Bryson grants Jesse his transfer request, will it solve the issue for the foreseeable future? Is there any reason to believe that Jesse won't have leverage to push for other transfers or promotions in the future? How will he handle other newly hired deputies with college degrees who want to transfer to patrol?
- What policies would you make to address this issue for future hires?

References

Bayley, D. H., & Shearing, C. D. (2004). The future of policing. In Q. C. Thurman, & S. Zhao-Jihong (Eds.), *Contemporary policing: Controversies, challenges, and solutions. An anthology* (pp. 355–369). Los Angeles: Roxbury.

British Association of Women Police. (2006). *Gender agenda 2.* Retrieved from http://www.bawp.org/Default.aspx?pageId=1239106.

Esty, K., Griffin, R., & Schorr-Hirsh, M. (1995). *Workplace diversity. A manager's guide to solving problems and turning diversity into a competitive advantage.* Avon, MA: Adams Media Corporation.

International Association of Chiefs of Police (IACP) Police Image and Ethics Committee. (2003). *Mobilizing the community for minority recruitment and selection: A strategy to leverage community assets to enhance recruitment and placement of minorities.* Retrieved from http://www.cops.usdoj.gov/files/ric/CDROMs/RecruitmentHiringRetention/Pubs/MobilizingtheCommunityforMinor.pdf.

Kostelac, C. A. (2008). *The changing face of police organizations: Trends in civilianization* (unpublished doctoral dissertation). Phoenix, AZ: Arizona State University.

Tapia, A. T., & Spence, B. (2012). *The emerging female-friendly 21st century: A gender revolution is under way.* Retrieved from http://www.diversitybestpractices.com/publications/emerging-female-friendly-21st-century-gender-revolution-under-way.

Whetstone, T. S. (2001). Copping out: Why police officers decline to participate in the sergeant's promotional process. *American Journal of Criminal Justice, 25*(2), 147–159.

Williams, Julie (2000). Mentoring for law enforcement. *FBI Law Enforcement Bulletin, 69*(3), 19–25.

Further Reading

Bocklet, R. (1987). Civilianization, it works in Santa Rosa. *Law and Order, 35*(12), 57–60, City of Berkeley (CA). 2002. Police Staffing Audit. Berkeley, CA.

Federal Office of Personnel Management (www.leadership.opm.gov/ecq.html).

Major Cities Chiefs and Federal Bureau of Investigation National Executive Institute (2003). *Report, Limited Duty.*

Major Cities Chiefs Human Resources Committee and Federal Bureau of Investigation National Executive Institute (1995). Conference on Recruitment, Hiring, and Career Development, February.

Major Cities Chiefs Human Resources Committee and Federal Bureau of Investigation (2001-2002). *Filling Vacancies,* p. 46.

Major Cities Chiefs Human Resources Committee, Hiring and Career Development.

Major Cities Chiefs and Federal Bureau of Investigation (2004). *Succession Planning.*

National Advisory Commission on Criminal Justice Standards and Goals. (1973). *Assignment of Civilian Police Personnel, Police.* pp. 258–262. Washington, DC: U.S. Government Printing Office.

Newcombe, T. (n.d.). Racing to Replace Retirees. www.govtech.net/magazine.

Snow, R. L. (1989). Strengthening through civilization. *Law and Order.* April.

Taylor, B. (2003). Pension crisis swamps cities and counties. *CAL-TAX DIGEST.* April.

Discussion Questions

1. What are the primary elements of the foundation blocks that drive succession planning? How can they be overcome?
2. How can you implement the Succession Planning Model?
3. How can you control the loss of outstanding employees?
4. How can we implement Workforce Development Planning?

7

Organizational Environment

LEARNING OBJECTIVES

1. The student will be challenged to provide a work climate in which every employee has the opportunity to mature as an individual and department member.
2. The student will be able to intelligently determine the "whys" of past behavior patterns.
3. The student will be able to predict change and control behavior patterns.
4. The student will become familiar with various behavior theories.
5. The student will recognize that in enhancing the importance of the individual, a higher level of professionalism—essential to a productive department—is achieved.
6. The student will first assess his or her own motivational needs for more effective utilization of assigned personnel.

Introduction

The study of organizational behavior is a search for answers to perplexing questions about human nature. What motivates people? How can the police manager make the best use of the behavior patterns found within organizations? Recognizing the importance of the human element in organizational behavior, this chapter develops a framework for police managers that can help them understand their employees better, enable them to determine the "whys" of past behavior patterns, and, possibly, allow them to predict, change, and control behavior patterns.

Police managers, having different types of personnel within their departments, must attempt to mold their people into productive units so that higher objectives may be set and reached. Only through the understanding of human behavior as it relates to the organization can managers make the most effective use of personnel within their departments.

An issue continually faced by police managers is that of **motivation**. Many managers believe that it is part of their job to help motivate subordinates; indeed, the author's own studies show that there are three essential aspects to developing motivated, highly productive officers. First, assuming that the officer has the ability to do the job, he or she needs time to develop; this time can be granted by the police manager. Second, officers need knowledge. This can be provided by the police manager through individual and group training programs. The third, and most important, ingredient is desire or motivation. This must come from within the individual. Without this motivation, the employee cannot be expected to grow and develop.

How, then, does a manager motivate employees? Usually managers attempt to serve as examples to subordinates. Police managers must be keenly aware that their performance is linked to the goals they seek. However, these goals are also controlled by officer performance. For example, a police officer who wishes to work in a certain patrol unit to gain extra time for continuing education would have a high performance level because he or she is strongly motivated to gain the potential reward. The manager, in turn, might work closely with the officer, giving him or her additional responsibilities for the ultimate outcome of higher productivity within the patrol unit. Because the two goals—that of the officer and that of the manager—are consistent, the manager's goals will probably be met and the employee would be considered to be highly motivated. However, once the individual officer's goal ceases to be important—if, for example, the officer were to drop out of school, graduate, or transfer to another shift where he or she cannot attend school—his or her performance level would probably drop. It is important for the manager to sit down with subordinates and discuss personal goals—that is, their reasons for working—and, whenever they are consistent with the manager's goals, help them to achieve these goals.

As stated previously, the officer's individual performance depends on ability as well as the drive or desire to succeed. It is also influenced by the officer's attitude, experience, and training. Assuming that an individual has ability, there will be a direct relationship between the manager's performance and goals and those of the individual officers. If motivation comes from within each individual, the police leader can play an important role in helping individual officers to achieve their ultimate goals.

In addressing the issue of motivation, the police manager must be careful not to attribute false motives to the behavior of others. Normally, when new behavior is distinctive—that is, when an officer has performed well in the past but suddenly changes his or her behavior—there is a tendency to attribute this change to factors within the officer. If, however, such a change in behavior is exhibited by several officers, the tendency would be to attribute this to external conditions and to take measures to improve the situation. Although it is possible to make certain assumptions about motivation, such assumptions must be tested by exploring them on a one-to-one basis. The police manager must understand that the greater the psychological difference between manager and subordinates, the more likely it is that motivational problems will be blamed on the officers. By being aware of individual differences, the police manager can check his or her assumptions and thus arrive at more effective final decisions.

Principles of Motivation

There are several motivational principles that the police manager should be aware of and understand. First, people cannot motivate other people. When a person is assigned a certain responsibility in the police department, three factors exist. To do a good job, the person needs knowledge, time to develop, and the internal desire to really want to perform. The police manager can provide the knowledge and the time, but the best he or she can do is open the doors so that the desires of this officer can be achieved.

The second principle states that all people are motivated, but they act for their individual reasons, not necessarily for the reasons given by the police manager. The third principle is that a person's strength, when overused, may become his or her weakness. For example, a police captain may have a great sense of humor, but if everything becomes a joke, he or she will not be respected as a true leader and much of the knowledge he or she has to offer may be discounted by the members of the department.

The last principle can be stated in this way: If I know more about you than you know about me, I can control the flow of communication. However, if I know more about you than you know about yourself, I can control *you*. For example, if I understand that you are the kind of individual who does not like to interact very much with people on a daily basis, then I can assign you to a planning and research position that may not require that kind of activity. If I place you in an appropriate position, I can achieve high levels of success. Alternatively, I could assign you to a public speaking position in community relations and end up burning you out in a short period. You might not fully recognize exactly what my intentions as a police manager might be, but by knowing as much as possible about you and what it is that you desire, I can control your degree of success and how quickly you might burn out.

Hierarchy of Effective Communication

Dr. Abraham Maslow (1954) described human behavior in terms of human needs. He developed a five-level hierarchy outlining these needs and emphasized that this system is the source of all motivation. In essence, as the first need is satisfied, the person then moves on to the second, then to the third, to the fourth, and finally the fifth. If a manager wants to motivate his or her personnel, the manager's actions must fit the needs of the employee. According to Maslow, only the unsatisfied needs become sources of motivation. Furthermore, having satisfied one level of need to some degree, an employee will advance to the next level. Certain conditions, however, may cause an individual to go back to his or her primary needs. For example, if an individual is satisfied with his or her present income, then the basic and safety needs are being met. However, if that employee loses his or her job, then the basic needs become primary until a new job is found.

Maslow has suggested that people have five basic needs that account for most of their behavior (see Figure 7-1). He goes on to say that, although a particular need may never receive complete satisfaction, there must be a degree of satisfaction before the need ceases to affect behavior. Once this minimum degree is reached, satisfaction is acquired and the person moves on to experience the potential associated with the next level.

Basic Needs

The bottom level of the hierarchy refers to the need for food and shelter. These **basic needs** have, for the most part, been satisfied in contemporary society. As they pertain to

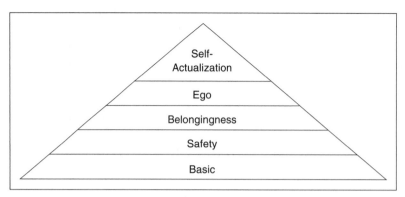

FIGURE 7-1 Maslow's Hierarchy of Needs. *Source: Maslow, Abraham H.; Frager, Robert D. (Editor); Fadiman, James (Editor); Motivation and Personality, Third Edition, © 1987. Adapted by permission of Pearson Education, Inc., Upper Saddle River, NJ.*

employees within a police department, these needs are sometimes reflected in the desire for added personal property and an increased salary—both directed toward increasing comfort. Once the officers receive adequate satisfaction of their basic needs through wages sufficient to enable them to live comfortably, they begin to move upward in the hierarchy.

Most police departments today, especially those in and around major population areas, provide adequately for the basic needs of their officers. Many rural police agencies, however, still struggle with 60- and 70-hour work weeks as well as salaries that place their officers in lower income brackets. Until these problems are overcome, these agencies will have difficulty progressing to professional standards.

Safety Needs

Once an officer has received adequate satisfaction of her basic needs, awareness of the **safety need** develops. She focuses on security, protection, and avoiding harm and risk. Within the police profession, the officer becomes concerned with issues such as fringe benefits, hospitalization insurance, retirement and pension plans, and consistent performance standards. Officers concerned with safety needs are likely to be unimaginative, constantly complaining, and lacking in creativity in their work activities. They generally exhibit little or no flexibility. Strict adherence to rules and regulations is important to these officers. The police department and police managers who overemphasize upgrading fringe benefits are, in essence, attempting to motivate the officers by satisfying their safety needs. If, however, the safety needs of the majority of the personnel are adequately satisfied, a different form of motivation is necessary. This is not to de-emphasize the need or the necessity of satisfying it, but only to caution police managers not to devote all their motivation programs to the satisfaction of the need to the exclusion of the next three.

Belongingness Needs

The third level of the need hierarchy deals with the desire of the officer for membership within a department, for acceptance by fellow officers, and for the feeling of belonging to an organizational family. These needs are manifested in the officer's wish for friendly peers with whom he can develop personal relationships. The police manager is beginning to find that through the creation and implementation of team-type policing, the need to belong is satisfied in members of the department.

The officer will usually look first to the organization for satisfaction of this need. If, however, his need cannot be met within the department, he will then become involved with a formal or informal group established either inside or outside the agency. This "need to belong" or **social need** has often been satisfied through active participation in chapters of the Fraternal Order of Police or through other social groups closely related to the activities of the police department. By instituting activities designed to reach organizational goals, police managers can often direct the enthusiasm and creativity of their personnel to benefit the department rather than losing these energies to outside interests.

Ego Status Needs

Once the officer has satisfied the need to belong, he generally demonstrates interest in achieving some special recognition or status for his contribution to the department. Some police departments have attempted to satisfy this need through the creation of such systems as "officer of the month," by special commendations and awards, or by giving the officer added responsibility. This ego status need usually drives the officer to find opportunities to show his competence, hoping that he will receive recognition from peers as well as achieve some material reward. These factors motivate the officer to contribute as much as possible to the organization in order to be recognized by its members. Usually, the officer attempts to receive assignments that are recognized within the department as more challenging. For example, some officers strive for assignment to specialized investigative units, such as homicide, or to administrative activities, such as planning, so that their contributions to the growth of the department will immediately be recognized.

Self-Actualization Needs

Although the ego status needs are difficult to meet and their satisfaction is often temporary, there are cases in which these needs are adequately met and the individual moves to the highest level of the hierarchy. At this level, the officer is concerned about improving his self-concept. He needs assignments that are challenging and meaningful, allowing him to be as creative as possible. The officer must be able to achieve a sense of growth and satisfaction through the performance of these activities. **Self-actualization** focuses on the personal satisfaction the officer receives from work. At this stage, he usually seeks out assignments that involve risk-taking and experimentation. Behavior patterns at the self-actualization level generally foster innovative and creative projects and provide the officer with a higher degree of self-satisfaction. The behavior prompted by this need produces the mature and constructive contributions necessary to accomplish the degree of professionalism sought by contemporary police departments.

The police manager's role is complex. The manager must first assess his or her own motivational needs, and then those of his or her subordinates. Only through these assessments can the police manager truly motivate and effectively utilize the personnel under his or her command.

It is the police manager's role to assist the staff through the hierarchy of needs. Generally, when a police chief examines his or her officers and finds them fixed at one of the lower levels, a careful analysis of this fixation may indicate that the constraints or barriers to reaching the next level are imposed by the structure of the organization and not by the quality of the personnel.

In testing police employees, a correlation has been found between Maslow's hierarchy of needs and the needs expressed by some of the officers. The highest need expressed was usually that of the ego, with the second being safety or security. Self-actualization was usually placed third. The expression of such needs, however, depended a great deal on the individual agencies tested. Where there were feelings of worth on the part of individual officers and managers, ego and self-actualization needs were higher. But where pay was higher than average, even though officers did not feel trusted or respected, the safety or security needs were rated highest.

Motivation-Hygiene Theory

The more mature the individuals become, the more important become their ego and self-actualization needs. During the 1950s, Frederick Herzberg (1966) conducted a series of studies emphasizing the difference between maintenance factors and motivation factors. His studies further dramatized Maslow's findings. As a result of Herzberg's studies, a theory of organizational behavior and motivation was developed.

Herzberg collected data on job attitudes from which assumptions concerning human behavior could be made. The **motivation-hygiene theory** was the result of his studies. More than 200 professional people were interviewed in an attempt to isolate the activities that gave job satisfaction from those that brought job dissatisfaction. From the information obtained by the studies, Herzberg defined two different categories of needs, independent of each other, that affect employee behavior in different ways. He found that if there was dissatisfaction, the employee emphasized the environment in which he or she worked. If, however, employees were satisfied with their jobs, they usually became more productive and had a stronger desire to help the organization grow. Herzberg titled the first category of needs *hygiene factors* and the second category *motivators*, feeling that satisfaction of the second category of needs brought about superior performance.

Herzberg listed such issues as policies, procedures, administrative practices, techniques of supervision, working conditions, interpersonal relations, salaries, and security as hygiene factors. These may not be intrinsic parts of every police officer's job, but they are surely related to the conditions under which the officer performs. Herzberg believed that hygiene factors do not produce growth in the individual or increase work output, but they do prevent losses in performance.

He defined as motivators the sense of achievement, challenge, professional growth, and recognition. Herzberg's use of the term *motivator* stresses that these factors have some positive effect on the employee, resulting in increased job satisfaction as well as total output capacity (see Figure 7-2).

There is a close relationship between Herzberg's theory of motivation and the hierarchy of needs developed by Maslow. Maslow refers to needs and motives; Herzberg deals with the goals and incentives that tend to satisfy these needs.

Wages would satisfy these needs at the basic level, and fringe benefits would satisfy them at the security or safety level. Interpersonal relations techniques are examples of hygiene factors that lead to satisfaction of social needs, whereas increasing employees' responsibility and authority, assigning them challenging work, and helping them to grow and develop are motivators that bring about organizational behavior and satisfy needs at the ego and self-actualization levels.

The basic, safety, and social needs, as well as a part of the ego needs, are hygiene factors within an organization. The ego needs are divided because there is a difference between status and recognition for a job well done. Status may be defined as the position one occupies through seniority, by promotions, or as payment for a political debt. Therefore, the status position would not reflect the individual's personal achievements or provide recognition for what he or she has earned. Recognition, as opposed to status, is gained only through the competence and achievement of the individual. It is earned by the individual and granted by others. Recognition is classified as an ego need and, along with self-actualization needs, is defined and classified by Herzberg as a motivator.

Hygiene factors relieve pain. They deal with the question, "How well do you treat the men and women of the police department?" Motivators, on the other hand, provide the opportunity to achieve and grow. They deal with the question, "How well do you use employees or police officers' skills?"

Hygiene Factors	**Motivators**
Salary	Challenging assignments
Fringe benefits	Increased responsibility
Security (civil service)	Recognition for work
Rules and regulations	Individual growth
Supervision	

FIGURE 7-2 Herzberg's motivation-hygiene theory.

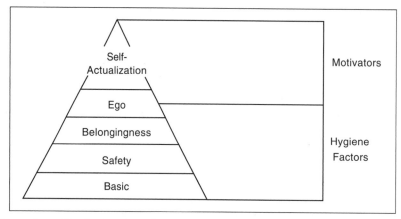

FIGURE 7-3 Comparison of Maslow's and Herzberg's theories.

The relationship between Herzberg's and Maslow's theories is shown in Figure 7-3.

The dynamics of hygiene are that people strive to avoid pain. Another dynamic is that there are an infinite number of sources of hygiene and, as a result, no police manager will ever satisfy every hygiene factor within the police department. Even when they are solved, they have a short-term effect. For example, a pay raise does not satisfy a person except for a specific period of time. Hygiene factors are cyclical in nature. They have a tendency to continually arise and have to be dealt with over the span of a specific period. A typical example is purchasing new vehicles. Within a few years, the department may again have to face purchasing newer equipment to keep up the performance of the police officers.

Hygiene factors have what is called an escalating zero point. If last year officers received a five percent pay raise, then they will strive to achieve at least five percent, preferably more, in the next year. This factor is demonstrated in the tactics that unions use in negotiating. In many instances, police unions would like to negotiate last with the city so that they can use as a minimum base the same percentages given to other city government employees. For example, if fire department personnel receive a seven percent pay raise, the police union begins with a minimum of seven percent.

The police manager must recognize that a dynamic of the hygiene factors is that there is no final answer. There is no way that a police manager will ever know that he or she has satisfied every hygiene factor in the agency.

There are dynamics about motivation as well. Motivators bring growth. They allow individuals to personally grow in the agency as a result. Motivation has a limited number of satisfiers, but this limited number has long-term effects and is cumulative to the individual. That is, if the manager gives responsibility to a subordinate—for example, a captain or a sergeant—then gives additional responsibility six months later, that individual becomes motivated and the added responsibility, assuming it is one that is desired, creates even stronger, lasting motivation.

Although there are answers for motivators, in many instances they become hampered by antiquated personnel and fiscal management rules.

However, the police manager sometimes finds it difficult to recognize the difference between hygiene and motivating factors.

Police managers will find that when hygiene needs are satisfied, dissatisfaction and work restriction will also be reduced, but the individual will have little desire to achieve superior performance. If, however, the police manager emphasizes satisfaction of the motivating factors and allows the individual officer to grow and develop, then he or she will witness an improvement in the officer's productivity as well as in the quality of his or her work.

Prior to Herzberg, most behavioral scientists dealing with worker motivation emphasized what is called **job enlargement**. The theory of job enlargement assumes that if the employees are given an increase in the number of tasks similar to or identical to those they are presently doing, they will gain more satisfaction from their jobs.

Herzberg disagreed with the job enlargement theory. He argued that, to satisfy the worker's motivation factors, management must take responsibility for enriching the job as well as expanding it. If the officer writes crime and traffic reports and then is allowed to write juvenile, property, and missing persons reports, the officer will be no more satisfied than if he or she had remained restricted to writing only one or two types of report. **Job enrichment**, on the other hand, implies that the officer is given the challenge of added responsibilities in all of his or her activities.

The attempt to implement motivating factors to enrich the officer's job does not always succeed in completely satisfying ego and self-actualization needs. If the police department hires an officer whose ability exceeds the demands of the police job, then job enrichment would have no effect in satisfying ego or self-actualization needs. Therefore, job enrichment must be equal to the ability of the police officer. If, for example, an officer is selected, trained, and prepared to deal with problems on a day-to-day basis and then is assigned to push the button to open the jail eight hours a day, even the additional step of enriching the job by adding the responsibility of walking the floors once an hour will not be a motivating factor.

Herzberg's studies of motivation produced interesting observations, which in some ways support Maslow's position and in other ways suggest that the satisfaction of lower-level needs may have different results than will satisfaction of higher-level needs.

Herzberg asked thousands of employees to describe situations that resulted in their feeling exceptionally good about their jobs. They were asked if the feelings of satisfaction in their work had affected their performance, their personal relationships, and their well-being. Finally, the nature of the sequence of events that returned the workers' attitudes to normal were elicited. Following this sequence, the interview was repeated, asking respondents to describe events that made them feel exceptionally bad about their jobs.

Events were evaluated in terms of situations that led to feelings of dissatisfaction. They were defined in terms of whether the effect was long or short. "Long term" was defined as two weeks or longer.

They identified five major factors that helped produce satisfaction. These included achievement, recognition, the work itself, responsibility, and advancement. They identified the five major factors that led to dissatisfaction. These included policies, supervision, salary levels, interpersonal relationships, and working conditions. Salary, however, was generally considered both a satisfier and a dissatisfier, depending on the way the money itself was used. For example, a 10 percent pay raise that keeps officers more or less at their present level both in terms of their work and of living standards tends to be seen as not bringing about dissatisfaction. However, a large pay increase—as might result from taking another job—is sometimes viewed as a satisfier because it allows the recipient to use the money for some specific growth goals such as furthering a child's education.

In studies of police personnel at the supervisory, middle-management, and management levels, the following results were noticed. Personnel at the lower levels of the department have a tendency to rank the following five factors as strong motivators: (1) feeling of achievement from doing a challenging job, (2) inner need to do a good job, (3) doing work that they felt was important, (4) having personal work-related goals, and (5) doing interesting work. Managers, on the other hand, ranked the following as the factors that they believed to be most motivating to subordinates: (1) doing work that they felt was important, (2) recognition and appreciation from supervisors and managers (the item ranked tenth by police officers), and (3) recognition from peers (ranked twelfth by subordinates). The possibility of promotion was ranked fourth by managers and sixth by officers. There is a slight difference, although recognition seems to play an important role in the eyes of both managers and police officers. The nature of the job itself is a motivating force for police officers, although such work-related motivation is not viewed as highly significant by police managers.

Theory X and Theory Y

Theory X and Theory Y were developed by Douglas McGregor (1960) during the 1950s. According to McGregor, the traditional organization is one that emphasizes centralized decision making and reflects the pyramid structure typical of most law enforcement agencies. It was McGregor's belief that traditional managers share certain basic assumptions, which he labeled **Theory X**. He has defined these assumptions in the following way:

1. It is management's role to organize resources—money, equipment, personnel—in a structure that requires close supervision of all employees and brings about maximum control. (The recommendation of one police sergeant for every eight police officers, without any regard for the ability of the officers or the sergeant, is an example of the Theory X type of control.)
2. It is management's responsibility to direct the efforts of the personnel of the agency, keeping them motivated, controlling all their actions, and modifying their behavior to fit the needs of the organization.

3. If management staff members do not take an active part in controlling the behavior of the employees, the employees will be passive, even resistant, to the needs of the organization.
4. The average employee is, by nature, lazy and will work as little as possible, as work is inherently distasteful to him or her.
5. The average employee lacks ambition, dislikes responsibility and authority, and prefers taking orders to being independent.
6. The employee is basically self-centered, has no feeling for organizational needs, and must be closely controlled and even coerced in order to achieve organizational objectives.
7. By nature, the average employee resists change.
8. The average employee does not have the ability to solve problems creatively.

Most police departments use these assumptions as a basis for developing rules and regulations. Police departments occasionally develop organizational structures in which a superior closely supervises each subordinate. Furthermore, most of the police manager's time is spent checking and rechecking the daily activities of immediate subordinates. The widespread practice of allowing patrol officers to perform only menial duties and of assigning any tasks that require intelligence to detectives or so-called specialized units is often viewed by personnel in the agencies as the practice of Theory X.

One of the first questions that police managers must ask themselves is whether the assumptions of Theory X are appropriate for use in running police agencies today. Educational and living standards in our country have risen immensely in the past decades. Among police officers today, the motivation for pay increases has greatly decreased.

Theory X assumptions about police officers are, for the most part, inaccurate and impractical. Many police agencies, in implementing such theories and assumptions, create serious management trouble, generally resulting in their failure to motivate personnel toward the achievement of departmental goals. Management by strong, centralized control will not usually succeed in our society. Theory X managers motivate people by attempting to satisfy basic and safety needs. Most people today, however, have reasonably satisfied these needs and seek motivation directed toward fulfilling belonging, ego, and self-actualization needs.

Douglas McGregor also developed a second theory of human behavior, called Theory Y, based on the assumption that it is management's role to unleash the potential of every member of the organization. If the individual can be properly motivated to obtain his or her own goals through the achievement of organizational goals, then the agency can be extremely effective.

McGregor's assumptions regarding **Theory Y** managers are:

1. It is management's role to organize resources—money, material, equipment, personnel—to reach organizational goals.
2. Work can be an enjoyable part of one's life if the conditions are favorable.

3. People are not by nature lazy, passive, or resistant to the needs of the organization, but have become so as a result of their experience working within the organization.
4. Management does not place the potential for development within the employee. Motivation, capacity for accepting responsibility, and willingness to work toward organizational goals are present within the individual. It is then management's responsibility to recognize this potential and allow the individual the freedom to develop his or her abilities.
5. People possess creativity and can solve organizational problems if encouraged by management.
6. The essential task of management is to develop organizational conditions and operational procedures that will encourage individuals to attain their goals by directing their efforts toward organizational goals and objectives.

Police managers who accept Theory Y assumptions usually have: (1) fewer levels in their departmental hierarchies; (2) controls with broad guidelines; and (3) minimal first-line supervision of police activities. The Theory Y police agency gives increased autonomy to middle management, first-line supervisors, and police officers. Allowing personnel to develop projects and programs involves them in identifying and overcoming obstacles to their goals. Police officers under a Theory Y organization achieve satisfaction for their ego and self-actualization needs.

Some police departments allow individual police officers to become involved in activities such as planning and problem solving on a daily basis. For example, agencies implementing **management by objectives**—in which top management has clearly defined the major objectives of the department for the coming year and has advised middle management and first-line supervisors of these objectives—assign the individual projects to the squads for development. Departments implementing Theory Y involve officers in many management functions such as developing training programs, hiring personnel, and even assisting in budget preparation. Some police agencies find that police officers are as satisfied by their jobs as they are by their hobbies and recreation. As a result, officers are spending off-duty hours preparing for the implementation of projects within their agencies. The police role begins to take on a different meaning to the officers and they, in turn, lighten the load of management.

Immaturity–Maturity Theory

As a result of the outdated management practices of many police departments and their emphasis on Theory X assumptions, the law enforcement profession still treats many police officers as immature.

During the 1950s, Chris Argyris (1957) conducted extensive studies of industrial organizations to determine the effect of management practices on the personal growth of the employees within the organization. Argyris listed seven changes that should occur in

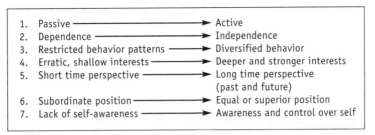

1. Passive ⟶ Active
2. Dependence ⟶ Independence
3. Restricted behavior patterns ⟶ Diversified behavior
4. Erratic, shallow interests ⟶ Deeper and stronger interests
5. Short time perspective ⟶ Long time perspective (past and future)
6. Subordinate position ⟶ Equal or superior position
7. Lack of self-awareness ⟶ Awareness and control over self

FIGURE 7-4 Seven Changes in Employees.

the employee's personality if he or she is to develop into a mature person and be an asset to the organization (see Figure 7-4).

First, individuals move from a passive state as infants to increased activity as adults. Second, as mature, thinking adults, they develop from a state of dependence on others to one of independence. Third, they increase their number of behavior patterns. Fourth, they move from erratic, casual, and shallow interests to deeper and stronger interests in specific directions. Fifth, the mature adult develops a time frame that includes the past, present, and future, as opposed to the child's frame, which emphasizes only the present. Sixth, as children they are subordinate to almost everyone, but as adults they assume equal or superior status to others. Finally, as children they lack self-awareness, but as adults they understand and are able to control themselves. Argyris postulated that these changes are normal and healthy, and they bring the individual from immaturity to maturity.

The major point is that although people rarely develop to a state of full maturity, as they grow older and learn from their experiences, they constantly move toward the maturity end of the continuum.

In many police departments, managers sometimes question the maturity of the personnel or even their desire to become mature. Apathy begins to spread through the department, and management immediately accuses the workers of being lazy and of having no interest in their jobs. Generally, when individuals come to work for an organization such as a government bureaucracy, the management practices utilized by the agency actually prohibit the employees from obtaining maturity. In many police departments, individual police officers are given minimal control over their job assignments and, in fact, are encouraged to depend on and be subordinate to the first-line supervisors and middle managers. As a result, these adults begin to behave immaturely, which, according to the assumptions of Theory X, is how many police agencies expect them to act.

The formal organizational structure of many police bureaucracies often forces the employee to remain immature. The emphasis of the organizational structure is toward fitting the individual to the job. The design for the organization always comes first, and this design is usually based on the concepts of scientific management-task specialization, chain of command, and span of control. Many police agencies attempt to increase the efficiency of the organization by using the police officers as interchangeable parts within the total structure.

Basic to these concepts is the fact that the authority and power to run the department rests in the hands of a very few individuals who are at the top of the organization and who make all major and most minor decisions. These decisions are usually made with little input from middle management and no input from the lower links in the chain of command. In fact, those at the bottom of the chain are strictly controlled by their superiors and by the rigidity of the system itself. Specialization of many police activities has resulted in oversimplification of duties, which soon become repetitive, routine, and unchallenging. This implies that in the task-oriented leadership of many police departments, supervisors and managers make frequent decisions about the work, and the police officers are responsible only for carrying out these decisions. As a result, the agencies have been overloaded with control measures such as strict budget practices, a performance evaluation system, and numerous other operating procedures that attempt to standardize operations so that initiative and creativity are carefully restricted.

This formal structure has led to certain assumptions about human nature that are directly opposed to promoting the maturation of the individual. In the Theory X type of police department, the needs of the mature employees cannot be satisfied due to the inflexibility of the formal organizational structure within which they must work. New police officers soon recognize that Theory X assumptions prevail and that management has designated childlike roles for them, frustrating their natural development. The officers are forced to turn to outside activities for fulfillment, to leave the department, or to change their profession.

The present challenge to police managers is to provide a work climate in which every employee has the opportunity to mature, both as an individual and as a member of the department. However, the police manager must believe that individuals can essentially be self-directed and creative in their work environments if they are motivated by management. Implicit here is the manager's acceptance of Theory Y and the Argyris theory, which allow the individual to grow from immaturity to maturity.

Management Systems

As a result of behavioral research studies of numerous industrial organizational structures, Rensis Likert (1967) developed a definition of management styles on a continuum, ranging from System 1 through System 4.

System 1

Under System 1, management has no confidence or trust in its personnel and seldom involves them in any part of the decision-making process. Top management makes a large majority of the decisions, sets the goals, and then issues rules, regulations, and orders through the chain of command. Subordinates are kept in line by the use of fear, threats, or occasionally by a reward, such as a letter of commendation. The emphasis within this system is on satisfying basic and safety needs. Usually any contact between the superior and the subordinate is brought about through the alleged mistakes or misconduct of the subordinate. The relationship between the first-line supervisor and the workers is usually one of fear and mistrust.

The trend in police departments today is to move away from System 1 and toward the other end of the continuum. However, some police organizations still place the control process in the hands of top management. This has affected the development of strong **informal organizations** within the agency, which, in many instances, oppose the goals of the formal structure. Most of the manager's time within System 1 police departments is spent in preventing conflict between the formal and informal structures.

System 2

System 2 management places some confidence and trust in the lower-level police officers, but the structure still retains many qualities of a master–servant relationship. Most of the decision making and goal setting occurs at the top of the organization. However, management has a structure through which input can be received from the lower levels, and it even allows the lower levels to make some of the less important decisions. Rewards and actual or potential punishments are the tools used to motivate employees. Usually the manager's relationship with the police officer is viewed as distrustful. Police departments with System 2 characteristics will usually have some communication between the top, middle, and lower levels, but generally the upward communication is carefully screened to feed information to middle and upper management that the lower level thinks they want to hear. The superiors still inject a large amount of fear and caution in their subordinates. Under System 2, the police department's control process begins to be delegated to the middle and lower levels. The informal organization existing in System 1 police agencies is still present, but it is not usually in direct conflict with formal organizational goals.

System 3

Police departments under System 3 demonstrate substantial but incomplete trust between management and subordinates. More decisions are made at the lower levels, but policies and high-level decisions still remain in the hands of those at the top. Communication flows both upward and downward, and rewards and occasional punishment are used to generate in the officer a greater interest in department goals. Because the amount of interaction between superior and subordinate broadens under System 3, confidence and trust begin to develop. Both the higher and lower levels feel responsible for controlling organizational activities. If informal organizations develop within System 3 police agencies, they will either support them or give them only partial resistance to their goals.

System 4

Under System 4, the management practices of the police department clearly indicate complete confidence and trust in the subordinates by top management and middle management personnel. Decision making, although well integrated, is widely dispersed and made throughout the department. Communication flows not only up and down the structure, but also horizontally among the peers. There is much participation and involvement in establishing goals; in improving techniques, methods, and operations; and in evaluating the success of the organization. There are friendly relations between supervisors and subordinates at all levels of the organization. The control process flows from the lower units to the top, and all levels are as fully involved as possible in decision making. The informal structure, if one develops, usually supports the formal organizational structure. As a result, the social forces that develop within the department support the efforts to achieve its goals and objectives.

In summary, System 1 may be defined as a highly structured, autocratic type of management, whereas System 4 is based on more participation, teamwork, and mutual trust within the hierarchy. Systems 2 and 3 are the intermediate stages between the two extremes, which closely approximate the assumptions of Theory X and Theory Y.

Expectancy Theory

The **expectancy theory** states that performance is a function of the officer's ability, multiplied by the motivation itself. Ability is a function of the officer's aptitude, multiplied by training and experience.

Performance is a function of the individual's ability, plus desire and perception. The police manager recognizes that personnel of the department will reach high levels of performance if they first have the ability—that is, if they have been trained and have the necessary skills. The second element is desire—the will to perform. Finally, there is perception—that is, the following question is answered: "If I give effort, can I meet my expectations?"

Officers have expectations about the likelihood that any effort they put forth will lead to intended behavior on the part of other people. They also have expectations about the likelihood that certain outcomes will follow as a result of their behavior. An officer's motivation to perform in a particular way will be influenced by his or her expectations about trying to perform at that level and the attractiveness of the goals involved. The police manager must consider that if the expectations of an officer performing at a particular level are low, or if there is a high probability that the outcomes will be negative, then motivation to perform will be low and the goals of the agency may not be met.

The police manager also performs using the expectancy theory formula (see Figure 7-5). The police manager says, "If I perform in a certain way, will I achieve my outcome?" However, the performance of others depends on the goals that the others seek.

Consider the police manager who desires an effective police department so that he or she can be considered a good leader, and his or her officers who desire a decent standard of living. If, due to economic difficulties and political reality, the salary and benefits for the officers are low, they do not feel obligated to perform at a high level because their goals will not be achieved. Another example would be when the police manager wants to produce leaders for the future. The goal for which he or she strives is a continuation of the values, beliefs, and principles presently exhibited by the leader. If he or she determines that the managers in the police department seek a higher skill level in dealing with other people, learning fiscal management responsibilities, and planning skills—and he or she provides them with these skills—they in turn will perform at a higher level, not just because of the training they have received, but because of the perception they have that if they do receive the training they can perform at a higher level, which is something that they personally desire.

The expectancy theory is the basis for career development programs and can be implemented by employing five steps. First, the expectations of all parties should be made known. It is easy for each party to define two sets of expectations—the expectations that they have of the other and the expectations that the other has of them. For example, the captain can say to the lieutenant, "I expect you to always be on time and produce credible reports, and you can expect me to support you and to give you immediate feedback." The lieutenant's expectations of the captain might be support, feedback, and a pay raise. The expectations that the captain can have of the lieutenant is that he or she will complete reports on time and give his or her best effort. In comparing the expectations, some conflicts will arise. For example, not being able to guarantee a pay raise can be addressed. In addition, this list of expectations can be used as a way to evaluate performance, thereby raising the overall quality of management in the police department (see Figure 7-6).

The second step involves making the work itself valuable. As long as department organizational goals complement the personal goals of people in the agency, the sworn and non-sworn personnel will believe that working toward these goals will help them achieve their goals and as a result there will be a higher level of commitment.

The third step involves making the work doable. Too often, the police manager assigns a responsibility without really finding out how the subordinate feels about this added responsibility. Making realistic assignments and asking in advance about what can be achieved by the other person in any specific assignment helps to identify obstacles before they arise.

Performance	=	Ability	x	Desire	x	Perception
(Training)		(Motivation)		Expectation		
My Performance [Your Performance—Your Outcome] My Outcome						

FIGURE 7-5 Expectancy theory formula.

(Sgt) Expect of You (Deputy)	You Can Expect of Me (Sgt)
Be honest	Be straight with you
Be loyal	Be supportive
Complete timely reports	Keep you informed
Adhere to our policies	Compliment and correct you
Dress sharp	Encourage your growth
Be on time	
Live up to your word	
I (Deputy) Expect of You	**You Can Expect of Me (Deputy)**
Be honest with me	Be honest
Maintain open-door policy	Keep you informed
Give me new responsibilities	Know procedures
Support me	Be professional
Keep me informed	Study hard
Respond when I need you	
Involve me in budget preparation	

FIGURE 7-6 Expectation agreement.

The fourth step is giving regular feedback. Feedback must be given as quickly as possible after the action is taken. It should be specific and should address behaviors that the other person can change.

The last, and probably the most important, step for the police manager is to reward his or her subordinates when they meet their agreed-upon expectations.

The factors that help determine a person's expectations and his or her perception of the likelihood of success include self-esteem, experience, the job situation itself, and the ability to share knowledge and receive input from others.

Some of the factors that help determine the likelihood of success include experience in a similar situation, self-esteem, the attractiveness of the goals, the belief in internal versus external control, the actual job situation, and the ability to communicate with others.

Conclusion

This chapter examines organizational behavior and the theories of motivation prevalent in contemporary management. Examples have been cited to provide a framework against which police managers may analyze and understand their own organizational behavior. Analyzing and understanding organizational behavior is a necessary start; but only if a manager implements decisions and develops his or her own style of leadership, utilizing the positive side of each theory, will he or she be able to advance the profession of law enforcement.

References

Argyris, C. (1957). *Personality and organization.* New York: Harper & Row.

Herzberg, F. (1966). *Work and the nature of man.* New York: World Publishing Company.

Likert, R. (1967). *The human organization.* New York: McGraw-Hill.

Maslow, A. H. (1954). *Motivation and personality.* New York: Harper & Row.

McGregor, D. (1960). *The human side of enterprise.* New York: McGraw-Hill.

Discussion Questions

1. What characteristics of team policing enhance the fulfillment of the "need to belong"?
2. According to Maslow's hierarchy of needs, there are five general levels of needs. Where are most students in this scale today? Where are most police officers? How about the police managers?
3. How does Herzberg's motivational theory relate to the way cities, counties, and police departments are organized today?
4. Are most police agencies oriented toward Theory X or Theory Y?
5. Which is best—Theory X or Theory Y? Should an organization have a little of both? If it is best to accept a bit of each theory, what criteria would you employ to decide when to use one approach or the other?

8
Transactional Analysis[1]

LEARNING OBJECTIVES

1. The student will be able to identify behavioral models and how they affect the overall change process.
2. The student will be able to identify how each of the ego states (parent, adult, and child) operates and to distinguish actions emanating from each ego state.
3. The student will be able to list and identify behaviors stemming from the parent and child ego states.
4. The student will be able to identify the types of transactions—complementary, crossed, and ulterior.
5. The student will be able to identify the four basic life positions.
6. The student will understand the concept of "stroking" and how it affects police organizations.
7. The student will be able to identify the six ways in which people structure their time.
8. The student will be able to identify organizational games.

Behavioral Models and the Change Process

Throughout this book, there is an emphasis on behavioral models regarding communication, leadership, motivation, and planning. Each of the models can assist the police manager in conceptualizing approaches to organizational problems. In addition, these models provide managers with a variety of approaches for making judgments as to needed changes in policy, procedure, personnel, as well as their own behavior. All models, however, are only approximations of reality. They are only useful when police managers can adapt the model to assist their understanding of the realities of the organizational environment.

Each of the models presented emphasizes the fact that the outcomes, in terms of results and side effects, show wide variance depending on the approach used in a given organizational situation. This emphasis on the dynamic character of organizational behavior highlights the complexity and importance of organizational development approaches to change. Thus, a change in leadership style may affect morale and relationships without having a major impact on production. Effective change comes only through the careful development of all aspects of the organization that influence the outcomes important to the manager. There are many excellent expositions of organizational development approaches. This chapter focuses on the police manager as an object of change and provides a model for conceptualizing this change process.

[1]Chapter 8 is included with the permission of Dick McMahon.

In most change approaches, the role of top management is singled out as the major force in the change process. Fortunately, most police managers are keenly aware of the importance of their leadership in change efforts. What is often absent, however, is the awareness of how their own personalities and established approaches to interaction with others interfere with their intentions. In many instances, the first change that must occur is a change in the behavior of the police manager.

There are few people who believe that significant changes in personalities or behavior can be accomplished by simply "willing" the change. However, most individuals who reach police management positions are reasonably competent, mature individuals capable of effecting behavioral changes in the interest of becoming more effective as managers. Such changes often occur as managers become more observant of their own behavior and more sensitive to the impact of their behavior on others.

This chapter provides a brief overview of a model that offers significant assistance to police managers in understanding their personal reactions and the nature of their interactions with others. With a little effort and study, this approach can provide a conceptual or "thinking" approach to managing personal change. The approach is called **transactional analysis**.

Since the publication of his bestseller *Games People Play* (1964), Eric Berne's psychological approach to human behavior has become more and more influential in a variety of settings in which behavioral change is deemed important. Transactional analysis (TA), as it is presented in this chapter, is a conceptual tool that may assist police managers in developing considerable insight into their own behavior. As a general model, it can assist them in determining the extent to which their behavior and attitudes are consistent with their managerial intent. The terminology used is simple and easily learned. Its effect can be powerful. Most of what Eric Berne says is not new; what is new is that he has taken much of the mystery out of human behavior through a language system to which most people can relate.

Ego States

As a result of broad experiences with both individuals and groups in a variety of treatment settings, Berne became more and more convinced of the importance of analyzing the interactions of individuals in terms of the way they go about obtaining satisfaction of their needs. He was particularly impressed by the fact that individuals in their interactions with others exhibit behavior that is, at times, reminiscent of childlike behaviors, at other times like behaviors one might expect from one's parents, and at other times rational and mature behaviors. Berne saw all these behaviors as psychological realities representing different states of the self or ego. Basically, the ego states are thought to be much like the sound tracks on an audiotape and, depending on which track is activated by the situation, the police manager responds accordingly. Managers have learned to relate various behaviors to feelings and situations that they have previously experienced. When these "tapes" are turned on, they respond with the behaviors that they have used to deal with these feelings in the past.

As a result of a person's unique personal development, his or her feelings, reactions, attitudes, and experiences become organized into three major influence systems or ego states. These ego states are referred to as *parent, adult,* and *child,* to call attention to the fact that the origins of their development come from different life experiences. If we know the nature of the experiences and feelings that make up each of these ego states, we can describe a given personality.

Transactional analysis is based on the belief that the ego states are consistent patterns of feelings and experiences faithfully recorded in the nervous system and evoked by stimulus situations we experience. How the manager interacts with others in relation to these ego states is important in understanding human behavior. Most managers have the capacity to identify many of the feelings and behaviors associated with each of the ego states. Through such analysis, police managers can develop the capacity to monitor these behaviors and work toward more effective performance. These ego states are shown in Figure 8-1.

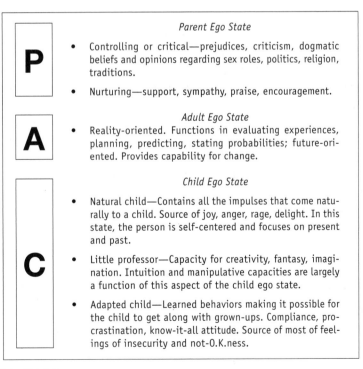

FIGURE 8-1 Ego state diagram.

Parent Ego State

The **parent ego state** contains all the attitudes, ideas, postures, gestures, habits, and reaction tendencies that were learned from parents, grandparents, older siblings, or other influential figures in the individual's life. Many of the assumptions, attitudes, ideas, and behaviors that characterize the parent ego state were learned through modeling and were incorporated into behavior patterns without critical examination. Therefore, in acting out the parental ego state, the police manager interacts with behaviors observed in his or her own parents or other authority figures.

The parent ego state tends to be filled with opinions and prejudices about religion, politics, traditions, sexual roles, lifestyles, the role of authority, proper dress and the manner of speech. The critical or controlling aspect of the parent ego state is expressed in a domineering and judgmental fashion. What is right is right, and there is no room for compromise.

The parent ego state, however, includes the feelings and behaviors that make it possible for the police manager to give support, praise, encouragement, or compliments to subordinates. This nurturing side of the parent ego state is particularly important in working with peers or subordinates, or in relating to individuals in difficulty. Some police managers have parent ego states that have very little capacity to nurture others; consequently, they have difficulty relating to situations that call for this type of behavior.

The parent ego state is particularly useful in helping to determine appropriate behavior when the manager has no other data available in providing support to subordinates. Managers who have had good "parental" guidance and nurturing behavior have many attitudes and actions that serve to make their interactions with others pleasant and effective. Other police managers have incorporated attitudes and behaviors that interfere with their effectiveness in dealing with conflict and change.

The content of each manager's parent ego state is unique. It is only through personal awareness of his or her own reaction tendencies that a manager can begin to change the behaviors that interfere with effective functioning. The nature of the parent ego state and the manner in which a manager expresses parent behavior can be modified through careful monitoring of gestures, feelings, and behavior. Thus, even though a manager cannot erase the parent "tapes," he or she can gain control through using his or her capacity to analyze situations objectively and testing the effects of his or her interactions with others.

Adult Ego State

The **adult ego state** comprises the capacity to reason, evaluate situations, gather information, and store information for future reference. It is not related to a person's age, even though the content of the adult ego state changes with age. A police manager who operates in the adult state is oriented toward present reality and the objective gathering of information. This aspect of the personality is well organized, adaptable, and provides the manager with the capacity to monitor his or her thought processes. Consequently, the adult ego state is indispensable in changing personal behavior. In the adult ego state, the police manager is detached from his or her own emotional and other internal processes. While in the adult state, the manager may be unemotional but able to appraise child and parent feelings. In the adult ego state, the manager considers past, present, and future. Thus, this ego state is essential for effective planning and overall management.

Child Ego State

The **child ego state** is essentially childhood preserved in its entirety. It contains the impulses that come naturally to the infant. It contains the recordings of early experiences, how one responded to them, and the positions taken about oneself and other people. A person who responds in an inquisitive, affectionate, selfish, mean, playful, whining, or manipulative manner is responding from the child ego state. There are three discernible parts of the child ego state.

The **natural child** is the part that is very young, impulsive, untrained, and expressive. When his or her needs are met, the manager responds out of the child state with affection. Angry rebellion at having his or her needs frustrated is also a reaction of the child state.

The **little professor** refers to the unschooled wisdom that we observe in children. It is the part of the child ego state that is able to influence the motivations and feelings of other people. It is through this aspect of the child ego state that the infant figures things out—when to cry, when to be quiet, and how to manipulate his or her parents. This aspect can indicate a highly creative mind, even though many of the child ego state creations might be impractical if not developed by the adult ego state. The police manager's capacity to create and fantasize is directly related to the degree to which he or she is able to permit the internal little professor to work.

The third aspect of the child ego state is the **adapted child**. This is the part of the child ego state that exhibits modifications of the natural child's inclinations. These adaptations of natural impulses occur in response to parental training and demands from significant authority figures. The manager who complies, procrastinates, acts like a bully, withdraws, or in other ways behaves as he or she did in response to the demands of his or her parents is acting from an adapted child state.

Each of the ego states is important to the manager's effectiveness in daily interactions with others. Effective decision making requires that the police manager be able to process data through the adult state without undue influence from the child and parent ego states. However, to have fun, a manager must be able to indulge in his or her child ego state. To give support to others or to exercise control of situations, he or she must be able to rely on the parent ego state. Good adjustment comes when the police manager is able to use the ego state that is appropriate to the situation.

Police managers can diagnose ego states in themselves and others by observing people's visible and audible characteristics (see Figure 8-2). Certain words, gestures, postures, mannerisms, and facial expressions are typically associated with each of the

	Parent Ego State	Adult Ego State	Child Ego State
Voice tones	Condescending, putting down, criticizing, or accusing	Matter-of-fact	Full of feeling; high-pitched, whining voice
Words used	Everyone knows that . . . You should never . . . You should always . . . I can't understand why in the world you would ever . . . I'll put a stop to that once and for all . . . If I were you . . . Stupid . . . naughty . . . ridiculous . . . shocking . . . poor thing . . . good girl . . . good boy	How . . . What . . . When . . . Where . . . Why . . . Who . . . Probable . . . In what way . . . I think . . . I seem . . . It is my opinion	I'm mad at you . . . Wow, terrific! (or any words that have a high feeling level) . . . I wish . . . I want . . . I dunno . . . I guess . . . Bigger . . . Better . . . Best
Postures	Puffed-up with pride, super-correct, very proper	Attentive, eye-to-eye contact, listening and looking for maximum data, continual action	Slouching, playful, beaten down, burdened, self-conscious
Facial expressions	Frowning, worried or disapproving looks, chin jutted out, furrowed brow, pursed lips	Alert eyes, maximum attention given	Excited, surprised, downcast eyes, quivering lip or chin, moist eyes, rolling eyes
Body gestures	Hands on hips, pointing finger in accusation, arms folded across chest, patting on head, deep sigh	Leaning forward in chair toward other person, moving closer to hear and see better	Spontaneous activity, wringing hands, pacing, withdrawing into corner or moving away from laughter, raising hand for permission, shrugging shoulders

FIGURE 8-2 Clues to ego states.

three ego states. Managers can also use their own emotional reactions and thoughts to help interpret the ego state that they have observed in another person. A parental reaction in the manager may mean that a child ego state is being observed in the subordinate.

Feelings of inferiority or rebelliousness in the subordinate may mean that the ego state being observed in the manager is that of the parent. These clues assist in determining the effect of behavior on others and the appropriateness of interaction. Awareness of these clues can be of assistance to the manager in understanding differences in approaches to various situations and may provide a basis for determining changes that may be necessary in interacting with others.

Any one of the ego states discussed can serve as the determinant of the police manager's personality at any given time. For a manager to be well-adjusted, he or she must be able to move from one ego state to another, using the proper ego state for a given situation. People normally develop some form of control that helps them in their movement from one ego state to another. This control may be lax—that is, there may be very little control from the adult ego state and therefore the manager may move very rapidly from one ego state to another: from child to parent or from parent to child. The other extreme is a manager who has a very rigid ego state boundary. In this case, there is very little free movement between the ego states.

The manager who has a rigid or constant parent ego state tends to treat subordinates as if they are children, refusing to accept their abilities or ideas. As a police manager, he or she might constantly go about trying to help officers carry out their everyday responsibilities. The manager who constantly uses the adult ego state has developed little in his or her personal relationships with people. He or she is extremely logical and requires hard-core data before making any kind of decision. This type of manager, although quite effective in such fields as research, might be ineffective as a commander of personnel within a police department.

The constant child refuses to accept responsibility and refuses to make decisions. This kind of individual rarely climbs the ladder of promotions within the police department and is satisfied with staying at the entrance level for his or her entire career. This is not, however, to imply that all people who remain at the entrance level are doing so because of their reliance on their child ego state. The constant child uses devices such as seeking direction for minor tasks for which he or she has been trained or constantly asking for reassurance before making any decision.

Police managers must also be aware of problems of **contamination** and isolation. Contamination means that the adult ego state is contaminated by either the child or the parent ego state. A typical example might be that of the police manager who refuses to have women under his command. He uses strong rationalization and attempts to prove his point by citing the possibility of injuries and even finds data to help to reinforce his position. The action may appear to be adult; however, careful examination may reveal that this police manager is highly prejudiced in his attitudes toward women. It is this prejudice, rather than the facts he has gathered, that governs his behavior. This can be tested by providing counterexamples to determine whether the individual manager is able to deal with the new data from his adult ego state. If he refuses to accept its importance, totally rejects it, and makes a judgmental decision strictly from his parent ego state, there is contamination.

Isolation means the complete blocking out of an ego state. If the child ego state is blocked out, the manager is also blocking out the spontaneous, fun-loving side of his or her nature. Managers who are only fact-seeking and are never able to laugh at life or accept humor within the daily operations of their legal responsibilities might have blocked out their child ego state.

If the parent ego state is blocked out, there is no conscience involved in the manager's decision. These managers show little remorse or shame. In many instances, they become criminal in their actions and may eventually be disciplined for dishonesty or unethical conduct. Managers who isolate the adult are usually in conflict with reality and may even have mental disorders severe enough to require hospitalization.

Of the three ego states, the adult state is usually the last to be effectively developed. Police managers who want to build a stronger adult ego state could follow some of the following principles from *I'm O.K.—You're O.K* (Harris, 1967).

1. Learn to recognize their child ego state, its vulnerabilities, its fears, its principal methods of expressing feelings.
2. Learn to recognize their parent ego state, its admonitions, injunctions, and positions.
3. Be sensitive to the parent, adult, and child ego states in themselves and in others.
4. Count to 10, if necessary, to give the adult ego state time to process the data coming into the brain and to sort out the parent ego and child ego realities.
5. Work out and develop a system of values. Once this system of values has been established, decisions can be made within its ethical framework.

Transactions and Communication

Police managers must understand their own ego states if they are to make transactional analysis (TA) work for them. However, it is the application of this knowledge in their daily interactions that is most useful. In TA, an interaction with another person is called a transaction. In all transactions, the person's ego state will determine his or her response to others. Three major patterns of interaction can be identified: *complementary transactions, crossed transactions,* and *ulterior transactions.*

Complementary Transactions

In many transactions, the police manager will find communication going smoothly; he or she will feel comfortable in the relationships and find it easy to continue the conversation. These transactions are most frequently referred to as **complementary transactions**. In complementary transactions, both parties in the interaction respond from ego states that are appropriate to maintaining the communication. In the example below, the manager tells a subordinate to have a report in on Friday, and the subordinate dutifully confirms that he will have the report in on that day.

MANAGER: John, I want that report by Friday, and you had better not be late. (The parent ego state is dominant, and the expectation is compliance from the child ego state in the other person.)

JOHN: Yes, sir. No problem. (Child compliance back to the parent in the manager.)

The manager's order is made in a demanding, uncompromising tone, indicating that he is coming out of his controlling parent ego state. The response of the subordinate indicates that he will comply without question. This response—from the child ego state— is the response the manager expected, and no apparent problem exists. Such transactions are referred to as *complementary* because the person who initiates the transaction communicates from a particular ego state and receives a response from the other person that meets his or her expectations. The following are examples of complementary transactions:

1st SGT: These new recruits just don't have any guts. (parent to parent—judgmental)

2nd SGT: You're right. I don't know how they expect us to do anything with these jerks. (parent back to parent)

OFFICER: Let's knock off early and get in a few games of bowling. (child to child)

2nd SGT: That's a good idea, where do you want to go? (child to child)

1st SGT: How many officers do you think we will need during the 4-to-8 period this Saturday? (adult to adult)

2nd SGT: From the data we have, I would say we need at least 12 additional officers. (adult to adult)

OFFICER: Sgt. Brown, I really screwed up this report, can you help me? (child to parent)

SGT: Certainly, son, I used to have a little trouble with those reports myself. (nurturing parent to child)

In each of the transactions illustrated above, the person initiating the transaction received a response that was consistent with the stimulus message. Such transactions set the stage for continuing communication between the two persons.

Crossed Transactions

In some transactions with others, the manager may immediately be aware that something has happened to disrupt the relationship. For example, after an initial exchange, he or she and the subordinate may glare at each other, turn their backs on each other, change the topic abruptly, or show confusion at what has just occurred. The behaviors suggest that the transaction has resulted in a disruption of communication. In most instances, the manager initiating the transaction has received a response that was inconsistent with his or her expectations. Such transactions are referred to as **crossed transactions**. A crossed transaction occurs any time the person initiating the transaction receives a response that is perceived as inappropriate or unexpected. As an example:

CAPT:	Have you spoken to the chief about the court schedule? (adult to adult)
LT:	No, and I'm not about to. He can go jump in the lake. (child to parent)

In the example above, the captain is communicating from her adult ego state, expecting a reasonable, adult reply. The lieutenant, however, responds out of her child ego state in an angry, rebellious manner. The lieutenant's response is directed to the parent in the captain. The subsequent conversation will largely be determined by the captain's response. She may choose to stay in the adult ego state and try to find out why the lieutenant is annoyed with the chief. If she moves to her parent ego state, she may either berate the lieutenant for her poor attitude or be sympathetic. In either case, the crossed transaction results in a change in the level of communication between the two. Other examples of crossed transactions are illustrated below:

CAPT:	George, you are changing shifts with Linda next week. (parent to child)
LT:	You're crazy. How did you make captain anyway? (parent to child)
LT:	Let's organize a card game this week. (child to child)
CAPT:	If you would quit trying to figure out ways to avoid work, we might get something done around here. (parent to child)

In the first example, the captain changes the shifts of one of his lieutenants and directs that the change be made. George responds from his parent state by making derogatory remarks about the captain. This transaction will probably lead to disciplinary action, which could have been avoided by an adult-to-adult discussion about the change of shift.

In the second example, the lieutenant expresses her wish to organize a card game and the captain responds in a critical, judgmental fashion. The lieutenant may not mention cards again, but she will also carry around a lot of hard feelings toward the captain. The captain could have avoided this by crossing the transaction to her adult state and saying something like: "I wouldn't mind discussing that later, but right now I have a lot of work to do."

In both examples, the crossed transaction results in consequences that are not productive as far as the police department is concerned. By paying more attention to their communications, the commanders in each instance could have avoided costly reactions on the part of their subordinates.

However, crossed transactions are sometimes useful and necessary to gain control of situations or to bring about a change in behavior that is inappropriate to the situation. The general rule is that a crossover to the adult state is likely to be the most productive. For example:

LT: That stupid lieutenant couldn't supervise if he had a seeing-eye dog. (parent to parent)
CAPT: What has he done to make you so angry? (adult to adult)

In this crossed transaction, the captain avoids getting into a parent-to-parent criticism of the lieutenant and begins to explore the problem between the two lieutenants. Although such a cross does not always lead to problem-solving behavior on the part of the responder, it provides a better chance than a parent-to-child or child-to-child interaction.

Crossed transactions leading to ill feelings, unproductive use of time, and organizational conflict can be avoided if police managers are aware of their tendencies and become more proficient in determining the appropriateness of the adult-to-adult pattern of communication.

Ulterior Transactions

The third type of transaction is called an **ulterior transaction** and has two messages. One, the overt message, is communicated at the verbal level. At the same time, the second, or covert message, is communicated subliminally. This second message is intended to elicit a response different from that called for by the first message. Managers may use ulterior transactions in attempting to sell a project. For example, the following, which on the surface sounds like an adult-to-adult transaction, may take place between a chief and his command staff:

CHIEF: This is a really good project I have developed, and I would like you to see if there is anything wrong with it.

The verbal message appears to be a straightforward request for constructive criticism. However, the implication is that the chief thinks highly of the project and is already committed to it; he is therefore probably not really interested in seeing the staff come up with alternative plans. These implications stem from the manager's parent ego state and are addressed to the staff's child ego state. If the staff members accept the ulterior message, they will respond from their child ego state and say "Yes, chief, that project sounds good." If the staff members do not read the ulterior message and question the chief, they may get a parent-to-child response from the chief, such as "You don't really understand the problem."

When a subordinate, overworked and looking discouraged, comes in with a report, her verbal comment "Here is the report" is on its face an adult-to-adult transaction. However, her demeanor may provoke the manager to say: "You look down, what's wrong?" The subordinate's physical appearance communicates a message from her child state that she wants encouragement and support from the manager's parent state. The manager, in acknowledging the report in her adult state, may or may not respond to the child needs of the subordinate.

An ulterior message is often involved when a person announces, seemingly from his adult state, that he has done something wrong or is having difficulty. For example:

LT TO CAPT: I've read this statute two or three
                                                 times, but I just don't understand it.

On the surface, this is an adult-to-adult description of the lieutenant's state of mind. However, the child message asks for either a put-down for being stupid or for support from the captain.

Ulterior transactions are sometimes used to communicate feelings or ideas when the individual wants to avoid a direct statement, being uncertain of the response he or she might otherwise receive. However, ulterior transactions are a poor substitute for honest ones and are the basis for psychological games, which will be discussed later in the chapter.

The police manager, in dealing with ulterior transactions, must be aware of the following:

1. In which ulterior transactions does he or she deliberately engage?
2. Which of his honest transactions may be interpreted as ulterior messages?
3. What ulterior transactions are others initiating?

Ulterior transactions can create major obstacles to effective communications in a police department; they prevent the agency from becoming as effective as it could be if honest transactions were more common.

Basic Life Positions and Organizational Sanctions

The police manager's ego states and the nature of the transactions that he or she customarily engages in are, to a large extent, determined by the manager's early life experiences. In all probability, one of the most important determinants of how we interact with others is how we view ourselves and other people. How we view our adult selves is very much a function of the view we held of ourselves as children. Likewise, the degree of trust we place in other people and our general beliefs about them are established on the basis of our early life experiences. In one way or another, at some time early in our lives, we made decisions about ourselves and others that determined the nature of our future interactions. These decisions are referred to in transactional analysis as **basic life positions**.

There are four basic life positions, which are determined by whether one has made positive or negative decisions about oneself and others. People whose life experiences have been rewarding and who have had a sufficient amount of praise and encouragement will probably see themselves in a positive light. That is, they consider themselves "O.K." If, on the other hand, they were constantly ridiculed, called dumb, or rejected by their peers, they will likely see themselves in a negative light, or as "not O.K." How other people behaved toward us determines whether we see others as "O.K." or "not O.K." All combinations of decisions are possible, and they, in turn, lead to one of four basic positions.

First Position: "I'm O.K., You're O.K." If realistic, this is the position of managers who are psychologically healthy, mature, and able to develop open, trusting relationships with other people. They see others as having the potential for development and assume responsibility for their own behavior. Although they may occasionally experience depression, they recognize that it is temporary and take steps to overcome their negative feelings.

Second Position: "I'm O.K., You're Not O.K." This is the position of managers who feel that others are out to degrade and persecute them. They blame others for their miseries and are unwilling to take responsibility for their shortcomings and mistakes. Their relationships are marked by a strong distrust of other people and a need to be in control of others and of all situations.

Third Position: "I'm Not O.K., You're O.K." Police managers in this position feel powerless. When they compare themselves to others, they come up short. Managers in this position are self-critical and overly concerned about their shortcomings and mistakes. They have a tendency to become easily depressed and are at times irrational in their decision making.

Fourth Position: "I'm Not O.K., You're Not O.K." Individuals in this position have given up on life. They see little good in themselves or in other people. They may be withdrawn, moody, and pessimistic, and it may be very difficult to develop any kind of effective working relationship with them. Usually they are not involved in steady employment at management positions in law enforcement due to the necessity of decision making in police departments.

The concept of the basic life positions is useful in understanding individual differences in responses to organizational sanctions and the differences in the use of sanctions by police managers. Most police departments have positive and negative sanctions that reward good performance and punish poor performance. However, people differ in their reactions to advancement, awards, and praise, as well as to negative sanctions such as suspensions, criticism, demotions, and transfers.

Managers who feel "O.K." about themselves and others seek and give as many forms as possible of positive recognition. Others who feel "not O.K." about themselves are more frequently in a position to receive negative sanctions than positive sanctions. Similarly, managers who take life positions that emphasize the "not O.K."–ness of other people have a tendency to impose as many negative sanctions as possible. In all probability, the difference between police managers who constantly look for opportunities to criticize, suspend, or demote and police managers who are conscientious in their efforts to provide positive sanctions has a great deal to do with their life positions regarding other people.

Both positive and negative sanctions are acts that recognize the behavior of other people. In TA, such acts are referred to as **strokes**. Everybody needs a certain amount of stroking, or recognition, to survive. Infants need physical stroking if they are to develop properly. After infancy, the need for physical stroking diminishes, and a need for recognition from other people becomes essential to psychological development. Whether the manager praises or punishes a person, his or her acts recognize the other person, which is the basis of a stroke.

To be psychologically sound and to relate meaningfully to others, people need positive strokes such as praise, compliments, appreciation, and attention to their ideas and feelings. Positive strokes make subordinates feel stronger, more competent, and more effective. Negative strokes, such as being criticized, ignored, or having ideas and feelings discounted make subordinates feel weaker, less effective, and less competent. The police work situation can be a major source of strokes. Unfortunately, some police departments give many more negative than positive strokes, and their officers are angry, unhappy, and less effective on the job.

Positive strokes can take many forms. Simple acts of recognition such as a friendly "good morning" or a welcoming handshake are important in maintaining a sense of "O.K."-ness. However, subordinates also need the more lasting strokes that come from having good work recognized, being given a chance to use their skills, and being rewarded for their service and hard work. At the deepest level, subordinates need the strokes that come from having an intimate, caring relationship with a manager they respect and trust.

Within police departments, managers and supervisors should be a major source of positive strokes. Many departmental change efforts result in different patterns of stroking. For example, placing decision making responsibility in the hands of officers at lower levels in the hierarchy is a way of recognizing their competence and importance and becomes a powerful positive stroke. Likewise, moving to team decision making gives every officer a chance to be heard, which for most is an important stroke in his or her relationship with others.

As police managers become more aware of their own stroking tendencies, they often find that they too frequently fail to give positive strokes in appropriate situations. On the other hand, they may ignore the negative stroking situations that they find during the course of a day. Such stroking patterns often create cautious, unhappy subordinates who may begin to feel incapable of making sound decisions. In addition, the officers and supervisors working in police departments where there is a deficit of positive strokes will frequently do only that which is required of them and use their energies and skills to obtain strokes in their time off or through sabotaging the efforts of the police command structure.

It is essential to recognize that all individuals need a certain amount of stroking and that they will find some way to obtain the strokes they need. For the "I'm Not O.K." individuals, negative strokes may be more important than positive strokes. However, most officers who make contributions to the police mission feel "O.K." about themselves and need positive strokes to maintain this "O.K." feeling.

Time Structuring

To obtain the strokes they need, subordinates structure their time in a variety of ways. The six ways that have been identified as providing opportunities for obtaining strokes are described below.

One way to structure time is to **withdraw**. The manager can withdraw through fantasy, by ignoring others and watching TV, or by going off by himself to a favorite thinking place. He may withdraw when he is uncomfortable, bored, or feeling "not O.K." In moderation, withdrawal is a healthy way to obtain vicarious strokes. The overuse of withdrawal may suggest that the manager is not getting enough strokes in his relationships with other people.

A second way to structure time is through **rituals**. Some rituals are social exchanges that we have learned from our parents, such as the proper ways to greet and introduce people, polite table manners, and so forth. Other rituals are unique to the culture or organizations to which we belong. There are many rituals in the typical police department. Some examples are the way in which subordinates address ranking officers, how seating is arranged at staff meetings, and how communication is formalized within the hierarchy. These are ritualistic in that they provide the structure for individuals in the various ranks to be recognized and respected by those below them in the rank structure. Observation suggests that the fewer opportunities for obtaining positive strokes in normal exchanges at work with the police department, the more important these ritual behaviors become. To be effective, a police manager must be aware of the importance of rituals within the department and within the community in which she works. She also needs to be wary when rituals become more important than results.

A third way to structure time is through **pastimes**. Pastimes include the general discussion between people of interests, values, and events. Pastimes are a rich source of strokes in the absence of other types of time structuring. Between casual friends, this is a major form of time structuring. An exchange of their latest "war stories" is a favorite pastime among officers. Managers can spend hours talking about the "new breed" of officer or how it was in the "good old days."

Being able to engage in pastimes is an important social skill in making new acquaintances, enjoying a luncheon, or relaxing with associates. Pastimes are also useful departmentally when there is informal discussion of issues relevant to the police organization. However, they can also be harmful, such as when supervisors get together over coffee and "knock" the police department—an example of a parent-to-parent pastime. Overuse of pastimes during work hours suggests that there is a lack of sufficient stroking for good police work habits.

The fourth time structuring approach is **activity**. Activities comprise all manners of time usage related to recreation and work. Home improvement projects, golf, tennis, or any other occupation in which an individual actively spends time is an activity. Activities are a primary source of gaining strokes. When the police department fails to provide enough strokes for the activity of police work within the department, many officers find activities outside of police work to gain the strokes they are missing. For instance, they take on second jobs. The dramatic increase in recreational activities in our culture suggests that police employees are highly motivated to gain strokes and use their work not as a primary source of strokes but as a way of earning the necessary income to engage in the activities in which they may obtain the strokes they need. The test of management is in the creation of a police department where police activities are a rich source of strokes.

Psychological games are the fifth way of structuring time. Psychological games are a devious way of obtaining or giving strokes. All have certain basic elements:

1. There is a series of complementary transactions that on the surface seem reasonable.
2. There is an ulterior transaction that is the hidden agenda or reason for the interaction.
3. There is a negative outcome or payoff that concludes the game and is the purpose for playing it.

Structuring time through games decreases the problem-solving capacities of the police department. Although games appear to have advantages, they are all destructive to some degree to effective work relationships. In departments in which officers are bored with their jobs, or the work environment is devoid of positive strokes, officers have more need to play games. The next section of this chapter describes some typical police department games.

The sixth way to structure time is through **intimate relationships**. Intimate relationships are free of games and free of exploitation. The relationship is straightforward and honest, arousing feelings of tenderness, empathy, and affection. It involves a genuine caring for another person. Intimate relationships require a sense of "O.K."-ness regarding oneself and others. The intimate relationship is a source of some of the most lasting and enriching strokes, but it is not the most typical form of structuring time in police departments.

Intimacy cannot be created or engineered by the manager. It must occur spontaneously. It occurs between people who may not even be expecting it, and it seldom occurs when the manager goes out in deliberate search of it. The experience of intimacy is the experience of feeling a massive dose of positive stroking. In an intimate relationship, people feel unconditionally stroked and accepted for who they are, not for what they can do, how they dress, how they look, or how important a position they hold.

The following conditions must exist for intimacy to occur:

1. All defenses must be down. This means the manager must give up some personal gains, ceasing to emphasize rituals and pastimes.
2. The manager must risk being vulnerable. A manager who lets down his or her defenses may get hurt, and this is what the adapted child in him or her may fear.

3. The manager has to feel positively, not negatively, toward the other person. His or her nurturing parent and natural child must feel "O.K." about the other person. The manager has to be in a state in which he or she moves toward and not against the other person.

4. The manager must accept the other person unconditionally. If he or she places demands or sets up rules that control how close others can come, then he or she blocks intimacy.

The time-structuring characteristics of managers in a police department provide important clues as to the changes needed in the work environment. Where withdrawal, rituals, pastimes, and games make up the major stroke-acquiring transactions, the department's effectiveness will be seriously curtailed. Most change efforts focus on making the activities of police work more meaningful sources of strokes.

The police manager's own time-structuring characteristics are important determinants in the effectiveness of such change efforts.

Organizational Games

Psychological games are played by individuals who have a need to receive or give negative feelings, which are the payoff in the games. A fairly typical game played in police departments begins by a supervisor asking his or her subordinates for suggestions:

Other commanders offer suggestions, only to be told that their ideas are "all right, but ..." The chief finally leaves with the comment that "I guess you can't help me with this problem." This leaves the commanders feeling that they have wasted their time and could not help. The chief leaves feeling that "These guys can't help with anything." The bad feelings the commanders have and the bad feelings the chief has toward them is the

CHIEF:	We're in a real pinch. Headquarters wants us to develop a better relationship with the community; any suggestions?
1st CAPT:	Why don't we approach all the business leaders on a personal basis and give them information about our department and have them submit their ideas and complaints?
CHIEF:	That's O.K., but it would take too much time.
2nd CAPT:	I think we should start with the schools and increase our contact with teachers, kids, and parents.
CHIEF:	That would be all right, but it doesn't relate to stopping crime.

payoff for the game of "Yes, but." The "Yes, but" player can be distinguished from one who genuinely requests help by the fact that the "Yes, but" player often asks for input but never accepts any ideas. The player will continue to play this game until his or her subordinates cease to offer suggestions.

Psychological games reinforce or confirm a person's basic life position about himself or herself and others. Thus, the police manager who is successful in playing "Yes, but" with his or her staff confirms his or her "O.K."–ness and the "Not O.K."–ness of other members of the staff. Games played from the "I'm O.K., You're Not O.K." position are attacks on subordinates and are designed to reinforce feelings that others are "Not O.K." Other games are played from the "I'm not O.K., You're O.K." position and reinforce negative feelings the police manager has about himself or herself.

Some of the other games played by people in law enforcement are briefly described below.

If It Weren't for Him/Her (Them). This is a game designed to blame someone else for one's own poor performance or production. The "him/her" or "them" usually represents a person higher in the department. The chief may point to the city council. The payoff is that the player takes himself or herself off the hook and places responsibility on someone else for his or her failure to perform. Basically, this game allows an individual to maintain his or her own sense of "O.K."–ness by placing others in a "Not O.K." position.

Now I've Got You, You SOB (NIGYYSOB). This is a game in which the player attempts to catch another individual or group in a mistake, a lie, or a violation of rules and orders so that he or she can discipline the person in violation. This might be played by anyone in the police department. For example, a lieutenant, knowing of the tendency for officers under his or her command to sleep on the midnight shift, might make a surprise check to catch sleepers. He or she then imposes disciplinary measures on both the officers and their sergeant. The game permits the lieutenant to get rid of angry feelings toward others and puts the sergeant in his or her place. This person is also confirming in his or her own mind that he or she is "O.K.," but that the others are "Not O.K." This game tends to destroy the lieutenant's chances of developing trusting relationships with these officers in the future.

Blemish. In this game, the player may review a report or performance evaluation and pick out minor flaws in an otherwise good report. This person is the "nitpicker" who always has to find something wrong and seldom comments on the good parts of the report. The payoff for the blemish player is the bad feelings he or she gives to others.

Corner. The players of this game put others in impossible binds. The corner player may ask for a report with an unreasonable deadline. When the report comes back with understandable omissions, the player returns the report with a reprimand. If the report writer turns the report in late to make sure it is complete and accurate, he or she is reprimanded for being late. The payoff is the reprimand the player gives to the report writer.

In addition to the games played for the purpose of punishing others or of proving their "Not O.K."-ness, there are a number of games that result in the player being put down or criticized or that are designed to provoke sympathy. Players of these games experience a keen sense of "Not O.K."–ness or inadequacy.

Poor Me. In this game, the players find themselves in a situation they do not like and spend hours griping to anyone who will listen. Usually the players get sympathy from the listeners. Players of "Poor Me" refuse to do anything constructive to remove themselves from the situation; if the conditions they gripe about were changed, they would find something else to make their lives miserable. "Poor Me" players see themselves as "Not O.K." and constantly find situations that confirm their dismal feelings.

Kick Me. Players of "Kick Me" constantly become involved in situations that provoke their managers or supervisors into taking some form of negative action against them. Some "Kick Me" players are chronically late for important assignments or turn in reports with errors. Even after careful instruction as to what is required, they continue to make serious mistakes. Hard-core players ultimately end up being "kicked out" of the police department by being fired. Others receive enough "kick" to prevent them from ever being considered for promotion and use this circumstance to play "Poor Me."

Stupid. This is a variation of the "Kick Me" game. In this instance, the players are constantly doing "stupid" things that provoke the supervisor or colleagues into commenting on their stupidity. "Stupid" players are usually bright enough to perform well, but constantly make mistakes or place themselves in jeopardy by their poor judgment. "Stupid" players may fail a sergeant's exam for years despite their intelligence and ability to pass the exam. They usually comment that they are probably too dumb to pass the exam.

Wooden Leg. In "Wooden Leg," the player finds some excuse to avoid success or accomplishment. It is a cop-out game in which a person uses a physical or social handicap to avoid being successful. A long-term officer who has failed to advance may say that he or she would try something else but is too old. The middle-aged sergeant might use the excuse of age to not attend college classes even though they may be necessary for further advancement. Any number of excuses can be used as a "wooden leg," such as family background, lack of education, age, or lack of physical capabilities. By using excuses, people escape from the challenge to grow and get ahead; thus they are able to maintain their "Not O.K." life position.

Although all the behaviors involved in these games can be exhibited by non-game-playing individuals, games can be recognized by the fact that they occur repeatedly and that the outcomes are predictable for the individuals involved. The kind of games a person plays seldom changes. The "Kick Me" player and the "Yes, but" player continue as long as there are people who allow them to get away with their games. The player of games from the "I'm O.K., You're Not O.K." position needs individuals in the "I'm Not O.K., You're O.K." position to make his or her games work. As in every game, certain players are necessary. Breaking up games requires straight adult-to-adult transactions. By pointing out organizational games and being unwilling to support them, it is possible to discourage the players. The police manager's task is to recognize the time-wasting games played in the department and to begin developing an atmosphere that discourages games and encourages direct, honest, problem-solving behavior.

Conclusion

This chapter summarizes the basic concepts of transactional analysis and provides a limited number of illustrations as to the implications of TA concepts in organizational and personal change efforts. The material presented primarily introduces the basic concepts. For interested police managers, further study and training are essential for these concepts to be of value in their management practice.

A substantial body of literature that covers in detail the theory and implications of TA to management practice has been developed. In addition, there are many consulting firms ready and able to provide training and consultation to police managers interested in implementing these concepts in their police departments.

There may be many who criticize TA on theoretical and practical grounds. However, the model has wide applicability, its major concepts are easily understood, and it provides an excellent set of concepts for giving direction to personal change. These comments in no way suggest that personal or organizational change is easy or that TA will solve all the problems for a police manager. Like all other models, it is a tool that can be effective in the hands of police managers who understand and believe in the approach.

References

Berne, E. (1964). *Games people play.* New York: Grove Press.

Harris, T. H. (1967). *I'm O.K.—You're O.K.* New York: Avon Books.

Jongeward, D., et al. (1974). *Everybody wins: Transactional Analysis applied to organizations.* Reading, MA: Addison-Wesley.

Further Reading

Berne, E. (1966). *Principles of group treatment.* New York: Grove Press.

Berne, E. (1963). *The structure and dynamics of organizations and groups.* New York: Grove Press.

Berne, E. (1961). *Transactional Analysis in psychotherapy.* New York: Evergreen Original.

Berne, E. (1972). *What do you say after you say hello?* New York: Bantam Books.

James, M. (1976). *The O.K. boss.* Reading, MA: Addison-Wesley.

James, M., & Jongeward, D. (1971). *Born to win.* Reading, MA: Addison-Wesley.

Jongeward, D., et al. (1974). *Everybody wins: Transactional Analysis applied to organizations.* Reading, MA: Addison-Wesley.

Meininger, J. (1973). *Success through Transactional Analysis.* New York: Signet Books.

Steiner, C. (1971). *Games alcoholics play.* New York: Ballantine Books.

Steiner, C. (1974). *Scripts people live.* New York: Bantam Books.

Discussion Questions

1. What are some common statements heard around a police department?
2. Do these statements usually come from the parent, adult, or child ego state?
3. What kinds of transactions exist in the daily operation of a police department?
4. Which ego state is most commonly used by police managers, and which ego state in their subordinates do they normally address?

5. Give an example of an ulterior transaction between a middle manager in a police department and the police chief.
6. What life position does most criminal behavior stem from?
7. What life position does most police behavior stem from?
8. What are some examples of negative strokes given in police work?
9. What are some examples of positive strokes that a police officer or police manager might receive?
10. What techniques might a police manager use to give as many positive strokes as possible?
11. Should a police manager ever give negative strokes?
12. What are some psychological games that are typically played in police departments?
13. As defined by transactional analysis, how do most police managers structure their time?

9

Understanding Personnel Through MBTI®

LEARNING OBJECTIVES

1. Students will understand themselves better.
2. The student will understand how others in law enforcement behave.
3. The student will understand functional behavior.
4. The student will understand different attitudes and behaviors.

Overview

How do the people in your police department get along? How do they feel about their superiors or their colleagues across the hall? Do they agree on how decisions are made and who should do what jobs? Probably not. Conflicts are inevitable in human organizations. These conflicts are believed to arise from personality differences, and they can be major obstacles to efficient operation. This chapter describes a method of helping police managers recognize these differences and use them to strengthen their agencies.

Personality, as used here, refers to the complex array of personal characteristics such as needs, motivations, values and morals that make people different. But these general terms do not describe the individual's basic attitude—or approach to life—that guides behavior and is reflected in personality (and sometimes conflicts with other approaches). As a result, psychologists have sought ways to identify what it is that makes up each person's preferred way of dealing with the world.

The Myers-Briggs Type Indicator® (MBTI) (1966) does just that; it is an instrument that specifically reveals a person's personal traits and makes it possible to compare differences in fundamental approaches among individuals.

The MBTI® frequently is used for management training and consultation. Police managers who have used it find that it helps them to recognize both compatible and incompatible styles. By understanding the differences in approach, managers can see how these differences affect relationships; thus they are better able to avert unproductive conflicts and improve the department's overall performance.

Functional Behavior

The MBTI® instrument identifies four basic preferences that relate to: (1) the way people become aware of the outside world; (2) the way they come to conclusions about what they become aware of—that is, how they make decisions; (3) their degree of flexibility; and (4) their orientation toward the external world. The theoretical direction for the MBTI® came from Carl Jung's theory of types (1923).

Jung believed that when we become aware of the world around us and make decisions on the basis of that awareness, we use a combination of mental processes:

- **Sensory** (through the five senses), symbolized by the letter S
- **Intuitive** (indirectly—through the subconscious, what is learned through the senses, and by pursuing the possibilities of the situation), symbolized by N
- **Thinking** (rational), symbolized by T
- **Feeling** (on the basis of a value system), symbolized by F

Ideally, the individual develops a command of all these processes and uses them throughout life. But because of differences in life experiences, people vary in the degree of their development of these processes and have different preferences and approaches to the situations that life presents.

Let us begin with awareness. People obtain their fundamental view of the world through using the sensory process, the intuitive process, or a combination of the two. The degree to which a person prefers one over the other can be visualized on a continuum that places total reliance on the sensory process at one end of the scale and total reliance on intuition at the other.

SENSORY   INTUITIVE

Most of us fall somewhere between the two extremes. Those who find themselves on the sensory side of the scale prefer gathering the observable facts of a situation; they tend to be "realistic, practical, observant … and good at remembering a great number of facts and working with them." (McCaulley, 1977, p. 2.) Those who rest on the intuitive side tend to value imagination and inspiration, are good at producing new ideas and projects, and like to solve problems.

What about decision making? When a person comes to settling, closing, or completing an issue, he or she primarily uses one of two processes: thinking or feeling. The person in whom the thinking (rational) process dominates tends to be logical, objective, and consistent, making decisions by analyzing and weighing the data. Those who rely mostly on the feeling process tend to make decisions on the basis of values, or "because it feels right." They also tend to be sympathetic, appreciative, and tactful in dealing with others. These processes can also be visualized on a continuum:

THINKING   FEELING

The processes of becoming aware and reaching conclusions develop independently. Thus, the processes of becoming aware and the processes of making decisions can be joined in the following combinations:

ST	(sensory plus thinking). People with this combination are mainly interested in facts; they make decisions by impersonal analysis. As individuals, they tend to be practical and matter-of-fact.
SF	(sensory plus feeling). People with this combination are interested in facts, but are also in tune with feelings in themselves and others. They are sociable and friendly.
NF	(intuitive plus feeling). People with this combination are interested not in facts, but in possibilities for the future—they base their decisions on personal feelings. They are enthusiastic and insightful.
NT	(intuitive plus thinking). People with this combination are interested in possibilities, but approach them with impersonal analysis. In decision making, they more or less ignore the human element.

Which combination of preferences an individual develops makes a difference in the types of work he or she will enjoy. An ST (**sensory-thinking**) person would prefer a job that requires gathering data and making logical, calculated decisions based on the data (a good example would be patrol). An SF (**sensory-feeling**) person would probably prefer a project that requires extensive dealings with people (working with juveniles), whereas an NT (**intuitive-thinking**) person might prefer abstract concepts or ideas (homicide investigation). An NF (**intuitive-feeling**) person would enjoy a job that deals with people and requires creativity and originality (training, community relations).

Another aspect of personality type identified by the MBTI® is whether a person prefers closure and having things settled or prefers to keep options open. People who choose closure over keeping their options open are referred to as **judgers** (Js); those who prefer to keep things open and fluid are **perceivers** (Ps). Judgers like to decide matters quickly. They live in a planned, decided, orderly way, wanting to regulate life and control it. Perceivers, on the other hand, like to keep their options open—they do not depend on order and stability. They are flexible and enjoy seeking alternatives, being spontaneously able to understand life and adapt to it.

The final trait measured by the MBTI® centers on relative interest in the outer or inner worlds—that is, on whether an individual is an introvert or an extrovert. **Introverts** concentrate on their inner world, and are more content in dealing with ideas and concepts. **Extroverts** enjoy focusing on the world around them and are more comfortable in action than in contemplation. Sometimes these words are given positive or negative connotations; in this context they merely describe individual preferences.

In terms of these four traits—preferred method of becoming aware, preferred method of reaching conclusions, preferred degree of closure, and preferred orientation toward the world—a person can be predominately:

1. S (sensing) or N (intuitive)
2. T (thinking) or F (feeling)
3. J (judging) or P (perceiving)
4. I (introverted) or E (extroverted)

Each preference contributes unique characteristics that help to shape the individual. People naturally tend to act and react in ways that are most comfortable for them. But one's preferred approach may not be the most appropriate for dealing with the situation at hand—or it may conflict with the approach preferred by a fellow officer. When this happens, knowing about and accepting the psychological preferences of both ourselves and those with whom we work can help to maintain healthy, productive relationships.

Generally, it is easier for police officers to develop the traits that are strongest in them. According to Jung, in becoming aware and in reaching decisions, most people rely on their dominant process instead of using their sensory, intuitive, thinking, and feeling capacities equally (Bates & Kiersey, 1978). But people usually have at least some overlapping characteristics. For instance, the dominant preference in extroverts pertains to the outer world, but the extrovert also has an auxiliary quality that provides a reasonable balance. Without the inner life, extroverts would become extreme in their extroversion and thus appear to be superficial to better balanced officers (Bates & Kiersey, 1978).

Introverts rely on their auxiliary as a connection with the outer world. If it is undeveloped, they will seem awkward and uncomfortable. Therefore, introverts who lack an adequate auxiliary tend to be at a greater disadvantage than extroverts who lack such a modifying quality (Bates & Kiersey, 1978).

To extroverted officers, introverts may seem aloof, but the introverts' reserve may stem from the fact that their energies are fueled by ideas and not by social contact (Bates & Kiersey, 1978). In ordinary dealings, introverts do not necessarily say how they really feel about an issue. Only when they feel strongly enough about something will they reveal their thoughts. Through understanding and a developed auxiliary, introverts can learn to deal effectively with the outside world without becoming full-fledged members of it (Bates & Kiersey, 1978).

Data Experience

Through a variety of programs, the Myers-Briggs Type Indicator® has been given to 1,164 law enforcement personnel from the ranks of sergeant through chief. Although a majority of these participants came from North Carolina, about 500 came from other areas of the country. Of the 1,164 officers, 58 were women. An analysis of the MBTI® data (Figure 9-1) provides a realistic profile of types of people in law enforcement.

A slight majority (51 percent) of those tested were introverts. That figure seems to carry no significance until it is compared with MBTI® figures for the general population. Across the country, approximately 70 percent of those tested were extroverted and only 30 percent introverted. In other words, law enforcement seems to attract more basically introverted (that is, inner-directed) people than people who are basically outer-directed and prefer to interact with others. In regard to preferred method of becoming aware, through the senses or through intuition, ratios among police officers ran about the same

Sensing Types		Intuitive Types			
With Thinking	With Feeling	With Feeling	With Thinking		
I S T J N = 374 %= 32.13	I S F J N = 53 %= 4.55	I N F J N = 8 %= 0.68	I N T J N = 48 %= 4.12	Judging	Introverts
I S T P N = 62 %= 5.32	I S F P N = 15 %= 1.28	I N F P N = 9 %= 0.77	I N T P N = 30 %= 2.57	Perceptive	
E S T P N = 34 %= 2.92	E S F P N = 17 %= 1.46	E N F P N = 33 %= 2.83	E N T P N = 27 %= 2.31	Perceptive	Extroverts
E S T J N = 322 %= 27.66	E S F J N = 42 %= 3.60	E N F J N = 16 %= 1.37	E N T J N = 74 %= 6.35	Judging	

	#	%		#	%		#	%
E	565	48.53	I	599	51.46	SJ	791	67.95
S	919	78.95	N	245	21.04	SP	128	10.99
T	971	83.41	F	193	16.58	NT	179	15.37
J	937	80.49	P	227	19.50	NF	66	5.67

FIGURE 9-1 Data analysis for 1,164 police managers.

as among people in general. Seventy-five percent of people tested, regardless of their occupation, prefer the sensory mode; 79 percent of law enforcement officers have this preference. The general population is about equally divided between those who reach decisions on a rational basis (thinkers) and those who decide on the basis of feelings (feelers). In this study, 83 percent of law enforcement personnel preferred thinking over feeling. About the same ratio existed in police preferences for judging (80 percent) over perceiving. The general population divides about 50:50.

The implication, then, is that the majority of law enforcement personnel are STJs—that is, they are logical in nature, designing their environment to close out issues as quickly as possible. They examine and direct issues on the basis of past and present experience, without much consideration of the future. Of the 16 types, two styles are common among police personnel: 32 percent of those tested are ISTJs and 28 percent are ESTJs; 60 percent of the total show a strong preference for one of these two related styles. Law enforcement managers must therefore consider how best to deal with these styles.

ESTJs are described as follows by Myers and Myers (1980, pp.85–86):

Extroverted thinkers tend to use their thinking to run as much of the world as may be theirs to run. . . . Ordinarily they enjoy deciding what ought to be done and giving the appropriate orders to ensure that it will be done. They abhor confusion, inefficiency, half measures, anything that is aimless and ineffective. Often they are crisp disciplinarians, who know how to be tough when the situation calls for toughness. . . . They act forcefully upon the basis of their judgment, whether well-founded or not.

On the other hand, according to the same authors (pp.105–106) **ISTJ**s possess:

a complete, realistic, practical respect both for the facts and for whatever responsibilities these facts create. . . . The interaction of introversion, sensing and the judging attitude gives them extreme stability. . . . ISTJs emphasize logic, analysis, and decisiveness.

Although these traits serve most decision makers very well, their high representation among police managers can account for some underlying problems in these officials' respective functions. Conflict can arise in working with citizens and fellow agency members who see the advisability of change. When dealing with a problem, ST commanders may not always be responsive to other points of view or sensitive to the emotional needs of others.

ESTJs are so in tune with the established, time-honored institutions that they may not understand those who might wish to abandon or radically change those institutions (Bates & Kiersey, 1978).

ISTJs also rely on time-honored institutions and base their decisions on the facts before them. On a day-to-day basis, this approach probably proves very useful, but in the long run it can produce a police department that resists adapting to new law enforcement techniques.

Some police managers' impersonal analysis of situations and lack of feeling can make them less aware in reaching a decision on others' personal needs. Because they may rely on the past in decision making, they may not be inclined to take risks or engage in creative or intuitive thinking. Consequently, their organization may tend to resist change. The police chief who fits this description may find an obstacle in an intuitive city manager; he or she may look for stability, whereas the city manager is inclined to be more experimental.

Temperament

Divergent types become departmental assets when the differences are recognized and put to use in problem solving. Even though there are some people who consistently fall in the middle of the continuum, nearly everyone has an enduring set of characteristics that give special quality to his or her behavior and relationships. This personal makeup is sometimes referred to as one's "**temperamen**t." It is this underlying quality that may determine one's leadership skills, teaching ability, and degree of successful participation in the departmental structure.

Specific temperaments have been associated with the four categories of Jung's typology (Bates & Kiersey, 1978). The **SPs** (ISTP, ESTP, ISFP, ESFP), who share the first type of temperament, are called negotiators. For the most part, SPs do not like to be tied down or obligated. They feel a sense of joy, living for today, barely glancing at tomorrow. SPs are impulsive—they do things because they want to. Of all temperament types, they are the most likely to "share and share alike." Resources are to be used; machinery is to be operated; people are to be enjoyed. SPs may have a flair for the dramatic and a disdain for detail. Frequently these people are described as exciting, optimistic, cheerful, and full of fun.

SJs (ISTJ, ESTJ, ISFJ, ESFJ) represent the second type of temperament. SJs are labeled as stabilizers. They feel a sense of duty and a need to belong. But this belonging must be earned. SJs do what they are required to do, and they want to be useful. As a type, they feel obligated, responsible, and burdened. SJs are the ones who are most inclined to save for future emergencies because they believe firmly in "Murphy's law"—whatever *can* go wrong, *will* go wrong. SJs and SPs make up over 70 percent of our population.

The third temperament group comprises all the **NTs** (INTP, ENTP, INTJ, ENTJ). They are referred to as visionaries. NTs have a sense of power and an urge to understand, control, predict, and explain realities. NTs want to be competent and make a fetish of intelligence. They are the most self-critical of all the types and are very sensitive to the credentials of their critics. To others, NTs may seem cold, remote, and sometimes arrogant. For the NT, work is work and play is work. NTs find SPs difficult to understand.

The fourth type of temperament is represented by the **NFs** (INFJ, ENFJ, INFP, ENFP). NFs are called catalysts. They have a sense of spirit, being basically involved in the search for self. NFs hunger to become better people, and their purpose in life is to have a bigger purpose in life. NFs feel they must have integrity: there must be no facade, no mask, no playing of roles—only one's genuine self. NFs also bring meaning and a heightened sense of drama to their relationships, which often become intense. The other types have trouble understanding the NF, and the NF, in turn, cannot really grasp the others' commitment to what seem to him or her to be false goals.

If we can identify the respective personality types found within a police department and then determine the behavioral characteristics associated with each, we may learn something about the climate within that agency. For instance, NT commanders may direct an agency that runs like clockwork, but in doing so they may demand too much of themselves and others. NT officers may be insensitive to the needs of others—namely, their peers and the community's citizens. SJ officers, the dominant type in police departments, believe strongly in rules, and they obey their superiors. SJs feel that they must be prepared for every situation. SP officers, on the other hand, may be just the opposite. They are very restless and do not like routine. They are not particularly disciplined, yet they work best in emergencies because emergencies open up new possibilities. NF officers are so people-oriented that they see good in everyone and want to bring out the best in each person. They are inclined to let their hearts rule their minds.

Of the law enforcement personnel tested, 68 percent preferred SJ behavior, 16 percent preferred NT, 11 percent preferred SP, and 6 percent preferred NF. When we tested other people in government, we found that about 50 percent were SJs, and slightly more SPs were found among non-law enforcement government employees than among law enforcement personnel.

The question then arose whether law enforcement work itself tends to change one's preferences from the time of entry into the organization until the time of promotion. To explore this issue, we examined a single agency. Officers with five or fewer years of service were asked to complete the MBTI.® Forty-four agreed. That testing showed roughly the same kinds of preferences as earlier tests—that is, a preference for introverted behavior and for sensing, thinking, and judging over intuition, feeling, and perceiving. Exactly one-half of the sample were of only two temperament types—14 percent were ESTJs and 36 percent were ISTJs.

These data suggest some possible implications for the future. It appears that law enforcement as a profession may continue to recruit the same kind of people it now attracts and may lack members of other temperament types. Apparently, the field attracts people who believe strongly in tradition, in accepting and fulfilling obligations, and in being well-prepared for tasks; moreover, these people are willing to live in a hierarchical structure and are strong advocates of fundamentals. The kind of person who has these characteristics will accept amounts of responsibility that sometimes are beyond his or her individual ability and energy to fulfill. These people will reward others who act decisively and will try to preserve the morals and ethics of the organization and the community. They may, however, attempt to decide issues too quickly. Today's activities need to be planned and implemented in a timely order if the goals of the future, five or ten years ahead, are to be reached. The kind of person who is attracted to law enforcement may have difficulty dealing with other types—for example, those who rely more heavily on feelings than on logic or are creative or intuitive in their approach to problems instead of drawing exclusively from the past and present.

In this study, however, managers in law enforcement or those promoted to key managerial positions differ from line officers in that they more often have an NT temperament. It is possible that a department with NTs as commanders and SJs at other posts throughout the organization will benefit from the strengths of each. This will be true if the department is able to call on one group for preservation of the past and on the other for direction to the future. NT managers may have a tendency to be critical of subordinates, especially when viewed by SJs from their more relaxed point of view. NTs may make too many assumptions about their fellow officers, some of which may be accurate and some of which may be inaccurate. With NTs in managerial positions, law enforcement may find that the profession will be able both to conceptualize the future and to perform adequately in the present.

NFs apparently are not attracted to law enforcement, and that may be the profession's loss. The special quality of NFs is that they seek to help all other people reach their potential. Whereas NTs emphasize how to reach goals, NFs think about the possibilities in people. Therefore, NTs may help an organization achieve the maximum and NFs may help individual people reach their goals. Without the NF's natural participation in task forces, group meetings are a little more difficult for the other three temperaments. NFs have a willingness to listen and are almost automatically empathetic and sincere in their relationships, and many people in law enforcement today must try hard to develop these qualities.

WHY IT'S IMPORTANT

Researchers have long tried to explain the complex concept of personality. This has proven to be a challenging task, but understanding the abstract preferences and interactions that make up a person's personality can be beneficial for police managers. It can be helpful for the manager to understand his or her own personality characteristics as well as those of subordinates.

Different people have different motivations and have varying preferences. Understanding these aspects of a subordinate's personality can help a police manager find tasks that are best suited to get the most out of the officer. In addition, it may lead to the subordinate experiencing a higher level of job satisfaction as well as appreciating the manager's efforts.

As people come to better understand their own personalities, they may also find the working situations where they can be most productive. Obviously, law enforcement does not allow officers managers to only seek those activities that only bring them satisfaction, and it does not provide subordinates who are not challenging to managers. However, understanding your own personality characteristics can help you determine which aspects of your behavior need to be accentuated when dealing with subordinate personalities.

The MBTI® has been used to assist a number of professions other than law enforcement. The Myers & Briggs Foundation (www.myersbriggs.org) reports that it has also been used in professions such as medicine, law, education, management, sales, sales and education. This inventory has become so widespread that it has become a commonly accepted part of management tools due to its usefulness.

Uses for the MBTI®

The MBTI® may be used in a variety of ways to improve working relationships. For example, the police department may use the test simply to learn more about itself. All officers and supervisors might take the test as part of an in-service training program over a 30-day period. By participating in the inventory, members of the department can improve their understanding of themselves, each other, the department's managers, and the citizens they serve. Police managers can share the results of their tests with supervisors and officers, giving their subordinates a better understanding of the managers' point of view.

Another example of the MBTI's® usefulness may come from the chief and subordinates seeking to improve their ability to communicate. Officers want a forum in which their views can be expressed and heard more readily. After taking the MBTI,® officers can discuss the results in relation to how their department operates. They may find that the chief is a sensory-feeling (SF) person, and the commanders below are predominantly sensory-thinking (ST) types. Therefore, most of the commanders' proposals may not address the issues of employee morale that the chief considers important. On the other hand, the commanders may become frustrated when their logical, precise proposals are consistently ignored.

A lack of feelers (Fs) in law enforcement may lead some officers to complain that they are not receiving enough praise or recognition for their work. Although the chief is an F, he or she may know little about these problems because the commanders (Ts) who report to him or her give little information about employee grievances. In addition, many of the commanders are also Js, who want to make quick decisions on the basis of given facts. Officers below them can become alienated because they are not allowed to participate in these decisions.

The Ss may disregard the intuitive Ns during decision-making sessions. They may dominate the discussions without really listening to the creative views of the Ns, who are thinking through the implications of the decisions and suggesting possible changes. After the MBTI® is discussed, the Ss realize the importance of including the Ns' viewpoints in proposals.

In some police agencies, communication issues may involve the preferences of the top commanders and the chief for extroversion (E) or introversion (I). Commanders who are introverts often assess situations in terms of their own reactions, often failing to pick up cues from others in the department. They may not seek contacts with their subordinates to determine sources of difficulty and therefore have little understanding of their subordinates' discontent. Inevitably, because it is the commanders who report to the chief, the chief also knows little about the complaints.

The three practical examples given above show five important uses for the analysis of personality differences through the MBTI:®

1. As a team-building tool. Those who take the inventory are able to recognize and accept the differences among them; improved communication can help them work together as a team, rather than as a group of individuals.
2. As an aid in looking at issues from different perspectives. People with diverse styles can make different and valuable contributions to the decision-making process. Groups often ignore ideas because the person who presents them has a preference type uncommon to the group—for example, when an intuitor presents ideas for change to a group of sensory-thinking people (STs).

3. As a database. To help develop strategies for improving communication and coordination between people with different personalities.
4. As a tool to help police managers understand the ways in which program proposals come across to officers who have different preferences in regard to decision making.
5. As an aid to officers in understanding why they may feel uncomfortable in certain job situations (for example, an ST would not feel comfortable in a job calling for creativity).

Another example of how the MBTI® can serve a police department involves the new chief who wants to build decision-making teams. The test can be used as a device to foster better understanding among team members, facilitate the decision-making process, and keep conflicts at a minimum.

Along with other instruments, the MBTI® has helped provide a composite of candidates vying for top management positions. City managers have used the inventory in choosing a police chief, but the results are not interpreted on a pass-fail scale. Instead, they help identify the kinds of interpersonal issues that can arise in a given environment. Then, once an applicant is accepted, any differences in style can be explained or ironed out. As an example, if the new chief is a heavy J (judger) and the manager is a P (perceiver), the two can: (1) realize that they do not operate in the same time frame; (2) accept that fact; and (3) thereby work more cooperatively.

Overall, when interpreted properly, the MBTI® is a valuable means of describing people—keeping in mind that it merely identifies preferences and does not label these as being either "good" or "bad." Everyone has different gifts, and it is management's responsibility to appreciate the possible contributions of all these traits. Once people understand that individuals vary, they can begin to understand that these variations are natural and that cooperation—rather than competition—can maximize their potential usefulness.

References

Bates, M., & Kiersey, D. (1978). *Please understand me.* Del Mar, CA: Prometheus Nemesis.

Jung, C. G. (1923). *Psychological types.* New York: Harcourt Brace.

McCaulley, M. H. (1977). *Introduction to the MBTI for researchers: Application of the Myers-Briggs Type Indicator to medicine and other health professions.* Gainesville, FL: Center for Applications of Psychological Type.

Myers-Briggs Type Indicator (MTBI) (1966). Palo Alto, CA: Consulting Psychologists Press, Inc.

Myers, I. B., & Myers, P. B. (1980). *Gifts differing.* Palo Alto, CA: Consulting Psychologists Press, Inc.

Discussion Questions

1. How can the MBTI® be used in a police department?
2. Are there any special types, as defined by MBTI,® that may make better police officers than other types?
3. Can the MBTI® be a useful tool in determining promotions and assignments?

Functional Aspects of Police Management

Once police managers understand the importance of the behavioral aspects of dealing with people within their agencies, they then must develop specific methods by which they can make effective decisions.

This section attempts to give police managers the tools they need to make the rational judgments necessary to maintain a stable organization.

This section opens with a discussion in Chapter 10 of the techniques of planning behavior. The police manager, in planning and implementing changes within a department, is responsible for balancing the concern for risk and the concern for the system. This section discusses the alternatives and their positive and negative features.

Chapter 11 describes a method of decision making that, if employed in the proposed step-by-step process, provides an effective tool for the police manager. This decision-making process is designed so that it can be implemented regardless of the police manager's style of management or communication process. This tool will help bring about effective staff work and give a clear-cut direction for all major decisions.

The management by objectives system discussed in Chapter 12 is a process by which a police manager can most effectively use the available resources. The process, which was designed for simplicity, has been tested and proven to be effective in both industry and government.

Chapter 13 deals with the issues of fiscal management, fiscal control, and the budgeting process for a police department. This chapter destroys the myths that many police managers may believe about budgeting and explains the destructive role that such misconceptions play in the development, execution, and implementation of a department budget. It is hoped that, with this knowledge, police managers will face future budgetary processes with an open mind and a positive attitude as opposed to feeling defeated before even starting. One of the major obstacles to effective police management seems to be insufficient time for the average police manager to perform all the required tasks.

By using a structured decision-making process, a specific management-by-objectives system, and wise use of time, the police manager can become more effective on a day-to-day basis.

10

Management Planning

LEARNING OBJECTIVES

1. The student will become aware of the importance of individual activities in terms of the overall purposes and goals of the department.

2. The student should strive for stability within the department—to reduce randomness and chance in departmental operations.

3. The student will be concerned with the functioning of the police department as a whole—integrating the technical systems (e.g., departmental training, communications) with the human and social systems operating within the police department.

4. In decisions pertaining to the degree of risk to be taken, the student will consider:

   a. Available information

   b. Logical decision making

   c. Assessments of the risk involved

   d. Estimates of the possibility of success

5. The student will become familiar with the four police management approaches to planning.

6. The student will become aware of the four criteria to be considered before the most appropriate management planning approach is selected:

   a. time

   b. severity

   c. frequency

   d. "ripple" effect

Planning is the foundation on which much of police management is based. The effective police manager, if he or she intends to reach specific goals and objectives, begins to develop managerial planning strategies in order to eventually produce effective action. Planning involves the aspects of problem solving, problem identification, problem prevention, and, most importantly, decision making (Educational Systems and Designs, 1968). It is the police manager's responsibility to seek out and weigh alternative solutions and to anticipate their consequences.

Planning should occur both formally and informally at all levels of every police department. Whether developed by individuals or teams, both short-term and long-term plans should be developed systematically. The quality of the final product depends in part on the ability of the people responsible for the planning and also on the influence that each has in solving problems and making decisions. The role of the police manager as a leader in developing planning strategies is important. Planning is strongly affected by the available facts and information and by the manner in which this information is used in identifying, evaluating, and solving problems.

The planning process can be approached in many ways, but we will discuss only the basic assumptions that can guide the police manager's thinking as he or she attempts to evaluate information, identify objectives, and use resources effectively.

Effective Planning and Use of Data

The quality and nature of police management planning revolves around two basic sets of concerns:

1. The concern for system, which includes purpose, stability, and entirety.
2. The concern for risk, which includes innovation and opportunity.

Concern for System

The three key ingredients within the concern for system are *purpose, stability*, and *entirety*.

Purpose. The first ingredient depends on how aware the police manager is of the importance of individual activities in relation to the overall purposes and goals of the police department. In the department, as goals or targets are established, there should be an attempt to establish a system of priorities, in the order of their importance, to the department's future.

Stability. The second ingredient within the concern for system is stability. The police manager should try to reduce randomness and chance in the operation of the department. It is a good policy to try to be in a position to anticipate and prepare for future problems. Standards, policies, rules, and regulations determine how the department should operate. The need for stability is reflected in the police manager's desire to establish some kind of order, sequence, and predictability in the police department as a whole and in the affairs of individual officers.

Entirety. The third major factor that the police manager should be concerned with is the functioning of the police department as a whole. The department can be thought of as a complex system consisting of subsystems and units within subsystems. In planning activities, it becomes the police manager's responsibility to link the information received from the uniformed operations with that from departmental records, communications, and training. In addition to the technical aspects, the police manager should be aware of the human and social systems within the agency.

The three ingredients—purpose, stability, and entirety—require careful coordination, for together they make up the concern for system, which the police manager should consider. The more aware the police manager is of the entire system, the better able he or she is to plan and work toward the department's stability and goals. Conversely, the manager who does not have an appreciation for the overall goals and purposes of the department may have difficulty carrying out his or her responsibilities effectively and making worthwhile contributions to the department as a whole.

The degree of the police manager's concern for the system can fall anywhere on a continuum, ranging from a high, or positive, concern to a low, or negative, concern.

The police manager should recognize, regardless of what level he or she has reached on the continuum, that a concern for the total system is necessary to maintain the direction and purpose that provides stability within the department. The manager may be at one end of the continuum, concerned only with the specific facts or elements within the total system and unaware of their interrelationship, or he or she may be concerned with events or a combination of elements without perceiving that they are part of a system or subsystem that eventually affects the total operation of the department.

The effective police manager, in creating plans within any system or subsystem, should be aware of the effects that his or her decisions and planning activities will have on the entire department.

Concern for Risk

The manager's concern for risk is demonstrated by his or her attitude toward **innovation** and **opportunity**. He or she should recognize that these factors are closely interrelated.

Almost every decision that the police manager makes involves some level of risk, opportunity, and innovation. The manager may take personal risks or risks that affect the department. The police manager who attempts to innovate by introducing something new into the department risks being rejected, laughed at, or, if the project fails, of receiving a reputation of incompetence. As far as the department is concerned, the risks of innovation include negative public reaction, higher costs, and a decrease in confidence among the personnel.

The decision pertaining to the degree of risk to be taken should be based on available information, logical decision-making, an assessment of the amount of risk involved, and an estimate of the possibility of success. An effective police manager is characterized by the willingness to take the risks appropriate to his or her level of authority and by a comprehension of the manner in which opportunity, innovation, and risk are interrelated.

The willingness to take risks is represented along the continuum shown in Figure 10-1. At the positive end of the scale, risk is viewed by the police manager as a challenge and an opportunity to utilize a given set of facts in the best interests of the entire police department. The negative end of the continuum represents resistance to risk. Thus, at one extreme, the police manager views risk as an opportunity rather than a threat, whereas the manager at the other end believes that the thrust of management practices should always be to avoid risk. From the middle, or the zero point, to the negative side, there are various degrees of avoiding and resisting risk, and from the zero point to the positive side, there are various degrees of accepting and welcoming it.

FIGURE 10-1 **Risk continuum.** *Source: Management Models—The Planning Process (Westport, CT: Educational Systems and Designs, Inc., 1968). Reprinted with permission of Educational Systems and Designs, Inc.*

What risks would a chief of police face if he stopped routine preventive patrol in several areas of his jurisdiction? That is the risk that Chief Clarence M. Kelley took when the Kansas City Preventive Patrol Experiment was undertaken in 1972. A task force of police officers from Kansas City proposed the idea of determining the effectiveness of police patrol. Chief Kelley agreed to conduct the experiment in cooperation with the Police Foundation. In this study, data were collected from 15 patrol beats in the city, measuring arrests, reported crimes, crime victimization, citizen attitudes, and police response time. Five of the beats were selected to have their regular police patrols removed. Those areas still received police service, but only as a result of calls for service; that is, police responded to calls in those areas, but did not conduct routine patrols. Five other beats received two to three times more routine patrol coverage than they had received prior to the beginning of the experiment. Finally, five beats had no change in their routine patrol coverage. This group functioned as a control group. The results demonstrated no appreciable difference in crime or the other variables that dealt with crime that were being measured.

This experiment caused quite a bit of surprise. Its effects and methodology have been debated for decades. However, it was a groundbreaking study. Consider the risks that Chief Kelley took in agreeing to partake in the experiment. This innovative mindset resulted in his agency being regularly discussed when considering patrol activities in agencies nationwide, but that could not have been foreseen at the outset. If serious violent crime had increased dramatically in the beats that were receiving no randomized patrol, could the Kansas City Police Department be held culpable? Even if the agency were not held legally responsible, the court of public opinion would likely not have been forgiving of the agency, and it would have forever been linked to a disastrous experiment with altering established police practices. Thankfully, none of that happened, but the agency had to accept the risks along with their innovative approach to learning about the effectiveness of police patrol.

- Could the Kansas City Preventive Patrol Experiment be carried out in modern times? Are the risks any different or greater than they were in 1972?
- If a modern agency were to try something similar to the Kansas City Experiment, would an agency be able to keep confidential the fact that some areas of a jurisdiction were not receiving patrol beats?

Management Planning Model

Explanation

An understanding of the police manager's alternatives in planning behavior is assisted by a model based on the manager's concerns for system and risk. The management model reflects the following key management issues:

1. To what extent the police manager should be concerned with system.
2. To what extent the police manager should be concerned with risk.
3. How the police manager should interrelate these concerns in his or her everyday activities.

The model (Figure 10-2) shows the four possible relationships between risk and system. The manager may exhibit a high concern for system, purpose, stability, and entirety as well as for accepting risk as a challenge and an opportunity. The manager may be more negative and resistant to risk but still maintain a concern for system. The manager may have a negative concern for system and a resistance to risk taking. He or she may accept risk as a challenge but may have a negative inclination toward system, purpose, stability, and entirety in his or her planning activities.

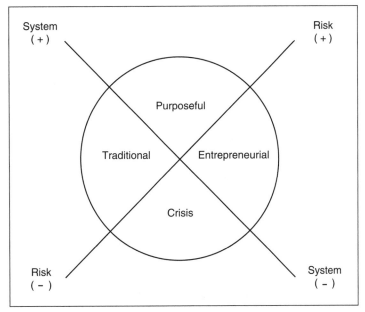

FIGURE 10-2 Management planning model. *Source:* Management Models—The Planning Process *(Westport, CT: Educational Systems and Designs, Inc., 1968). Reprinted with permission of Educational Systems and Designs, Inc.*

Police managers should be aware that they may have to move from one approach to another, depending on the issues they face. In addition, there are varying degrees of system and risk within each approach. For example, although two managers may be concerned with system and accept risk as a challenge, one may view the challenge of risk more positively than the other.

The four segments of the model represent the different approaches of police management to planning: (1) purposeful approach, (2) traditional approach, (3) crisis approach, and (4) entrepreneurial approach.

Purposeful Approach. In this approach, the police manager is concerned with system, is willing to take risks, and wants to take advantage of opportunities. Under this approach, the police manager integrates purpose, direction, innovation, and creativity within the system to contribute to the growth of the department. The police manager who uses this approach does not view systems or stability within the department as ends in themselves or as means for minimizing risk, but as ingredients important in maintaining a sense of direction and purpose. This manager will weigh the risk against the opportunity, taking into consideration the effect of the outcome on the entire police department.

Traditional Approach. The police manager who exercises this approach shows a high concern for system and stability and a desire to avoid risk, innovation, and creativity. This police manager wants to maintain the department in its present form, to support its traditions and precedents, and to minimize risk. Tradition, precedent, and stability are highly regarded. The philosophy of this approach is best described by the statement "We plan to stay on the same path, avoid rocking the boat, and eliminate any risk to our system."

Crisis Approach. This type of police manager demonstrates minimal concern for system and a desire to avoid risk. He or she considers every problem, regardless of its importance to the functioning of the department, as a pressing issue that must be solved immediately. Each issue and incident is regarded as requiring quick and firm handling and is normally dealt with on the element or event level with little or no regard to the subsystem or system. Police managers using this planning approach attempt to minimize risk by maintaining constant surveillance of subordinates and their activities, even if such surveillance stymies the department in its attempts to reach its goals.

Entrepreneurial Approach. This approach exhibits a low or negative concern for system and stability coupled with a strong willingness to accept risk and take advantage of opportunities.

The members of police departments emphasizing this managerial approach are overly concerned with exploration and speculation. In many instances, they take inappropriate risks and may overtax themselves or the department with projects unrelated to specific purposes or goals. Police agencies involved in federal funding projects that distract them from their long-term direction and goals exhibit the entrepreneurial approach to management planning.

Responses Within Each Management Approach

The differences between the four approaches to police management planning can be further clarified by comparing the attitudes and actions of police managers supporting the different philosophies. The manner in which each management approach relates to the following activities will be described:

1. Planning in general
2. Long-range planning
3. Establishing priorities
4. Structuring the organization
5. Using information
6. Controlling activities

Purposeful Approach

1. Within the purposeful approach, the planning activity is designed to bring about sound direction and to help provide stability to the police department. If the opportunity for risk can contribute to the department's overall achievements and purposes, such opportunities are welcomed.
2. Long-range planning is both systematic and flexible to encourage innovation and creativity as new facts and opportunities arise.
3. Priority is placed on building for the future while maintaining sound direction.
4. The department is organized so as to promote the flow of information among its members. Furthermore, the department's organization helps to handle short- and long-range problems and helps to balance risk-taking with the concern for system.
5. The basis for future planning is contained in the information collected by the department. This information is used to provide control and direction for the department as it grows.
6. The department's goals are examined first, and then plans are implemented with systematic controls consistent with the overall purposes. These controls are sufficiently flexible to allow the individual members of the department to exercise initiative in making decisions that will further the department's goals.

Traditional Approach

1. Planning is designed to produce stable and sound direction. This requires specific procedures and steps, as well as checks and balances, so that the command level of the department can be assured that the action taken by subordinates is in strict conformity with the established plan.
2. Long-range planning is systematic and based on present practices and tradition. Whether these practices benefit the department is not taken into consideration.

3. The highest priority of the traditional approach is to create a stable organization by developing rules and regulations to minimize risks.
4. The department is organized so that there is a clear-cut chain of command with a distinct delineation between staff and line operations. The staff functions are responsible for the creation and maintenance of the department's stability. The line operations are permitted to act only on opportunities approved by the command staff.
5. Much detailed information is collected on a systematic basis to reduce the risk of any chance occurrence within the department.
6. The established practices, procedures, and systems are designed to allow minimal deviation, thereby guaranteeing the staff close control of the entire department.

Crisis Approach

1. In the crisis approach, there really is no need to plan. Most situations that arise are emergencies, and they are dealt with on a day-to-day basis.
2. There is no long-range planning because in law enforcement, the future is totally unpredictable.
3. Priority is placed solely on current needs, problems, and issues.
4. The department is organized so that command-level personnel will be alerted when a problem arises in order to handle any emergency situation.
5. The information collected usually relates only to the problem at hand. It is designed to identify the cause of the problem, to provide solutions for it, and to prevent it from recurring.
6. Personal inspection by the manager is used as a control mechanism to guarantee that whatever mistakes do occur do not have any effect on the police operation.

Entrepreneurial Approach

1. In the entrepreneurial approach, action is the key to the department's success and plans restrict its freedom. Activities of the department are basically random and unconnected; therefore planning is impractical.
2. If the department is composed of sensitive and creative personnel who see opportunities and take appropriate actions, there is no need for long-range planning.
3. Priority is placed on discovering opportunities for improvement and growth.
4. Formal structures, such as organizational charts and job descriptions, are avoided because they tend to restrict the freedom and flexibility of the police personnel in responding to emergency situations.
5. Risk-taking is promoted and trust is placed in the judgment of the department personnel. Therefore, only a limited amount of information is needed to assist them in solving problems and exploring opportunities.
6. Loose control is sufficient if personnel possess the imagination and initiative to deal with problems effectively.

Selecting a Management Planning Approach

Before selecting a management planning approach, the police manager should evaluate its positive and negative features and its influence on the future of the department. The amount of energy expended in planning and problem solving should be in reasonable proportion to the potential gain to the department. If the energy expended is excessive, a quick solution to the problem may well be advisable. The manager should evaluate the potential gains in making a quality decision as well as the amount of effort necessary to obtain additional information. He or she should also be aware that the delays resulting from a long study sometimes slow the achievement of the overall goals of the department.

The potential gain or loss that the department may experience as a result of management planning is affected by specific criteria that the manager must weigh prior to selecting the most appropriate management planning approach. These criteria are *time, severity, frequency,* and *"ripple effects."*

Time is an important factor. Some problems that the police manager faces require an immediate solution. For example, a civil disturbance or the investigation of a serious crime must be dealt with as quickly as possible. In addition, long-range management planning is necessary to help identify the causes of problems, to develop plans and strategies for resolving future problems, and, if possible, to prevent their occurrence.

The time demands in solving a specific problem often cause the police manager to consider different approaches to management planning. He or she may need one approach for short-term needs, another for those in the middle range, and still another approach for long-term needs.

Severity is the second criterion affecting the decision about the best approach to use. Usually, when the issue is pressing, such as an immediate threat, then the management approach that accomplishes the quickest results is the most effective. With a less severe problem, however, the manager may be willing to extend the amount of time in which to reach a decision, thus permitting the accumulation of additional information and an examination of alternatives.

Frequency is a third factor. If the issue arises only once, it often will affect only a few people. In this case, almost any of the approaches may be used. However, if the issue comes up with greater frequency, the purposeful approach may be more effective.

Ripple effects—that is, both positive and negative side effects—should be taken into consideration. The police manager should be aware of the possible results of using a specific approach to reach a decision. For example, if the department elects to implement a new field reporting system, then the manager should be sensitive to the effect of the system on other members of the department as well as the operational personnel. In this case, the purposeful approach is the best management planning approach to use because it promotes the flow of information among the employees.

The police manager should realize that the selection of an approach should be based on whether it will promote or hinder the achievement of goals within the department.

To select the proper management planning approach, the factors of time, severity, frequency, and ripple effects must be taken into account.

Conclusion

For many years, police management has defined planning as the development of a set of procedures and practices. The implication is that there is only one correct way to plan. This discussion has focused on the variety of approaches to management planning that are available to the police manager. The approach selected is determined by the manager's attitudes, assumptions, and concerns. The management planning model built around the two basic sets of concerns shows the responses elicited by each approach.

Although this discussion emphasizes that the purposeful approach is generally the most effective, the police manager should realize that only through an analysis of the situation and careful consideration of the criteria can he or she accurately decide which approach is best for the department.

Reference

Educational Systems and Designs. (1968). *Management models—The planning process.* Westport, CT: Educational Systems and Designs.

Discussion Questions

1. Discuss the level of expertise that, in your opinion, exists in the average police department today in relation to the manner in which commanders conduct planning.
2. Do most police managers feel more inclined to accept risk as a challenge or are they strongly resistant to risk?
3. According to the management planning model, which style is most prevalent in law enforcement agencies today? Which style should be used more, and how would you develop it? What technique should be developed for implementing the new style?

11

Problem Identification and Decision Making

LEARNING OBJECTIVES

1. The student will become aware of the differences between the management activities of problem analysis and decision making.

2. The student will become aware of the distinctions between the types of management decisions: (a) routine, (b) resolving issues, (c) generating new ideas and techniques, as well as the most effective techniques by which they can be implemented.

3. The student will employ the four basic dimensions of a problem (identity, location, timing, and magnitude) as he or she searches for deviations within a problem.

4. The student will recognize the importance of and implement the management tool known as *means-ends analysis.*

5. The student will become familiar with and implement the seven steps of the decision-making process.

6. The student will become aware of the pitfalls common to the decision-making process.

Problem analysis and decision making are probably the most important issues that the police manager faces. On a day-to-day basis, the manager is continually thrust into situations that require logical, sound, and realistic decisions that, if successfully implemented, will lead to the resolution of problems and the achievement of specific objectives. Often, however, police managers are never quite prepared to adequately handle the rational aspects of problem analysis and decision making.

Problem Analysis

Many police officers and police managers are not aware that there is a difference between the management activities of problem analysis and decision making. They progress through their management careers using these terms interchangeably, and they attempt to apply identical approaches in dealing with each. **Problem analysis** is a careful examination of the facts to determine the cause of a problem, so that positive action can be taken. The problem is defined as the difference between what should be happening and what is happening.

There are four basic steps to problem analysis: (1) recognizing problems, (2) separating and setting priorities, (3) specifying the priority problem to be analyzed, and (4) testing for cause.

Recognizing Problems

In the real world, things all too often are not the way we hope they will be. This is especially true in the day-to-day operations of the average police department. The behavior of police officers, supervisors, and civilian personnel often varies over a given period, as do equipment and the systems for effective use of equipment and personnel. Many times these variations are small and may go unnoticed. In fact, small variations in our daily activities are expected, and they do not arouse a strong concern for problem analysis or decision making. Sometimes, however, small deviations, such as damage of a police vehicle or the excessive use of emergency equipment, may be a warning of a trend of deterioration. Such deviations then become significant factors, and their causes should be sought through systematic analysis. The key point in the first major step of problem analysis is to be aware of relevant problems.

To help identify the problem more clearly, the manager should ask the following questions:

1. Who or what is the cause or what is the identity of the problem being analyzed?
2. Where does the problem occur?
3. When does the problem occur?
4. How serious is the problem?

Separating and Setting Priorities

Of the many problems that the police manager handles, only a few demand immediate attention and action. For example, although Part I crimes may be rising at a slow rate, robbery may be rising at a rate twice that of any other crime. If the police department gives the same attention to the robbery problem that it does to the less demanding Part I crimes, the consequences could be disastrous. Problems with urgent and critical demands for attention should be given the highest priority. Other problems can be ranked by their relative importance. The criteria to use are different in each situation, and each police manager should establish his or her own priorities. Some criteria that can be used are (1) the growth rate of the problem; (2) the financial cost of the problem; (3) the effect the problem has on reaching stated objectives; and (4) the effects the problem has on such issues as condition of personnel, turnover rate, or morale. A small problem, when ignored, may grow rapidly to large proportions.

Specifying the Priority Problem to Be Analyzed

Once a problem has been selected for analysis, the next step is to describe it accurately. Every problem has four basic dimensions: *identity, location, timing,* and *magnitude.* Any thorough description of a problem should include detailed information regarding these four dimensions. Because the heart of problem analysis is the systematic search for deviations, it is essential that the basis for that search be carefully prepared. An accurate description of the four dimensions of the problem provides this basis.

The following six questions, when properly answered, can help analyze the problem and identify its priority:

Identity:	1. What or whom does the problem concern?
	2. What is the nature of the problem?
Location:	3. Where, geographically, does the problem occur?
Timing:	4. When does the problem occur?
Magnitude:	5. What is the extent of the problem?
	6. What is the trend—is the problem growing, stabilizing, or diminishing?

The matrix shown in Figure 11-1 is a tool the police manager can use in analyzing these important questions.

Testing for Cause

The cause of a problem can be determined from careful examination of all the possible causes. Each possible cause must be tested for a logical relationship with the facts. This is done by tentatively assuming a possible cause to be the actual cause, then testing it against the problem specification (six questions) and its four dimensions. If any of the

Problem _____ _____ _____	Is	Is Not	*(a)* Differences	*(b)* Changes (Date & Time)	*(c)* Possible Causes	*(d)* Most Probable Cause
Identity 1. What or whom does the problem concern? 2. What is the nature of the problem?						
Location 3. Where, geographically, does the problem occur?						
Timing 4. When does the problem occur?						
Magnitude 5. What is the extent of the problem? 6. What is the trend—is the problem growing, stabilizing, or diminishing?						

(a) What is unique or distinct about the "is" of the problem as opposed to the "is not" of the problem?
(b) What circumstances were new, improved, modified, added to, or changed to bring about these differences?
(c) What was there in, around, or about these changes that could have triggered or created the problem?
(d) If this possible cause is the most probable, how does it explain both the "is" and "is not"?

FIGURE 11-1 Problem analysis matrix.

facts of the specification discredit the possible cause that is being analyzed, that possible cause should be disregarded. This test is applied to each cause until one cause, or a combination of causes, is found to fit the facts of the problem specifications.

To find the most likely cause, the police manager must ask, "If this possible cause is the most likely cause, how does it explain both the variations and the stable factors?"

The final test for cause is demonstrating that the cause actually triggered the problem in question. In the world of tangible objects, this testing or verifying is done through some sort of physical proof such as chemical analysis, measuring, or examining control areas. Less tangible problems centering around human behavior are often more difficult to verify. Reasons for problems in department morale must be found through more indirect means, such as in-depth interviews by a skilled counselor.

In verifying the cause, the police manager should answer the following questions: "What tangible, factual, scientific steps or research can I undertake to prove that this possible cause is the actual cause?"

Decision Making

General Principles

Three general principles can be applied to the philosophy of decision making. The first rule is *make the decision*. It is extremely important that decisions be made: an effective manager will soon be evaluated on his or her ability to make a decision rather than by the number of correct decisions that are made. The second general principle is *once the decision has been made, do not worry about it.* Implement it. The only times a manager should change the original decision is if it has been proven wrong or if a new and more effective approach has been established. The third rule deals with the question of consideration: *the manager should not try to satisfy everyone.* Managers are required to satisfy the people to whom they are responsible. A manager who attempts to satisfy everyone will not be able to make a sound decision or perhaps make any decision at all.

Types of Decisions

The decisions of effective police managers are few in number but concentrate on solving important systemwide problems and deal with a high level of conceptual understanding. The police manager is not normally put in the position of making decisions quickly but instead is required to evaluate and manipulate many variables to arrive at an important decision which, when implemented, will strongly affect the day-to-day operations of the agency. The professional police manager wants to make sound, rather than clever, decisions.

Before analyzing how to make a decision, a conceptual framework must be established. In essence, before the police manager begins to make a serious decision, he or she must first place that decision in its proper perspective.

The first type of management decision is classified as *routine*. Routine decision making is an important daily activity of any police manager. Only through routine decision making can a police department continue to function while allowing the manager the time he or she needs to solve major problems and make new innovations. Indeed, one criterion of an effective police manager is the ability to develop ways in which the routine and unimportant details of daily police activities can be handled. The police manager who is able to delegate as many decisions as possible to subordinates is the one who will not be spending a majority of time in routine decision making.

The second type of decision deals with **specific issue resolutions**. These issues result from actions taken by members of the police agency or from internal problems identified by external sources. An illustration might be the city manager who feels that the police department is not adequately and effectively using its present resources and who advises the chief to reduce crime as quickly as possible and develop a new patrol allocation plan.

In this type of decision making, the total police system is examined, and isolated portions of the system are brought out for revising and revamping. An example of this occurs when the police chief recognizes that he or she does not have sufficient information with which to plan and make sound decisions. After careful examination of the total system, the chief realizes that the record-keeping function is outdated and neither collects nor analyzes the type of data that are needed to make decisions on a day-to-day basis. Pressure is then placed on the whole system; this pressure rebounds and directs itself to the records center. The result is the discovery of a serious problem in the records center, and action is finally taken to develop a new system of recordkeeping so the necessary information can be collected, analyzed, and properly used.

The third type of decision is designed to *generate new ideas and innovative techniques.* Innovative decision making in law enforcement is more difficult than routine decision making or problem solving. In many cases, the police manager lacks hard information to help reach adequate decisions. This type of decision making requires the manager to take some risk, because not all innovations or new techniques and ideas will be completely successful. This type of decision making brings about progress in the profession and is extremely important for vibrant, growing police organizations.

Means-Ends Analysis

One of the key factors in decision making is developing a clear picture showing the relationship between the objectives the department is trying to reach and the various alternatives the department must implement. To build a chain that links the objectives or ends that have been set with the various methods available, a management tool called ***means-ends analysis*** is used. For example, assuming that the problem involves poor performance on the part of records clerks and the records function in general, a specific objective—to improve the performance of records clerks—is set. The first question asked is "Why improve their performance?" The answer is to help increase overall departmental efficiency, cut costs, to avoid conflict that may exist between line and staff activities, and to provide quality information for line operation. Through answering the question, specific broader goals or objectives have been identified at the level above the original objective.

Once the broader goals have been identified, we can proceed to the question of how they and the original objective can be achieved. The answer generated may be better or more supervision, an increase in the number of clerks, or retraining present clerks.

The final means-ends analysis to meet the initial stated objective of increasing the production of records clerks is shown in Figure 11-2.

As shown in this illustration, the mechanics involved in developing a means-ends chain are not complicated. The first question involves the objective to be achieved. A move up the chain answers the question "why?" and a move down the chain answers "how?"

There is some value to developing a means-ends chain before entering into decision making. First, the means-ends analysis helps show the relationship of an objective at one

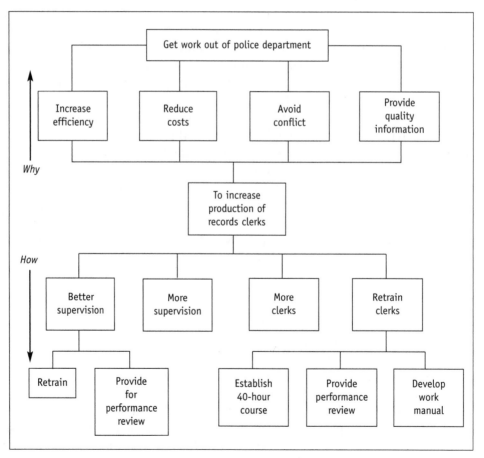

FIGURE 11-2 Means-ends analysis.

level to the goal at a higher level, so that meaningful objectives can be set. Second, the means-ends analysis helps stimulate the development of a series of possible alternative solutions to a single problem. Third, it helps develop and translate rather broad objectives, such as increased efficiency, to some very sound actions at the bottom of the chain that can be specifically delegated to individuals—for example, establishing a 40-hour course for record clerks.

Fourth, the means-ends chain helps depict the numerous relationships and dependencies that the police manager must consider in the overall decision. Fifth, it helps to narrow the field of information and data that must be collected to make the decision final and to make the decision that can be most effective for the police department. Finally, it helps highlight discrepancies between the objectives that have been set and the work that can be done at the bottom level of the workforce.

Consider the overall goal or objective of trying to reduce costs for the department and the action of increasing the number of clerks at the bottom. They are inconsistent and may require either restating or eliminating the objective or eliminating the alternative solution of employing more records clerks.

The manager should realize that the means-ends analysis does not help select alternatives, nor will it dictate all the alternatives available. Means-ends analysis is nothing more than an organized method of brainstorming to help bring out objectives that should be achieved, along with the methods that can be used to achieve them.

The Decision-Making Process

Once the means-ends analysis is completed, the following seven-step process can begin: (1) setting the objective, (2) identifying obstacles in the way of the objective, (3) collecting and analyzing data, (4) developing alternative solutions, (5) selecting alternatives to be implemented, (6) developing and implementing a plan, and (7) evaluating the results of implementation. This process can apply regardless of the type of decision being made. The importance of the decision, the time, and the information available for making the decision all affect the way the process is used.

Setting the Objective

Many management decisions become ineffectual because the process starts with a so-called problem that, when ultimately solved, does not contribute to the achievement of any objective. In this part of the overall process, the police manager determines the purpose and direction that the total decision-making process is to take by setting objectives.

Too many times, police departments devote the majority of their day-to-day activities to solving "problems." When the whole operation is carefully examined, a question is raised: "Why is so much time spent solving many little problems that constantly send you in numerous directions?" The police command level should establish specific directions before becoming involved in the issue of decision making. Consider the police department that revamps its records system without first establishing the purpose and necessity of the records. Money is spent for sophisticated hardware, consultants are hired, new personnel are employed and trained, physical space is revamped, problems generated by the change itself are solved, and the new records system is implemented. After a short time, the police manager recognizes that the information received from the new records system is really not very different from the data generated prior to the expenditure of large amounts of money, time, and effort. The efficiency of the records has improved, but the new system has not contributed to the overall purpose of the police department and in many instances may even be preventing it from reaching major goals.

The **objective** is a statement of reason or purpose, indicating that the police manager wants to solve problems and make decisions. These objectives should be tested for consistency with the department's overall goals.

Identifying Obstacles

The second step of the decision-making process is to define and identify conditions that obstruct and prohibit meeting objectives. There are two parts to obstacle identification. The first is the ability to recognize deviations within the obstacles, and the second is to separate and set priorities to handle these deviations.

Sometimes it is appropriate at this point for the police manager to go back to the steps outlined for problem analysis. In many instances, however, obstacles or stumbling blocks are fairly definitive and can be identified easily.

Collecting and Analyzing Data

When the objectives have been stated and the obstacles have been identified, the police manager should begin to determine the data relevant to the issue or the data necessary to make an effective decision. Facts and information should be obtained and organized. The police manager should determine which resources of time, money, and personnel are available and then determine the type and amount of information to be collected. It is possible to achieve an endless supply of information, but only if its limits have been defined can it be used effectively.

The police manager should determine how the information necessary for making a decision is to be obtained. How many times are police managers faced with the situation of examining reams of computer printouts when really only two or three percent of the data involved is necessary in making the decision? The police manager must determine in advance which criteria are to be used in making a final selection of alternatives. The data that will be useful in examining each of these criteria should be collected.

Developing Alternatives

In this step, alternatives for reaching the objectives are determined and identified. If a thorough means-ends analysis has been prepared, alternative solutions will be delineated in the original means-ends chart. The manager should be careful at this point not to restrict the number of alternatives or give consideration to whether they can be implemented. The major purpose of this step is to identify as many alternatives as possible, creating a clear picture of the total environment. The police manager can then select the most effective alternatives for resolving the issue.

Another way of describing this step is that the police manager is now in the process of searching for all possible solutions—not determining which is the best or most appropriate solution. The question being asked is "What are the various solutions that can be considered?"

Most police managers recognize that if a solution is not included in the array of possible alternatives, then that solution cannot be chosen. Too often in practice, however, insufficient time is given to developing a comprehensive list of possible alternatives or solutions. As a result, the effectiveness of the total decision making process is hampered because only a few hastily identified alternatives are examined. Other solutions that may be even more appropriate for that police department are never examined.

Consider the police department that has stated the objective of reducing the number of armed robberies by a specific percentage and carefully identified some of the obstacles to that objective. The next step might be to collect and analyze only information concerning successful projects or programs in other areas and not information available from the department itself. Too often the decision-making process comes to an abrupt end at this point. The police department decides that a program that was somewhat successful in another city will be highly successful in its city. In such a case, the number of alternative solutions has been greatly reduced by the narrow approach taken by the police manager.

Selecting Alternatives

When alternatives have been identified, the advantages and disadvantages of each should be carefully examined and weighed before selecting which alternative or series of alternatives is to be implemented.

The key factor in this step is establishing criteria for selecting the best alternative or alternatives.

A **decision-making criteria chart**, shown in Figure 11-3, can be an asset to the manager in the analysis of alternative solutions. Four major criteria normally considered in most decisions are included in the chart. First, does the alternative really contribute to the objectives? Second, how much will be spent if the alternative is implemented? Third, is it feasible—are the people available, does the manager have the authority, and is this alternative within the control of the manager? Finally, how does the alternative affect the entire system, considering the positive and negative side effects?

In completing the decision criteria chart, the police manager weights each of the alternatives as they are compared with each of the criteria. The weights can either be in a simple designation of high, medium, or low, or can even be given a numerical value of 1 to 10.

Statement of Objectives: _____

_____

_____

_____

_____

_____

_____

Alternative	Contributing to Objectives (Output)	Cost (Input)	Feasibility	Side Effects	
				Positive	Negative

FIGURE 11-3 Decision criteria chart.

Developing and Implementing a Plan

This step requires programming the decision. Before implementing the decision, the resources of the department, especially the personnel, should be taken into consideration. A plan for the orderly process of implementing the selected alternatives should be established. This plan should provide for standards and controls, along with a feedback system. The controls, measurements, standards, specific objectives, time limits, and feedback system are necessary to allow the decisions to be carefully evaluated.

The plan should contain the data to be collected and analyzed in order to evaluate the total process. Ideas become great through implementation. The police manager should continually strive to implement his or her carefully analyzed decision. The implementation process is the heart of the decision-making process. It is at this point that the decision or ideas generated earlier become realities in the day-to-day operations of the police department.

Evaluating the Results

The decision-making process and its divisions should be evaluated in terms of predetermined objectives and criteria. Evaluation begins the recycling process at the end of any of the steps developed earlier. For example, the collection of data as defined in Step 3 may result in the need to establish new objectives (Step 1). There is no straight line from the stated objective to the evaluation of the decision that was made. Examination and evaluation must occur at each step.

The evaluation process includes specifying measurable objectives, formulating a practical evaluation design, specifying data collection procedures, and specifying data analysis methods.

Pitfalls of the Decision-Making Process

There are pitfalls that police managers will encounter if they are not careful in the overall decision-making process. It is possible to establish objectives that do not provide a framework within which decision making can take place. Objectives using superlative terminology, such as "best," do not create a clear picture of what the department seeks; as a result, no real guidelines are developed.

There could be an inappropriate statement, or no statement at all, of what can be expected in the way of obstacles to be overcome. The police manager could define the obstacle in such a way as to limit the possibility of alternative solutions. Consider the police manager who decides that the only obstacle to reducing robberies is the judge who hears such cases. In essence, this manager has listed only one or two possible solutions, none of which may be under his or her control. The result will probably be no action at all.

Another pitfall common to the decision-making process is the failure on the part of the police manager to re-examine the previous steps as each succeeding step is developed. As data are organized, gathered, and analyzed, new obstacles may be discovered and perhaps a new objective established. There may be times when the data that the police manager collects in the decision-making process are irrelevant. Consider the police manager who constantly examines computer printouts to design a project to reduce robberies when a careful examination of just a few of the elements—time of day, location, day of week—may be sufficient to develop programs that can be effectively implemented to reduce robberies.

There is also a tendency to begin to select alternatives before all the possibilities have been presented, thus limiting the solutions. As personnel work around and near such managers, it quickly becomes obvious that the alternatives that are developed and selected are the alternatives that the manager wants to implement.

The police manager should be aware of the need to establish specific criteria on which to base the numerous alternatives from which those to be implemented will finally be selected. If, for example, cost, time, and side effects are disregarded in the decision-making process, the resulting program will be doomed to failure long before it is implemented.

The final pitfall that should be avoided is failing to follow up on decisions to guarantee that they have been implemented. This means developing checkpoints within the implementation process to guarantee that projects are implemented, evaluated, and adjusted when necessary.

Conclusion

When police managers have identified a problem, there are a number of steps that are involved in addressing problems. The decision-making process for police managers involves taking into account a number of factors such as budget concerns, personnel issues, and even working with agents of other branches of the criminal justice system. Being prepared for the challenges by understanding how problems are identified and how solutions are implemented will maximize the solution's benefit for all the department's personnel.

Discussion Questions

1. What models are available for decision making?
2. Should all managerial decisions be made using the special format?
3. What makes an effective decision maker?
4. Should there be a special format for decisions reached by all top managers of a police department?
5. Is the decision-making process in a police department similar to that within industry or other phases of government?
6. What are examples of some of the most difficult decisions a police manager has to make?

12 :::: Management by Objectives

LEARNING OBJECTIVES

1. The student will become familiar with the management by objectives (MBO) principle as an important tool in the decision-making process.
2. The student will become familiar with the specific guidelines for setting objectives within the context of the MBO system.
3. The student will be able to establish an evaluation system to determine the effectiveness of the individual program level, the goal level, and the objective level within the department.
4. The student will be able to implement the MBO system on the basis of the assumptions of McGregor's Theory Y.
5. The student will become familiar with the drawbacks of the MBO system.

Introduction

Management by objectives is a functional process that has been discussed by many people who have provided similar, but not identical, definitions.

A complete volume on this subject, called *Policing by Objectives* (Lubans & Edgar, 1979), has been prepared by Social Development Corporation of Hartford, Connecticut, under the direction of Val Lubans. It now appears as a prescriptive package distributed by the National Institute of Law Enforcement and Criminal Justice of the Department of Justice.

The system described in this chapter has been implemented effectively in various police departments. It is by no means the only management tool and can and should be adjusted to meet the needs of the individual police agency.

Management by objectives, or MBO, as it is more commonly known, may be viewed as a management tool that aids in the decision-making process. The numerous principles developed under decision making also apply to MBO. MBO is a method by which police managers and their subordinates can identify areas of growth, set standards to be reached, and measure the results against the standards that have been set. MBO relates directly to what is expected of the department and is usually expressed in terms of objectives. It relates to the development of teamwork within all levels of the department by establishing common goals and projects.

The concept of management by objectives is based on a number of behavioral science assumptions. The police manager who emphasizes MBO assumes that all officers want to know what is expected of them and whether they are performing satisfactorily. The

171

manager further assumes that the officers want to participate in and influence decisions that affect the overall purpose and goals of the police department.

MBO may also be viewed as a method of changing the present system of decision making. It is an important tool in the decision-making process and provides a control component for monitoring progress toward the specific goals of the department. MBO can also be used as a training and development tool. It is a method of maximizing utilization of all personnel within the police department. MBO has also been used as a method of enhancing communication within police departments.

An examination of a police department includes three broad areas of analysis. The first, the **input process**, consists of the elements that must be present before the department can begin to achieve any goals or objectives. The inputs include personnel, money, time, and equipment. The second consists of the **activities** of the people within the department. If something can be described as "doable," it must be included as an activity. Examples include typing, driving, developing plans, patrolling, and investigating. The third area involves **output**, which is the result achieved by the input.

MBO addresses all three areas. It starts with the result, or output, area. The MBO process requires police managers to carefully define the results they are attempting to achieve in a specific period, usually of three to five years. This careful analysis of goal and objective setting before agreement on projects is an effective way of increasing the efficiency of the activities within the agency.

Under the MBO process, not every activity of the department should be included. The MBO process is designed to help bring about the changes necessary to upgrade departmental performance. MBO may be viewed as a tool of change and should be directed toward approximately 20 percent of the activities within a police department.

MBO can best be implemented in line operational functions, as opposed to staff or administrative functions. This is because it is easier to set objectives and to define the results. This does not, however, imply that MBO cannot be used in staff functions, but it is generally better implemented first in line operations with the assistance of staff personnel. The disadvantage of this implementation process is that it generally has a tendency to force line personnel to possibly downgrade the role that staff plays in the overall operation of the police department.

Some police managers attempt to implement MBO as a "system of management," claiming that it fulfills all the broad managerial purposes of planning, organizing, controlling, communicating, and staffing. This is not necessarily true. In fact, when MBO is viewed as a system of management, it tends to downgrade the routine activities of the police department.

In viewing MBO, police managers must constantly keep in mind its role as a tool to aid and assist them in making the broad managerial functions of planning, organizing, staffing, and implementation easier. It does not, however, take the place of these functions. Furthermore, by ceasing to place emphasis on other activities of the police department and by spending too much time attempting to implement MBO, managers may fail to achieve the actual purposes of the department. This has been one of the major downfalls of MBO in some agencies in which police chiefs have attempted to implement MBO as a strong control tool instead of using it as a rational tool to assist them in long-term, short-term, and everyday planning.

There is a distinct difference between MBO and **program budgeting**. A description of what constitutes a program budget will help to clarify the MBO philosophy and system.

Plan-program budgeting is essentially a method of controlling budgetary expenses, with an emphasis on programs, such as suppression of crime or investigation of criminal activities. The program budget attaches a dollar amount to every activity within the police department. Under this budget, activities are grouped together in broad categories such as investigation, patrol, management services, and technical services.

The major differences between MBO and program budgeting are as follows: (1) program budgeting does not have specific objectives attached to the programs, and (2) program budgeting refers to all departmental expenditures, whereas the MBO portion may amount to only 20 percent of activities within the department.

The cost of implementing an MBO project does not necessarily correspond to the total amount given to the department. For example, if a police department operating under a program budget is given $500,000 for control and reduction of crime, that amount must cover the cost of prevention, suppression, investigation, apprehension, prosecution, and recovery of property. In this same department, an MBO program would direct this broad budgeting toward specific objectives, such as a 10 percent reduction of robberies. An evaluation of this reveals that the objective under the MBO program would cost the department only a small portion of the total amount allowed under program budgeting for control and reduction of crime. The manager is able to evaluate the total cost of the broad activity as well as the smaller cost of reaching a specific objective.

MBO is a tool to be used for bringing about the desired growth of the organization; it is not a control mechanism for expenditures.

Police managers who accept MBO must also respect the personnel in the department and have faith in them. Their philosophy must be consistent with the means structure as defined by Maslow and with the assumptions of Theory Y as defined by McGregor. They should be able to recognize the potential for contribution by the people in their command.

The MBO System

MBO can best be described as a seven-part process. These parts (shown in Figure 12-1) are:

1. Recognition of community values and departmental beliefs
2. Statement of departmental mission
3. Establishment of long-term goals
4. Establishment of short-term objectives
5. Project development

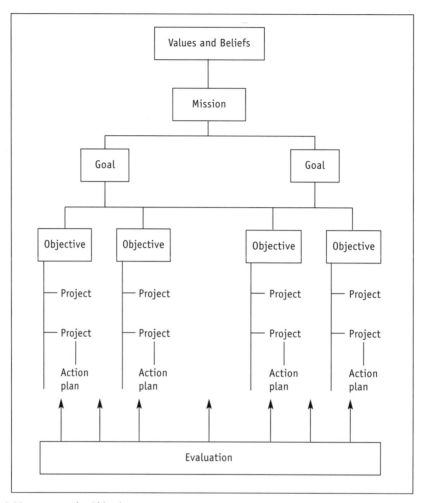

FIGURE 12-1 Management by Objectives system.

6. Development and implementation of action plans
7. Evaluation of the system

Values and Beliefs

Values are defined as the social principles that have been accepted by the community. These include attitudes about honesty, community ethics, level of service, crime, vice conditions, and traffic problems. The values of the community are usually exhibited through the policy statements issued by the city council. The police chief should help to establish and interpret these policies as they apply directly to the police department. These policy statements are often issued in the form of departmental beliefs.

Examples of belief statements dealing with the issue of crime might read as follows:

Criminality resulting from poverty, unemployment, and slum conditions is a community problem, not a problem for the police alone. The police have a responsibility to prevent and suppress crime and to solve crimes once they have occurred, but the police cannot prevent or solve every crime that occurs. The police must have the active cooperation, assistance, and moral support of the community that they serve.

For a crime to occur, two factors must be present: opportunity and desire. It is the function of the police department to minimize the opportunities for crime by such means as open, conspicuous, and aggressive patrol. Desire, however, is a factor controlled by potential offenders and those who influence their thinking. It is a factor over which the police have little control. Each police officer is chief of police within the area to which he or she is assigned. Officers are accountable for the crime and vice that exist on their beats, and they have a responsibility to prevent crime whenever possible.

Mission

The **mission statement** is the broadest, most comprehensive statement that can be made about the overall purpose of the police department. Another way of viewing the mission statement is that it spells out the primary responsibility of the police department, which justifies its continuing support by society and provides initial direction for the management of the police organization. The main purpose of a mission statement is to provide a focus for the resources of the police department and for the development of goals, objectives, and projects.

A simple mission statement for a police agency might be the following:

Our mission is to ensure the safety and protection of both the property and person of all of the inhabitants of our community and to regulate and control the flow of traffic in order to facilitate the movement of persons and goods within our city and to reduce the impact of crime on the inhabitants of our city through investigation, apprehension, and adjudication of persons involved in criminal offenses.

Goals

Under an MBO system, **goals** may be viewed in two different ways. The first is that goals should be idealistic—perhaps impossible to achieve. An example of this view would be a goal to eliminate crime. The second and more popular view is that goals should be measurable and within reach, even though they may require a long period for implementation.

Goals, although broad in nature, may be specific in terms of the major accomplishments desired by management over two years' time. Examples of such goals might be: "the reduction of Part I offenses by 10 percent within the next two years," or "the reduction of the average monthly traffic accident rate by five percent within the next three years."

Objectives

Objectives are considered short-term achievements. They must be attainable within a given period. The maximum period for accomplishment of objectives within the MBO system is one year. The objectives themselves must be tied to specific measurements. An example of an objective is: "to reduce the number of robberies in the eastern sector of the city by five percent within the next six months."

In establishing objectives, it is mandatory that the manager stay away from superlative phrases such as "finest" or "best." Within the MBO system, there should be a minimum of one and a maximum of six objectives for each established goal. Objectives should be used as guides in planning and implementing specific projects. They should be seen as tools for measuring the progress that is being made toward the achievement of goals. Objectives should define the results that are to be achieved, not activities that are to be performed.

In addition to being measurable, objectives must satisfy two other conditions—they should be both feasible and cost-effective. The levels of accomplishment within each project must be practical in the sense that they are attainable. The goals and the objectives must also be cost-effective; that is, the expected contribution to the individual project objectives, as well as the overall objectives of the MBO system, must justify the cost of the individual projects.

The following guidelines for setting objectives will help the police manager achieve the most from the MBO system.

1. Define *results* to be achieved, not activities. In stating objectives, the result should be described, not the activity necessary to meet this result. For example, an objective of "putting the stakeout squad in high crime areas" is really an activity that should be designed to meet a stated objective, such as "reduce robberies by 10 percent within the next six months."

2. Relate the objective to goals at the next higher level. As objectives are established, it is important that the police manager focus on the overall good to be achieved and that the goals be balanced with the major purpose of the police department, which is the protection of life and property. There is a natural tendency for police managers to set objectives that they feel will be interesting, and they may ignore objectives that are necessary. The police manager, especially if at the middle level of the department, should view his or her role as it fits into the total MBO system and then assist in establishing objectives that can best contribute to the stated overall goals of the

department. He or she must be careful to avoid establishing objectives that are based on what he or she can or would like to obtain.

3. Set objectives at a reasonable level. The objectives should be challenging and should call on the police managers to do better in the future than they did in the past. There is sometimes a tendency for police managers to establish objectives at such a high level that they may be impossible to achieve. In writing objectives, managers should be careful to balance the need to challenge with the need to achieve. Police managers should not set impossible objectives for themselves or their subordinates.

4. Use language that everyone will understand. Objectives should be written clearly and simply in language that both subordinates and supervisors can understand.

5. Emphasize realism. Objectives are valuable as guides for action only when they are prepared in a realistic manner. The police manager at the middle level should not try to impress superiors by establishing objectives that are unrealistic.

Projects

Once objectives have been determined, it is time to begin to put into action the **projects** that have been designed to meet these objectives. Projects involve establishing a step-by-step process that will be used to reach each of the objectives. A single project may have an effect on more than one objective. For example, if the objectives to reduce robbery by 5 percent and burglary by 10 percent have been established, a project using a tactical unit in certain areas of the city may have an effect on both objectives.

Every project that is implemented under an MBO system must be specifically designed to attain one of the already established objectives. Within the individual projects themselves, objectives can be set that define the period needed for implementation of the project and the results that are to be achieved by that project. For example, how long will it take to assign personnel to the tactical unit, to have the unit analyze present crime trends, and then to begin to take positive action toward reaching the objectives of reducing robbery and burglary?

Projects should also be designed for the short term. If the objective is to reduce robbery by 10 percent within a 12-month period, then there may be three or four projects during this 12-month period that are part of the attempt to reach the stated objective. Each project may require only two or three months. They may overlap, or some may begin immediately and continue throughout the entire 12-month period.

Even though a long-range goal and a series of specific objectives have already been determined, it is important that individual accomplishments also be included with each project. These steps for accomplishment are the objectives within the individual projects. It is really these project objectives that are carefully evaluated at the beginning of the process and later analyzed to determine the success or failure of the objectives of the overall MBO system.

Action Plans

Action plans are the detailed steps of activities necessary for the completion of individual projects. They dictate the responsibility that has been assigned to particular people, define the mutually acceptable target date, and determine how the task itself will be verified once it has been completed. All action plans relate directly to the projects to which they are assigned.

A simplified form, such as that shown in Figure 12-2, can be used for the development of action plans.

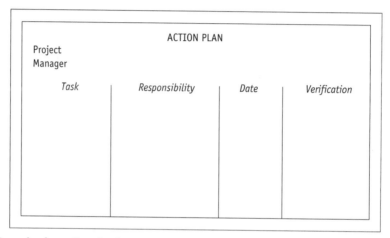

FIGURE 12-2 **Example of an action plan form.**

Evaluation[1]

Evaluation in the MBO system is considered one of the most important steps. Evaluation is the process of determining the amount of success in achieving the predetermined objectives. Evaluation may be interim, to determine the amount of progress that has been made, or final, to determine the ultimate level of accomplishment.

Evaluation information is required for three different types of measurement: (1) **external measures** that determine the amount of success or failure in achieving the predetermined objectives and goals; (2) **internal measures** that determine (a) the efficiency and effectiveness of the individual and (b) the difficulties or stumbling blocks that were encountered and describe how they were overcome or why they could not be overcome; and (3) **research measures** that yield insight into cause-effect and other relationships that are useful as empirical and theoretical bases for future program planning.

The police manager should realize that the best evaluators of the projects that are implemented by police personnel are the individuals who conduct the implementation and

[1]Developed for the Atlanta Impact Program (LEAA) by Norman Baker, Edward Unger, Terry Sprott, Thomas Buskirk, and Gordon Miller.

manage the organization itself. As individual projects are developed, evaluation criteria can be established for each. Consider the attempt to evaluate a special stakeout unit designed to reduce armed robberies. The criteria for determining the success or failure of this project would be how many robberies actually occurred; how much time, money, and effort was placed into the project; and how long it took to reach the success level that was finally attained.

Police managers can help evaluate this project. First, the area of the city in which the special stakeout unit is to be employed should be examined for its present robbery rate. Then, at the end of the project, the number of robberies must be determined. The manager should also use another area of the city as a "control" area to be evaluated in terms of any reduction or increase in robberies. The police manager should determine whether other crimes in the stakeout area have increased or decreased. The rates of apprehension should also be examined, both in the control area and the experimental area.

Many criteria can be used to determine the success or failure of a project, but the most effective approach is to decide on only a small number of criteria as a measure.

The police manager can establish an **evaluation criteria chart** similar to the chart for the decision criteria discussed earlier. The projects can be listed on one side, and the criteria—such as implementation gained from each and feasibility—can be listed across the other. Information gained from each project can be evaluated against the stated criteria. The police manager then has a simplified evaluation system to use in determining the effectiveness of the individual program.

In addition to the careful evaluation of individual projects at the project level of the MBO system, evaluation must be conducted at the objective and goal levels. Evaluation at the objective level can be based on analyzing the effect of complementary and duplicate projects designed for achieving the same objectives. Whenever possible, the police manager should establish both evaluation and control groups to isolate the effectiveness of the individual project from any external effects. In addition, projects that are directed toward the same objective should be separated, either in time or space, so as to avoid a subjective decision concerning which project had the greater effect on the stated objectives.

Evaluation of groups of projects is also necessary to determine which strategies proved to be most effective in achieving the objectives and goals. In larger cities, projects can be grouped by geographic areas, concentration of target population, or type of area, such as residential or commercial.

Evaluation includes a series of activities: (1) specifying measurable objectives, (2) formulating a practical evaluation design, (3) specifying data collection procedures, and (4) specifying data reduction and analysis methods.[2]

This overall process is shown in Figure 12-3 and applies whether the evaluation is being conducted at the goal, objective, or individual program level.

---

[2]Developed for the Atlanta Impact Program (LEAA) by Norman Baker, Edward Unger, Terry Sprott, Thomas Buskirk, and Gordon Miller.

FIGURE 12-3 A schematic flow model of the evaluation process. *Source: Norman Baker, Edward Unger, Terry Sprott, Thomas Buskirk, and Gordon Miller. Developed for the Atlanta Impact Program (LEAA).*

Specify Measurable Objectives

To have proper output from this first step in the evaluation process, the objectives should be "measurable." Therefore, the output should clearly identify the individual data elements that must be used to determine the amount of success.

In Step 1, the objectives must be converted to numerical terms. For example, if the objective was the reduction of robbery by 10 percent within a six-month period, then the 10 percent must be translated into numerical figures—from 60 robberies per month to 54 robberies per month.

In addition to translation to numerical figures, there should be an identification of the performance measures that will be examined in the individual projects being directed toward the objective. Using the 10 percent robbery reduction as an example, the basic performance measures may include such broad factors as location, time, and whether the robbery is classified as commercial, residential, or open-space. Once these performance measures have been identified, data elements can be collected and analyzed for each of the performance measures. Data elements for location may be the specific address, reporting area, census tract, patrol beat, or any combination of these. The data elements for time may include the month, day of the week, and hour of the day designated in groups of four hours, eight hours, or individual hours. The data elements for commercial robbery might include banks, gas stations, food markets, and liquor stores. For residential robbery, the data elements might include house, apartment, hotel, or motel; for open space, they could include street, alley, parking lot, or park.

If evaluation is to be conducted, the objectives should be measurable, feasible, and cost-effective.

Step 1 is described in Figure 12-4. As this figure indicates, the output of Step 1 is a measurable objective that is feasible and cost-effective and internally consistent with criteria, performance measures, and basic data elements.

FIGURE 12-4 A schematic flow model of Step 1: Specify measurable objectives. *Source: Norman Baker, Edward Unger, Terry Sprott, Thomas Buskirk, and Gordon Miller. Developed for the Atlanta Impact Program (LEAA).*

Formulate a Practical Evaluation Design

The important words in this step are "practical" and "design." The purpose of the evaluation design is to assure the police manager that it is possible to distinguish between changes caused by the projects and other changes that may have occurred within the department. Therefore, the evaluation design must distinguish the impact of other projects from the effectiveness of the projects being evaluated.

The manager has two types of designs from which to choose in evaluating individual projects. The first is referred to as "before-after" design and the second as "control group" design.

Use of the **before-after design** is the more common method of evaluating projects in terms of success or failure. This approach involves only one step—comparing the level of activity prior to the implementation of the projects to the level of activity after the projects have been implemented. A simple example is the comparison of robbery rates in a certain area of the city during the first six months of Year I (prior to the implementation of the MBO system) and the robbery rates of the same area of the city during the first six months of Year II (after the projects have been implemented). The difference in the robbery rates during these two periods indicates the success or failure of the MBO system.

The **control-group design** is based on the assumption that it is possible to identify two environments—two geographical population areas—that have similar characteristics. One area is designated the experimental group, and the other the control group. Basic data elements are collected for both groups, with the further assumptions that the factors influencing one group (except for the projects being implemented in the experimental group) also influence the other. The assumption is that the only difference between these two groups during the period of program implementation is the project activity. Therefore, it is safe to assume that the difference between the performance measures found in the experimental group and those in the control group can be attributed directly to the projects that are implemented in the experimental group.

At least one of the approaches should be used to guarantee some valid evaluation; however, in many instances it is impossible to use both the control group and before-after approaches.

The evaluation design must also be practical. It should be possible for the police manager to collect and manage the required data elements so that careful evaluation can be made. In this instance, the manager should consider such questions as: (1) Are the data we need currently being collected for some other reason? (2) If the answer is no, then can these data be collected only by implementing minor modifications of the present data collection system? (3) Is it necessary to develop a completely new data collection system?

The manager must also examine the cost of obtaining this information and whether it will be reliable and valid.

Step 2 is shown in Figure 12-5. The results of this step are: (a) practical evaluation design, (b) identification of required basic data elements, (c) specification of interim goals and objectives, and (d) timetable for the accomplishment of these interim measurements.

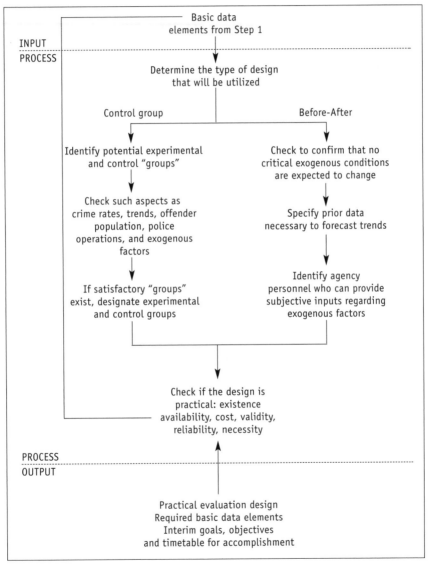

FIGURE 12-5 A schematic model of Step 2: Formulate a practical evaluation design. *Source: Norman Baker, Edward Unger, Terry Sprott, Thomas Buskirk, and Gordon Miller. Developed for the Atlanta Impact Program (LEAA).*

Specify Data Collection Procedures

Within this step, the police manager should perform the following activities: (1) determine how the data will be collected, (2) specify by whom the information will be collected, (3) decide on the frequency with which the information will be collected, and (4) design forms that will be used to collect the information.

These activities should be formulated for all of the required data elements that will be collected and analyzed.

The information system presently in use should be examined in considerable detail, and it should be used as much as possible. In some instances, the police manager may determine that the information necessary for evaluation is being collected but is not being used for output purposes. Therefore, minor adjustments should be made that will produce this information in the output process. For example, if the manager wants to know whether robberies have been directed toward gas stations, liquor stores, or banks, he or she may find this information in the field reports. The manager would then only have to take this information from the field reports and have it analyzed on a monthly basis. If, however, the information is not currently available, then the manager must take the necessary steps to guarantee that the information will be collected and analyzed.

The process of Step 3 is shown in Figure 12-6, with the output being the specification of the information collection procedures.

Specify Data Reduction and Analysis Methods

This step is necessary to enable the police manager to measure the success of projects in reaching goals and objectives. This step also helps to describe relationships between projects, and it provides knowledge that may be useful in future planning and project activities.

The success of each project must be measured so that the police manager will have a way of monitoring, controlling, and directing the activities within each project from its inception to its conclusion. By assessing the program's failure or success and that success's contribution to the overall objectives and goals of the MBO system, the police manager can make recommendations as to whether the individual project should be continued, modified, or eliminated. In addition, the description and explanation of the data produced from the projects can be used to analyze the reasons for the degree of success or failure of the total MBO system. The manager can use this analysis to improve management practices and upgrade the operation of the entire department.

With regard to the measures of success, the police manager should attempt to determine the degree to which the projects have achieved their individual goals and objectives as well as the objectives of the MBO system. This data analysis can also help to formulate a value judgment as to whether the projects should be continued or expanded to other units within the department.

The data reduction and analysis methods include such activities as weekly reports, monthly reports, before and after comparisons, comparisons of the control group

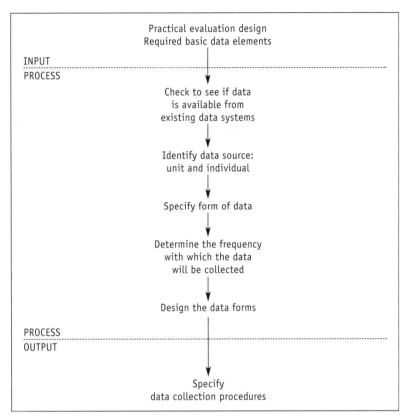

FIGURE 12-6 A schematic model of Step 3: Specify data collection procedures. *Source: Norman Baker, Edward Unger, Terry Sprott, Thomas Buskirk, and Gordon Miller. Developed for the Atlanta Impact Program (LEAA).*

with the experimental group, and the use of maps, charts, and graphs. In larger police agencies, data reduction and analysis includes the use of computerized information systems and highly technical procedures for summary evaluation of the information.

In addition to specifying the data reduction analysis methods to be used, the police manager should identify the individual responsible for the evaluation analysis. In many instances, this can be personnel who have already been assigned to activities such as operations analysis, research and development, or crime prevention. The manager should also determine when interim evaluations will be conducted. The number of interim evaluations depends on the length of the project, its cost, and its complexity. Within this step, the police manager should also specify how the evaluation results will be used, especially with regard to the overall management practices and procedures of the department.

Step 4 is described in Figure 12-7, with the output being the full specifications of the evaluation process.

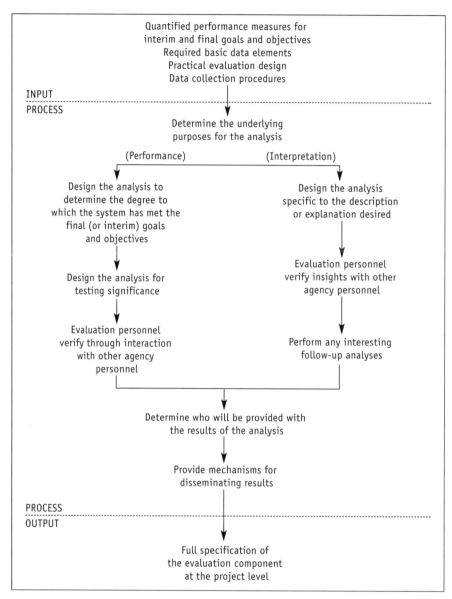

FIGURE 12-7 A schematic model of Step 4: Specify data reduction and analysis methods. *Source: Norman Baker, Edward Unger, Terry Sprott, Thomas Buskirk, and Gordon Miller. Developed for the Atlanta Impact Program (LEAA).*

Implementation

Once the manager has an understanding of the MBO system, he or she must develop MBO and begin to implement it within the department. The MBO system is most effectively put into practice through the use of 9,9 team management. It must also be based on the assumptions of Theory Y (discussed in Chapter 7).

Establishment of Goals by Top Managers

It is the responsibility of top-level managers to determine long-range goals and to give direction and set parameters for the managers at the middle level. It is the middle managers who are responsible for developing and implementing the objectives and projects.

Establishment of Objectives for Each Goal by Middle Managers

Once top management has determined the goals for the agency, middle management must submit a series of objectives for each stated goal. In this step, the managers at both levels must have an opportunity to clarify the stated goals and proposed objectives through effective communication.

Selection of Objectives by Top Managers

In this step, top management reviews the objectives with middle management. Depending on the ability of middle management to implement the management by objectives system, top management selects one to six objectives for each stated goal. The selection of objectives by top management should follow as closely as possible the priority listing of objectives by middle management. It is top management's role to carefully evaluate each of the objectives submitted for inconsistencies and to adjust the measure of achievement in each objective if they feel it is either too low or too high.

Objective Finalization by Middle Managers

In this step, middle management is given the responsibility of finalizing all stated objectives, even though top management can place certain guidelines on how each objective is to be stated. For example, they may require the objective to first state what it will accomplish (reduction of robbery by 10 percent); second, the cost of the objective (not to exceed limits already established within the budget); and third, its completion date (within the next six months).

Overview of Projects for Each Objective Submitted by Middle Managers

In this step, middle management is required to submit for approval by top management a list of projects to be implemented in order to reach each objective. This step requires close coordination between top and middle management as well as horizontal coordination between the middle managers. The projects should be carefully screened to avoid duplication and to evaluate all possible consequences and side effects. Consider a project to implement a special tactical unit in one control area and a special stakeout squad in another high-crime area. If both projects are implemented at the same time, even though both have merits and will have some effect on the overall objective of robbery reduction, the effect of transferring personnel within the patrol force to handle both projects may seriously hamper the overall operation of the uniformed forces. The negative side effects may cause more harm and prevent the department from reaching its overall goal of reducing robbery.

Development of Detailed Projects by Middle Managers

After the projects have been approved by top management, the middle managers must develop specific formats for the implementation of each project. The middle manager should refer to the seven-step process developed in the section titled "Decision Making" in Chapter 10 and use it to develop the individual projects. Each project has its own objectives, defines the obstacles to completion of the project, and determines the data that is to be collected and analyzed. In this case, it would not be necessary to develop alternative solutions because the project has already been selected. But the manner in which the project is to be implemented can be developed according to how it will be evaluated.

A simple one-page information sheet can be developed to give all necessary data concerning each project. This information sheet should include such items as: (1) who will be responsible for the project; (2) the stated objectives of the project; (3) which overall objectives the project might affect, as well as its effect on the objectives of the MBO system; (4) what results are expected; (5) what steps are to be taken and who is responsible for each step; and (6) the beginning date, the interim evaluation dates, and the ending date.

This form should also include such items as: (a) staffing—the personnel who will be involved with the project in each of its steps; (b) coordination of the individuals from within the department, as well as those outside the department whose services will be necessary for the successful completion of the project; (c) training—what additional training is necessary; and (d) evaluation—the determination of the overall success or failure of the project.

Evaluation

Steps within each project should be carefully evaluated on review dates for success as well as failure and for determination of changes that may be required. This evaluation should be flexible enough to allow project directors to initiate changes they deem necessary or recommend that the project be cancelled due to lack of success.

This step-by-step implementation process forces the police agency and the manager to plan systematically.

Additional Use of the MBO System

As a police department evaluates its direction, it views numerous issues to help define where it is, and it examines its values, beliefs, problems, environmental factors, and the elements of the evaluation process. To define direction, it establishes a mission statement, goals, and objectives. To analyze and describe how it is going to achieve the mission, goals, and objectives, projects and action plans are developed.

Environmental factors may also affect the MBO system. Environmental factors are defined as those over which the police department has no direct control. Typical examples might be the appointment of a new city manager, who emphasizes values and beliefs different from those already established by the police department, or a new governing board that has different priorities—or it could be a new law that requires a different course of action or that changes present procedures in the police department. Such environmental factors can easily be integrated into the MBO system.

Specific problems that require immediate action might also arise during the implementation of the MBO program. These can easily be integrated into the total MBO system. The police manager must recognize that if serious problems do arise—for example, a high turnover rate, a reduction or freeze in spending, or a type of crime that drastically increases—he or she will be able to use the MBO system at any level to take positive action to overcome the problem.

Assume that armed robberies suddenly increase at an alarming rate. Within the MBO system, there might be an objective dealing with armed robberies. However, the objective might be too low-priority or the projects themselves might not really deal with the areas of the community in which the problem exists. With new information developed through the evaluation process, a new objective can be established, an old objective can be changed, new projects can be implemented, or old projects can be upgraded to help meet the newly established objective that is designed to overcome the problem.

When MBO is viewed as an ongoing system of assisting in day-to-day operations, it takes on a new meaning. The total picture of how the MBO system operates is shown in Figure 12-8.

Drawbacks of Management by Objectives

Management by objectives is not a panacea for all management ills. The police manager must realize that he or she is responsible not only for implementing projects designed to meet specific objectives and goals, but also for day-to-day implementation of the many functions and activities necessary to bring about a successful police operation. The police manager cannot seriously deplete organizational units such as the patrol force in order to emphasize implementation of or meeting a specific objective.

The manager cannot allow MBO to override the responsibilities of day-to-day activities. The police manager's job is to decide which objectives are to be sought, at what point

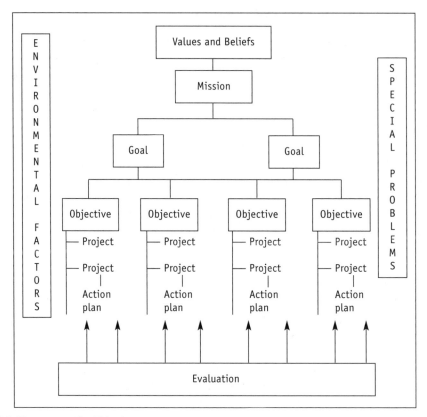

FIGURE 12-8 Management by Objectives system.

in the organization they are to be implemented and by whom, and to what degree the total effort of the organization should be devoted to reaching stated objectives.

Another pitfall in the implementation of MBO is the attempt to involve every member of the agency in some way in attempting to obtain the objectives. This may upset the stability that has already been created and may do more harm than good. Consider the police department that has an adequate records and information system. To force them to revamp their present practices and procedures for the sole purpose of doing a "better job" may be expensive, frustrating, and, in the long run, bring about more negative than positive effects.

In summary, the police manager, in the implementation of an MBO system, should determine the time and effort that can be devoted to bringing about change in the department, who can devote this time, and who can determine what effect the implementation of change will have on the stability already created within the organization.

References

Gazell, J. A. (1974). MBO in the public sector. *Business Review, 27*, 29–35.

Lubans, V., & Edgar, J. M. (1979). *Policing by objectives: A handbook for improving police management.* Hartford, CT: Social Development Corporation.

Further Reading

French, W., & Hollman, R. (1975). Management by objectives: The team approach. *California Management Review, 17*, 13–22.

Humble, J. (1972–1973). *How to manage by objectives.* New York: AMACOM.

Kirchoff, B. A. (1975). A diagnostic tool for MBO. *Personnel Psychology, 23.*

McConkey, D. D. (1965). *How to manage by results.* New York: American Management Association.

Morrisey, G. L. (1970). *Management by objectives and results.* Reading, MA: Addison-Wesley.

Discussion Questions

1. Is MBO an effective tool?
2. Should MBO be used by every police department?
3. When should MBO be implemented and when should it be eliminated from the managerial process?
4. How can MBO be a detriment to the police department?
5. What are some methods of implementing MBO?
6. What are other MBO models?
7. Should the police department be the strong driving force for the implementation of the MBO system citywide?

13

Fiscal Management

LEARNING OBJECTIVES

1. The student will be able to define budget and distinguish budgeting from other functional areas of police management.
2. The student will be able to discuss the purposes of fiscal management.
3. The student will understand and be able to explain the stages of the budgeting process.
4. The student will know the differences between the three basic types of budgets, their formats, and their purposes.

The police department's annual budget is one of the most important policy statements made by the department. It reflects the predominant values and thinking of the managers of the police department, the city or county administrator, and local political leaders.

Budgeting

The most common definition states that a **budget** is a plan, expressed in dollar terms, by which a set of **programs** is authorized for a future period, usually one year. This definition is often questioned. One of the first issues raised is whether the budget really is a plan, or whether it is just an **agreement** or contract between the governing board and the department heads on how much money they may spend in the upcoming year. Although the budget is expressed in dollar terms, it is seldom viewed strictly as a fiscal device. In some instances, it is a device used to indicate priorities and to indicate the role that department heads may play in conjunction with other department heads, the city manager, and the governing board. Under a strict economic definition, a budget is an allocation of resources among competing demands from different departments, including the police department.

A better definition is that a budget is a **comprehensive plan**, expressed in financial terms, by which an operating program is effective for a given period. It includes estimates of services, activities, and projects included in the program; the resultant expenditure requirements; and the resources available for their support.

CASE STUDY

Midvale, Utah, a town just south of Salt Lake City, faced a fiscal crisis. Nearly half of the city's annual $19 million budget paid for some form of public service, such as police or fire department service, and the costs were increasing. Overtime costs were hitting the 56-officer police department hard, and the vehicle fleet was aging and in need of repairs. After much consternation, the city decided to join the police department with a regional consortium of law enforcement agencies including the Salt Lake County Sheriff's Department. This merger of agencies turned cities and towns into precincts of the unified police force (Johnson, 2012).

This merger was the result of the economic recession that began after loosely regulated banks had a financial collapse in 2008. The recession caused similar difficult decisions in law enforcement agencies throughout the United States. Agencies have been consolidating a range of integrated service options to deal with budget shortfalls. Some agencies select full-scale departmental mergers like the one in Salt Lake County, but others are integrating specific services such as crime laboratories, tactical teams, and dispatch responsibilities. The International Association of Chiefs of Police and the Major Cities Chiefs Associations each independently found that law enforcement agencies throughout the country were providing various forms of support to other agencies.

In Midvale, the efforts benefited the police department by saving millions of dollars in budget projections. Other benefits include shorter response times and a more culturally diverse agency with more speakers of Spanish. However, some officers have concerns that this collection of agencies from varying jurisdictions will eventually lead to law enforcement decisions being made by politicians. Do you see any other potential benefits or drawbacks?

- What community reactions might occur when small agencies merge with larger ones? Would they be negative?
- Assuming the police department merger trend is a short-term event dictated by economic circumstances, if the budgets are eventually balanced, how will the saved money be spent? Will smaller agencies benefit from once again becoming independent?

Purposes of Budgeting

The budget is significant from several standpoints. First, it encompasses comprehensive reviews of police department activities, usually on an annual basis. Second, it specifies limits as to what the police department can do; in this sense, it serves as a legal document. Third, it is used to accomplish managerial ends such as designating who is responsible for what activities, setting a pattern for centralization or delegation of authority within the police department, and mandating economies that must be brought forth in the future. It sets out what the police department will accomplish or attempt to accomplish. In this sense, it is a **workload plan**. It is used to enact new programs or significantly change existing programs within the police agency. It helps bring information to the proper level for decision making and, when implemented correctly, provides information upward and downward, so that these decisions may be properly carried out at all levels within the police department.

There are two overall approaches to the establishment of a budget as far as the chief of police is concerned. At one end of the spectrum is *incremental budgeting* and at the other end is *zero-base budgeting*.

Under incremental budgeting, there is an assumption that activities that have occurred within the past fiscal year are presently effective and will become the foundation for the future. This budget focuses on **revenue growth**. A typical example might be the police chief who is obligated to submit the budget in a format that discloses how much was spent last year on a certain item (such as new vehicles), how much will be needed this year, and the difference between these two figures. For example, if the chief requires an additional $3,000, justification is needed for the additional expense. The assumption is that the amount of money spent for purchasing during the last year was spent in an efficient and effective manner.

Zero-base budgeting, on the other hand, implies a review of the entire budgeting process. It requires setting priorities; communicating to the police department the relationship between these priorities and their costs; and establishing goals not only for the upcoming year, but also for at least three to five years into the future. In essence, the police department must know where it is headed and how it will get there; it will then be able to measure its effectiveness. This budget explains, on an annual basis, why the police department exists.

In practice, no budgeting system is 100 percent incremental or 100 percent zero-base. Budgets are usually built on a few aspects of each system.

Stages in the Budgeting Process

There are four stages in the budget process. The first is the **preparation stage**, which is the responsibility of the executive branch of the government, including the police department. The budget calendar is usually established by the city manager, who works backward from the legal data required for the enactment of a budget. For example, if a budget must be enacted by July 1, the city manager may demand that the police department's budget be submitted at least 45 days in advance. It then becomes the police department's responsibility, under the direction of the police chief, to establish its requests. The police chief must first know the date required for submitting the initial budget requests to the city or county manager, the budget director, or whoever may be responsible for first reviewing the police department's budget. Depending on the size of the police department and the amount of involvement required by members within the department, the commanders of the police agency can establish a budget schedule designed to meet the required date for initial budget requests.

The second stage in the budget process is **adoption**. This is a legislative function that requires some legal action, such as a special ordinance passed each year or a resolution by the governing board. Each police chief should carefully review the statutes governing the budgetary adoption process for his or her individual community so that he or she will be aware of the legal requirements and the formal process that must be followed.

The third stage is **execution**. This is an executive function and is a fairly detailed process of the establishment of a fiscal control system, usually at the direction of the city or county manager. The police chief, therefore, need not be concerned with the development of an execution process. His or her primary concerns should be to have a clear understanding of how the budget forms are to be used, what forms are to be submitted for what types of requests, how the summary information can best be used to upgrade the police department, and how well the department is proceeding in implementing the programs and expenditures of its approved funding.

The execution process includes the development of purchase orders, preordering, receipts to be received for merchandise purchased, and the disbursement of funds. Each of these procedures is generally citywide or countywide in nature; the individual police department is usually not responsible for developing special procedures for the police agency.

The fourth major stage in the budget process is the **postaudit stage**, which is a legislative function by which, on an annual basis at the close of each budget year, an audit is taken to show that the funds have been properly expended, that the police chief has not

FIGURE 13-1 Stages in the budget cycle.

overextended the department's budget, and that the budgeting has proceeded in a proper manner. This also has the effect of protecting the city and the department from potential accusations of misappropriation of funds.

These four stages and their relationship are shown in Figure 13-1.

Types of Budgets

There are three basic types of budgets. The first is the *line-item* or *object budget,* the second is *the performance budget,* and the third is *the program budget.*

The **line-item** or **object budget** groups expenditures by classes or objects. It concentrates primarily on efficiency, focusing the dollar amounts on inputs (what the police department intends to purchase), not on outputs (what the department intends to achieve). Normally, only an *increase* in any specific amount is questioned by the budget director, city or county manager, or governing board. This type of budget forces the police chief to concentrate on the incremental philosophy of budgeting. The line-item or object budget was created to resolve problems of corruption that existed at local levels many years ago. Today it is used as a strong control tool by fiscal managers; it really does not assist in developing departmental programs or explaining the purpose of the individual police department.

The police manager must recognize that a line-item or object budget will always be present somewhere within the budgetary process. It may be the sole budgetary style, or it could be part of a different type of budget, such as the performance or program type. It may be used as a planning tool or as a means of auditing expenditures. Therefore, it is important for all police managers to understand the line-item or object budget. Although this type of budget may, on the whole, be more negative than positive in nature, it is one of the more common types of budgets in law enforcement today. In addition, a clear understanding of its value can assist the police chief in the overall fiscal management of the department.

Line-item budgets are usually divided into the following four major categories: (1) **personal services**, which includes salaries, fringe benefits, and other costs relating directly to people; (2) **operating and maintenance**, which includes supplies, such as gas, oil, forms, pencils, and even paper clips; (3) **charges and services**, which covers special contracts, rentals, travel funds, and training; and (4) **capital outlay**, which is the money expended for the purchase of equipment such as cars, desks, and weapons.

An example of the format of a line-item or object budget is shown in Figure 13-2.

A **performance budget** specifies activities of the police department, the performance data being the information by which the police chief determines the necessity for incremental increases or decreases. The format is much like that of the line-item or object budget. It normally measures activities such as number of tickets written, crimes solved, property recovered, and calls for service handled. It is divided into these types of services by organizational unity. For example, it compares the number of calls for service handled by the Uniformed Operation Division to those handled by the Criminal

Item	Amount
Personal services	$25,000
Contractual services	5,000
Supplies/materials	5,000
Miscellaneous items	500
Capital outlay	10,000
Total	$45,500

Sample—Object Budget with Divisional Breakdown

Item	Amount	Total
I. Personal Services		
A. Salaries		
Headquarters	$5,000	
Patrol	5,000	
Detective	5,000	
Services	5,000	
		$20,000
B. Fringe		
Headquarters	$1,250	
Patrol	1,250	
Detective	1,250	
Services	1,250	
		$ 5,000
	Total personal services	$25,000

Note: Contractual services, supplies/materials, miscellaneous items, and capital outlay categories would all have similar breakdowns.

FIGURE 13-2 Line-item or object budget.

Investigation Division. An example of a performance budget format is shown in Figure 13-3.

Program budgeting, developed by the RAND Corporation for the U.S. Department of Defense, demands an analysis between **cost-benefits** and **cost-effectiveness**. This first requires a statement of the goals of the police department, such as what effect they will have on crime and calls for service. It then focuses on what programs and activities will be used to achieve these goals. Finally, it emphasizes **output measures**. Budgeting becomes a planning tool in the everyday operation of the police department. It demands a justification for expenditures for new programs or for deleting old programs that have not met their objectives and are no longer effective because of changing conditions within the police department. Program budgeting requires that decisions for implementation be left with the police department and not controlled by an outside agency.

The program budget is also a means of planning future costs on the basis of past experience and predicted events and conditions.

There are numerous programs in which law enforcement can become involved. Some of these include prevention of crimes, investigation of crimes, apprehension of violators,

Accident Investigation		Amount
Personal services		$85,000
Contractual services		5,000
Supplies/materials		1,250
	Total	$91,250
Performance Statistics		
Investigate (initial)		
Property damage		$ 2,000
Personal injury		500
Fatal		10
Arrest and follow-up		$ 2,400
Cost per accident		
Property		$ 25
Personal injury		75
Fatality		375
Issue summonses		
Hazardous violations		$20,000
Nonhazardous violations		15,000

FIGURE 13-3 Performance budget.

presentation of criminals for judicature, services to the public, and career development of personnel. An example of a program budget is presented in Figure 13-4.

The police department shares the broad responsibilities of its overall program with such other agencies as public works, traffic engineering, and the fire department. Each agency contributes to the **program objectives** and needs to show those expenditures in its budget.

Regardless of whether the budget is designed as a performance or a program budget, a line-item budget must be prepared to support the theories behind the overall budget process. The line-item document may be developed and kept at the police department level, or it may be a separate document helping to support the performance or program budget request.

The Budgeting Process

The budgetary process is by no means completely under the control of the police department. Numerous parties are involved, each playing a separate role and each affecting the decisions of the others.

The first important person in the budgetary process is the chief of police. Working with other members of the police department, his or her budget reflects the professional or expert approach to resolving problems that face the police department. The police chief is oriented primarily toward successful completion of his or her mission. His or her

```
                    Program—Community Safety
Subprogram—Crime Prevention and Suppression              $100,000
Program Elements  (a) High school education                10,000
                  (b) Preventive patrol                     50,000
                  (c) Crime prevention, security-oriented   25,000
                  (d) Crime prevention, treatment-oriented  15,000

Subprogram—Investigation and Apprehension                $ 25,000
Program Elements  (a) Crimes against persons                7,000
                  (b) Crimes against property              15,000
                  (c) Community security                    3,000

Subprogram—Movement and Control of Traffic               $ 30,000
Program Elements  (a) Traffic patrol                       15,000
                  (b) Accident investigation                7,000
                  (c) Traffic regulation                    3,000
                  (d) Traffic safety education              5,000

Subprogram—Maintenance of Public Order                   $ 10,000
Program Elements  (a) Civil disturbance prevention         $3,000
                  (b) Noncriminal investigation             7,000
                                           Total         $165,000


             Program—General Management and Support

Subprogram—Staff Support                                 $ 80,000
Program Elements  (a) Information services                 20,000
                  (b) Technical services                   10,000
                  (c) Discretion and supervision           40,000
                  (d) Planning and evaluation              10,000

Subprogram—Employee Development                          $ 20,000
Program Elements  (a) Employee training and education      12,000
                  (b) Employee recruitment                  8,000
                                           Total         $100,000
                                     Grand Total         $265,000

Note: Each program element contains the "objective" and cost summary by
object—personal services, operating and maintenance supplies, charges
and services, capital outlay.
```

FIGURE 13-4 Program budget.

responsibility is to initiate most of the policies that are eventually accepted into the budget.

The second key person is the budget or finance officer. He or she is usually an administrative generalist and is oriented to financial and managerial norms. The budget or finance officer tends to be more restrictive in budgetary recommendations and carefully considers the progress of the police department, the goals it has established and whether they are being met, and how well guidelines established within the present budget have been met.

Unexpected Expenses

Police executives can benefit from having alternate budget plans in the event of unexpected costs. Agencies throughout the country had to deal with this problem as gas prices began fluctuating unpredictably in the 2000s. This forced agencies to come up with innovative solutions to this problem. Agencies typically draw money from budget areas that are non-essential or that have surpluses to make up for the shortfall of resources in essential areas like patrol fuel. Some agencies have begun adding fuel surcharges to traffic citations (Orrick, 2008). This has the benefit of increasing revenue without taxes on an entire population, only on offenders.

Another approach is to modify services that the agency provides. Some agencies have made their officers get out of the cars and conduct more foot patrols. This has added the extra benefit of providing improved public relations for departments. Agencies that typically have one officer per car can put two officers to a car in jurisdictions where fewer cars are necessary. Burglar alarm response services could be modified by having dispatch personnel call the location to investigate the alarm instead of automatically sending a patrol officer. Agencies can also employ problem-oriented policing to try to address crime problems with lasting solutions that communities can implement on their own with limited police assistance.

All public agencies will struggle with budget shortfalls at some point. Law enforcement agencies present particular challenges because the public expects prompt, professional service from police. This often means the public expects to lay eyes on an officer. For this reason, as well as the urgent nature of the situations to which police often respond, patrol gas budgets are among the largest expenditures of local budgets. It is important that police managers be able to come up with innovative ways to overcome these challenges and to be prepared for the unexpected budgetary stressors.

Successful Budget Requests

One of the primary considerations in budgeting for police departments is determining how to effectively persuade councils, boards or mayors of the importance of keeping agencies adequately funded. Coe and Wiesel (2001) researched the strategies that police chiefs across the United States used to increase their budgets. They conducted this research with a nationwide survey of 490 municipal police agencies, and a follow-up focus group with the chiefs from some of the agencies. The focus group participants were selected partially on their ability to substantially increase their budgets over a two-year period.

In comparing budgetary changes in police departments, they found that the agencies with increases of 20% or more over the two-year period of interest were not statistically different from agencies that did not see such budget increases when compared by police chief tenure, the size of the agency, the political structure, the number of calls for service or even the crime rates. Although, departments that successfully increased their budget sizes significantly had experienced sizable increases in population, but that growth did not necessarily result in increased crime.

Police chiefs also cited the judicious use of crime data to justify increases in their budgets. The issue of public safety, crime and fear of crime give police chiefs a strong position to argue for a solid budget. The crime issue can be used in a variety of circumstances. Increased crime can act as a justification for an increased police budget. For example, when crime rates rise, a police chief can make the argument that his or her agency needs a healthier budget to protect the public. However, how can an increased budget be justified if crime rates have been falling for consecutive years? Coe and Wiesel's (2001) research indicates that successful police executives point out that much of their agencies' workloads are for calls that are not related to crime. If an agency is increasing community outreach and administrative duties, and is receiving a high percentage of service or maintenance related calls, the police chief can still justify an increased budget. Because a relatively low percentage of police calls are directly crime-related, police managers tend to agree that calls for service are a more accurate indicator of workload than crime rates (Coe & Wiesel, 2001). Therefore, it is important that police executives note all the other important services that police departments provide to their communities.

An additional concern with crime rates occurs when the overall crime rate of a jurisdiction drops, but specific types of crime increase. For example, gang activity may be increasing in one part of town, or a new type of drug may be leading to more arrests throughout the jurisdiction than previous years. These pieces of information can be helpful for agencies to point out to budget providers. These types of crime may be harbingers of a soon to grow crime rate that could still be controlled if the issues are addressed before they grow too large. Chiefs have successfully used this strategy to note specific crime problems among juveniles, crime in commerce districts and vehicular accidents (Coe & Wiesel, 2001).

Agencies can also take advantage of highly publicized crime events or critical incidents to note the need for increased budgets. Sometimes these incidents are national events, sometimes they are in nearby areas, and sometimes they occur in the agency's jurisdiction. Natural disasters or single, high-profile crimes may reveal the need for greater training, equipment or manpower for an agency. However, the savvy police manager should be careful in using such events, particularly if they occurred in his or her own jurisdiction. Pointing out the shortcomings of the agency response may cause some to question whether the police chief should have been better prepared before the incident occurred. Additionally, a police manager should use critical incidents as a way to prepare his or her agency for potential catastrophes instead of just as a means of increasing the departmental budget.

Chiefs have also been successful in increasing budget requests by having long-term strategic plans. These are usually looking forward for the next three to seven years. Coe and Wiesel (2001, p.723) state, "A long-range strategic plan enables governing board members to make better one-year, operating-budget policy decisions." Additionally, police department long-range plans can be implemented with total local government budgetary plans for board members or mayors who also make long-term budgetary plans.

LEARNING EXERCISE

Chief Al Ridpath has never seen anything like it. He has been managing his large department's budget for 12 years without any major financial problems. He has been able to figure out how to balance the budget while phasing in new, more expensive sidearms; kept the vehicle fleet modern; and slowly increased his department's staff over the years. Today, the challenge is different. He is sitting in the office of the City Accountant, Burton Henry. They are trying to figure out where to get the money to finance his department's patrol officers until the next fiscal year, which is still two months away. The problem this year is the fluctuating price of gasoline. He budgeted $45,000 for it, which was more than the previous year, but that budget is nearly exhausted.

Chief Ridpath explains, "I've instituted a hiring freeze, so we're not replacing personnel when they leave. I've cut back on overtime. I don't know what else to do."

The accountant nods his understanding and says, "I understand, Chief, but the whole city government is coping with the same predicament. The Public Works Department is struggling to get to water leaks in the sewer system and how to pay for parts when they get there. The Parks Department has cut back on mowing the grass in the parks because running the mowers is so expensive. The city is just out of money for this fiscal year."

In exasperation, Chief Ridpath asks, "What am I supposed to do? Grass getting cut in the parks isn't as important as having my officers out there answering calls about crime!"

"I agree, but every department that has vehicles is cutting back because no one anticipated gas prices jumping around like they do now."

Chief Ridpath and the accountant sit silently for a few moments. Finally, Henry says, "I'll tell you what. You go speak with your people and see if anyone has any ideas and I'll see if we can divert some money from somewhere else in the budget to pay for gas for the patrol vehicles."

Ridpath agrees and returns to his office. He calls the captain over the patrol division. "Are you busy? Do you have a few minutes?" The captain agrees to come to the chief's office.

When he arrives he says, "Hi, Chief. What's going on?"

Chief Ridpath explains the exhausted gas budget to the captain. He says, "We need to come up with a way to keep our officers out there until the next fiscal budget. Do you have any ideas about how we can do this?"

- If you were the captain of the patrol division, what ideas could you offer to deal with this situation?
- If you were in Chief Ridpath's position, what ideas can you come up with to deal with this situation?
- What can police agencies do to prepare for such unforeseen fiscal shortfalls in future budgets?

Conclusion

This chapter was designed to give the police manager an overview of the budget process, the types of budgets available, and the roles that different people play in the budget process. This has a strong effect on how the police department obtains its funds and how much flexibility is given for day-to-day operations.

Police managers should not be overwhelmed by the budgetary process. It can and should be carefully studied, analyzed, and understood by all commanders in a department so that they will be able to assist the chief of police in preparing the police department's budget, negotiating its approval, and executing its mandates.

References

Coe, C. K., & Wiesel, D. L. (2001). Police budgeting: Winning strategies. *Public Administration Review, 61*(6), 718–727. http://dx.doi.org/10.1111/0033-3352.00142.

Johnson, K. (2012, February 24). Cities find benefits in mergers of police. *USA Today*, p.4A.

Orrick, W. D. (2008). Controlling costs: Fuel: Today's economic crisis. *The Police Chief Magazine*. Retrieved from http://www.policechiefmagazine.org/magazine/index.cfm?fuseaction=display&article_id=1688&issue_id=122008.

Discussion Questions

1. How do most police managers feel about developing the department budget?
2. Should the city manager or budget director be allowed to develop the police department's budget?
3. Why should a police department request more funds than it actually needs to accomplish its mission?
4. Assuming that the city government has a tradition of asking for more funds than are necessary, should the police department adhere to this practice or should it attempt to break from tradition?
5. Who should receive copies of the police department's budget and why?
6. How much authority and flexibility should a team commander using team policing have over the development and implementation of the group's budget?

Modern Police Management: Major Issues

Once police managers understand the psychological and functional aspects of their roles as chiefs of police or commanders, they are ready to begin making changes. This section shows police managers how such changes may be instituted.

In Chapter 14, the manager is made aware of the issue of *power*— defined as the ability to influence others so that the goals of the police department may be met. In this chapter, the police manager is given information concerning the types of power, techniques for using power, and the reasons for seeking power or influence.

One of the major liability issues facing law enforcement today is the improper use of force. Chapter 15 deals with this issue. The chapter discusses both deadly and non-deadly force, canines, and stun guns. It also discusses legal decisions that affect the rights of officers in their use of force.

A major issue facing police managers today is civil liability. Chapter 16 covers this important topic in a broad manner so that police managers will be able to deal with their roles within the framework of law. This chapter is not meant to be a complete text on legal responsibilities, only an overview, giving police managers some understanding of the issues that must be dealt with in the broad context of civil liability. The chapter also discusses accreditation and details the history of civil liability, giving a complete picture of the entire process with a discussion of the major benefits to be achieved.

Chapter 17 is designed to excite the student's inward values and beliefs. It discusses a historical background of ethics and, more importantly, shows the effects of an ethical system on a police agency and how they are employed by police managers.

Chapter 18 discusses School Resource Programs. Topics include student safety, building positive relationships with students and school administrators, and how to implement such a program. The system created by an accredited law enforcement agency is presented with appendix items for clarification.

One of the most challenging issues, and one that can have serious repercussions, is that of promotion. Chapter 19 deals with the latest techniques for designing an effective promotion process. It discusses the role of assessment centers and how they can help police managers run their departments more effectively.

Chapter 20 is a summary of the role an effective police chief must take in being successful in the running of a small- or medium-sized police agency. This includes examples and discussion of rural law enforcement agencies.

14 ▦

Use of Power

LEARNING OBJECTIVES

1. The student will be able to identify the two types of power.
2. The student will understand the approaches of power.
3. The student will understand why people want power.

Police organizations use the terms authority and power interchangeably. **Authority** is defined as the formal power that goes with a given position in the department. For example, the chief has more authority than the captain. The fact that such authority exists does not, however, mean that the chief will be more influential than the captain in the running of the police department.

Power is defined as the ability to influence others toward stated goals and purposes. This chapter discusses the three major issues relating to power: (1) types of power—formal and informal, (2) approaches to the use of power, and (3) reasons for seeking power.

Types of Power

Formal Power

There are two basic types of power—*formal* and *informal*. **Formal power** is granted to police managers by the nature of their position in the organization. Formal power has certain distinguishing characteristics.

Formal power is acquired in an instant. Police managers can point to the date, time, and place when they received this power and the position that went with it. However, they are generally aware that this power can also be lost in an instant—when they are demoted, dismissed from the police department, or retire. Such people no longer have the formal power associated with their positions in the department. Police managers recognize that formal power comes from outside. It is therefore entirely controlled by the manager's actions or behavior.

Police managers who rely heavily on formal power may become caught in the trap of believing that they are more important than they really are. The result is that subordinates tend to play organizational games, making the formal power of the police manager less effective.

Informal Power

The second type of power, **informal power**, is power that one earns over a long period. Whereas formal power can be granted in a moment, informal power can only be earned through long-term relationships and the kind of reputation necessary to demonstrate that one is capable of dealing with the issue of power.

Informal power is internal in nature and is long-term in both development and use. It does not relate directly to one's position within the police department.

Police managers who may hold the rank of lieutenant or captain and teach in the police academy may have greater degrees of informal power than others of higher rank within the same agency. It often happens that people with informal power are able to reduce conflict and bring about changes in a police department even though they are not directly related or involved in the conflict or change. The police captain who, in training, is able through informal power to influence the actions of other captains and commanders by bringing them together to resolve a conflict, may have a greater effect on the outcome of patrol operations than individuals who are directly involved in the patrol division.

Effective informal power gets things done through other people. It does not depend on wealth or status and it cannot be bought—it must be earned. Informal power might require sitting at a large desk in a large office, but it is not directly related to the size of the desk, the number of phones, or even to the office's position in the building or the number of people being managed. Instead, people with strong informal power have the ability to use such power for good purposes. Police leaders with informal power clearly show that they know what they are doing, how they are doing it, why they are doing it, and what other people are doing about it.

Informal power helps bring out creativity within the individual and his or her co-workers. It also tends to foster a high degree of self-confidence. When police managers are able to blend both formal and informal power in day-to-day operations, their level of influence on both subordinates and superiors seems boundless.

Police managers who receive formal power should feel confident in accepting such power, but they should not take the acceptance or maintenance of formal power alone as a great and serious matter. If, instead, they see it as something they could easily put aside, they will never become slaves to it. The growth of formal power is fostered by adherence to sound values and the use of this power to help others grow.

To keep developing informal power, police managers must first learn to establish priorities and be willing to learn about the various approaches to this end. There are three major steps in developing informal power:

1. **Being visible.** That is, making themselves available so that subordinates can get to know them as human beings. Being visible means being available. When something must be done, the leader with informal power is available and usually knows what to do.
2. **Maintaining integrity.** Integrity is the willingness to be open and maintain one's values and principles. Leaders who strive to develop informal power have a clear idea of their strengths, weaknesses, and goals. They also have a clearly defined system of values. They do not appear lazy or dependent on others. When they value a principle, they have chosen it carefully, cherish it, and pursue it on a day-to-day basis. Police leaders with informal power know how to trust themselves as well as others.

3. **Maintaining performance.** Performance is the ability to listen, to be open and honest, and to live up to one's word. This, the production side of management, is especially important in developing informal power. Police leaders with power are capable of doing a job well. They are dependable and willing to take on a variety of tasks within their police departments. For example, the effective police leader who attempts to build an informal power base is willing to accept assignments in almost any unit within a department.

A technique common to many informal police leaders is to carry a small notebook or set of blank index cards with them at all times. When discussing issues in the hallway or in someone else's office, they make note of dates and commitments so that they can follow up on this information later, making sure that they keep their word and perform. Police managers who have a high degree of integrity, and can be counted on to perform, develop an informal power base that is almost impossible to destroy.

With regard to relationships within a police department, the formal power of police leaders is not of primary importance. Power or influence is the capacity to get things done, and police leaders clearly recognize that such power is unevenly distributed among their personnel.

Police managers who take over new sections or departments have to consider the methods that were in use before their arrival. For example, if someone takes over as chief of police and finds that the agency has previously responded to the formal power structure, the new chief will have relatively more formal power and may be able to initiate rapid changes. In instances in which departments have been more responsive to informal power, the new police chief does best to work closely with the most influential (informally powerful) people so that they will help to initiate needed change. Normally, a new police chief can transfer and possibly even dismiss or force into retirement people who have depended on formal power in the past. But trying to use the same techniques on those with informal power tends to undermine the implementation of change, creating conflicts between the new chief and informal leaders.

Approaches to the Use of Power

There are six basic approaches to the use of power: (1) control, (2) manipulation, (3) threat, (4) referent, (5) needling, and (6) coordination.

Control

Control is formal use of power. It emphasizes rank and organizational position and involves the use of authority in controlling other people's behavior.

At first glance this approach may seem negative; however, like all approaches, it has advantages and disadvantages.

The advantages to the use of control include the ability to manage a situation quickly, to coordinate activities in the manager's department, and to coordinate activities with those of another department. It also allows the police manager, when necessary, to conceal the motives for the use of such power. This approach brings about conformity and can affect many people simultaneously. It is effective in short-term projects or emergency situations.

When a police department is ordered to perform in a certain way, such as by court decision, the use of formal authority as an approach to power is an effective method.

There are negative features as well. Accuracy is sometimes lost in relying on control. It tends to create moral issues, especially when the decisions reached under this approach affect the lives of individuals and groups within the department. It sometimes creates frustration and, when relied on exclusively, tends to generate organizational game-playing. Additionally, if this approach is uncompromisingly and rigidly implemented, it becomes difficult to reverse or modify.

Manipulation

The second approach is manipulation—which depends largely on more or less indirect methods of ensuring cooperation and getting things done. Manipulation may be either positive or negative, depending on how it is viewed by those who are being manipulated. It has five main aspects:

1. The withholding of full information as to the reasons behind certain actions. For example, an officer may be asked to undertake advanced training without being told that this step is connected with plans for his or her future promotion.
2. Dependence on long-term personal relationships. For example, a police lieutenant may be able to persuade a police sergeant to observe departmental principles or rules on the basis of an earlier project in which they both cooperated.
3. Reliance on hierarchy. For example, it is difficult for a lieutenant to manipulate a captain or major; **downward manipulation** is generally easier.
4. Ability to exploit others' needs for approval or participation. For example, a police commander may announce that meetings will begin at a certain hour and that people who are late will be excluded. By closing the door once, the commander will have threatened the latecomers' sense of participation. This tactic can be very effective in preventing subsequent tardiness.
5. Dependence on cumulative effects. The use of power through manipulation is built on one example after another. It is difficult to manipulate people to a great degree during the first few days of a relationship, as when an officer is new to a department. But as the newcomer becomes accustomed to the new milieu, this approach may become more useful.

Manipulation can be negative when it is used in a predominantly self-serving way, to aggrandize the manipulator rather than to get things done while also considering the needs of others.

Threat

Threat is the third approach. It is unlike manipulation because, in this approach, the police manager goes outside the rules. Police managers use this approach when they try to influence the behavior of subordinates by suggesting that failure to comply may bring about personally damaging consequences. For example, a captain may try to coerce a police sergeant to perform an unethical—although not illegal—act by threatening to have the sergeant transferred to a less favorable post should he or she fail to cooperate.

People who are tempted to submit to threats must recognize that they have control of their own behavior and that they must decide whether they should submit to the coercion. People who try to use this approach to implement their power are usually recognized fairly quickly and disciplined by way of disgrace, demotion, or dismissal, and a consequent loss of power.

Referent

In the referent strategy, a police manager uses the name of someone who has formal or informal power, such as the chief. The manager then implies or states directly, that he or she is representing the more powerful person. An example would be a captain, who strongly desires that a certain task be completed in a certain way, referring often to the police chief during a meeting about this task.

Sometimes referent power is presented in an indirect way. Consider the person who attempts to have his or her office placed next to the boss' office. People might assume, sometimes correctly, sometimes incorrectly, that this person has the total support of the chief.

Another example of the use of referent power is when one is seen with the chief as much as possible. For example, accompanying the chief to larger staff meetings or attending speeches given by the chief may give an impression of power that may be illusory rather than real.

Needling

Needling is a strategy in which the police manager constantly makes suggestions or takes advantage of every opportunity to show how a decision reached by someone else is not working adequately or why his or her idea should be implemented.

A manager with certain formal power, such as a chief of police, may desire to achieve something special for his or her department. Unable to get this formally approved through the channels, the chief constantly talks about how the police department could be more effective if only it could be allowed to implement the original suggestion.

This technique is only successful if the person employing the strategy has a secure position. Such techniques generally tend to irritate other people and, in many instances, make enemies who are more powerful than the person using the strategy.

Coordination

Coordination involves sharing power. It includes involving other people and is the most effective use of both formal and informal power, although it is also the most time-consuming. This approach is best used when attempting to bring about change and in resolving conflict.

Some people see their power as limited, believing that if they delegate part of it, they will be left with less. The truth is that power can be seen as related to an issue such as love. The parent who has one child and then has a second does not have less love for the first child as a result; instead, the circle of love simply grows. The same is true of power. The police manager who is willing to share power with subordinates as well as superiors usually becomes far more powerful and influential within the entire community, both directly and indirectly, than one who is unwilling to share power and authority with others.

Reasons for the Use of Power

There are three basic reasons for using power: personal, social, and survival.

Although these three may seem mutually exclusive, police managers in day-to-day operations generally balance them and do not usually use their power for any one of these reasons alone. They usually follow a set of priorities, however, and will use their power primarily for one of these reasons, and less often for the others.

Personal

The manager who uses power for personal reasons is generally trying to enhance his or her own status; therefore, personal power is essentially self-serving. Although this may seem negative, it can sometimes be justifiable. For example, if the police manager recognizes that he or she may have to stand on his or her own reputation in a conflict, as with a community group or another department head, personal power may help carry out not only his or her personal goals but also those of the police department. Another example would be that of the police official who has developed an influential base in the community and therefore can effectively defend the police department against arbitrary or unjustified attacks from the media.

Social

Social power is exercised when a police manager uses his or her influence over others to achieve some common good. In this situation, power is used mainly to influence people within the agency, at other levels of government, within the criminal justice system, or in the community. An example would be the police manager who uses his or her unique background to educate the community on the subject of crime and crime prevention.

Survival

The third reason for the use of power is for survival. For example, a chief might be willing to use his or her power to implement the plans of the city manager even though he or she does not favor these plans. In other words, the chief "goes along" in order to retain his or her position as chief. Another example might be that of a police executive who agrees to implement performance evaluations within his or her department, even though such evaluations seem unnecessary and unconstructive, simply because he or she considers it politically risky to oppose them.

In studies throughout law enforcement agencies, it appears that most police managers tend to place a higher priority on social power than on the other two. Personal power usually ranks second, with survival being lowest. The only time survival power seems to come higher in the order of priority is when the chief of police feels the need to survive for a short period—for example, for the two or three years prior to retirement.

Data indicate that people with a strong need for personal power exhibit certain common characteristics.[1] These include: (1) dominance—the desire to be in charge of a situation; (2) aggression—willingness to criticize others rather than defend their own principles; and (3) exhibitionism—the need for personal attention. Police managers who strive for power for personal reasons usually have low needs for (1) nurturing—caring for others; (2) perception—understanding the reasons others behave as they do; and (3) deference—the willingness to defer to others solely because of the others' position.

Police managers who demonstrate a strong need for socialized power usually score high in perception, achievement, the desire to excel, and dominance. They scored low in abasement, the need to accept guilt for their own or others' behavior, and aggression.

Police managers who sought power for survival reasons usually had high scores in guilt, nurturing, and deference, with low scores in dominance and achievement.

Conclusion

All police managers must be skilled in the use of power. Police managers depend on the activities of other people—peers, subordinates, and superiors—as well as those who attempt to influence the operation of the department from the outside.

Power is established in a personal relationship through the ability to lead, especially during a crisis. Therefore, police managers are evaluated on their professional reputations and track records and through the ideas they implement within their departments.

In conclusion, in using power at any time, either formally or informally, successful police managers are sensitive to what others might consider to be legal, ethical, and moral considerations. Police managers need a good intuitive understanding of power and influence and how their power affects other people. Successful police managers develop

---

[1]Tests conducted from 1980 through 1990 by the Institute of Government at the University of North Carolina.

different types of power and are good at using the appropriate methods in dealing with various situations. They are able to take advantage of their resources and do not feel that power should be used to avoid risks. Instead, they look for opportunities that will help them to enlarge their base of influence in a prudent way. Finally, effective police managers recognize and accept the fact that they, by the role they play, influence the behavior of other people.

Discussion Questions

1. Why must a police chief have power if he or she is to be effective?
2. What are some techniques that may be useful in building an informal power base?
3. Is it necessary for a police chief to have a great deal of formal power?
4. Why do police chiefs seek power?

15 The Use of Force

LEARNING OBJECTIVES

1. Understand the need and value of the laws governing use of force.
2. Be able to understand the role of the U.S. Constitution as it relates to the use of force.
3. Understand the significance of Supreme Court cases dealing with use of force.
4. Recognize the different types of action the police may take in the use of legal and effective use of defensive force.

Introduction

Perhaps no other area of law enforcement work is more controversial than the use of force. Agencies often have to deal with lawsuits after serious **use-of-force** incidents. This chapter addresses some of the considerations of which police managers should be aware when addressing this issue.

Frequency of Use of Force Incidents

There have been a number of researchers who have examined police use of force incidents and they have come to similar conclusions in terms of the infrequent use of force by police and the circumstances and types of calls that most frequently result in police use of force. The Department of Justice conducted two national use-of-force surveys with participants who had contact with police in the previous year (Langen, et al., 2001; Greenfeld, et al., 1997). The results demonstrated that most force incidents involved traffic stops, disturbance calls, felony arrests, and domestic violence reports. Predictors of police violence included **verbal resistance** from suspects and **physical resistance** during searches and arrests. Ross (2005) revisited 43 use-of-force studies in the United States and also concluded that felony arrests, traffic stops, and disturbance and domestic calls resulted in police force more often than other types of calls. Performing similar research, Hickman, et al (2008). concluded that a suspect's level of resistance or attempted escape was the biggest predictor of the amount of force a police officer uses. The International Association of Chiefs of Police (IACP) began studying police use of force in 1991 by examining police records and found similar results in their analysis. According to their data (IACP, 2001), arrests were the most frequent predicator to police use of force, followed by traffic stops and domestic violence incidents. Not surprisingly, alcohol intoxication predicted physical altercations at traffic stops.

The IACP research also demonstrated the relatively rare use of force by police when considered in the context of all the dealings with the public with which police are involved on a day-to-day basis. Association data revealed that police use-of-force incidents occur 3.61 times for every 10,000 calls for service, demonstrating just how rare it is. Ross's research also showed how seldom police use of force occurs, concluding that force is only used in three percent of all arrests, and that excessive force occurs in less than one percent of all arrests. The reader should remember that police answer many calls for service that do not end in arrest, so the overall ratio of use-of-force incidents in relation to calls for service is even lower.

Use-of-Force Law

It is not possible, or even perhaps desirable, for law enforcement officers to try to commit to memory the criminal statutes or codes of their respective jurisdictions. There are, however, some laws that ought to be memorized. In addition, they must be studied and analyzed to the extent that it enables the law enforcement officer to apply and observe the legal rules in an emergency action without hesitation.

The law enforcement officers who are forced to make decisions that could have an adverse result are putting their careers on the line as well as having an adverse impact on themselves, their departments, and their families. Officers who fail to observe the legal rules in the application of force may find themselves subject to administrative discipline, criminal charges, and/or civil actions under both federal and state laws. This chapter outlines and discusses the substance of state and federal law concerning the lawful use of force.

When discussing the use of force by law enforcement officers, which may vary from jurisdiction to jurisdiction, one should first look to legal sources for an understanding and application of the term *use of force*. The *Black's Law Dictionary* definition of "force" says usually the word occurs in such connections as to show that unlawful or wrongful action is meant. The United State Supreme Court, as well as federal and state courts, distinguish among **deadly force**, lethal force, or fatal force, as they apply to law enforcement officers in their daily duties of encountering, interviewing, and stopping suspicious people, or making an arrest and applying force.

Whenever an officer restrains the freedom of a person to walk away, he has seized that person according to *United States v. Brignoni-Ponce* (1975). While it is not always clear just when a police interference becomes a seizure, there can be no question that apprehension by the use of force is a seizure subject to the reasonableness requirement of the **Fourth Amendment**. One of the factors is the extent of the intrusion, but reasonableness depends on not only when a seizure is made, but also how it is carried out.

An arrest is the seizure of a person based upon reasonable probable cause. The Fourth Amendment to the U.S. Constitution does not prohibit arrest without a warrant for misdemeanors, felonies committed in the presence of an officer, or for felonies that have been committed, are being committed, or are about to be committed, and the officer has probable cause to believe the person to be arrested has committed the felony or is about to commit the felony. This means the force used to effect the arrest must be reasonable.

Non-deadly force is any use of force other than that which is considered deadly force; this will include any physical effort used to control or restrain another or to overcome the resistance of another.

Deadly force is any use of force that is reasonably likely to cause death or serious bodily harm, while **lethal force** is considered to be any action that causes death or that is likely to cause death.

Excessive force is force that goes beyond what is usually necessary, proper, and should be considered to be an inordinate, extreme kind of action.

Objectively reasonable is the standard determining the necessity for force and the appropriate level of force. The officer must evaluate each situation in light of the known circumstances, seriousness of the crime, the level of threat or resistance by the subject to the officer and the level of threat to the community.

Deadly Force

The U.S. Supreme Court addressed the legal use of deadly force in the case of *Tennessee v. Garner* (1985), but the events that led to the decision occurred several years earlier. In 1974, 15-year-old Edward Garner and a friend entered an unoccupied dwelling in Memphis, Tennessee. A neighbor called the police department and reported the young men as burglars. When police officers arrived at the scene, the suspects fled. The officers shouted warnings, but Garner and his friend continued their escape attempt. One of the officers fired shots at the suspects, and a bullet struck Garner in the back of the head, killing him. At the time, the police department allowed officers to use deadly force to prevent the escape of felons who were fleeing. The officers believed Garner was unarmed, but they believed that if he got over a fence he would escape. Burglary was a felony, the officers saw him fleeing the crime scene, and they believed he would escape if they did not stop him, so the officers believed deadly force was authorized.

Garner's father, believing that his son's constitutional rights had been violated, filed suit. The case finally made its way to the Supreme Court in 1985. The **fleeing-felon rule** was an artifact of English and American common law that developed when many more crimes were capital crimes. However, many law enforcement agencies had already detected the outdated nature of the rule and had begun implementing alternative use-of-force policies. In the *Garner* case, the Supreme Court ruled that, despite the historical and widespread use of the fleeing-felon rule, deadly force was not warranted in this situation. Their ruling nullified the long-standing rule. The new rules allow deadly force on fleeing suspects if they are posing a threat to the lives of officers or other citizens; however, officers should announce their authority to arrest and warn of the intent to shoot.

Deadly force restrictions also imply that officers may use deadly force to destroy an animal that is a threat to public safety, or may use deadly force to destroy an animal that is seriously injured, when the officer is reasonably sure that deadly force can be used without harm of injury to the officer or others.

Warning shots are generally prohibited but may be fired if the officer is authorized to use deadly force and only if the officer reasonably believes a warning shot can be fired safely in light of all circumstances governed by the situation encountered and must be authorized pursuant to departmental orders. Shooting at or from a moving vehicle is generally prohibited but is governed by the department's use-of-force policy.

Non-deadly Force

Use of non-deadly force occurs when deadly force is not authorized, and the officers may use only the level of force that is reasonable to bring an incident or suspect under control. Officers are authorized to use department-approved non-deadly force techniques and issued equipment to protect the officer or others from physical harm, to control an unlawful situation, and to bring the unlawful situation under control safely and effectively.

Devices that may be used by law enforcement personnel to control subjects may include handcuffs, flex-cuffs, body chains, leg irons, hobbles/nylon restraints, ankle chains, or impact weapons such as the baton, side handle baton (PR-24), expandable baton (Asp), and nunchaku "nunchucks." Chemical agents including chemical mace (tear gas-Cn/Cs) and pepper spray (OC) (three types of spray—mist, direct stream, and foam) are also used.

Conducted Energy Weapons (CEW), Tasers/stun guns are electronic restraint defense weapons designed to restrain individuals, where conventional restraint tactics are reasonably likely to fail. The Taser discharges an electrical current (50,000 volts) into the person by means of two electrical contact barbs, connected to the conducting device by two wires. Stun guns discharge 50,000 volts by direct contact with the subject. These weapons are most likely to be used by law enforcement officers when detaining and arresting a subject, controlling a pretrial detainee, or controlling a convicted person.

The stun gun is the weapon that draws the most criticism. Police argue that the weapon is not the use of deadly force and therefore can be used to restrain uncooperative subjects. Others state that it is a deadly weapon and should only be used at a much higher use of force by the subject. In some states the issue of what constitutes a deadly weapon is defined by statute.

Force Continuum

There is no single standard for assessing the validity of force, as spelled out in the United States Supreme Court case of *Graham v. Connor* (1989). The specific constitutional amendment that applies is the Fourth Amendment; therefore, the detention, arrest, and whether the force used was reasonable will be judged by this standard. The Fourteenth Amendment standard (due process) states that no one is to be subjected by anyone acting under color of law to the intentional and wanton infliction of physical harm.

Written guidelines to assist the officers in the decision to use force are usually identified in the "use of force continuum/matrix." The decision to use the Taser/stun gun should not be deployed at the level below where impact weapons would be used. This weapon is governed by the Gun Control Act of 1968, Pub. L. No. 90-618; 18 § U.S.C.

921(a)(3)(A), Chapter 44–Firearms; the National Firearms Act, 26 U.S.C. 5854(e); and various state laws.

CASE STUDY

Former Los Angeles Police Department (LAPD) Sergeant Stacey Koon was the supervising officer on the scene of the Rodney King beating in 1991. In his book *Presumed Guilty* (1992), he explains that King's brutal treatment was the result of King's refusal to obey officer commands to lie down as well as administrative decisions that limited police use-of-force options. Koon states that a chokehold maneuver had been removed from the LAPD use-of-force continuum during the 1980s. He believes that if this option had been available to police, they could have applied it to King, rendered him unconscious, and avoided the videotaped beating that later led to riots fueled by citizen outrage. He maintains that the use-of-force continuum that LAPD officers were trained to follow was obeyed, including the portion of the confrontation during which several officers simultaneously struck King with their batons. King was still able to defend himself and, according to Koon, even able to make aggressive moves. It was not until after several minutes of beating that King finally relented and was able to be handcuffed. Koon further supports his point by noting that King was not harmed when he began complying with officer commands and that neither of the passengers who were in the vehicle with King prior to the beating was harmed.

The Rodney King beating is an interesting case for police officers to examine in order to understand the sometimes blurred line between necessary and unnecessary force. Yet the ultimate responsibility for street level officers' understanding lies with police managers who have to give them guidance on the proper use of force. The questions are not always easy to answer. Koon contends that his officers obeyed the use-of-force policies set forth by their agency. However, when videotaped footage of the beating made its way to national news coverage, the agency did not support the officers. Perhaps it is this type of confusion that led to contradicting verdicts in the officers' state and federal trials. Regardless, it is important for police managers to note the importance of providing a clear guide for street-level officers in terms of how and when to use force properly. Yet, it is also important to note that no strict set of rules on use of force can account for every possible scenario in which police may have to apply force in order to gain compliance. A clearly arranged use-of-force continuum is the best tool agencies have for this challenge, but as the Rodney King case demonstrates, it is not perfect.

Canines

Law enforcement canine deployment should be regarded as any other tool in the law enforcement officer's use-of-force arsenal. On a "continuum/matrix," deployment of canines should be considered a use-of-force option between that of deadly force and impact weapons if it is a K-9 bite/hold situation. Decisions to deploy a canine should be based upon the following three factors as established under *Graham v. Connor* (1989): (1) severity of the crime, (2) whether the suspect poses an immediate threat to the safety of the officers or others, and (3) whether the suspect is actively resisting arrest or attempting to evade arrest at the time.

It is imperative to remember that canines act in accordance with their training—to grab an arm or any other reachable part of the body and hold until called off by the handler. Sanctioning indiscriminate use of dangerous police dogs (canines) to subdue non-dangerous suspects may well meet the objective reasonableness test set forth in the *Graham v. Connor* decision and could be considered excessive use of force.

GRAHAM V. CONNOR (1989)

Graham, a diabetic, asked his friend Berry to drive him to a convenience store to purchase orange juice to counteract the onset of an insulin reaction. Once in the store, he observed a long line at the checkout counter, decided to put the juice container down, and ran out of the store. Graham requested that his friend drive him to another friend's house for assistance.

Officer Connor of the Charlotte, North Carolina, police department observed Graham hurriedly exiting the store and conducted an investigatory stop. During the stop, Berry informed the officer of Graham's condition, and the officer ordered Berry to wait while he performed a check and summoned backup. During the check, Graham exited the vehicle, ran around it twice, and passed out. Several officers responded, and one rolled the unconscious Graham over and secured him with handcuffs. Berry attempted to explain that Graham was experiencing an insulin reaction, but officers ignored him. One officer thought Graham was drunk and needed to be locked up, while another officer stated "Ain't nothing wrong with him, I've seen a lot of diabetics that never acted like this." The officers picked Graham up and slammed him headfirst into the hood of the car. The officers shoved him into the police car, where he sustained a broken foot, cuts on his wrists, a bruised forehead, and an injured shoulder. Berry attempted to give some orange juice to Graham while in the squad car, but the officers refused to let him have it. Later, Officer Connor returned to the store and found that no crime had taken place and the officers drove Graham home.

Graham filed suit, claiming that the officers used excessive force during the arrest. Relying on the *Glick* test, officers prevailed at trial and the Fourth Circuit Court of Appeals affirmed. The Supreme Court granted certiorari and found that the lower courts had improperly applied the appropriate standard in determining the excessive force claim. The Court remanded the claim to the district court for reconsideration under the Fourth Amendment standard. The jury, using the Fourth Amendment reasonableness standard, found in favor of Graham. The officers' use of force was unreasonable, because Graham was unconscious when apprehended. This was further compounded by his medical condition, as officers failed to acknowledge warnings by Berry that Graham was experiencing an insulin reaction.

This case is significant because the Court ruled that the appropriate standard of review of excessive force claims arising from an arrest is "objective reasonableness" in accordance with the Fourth Amendment. The Court established the following factors of legal review: the severity of the crime at issue, whether the suspect is actively resisting arrest, whether the suspect is attempting to evade the arrest by flight, and whether the suspect is an immediate threat to the officer or others. The Court noted that officers are often forced to make split-second decisions regarding force and that the reasonableness of such decisions must be based on the perception of the officer and not through hindsight. Determining whether reasonable force was used will be made by courts on a case-by-case basis, in light of the facts and circumstances the officer faced at the time force was required.

Source: Ross, Darrell L. (2013). *Civil Liability in Criminal Justice*, 6th ed. Boston: Elsevier / Anderson Publishing.

Fourth Amendment

The courts have basically set forth a standard that all law enforcement agencies must take into consideration when developing a written departmental policy on the use of force—especially in regard to the use of deadly or lethal force. Where departmental policies and procedures serve as written guidelines it must be taken into consideration that the written policies do not supersede the applicable state statutes or codes and are but one matter to be considered by a law enforcement agency and its administrators. The use of force continuum/matrix contains executive standards set forth in departmental policy manuals, but it is not the law and has no legal standing and therefore it is an incorrect assumption that a departmental policy controls the legal use of force and its legal application.

A law enforcement officer's use of force is subject to the requirements of the United States Constitution and because of the Constitution's supremacy clause, a state or other lower governmental political subdivision cannot attempt to create a use-of-force standard that is less restrictive than the standard defined by U.S. Supreme Court and federal case law as it pertains to local jurisdictions.

Historically the standard for criminal law in the United States was the "common law," but in most states today, the criminal laws have been codified by the states as a felony, misdemeanor, or violations of a city or county ordinance. The common law also developed a privilege to protect one's personal property and self—that being by the reasonable non-lethal use of force. Slowly both the civil and criminal law came to recognize and adopt the view that no crime or tort should result from the legitimate use of force in self-protection. The need to use force must be justifiable and the amount of force used should be proportionate to the force being used against that person. The level of force that a law enforcement officer is allowed to use when making an arrest or defending himself or herself will depend on the nature of the resistance to the action being taken by the officer.

As the U.S. Supreme Court stated in its decision in *Graham v. Connor* (1989): "Our Fourth amendment jurisprudence has long recognized the right to make an arrest or an investigator stop necessarily carries with it the right to use some degree of physical coercion or threat thereof to effect it." The Court stated the proper constitutional standard to determine whether the use of force is excessive is the "objective reasonableness" test under the Fourth Amendment. This applies to all alleged law enforcement excessive force claims (deadly or not). In determining the necessity of using some force to make an arrest, which involves an arrestee's constitutional rights, the Court must evaluate a number of factors:

1. **Severity of the crime** at issue. Judging whether the person poses a threat of serious physical harm to the law enforcement officers or to others, thus justifying the use of force up to and including deadly/lethal force, must be considered. What kind of force was used and what was the nature of the place and the circumstances surrounding the use of force?

2. Whether the suspect poses an **immediate threat** to the safety of the officers or others. Law enforcement officers are permitted to protect themselves and others from threats to their safety. The use of force must be evaluated as to the actions or the threats that caused the use of force, the officer's assessment of the situation as to whether the person to be arrested is armed or unarmed, and to the level of resistance being directed toward the officers. Did the suspect have, use, or display a weapon?

3. Whether the suspect is actively resisting the arrest. The likelihood of gaining control of an individual, the likelihood of injuries, and certain circumstances may warrant a reaction by the officer to use a higher degree of force when initiating a contact with a violent or dangerous person.

4. Whether the suspect is attempting to evade the arrest by flight. Force used must be reasonable, and courts must examine the need for the application of force and the relationship between the need and amount of force used and the extent of the injury if inflicted.

The *Graham v. Connor* decision restricts a Fourth Amendment claim to those who have been allegedly seized, arrested, or detained by law enforcement officers when the officers acted in a reasonable manner. Where a person is subjected to the use of force, but is not being seized and is not already in custody, the person may have a cause of action for deprivation of life or liberty in violation of his or her deprivation of life or liberty in violation of his or her Fourteenth Amendment (substantive due process) rights as spelled out in the U.S. Supreme case of *County of Sacramento v. Lewis* (1998).

Evolving Role of Technology

In the early 1900s, police had few options in terms of the force they could use. They often relied on sheer, brute force. When weapons were used, they typically had a night stick or flap jack, and a sidearm. Unfortunately, this led to many injuries and even unnecessary deaths. This often resulted in public discontent with police.

Technological advances of the twentieth century gave officers a multitude of options to use in gaining compliance from resisting suspects. Metal handcuffs were once the only option to restricting a suspect's hands, but flex cuffs are small, light, and effective enough that police can carry many of these as a way of controlling multiple suspects. Variations of the night stick are still used, but now they often take the form of extending batons. These are small, handheld batons that can be carried and extended when the officer is threatened. Chemical and pepper sprays now give officers more options for subduing uncooperative suspects. The irritants in the sprays inhibit uncooperative suspects' vision and breathing, thereby making them more cooperative. Stun guns and Tasers use electricity to induce cooperation from suspects who might otherwise be inclined to resist arrest. These devices send an electric shock through the suspect in short intervals and at the manual manipulation of the officer, thereby providing the suspect the opportunity to cooperate before serious injuries occur. Many officers have found that otherwise aggressive suspects lose their pugilistic aspirations when they have their first Taser experience.

Police use of force will always be controversial. It is vital that police managers properly train and equip their officers for the range of use-of-force incidents that can occur. Technological advances now give police more options than previous generations of police, which can save lives and spare suspects as well as officers from serious injuries if used properly.

Identifying Problem Officers

Research has shown that use-of-force incidents are not typically evenly distributed throughout police departments; a relatively small number of officers account for high proportions of the events. For example, in 1991 the Independent Commission on the Los Angeles Police, also known as the Christopher Commission (Independent Commission on the Los Angeles Police Department, 1991), noted that allegations of excessive force had been made about 1,800 police officers in the LAPD during a four-year span. The vast majority of those officers—more than 1,400—had two or fewer accusations made against them. Yet the remaining officers had far more allegations made against them in the same time period: 183 officers had four or more allegations, 44 of them had six or more, and an additional 16 had eight or more complaints. One officer had 16 allegations of excessive force made against him in the four-year span.

Toch (1995) arrived at a similar conclusion, noting that some officers, whom he refers to as "chronic deviants," are more likely than the majority of police officers in a department to use force. He notes that these chronically deviant officers receive this label because of the number of problems they cause for police managers and coworkers. These problem officers are disrespectful, abusive of their powers, and have difficulty interacting with the public.

It is advisable for police managers to be vigilant of those officers whom they suspect to be these chronic deviants and develop a disciplinary system to address their problems before they contribute to major problems in the agency. Some agencies grade their officers on criteria such as citizen complaints, use-of-force events, reprimands, and firearm discharges. Managers review their subordinates' records on the criteria and work on ways to reduce problems, including disciplinary measures. The Miami-Dade Police Department, the New Orleans Police Department, and the Minneapolis Police Department all implemented these types of systems and saw reduction in citizen complaints according to Walker et al. (2011).

Use-of-Force Policy

Police departments are the only agencies that are allowed to use force legally to gain compliance. This extra power provides for many potential problems for police managers. For example, when a police officer uses force against a suspect, there is an increased risk of a civil lawsuit and bad publicity. The agency and officer may win the civil case and therefore be vindicated, but the time and effort put into the case is frustrating for officers and their managers.

To guide the use of force, many police agencies now write policies meant to guide their officers. The use-of-force continuum discussed in this chapter is a partial implementation of these types of policies. Many departments spell out other use-of-force considerations in an attempt to guide officers without inhibiting their ability to defend themselves and others. McEwan (1997) researched use-of-force policies from throughout the country. His findings can assist police managers in creating their own policies. For example, he found a number of consistencies among the sampled agencies. Almost all of the agencies' policies included purpose statements acknowledging that police work often requires the use of force, but that it should be restrained. Some agencies provide guidance about the weapons that officers are allowed to use, but the police manager should note that if the agency provides the weapon, it is the agency's responsibility to train the officers on proper usage of the weapon. Furthermore, agencies benefit from including wording that suspects who are injured by police force will nonetheless receive medical treatment. Obviously, all of these advantages to departmental use-of-force policies also assist in limiting a police agency's civil liability.

Agencies can shape their use-of-force policies on successful policies that other agencies have used. The Commission on Accreditation for Law Enforcement Agencies (CALEA) is also a useful resource for procuring information and ideas about helpful use-of-force policies that protect officers, their supervisors, their agencies, and the public.

Conclusion

The use of force is an integral part of a law enforcement officer's job, particularly when stopping, interviewing, or arresting a criminal suspect, and is one of the most dangerous functions performed by officers. The subject may be wanted for a crime of which the officer is not aware and the officer must make the decision as to the sufficient level of force necessary to take the suspect into custody. Every encounter is different—therefore, no single set of rules or prescribed course to be followed in every instance can be set forth, but certain basic fundamentals can be brought to the officer's attention to assist him or her in situations as they may arise.

Any person, even if he or she is being lawfully arrested, has a constitutional right to be free of excessive force. A law enforcement officer is entitled to use such force that a reasonable law enforcement officer would think is required to take an arrested individual into custody. This may include force that is reasonably necessary to subdue a person who is physically resisting the officer's efforts to take him or her into custody.

One must consider the issues and criticisms of the use of force and controversies facing law enforcement officers and their departments. The concern about specific tactics involving the use of non-lethal or less-than-lethal weapons is continuing to grow, and a great number of cases involving law enforcement officers' use of force are those in which it is alleged that the person resisted or attempted to evade arrest. The legal questions under the Fourth Amendment are whether the use of force was objectively reasonable. The officer's intent or state of mind does not become relevant or a factor to be considered in determining whether the officer's actions were reasonable.

A law enforcement officer's subjective intent, motivation, or good intentions will not offset an unreasonable use of force beyond what is privileged and may render both the department and the officer liable to an injured person. There must be an awareness on the part of the departments and the officers charged with enforcing the laws of their jurisdiction that going beyond acceptable levels of force can have serious legal and financial results. What may be considered to be a reasonable use of force will depend upon the facts and circumstances of each individual situation. Education and training in the use of force must be ongoing—not only in techniques, but on changes in the law and court decisions and continued training that includes practical, "shoot–don't shoot" decision making, firearms training, agency-authorized judgment simulated training, discretion, and judgment in the use of lethal force. Continuous training and exposure in the use of reasonable force—both physical and non-physical—to ensure compliance and overcome resistance, certification in the use of chemical agents, the use of impact weapons, and driver training refresher courses should be considered a high priority of the police agency.

The Supreme Court has held that the level of force that law enforcement officers may use to effect an arrest or investigative detention of a suspect must be reasonable and conform to the requirements of the Fourth Amendment. Law enforcement administrators, policy makers, and instructors must be knowledgeable about court decisions. Policy and training should have an appropriate balance between the constitutional rights of all citizens to be free from unreasonable seizures and the interest of communities in maintaining professional, effective law enforcement and at all times protecting the law enforcement officers who perform these duties.

References

County of Sacramento v. Lewis, 523 U.S. 833 (1998).

Graham v. Connor, 109 S. Ct 1865 (1989).

Graham v. Connor, 490 U.S. 386 (1989).

Greenfeld, L. A., Langan, P. A., Smith, S. K., & Kaminski, R. J. (1997). *Police use of Force: Collection of National Data*. Washington, D.C.: Bureau of Justice Statistics.

Hickman, M. J., Piquero, A. R., & Garner, J. H. (2008). Toward a National estimate of Police Use of Nonlethal Force. *Criminology and Public Policy, 7*, 563–604.

Independent Commission on the Los Angeles Police Department. (1991). Report of the Independent Commission on the Los Angeles Police Department. Los Angeles, CA

International Association of Chiefs of Police (2001). Police use of Force in America. Alexandria, VA: IACP.

Koon, S. C., & Deitz, R. (1992). *Presumed guilty: The tragedy of the Rodney King affair*. Washington, D.C.: Regnery Gateway.

Langan, P. A., Greenfeld, L. A., Smith, S. L., Durose, M. R., & Levin, D. J. (2001). *Contacts Between Police and the Public: Findings From the 1999 Survey*. Washington, D.C.: Bureau of Justice Statistics.

McEwan, T. (1997). Policies on less-than-lethal force in law enforcement agencies. *Policing: An International Journal of Police Strategy & Management, 19*(1), 36–39.

Ross, D. L. (2005). A Content Analysis of the Emerging Trends in the Use of Non-Lethal Force Research in Policing. *Journal of Law Enforcement Executive Forum, 5*, 121–148.

Ross, D. L. (2013). *Civil liability in criminal justice* (6th ed.). Boston: Elsevier/Anderson Publishing.

Toch, H. (1995). The "violence prone" police officer. In W. Geller, & H. Toch (Eds.), *And justice for all: Understanding and controlling police abuse of force* (pp. 99–112). Washington, D.C: Police Executive Research Forum.

United States v. Brignoni-Ponce, 422 U.S. 873 (1975).

Walker, S., Alpert, G. P., & Kenney, D. J. (2011). *Early warning systems: Responding to the problem police officer*. National Institute of Justice: Research in Brief. Retrieved from https://www.ncjrs.gov/pdffiles1/nij/188565.pdf.

Learning Exercise

Officer Duplain responded to a call late one night from a resident who stated that someone was trying to break into his house. The suspect was beating on the back door and loudly demanding to be allowed inside. However, the complainant hung up during the phone call, so the dispatch officer was not able to confirm that the suspect was not in the house. After arriving at the residence, Officer Duplain walked around the house toward the back door and found a male standing in the shadows near a tree with both hands in his coat pockets. Duplain pointed his sidearm at the suspect and ordered him several times to reveal his hands. The suspect looked to his left and right and charged at officer Duplain without removing his hands from his pockets.

- If you were a police manager, and you were using this scenario as a training tool, how would you advise your subordinate officers to react? Why?
- How should Officer Duplain have reacted? Keep in mind that no weapon has been seen and even if the suspect attacks Officer Duplain, there are varying levels of force that can be used.
- Create a use of force policy for a police department that guides officers on how to use force in these types of situations.

This scenario is a summary of the case *McKinney v. Duplain* (2008). Officer Duplain shot and killed the suspect with four shots fired in less than two seconds while the suspect was charging him. As it turned out, the suspect was not armed, but the court determined that Duplain's use of force was justified. Do you agree with this decision? Why?

Discussion Questions

1. Discuss the importance to the police of understanding the limits on the use of force.
2. Which Supreme Court cases are especially important for police regarding the use of force? Why?
3. Discuss what tools are given to police to protect themselves and which you think should be issued.
4. What is your position on the use of stun guns? Why?

16 Civil Liability and Accreditation[1]

LEARNING OBJECTIVES

1. The student will understand the police agency's need for protection from civil liability.
2. The student will understand issues of liability.
3. The student will be able to identify ways in which to reduce the police department's potential liability.
4. The student will be able to identify the origins of the National Accreditation Process.
5. The student will be able to relate the accreditation process to issues of liability.

Introduction

The role of the police manager has been in a state of flux for some time, and although some challenges have been completely met and conquered, new challenges for the law enforcement manager constantly emerge.

There was a time when police managers could count on exercising some degree of control over the crime rate and keeping their agencies scandal-free; this gave them a sense of security. Today, however, they have additional and more pressing problems while still having to contend with the old ones. Many of these problems have already been addressed in this text. But recently, more police managers have been troubled by the presence—very real and very expensive—of **liability** for the actions of their personnel and of judgments against their agencies that in some cases run into millions of dollars. But before addressing the more specific ways of confronting the liability issue, we should think in terms of the multiple layers of protection offered by policy, support, training, discipline, supervision, and evaluation. Each item will add more protection; any single item alone will not offer enough protection. It is only by depending on the interaction of all these factors that the police manager can feel secure.

Another approach is to make sure that the manager selects, appoints, trains, supervises, entrusts, retains, and directs personnel so that an officer's misconduct on the street at 2:00 A.M. can be shown to have occurred despite the manager's best efforts. The trail of evidence that might indicate culpability should not necessarily lead to the police manager's door. If it appears that the officer acted independently, there will be no **vicarious responsibility**. Liability has increased for a number of reasons—the greater number of lawsuits in our society, more intense scrutiny given to the actions of police officers, and greater accountability demanded by the public and recognized by the courts.

---

[1]Chapter 16 is included with the permission of G. Patrick Gallagher and Jay Leffert.

Years ago, police officers were rarely sued, but today suits are filed almost automatically if there is any possibility that the actions of the officers fell below the standards required by the courts. Perhaps these lawsuits for "**police malpractice**" are a sign of the profession's coming of age.

Police managers must be familiar with current terms, concepts, and trends in the civil courts; they must keep track of recent decisions so as to understand what is expected of them and their personnel. By monitoring the decisions of various courts, the manager can learn valuable lessons and avoid potential lawsuits.

The following story concerns a question given to candidates for a sergeant's promotional examination in England:

Q. You are on duty in the High Street when there is a large explosion, which causes a large crater in the middle of the road, a main trunk road in fact. The explosion blows a van onto its side and upon investigation you discover in it a man and a woman, the woman being the wife of your sergeant, who is currently away on a course. Both are injured. At this point two dogs, neither of which is wearing a collar, begin to fight in the middle of the road, and they are encouraged by drinkers from a nearby public house who are quite obviously inebriated and disorderly. In the confusion, a car and a coach collide and you discover that the car is being driven by your chief constable and that the bus driver has taken a shotgun from his cab with obvious intentions of using it. A man runs from a house shouting for a midwife and a woman informs you that there is a fire in the large garage around the corner. You then hear someone shouting for help from the nearby canal where he has been thrown by the original explosion. Bearing in mind the provisions of the Justices of the Peace Act, the various Mental Health Acts and particularly, section 49, Police Act, 1964, what should your course of action be?

A. Immediately—immediately remove your helmet and mingle with the crowd.

This is not an option for us. The plaintiff is interested in a defendant with "deep pockets." The "deep pocket theory" makes it advantageous for the plaintiff's attorneys to name as many defendants as possible, from the officer who committed the alleged act to the supervisor to the chief. Therefore, the chief, as the agency head, must be able to avoid liability by proving that he or she did everything that could be expected to supervise and train the highest-quality officer.

One of the ways a police manager can proactively address these potential claims is the accreditation process. As you will read in this chapter, the accreditation process requires each applying agency to go through a rigorous examination of its resource allocation as well as its policies and procedures. Having these approved by an accrediting body can help a police manager answer any hindsight criticisms that may come with civil lawsuits.

Due to the increase in the number of lawsuits, there are now newsletters and other publications that discuss police liability and highlight cases and damage awards. *Police*

Misconduct: Law and Litigation (Avery & Rudovsky, 1980), for example, is a valuable tool for the police manager because it indicates the course of action, the points of attack, and the ease with which liability suits can be filed.

So, given the magnitude of the problem, it is necessary that police managers achieve a greater familiarity with the concepts, terms, and principles guiding the courts as well as with rules of litigation; that they have a comprehensive overview of the latest information on liability issues from jurisdictions around the country; that they glimpse a projection of future trends and issues; and that they understand the major areas of liability—civil rights violations and negligence. Finally, and most importantly, managers must know how to develop liability protection programs for both themselves and their agencies. This will minimize the risk of "self-inflicted wounds," such as those from which the profession now suffers.

Lawsuits resulting from police misconduct fall into two major categories: civil rights violations and negligent employment and supervision. Police managers must become familiar with the ways in which lawsuits in these categories can be filed, and the decisions of the courts. Although not always consistent from jurisdiction to jurisdiction, these decisions should be tracked to monitor trends. The emphasis in this chapter is on managing liability; the technical and legal aspects of civil rights and negligence will be covered in outline form only.

Civil Rights Violations

Civil rights violations that allege the deprivation of a person's rights under the Constitution when an officer is acting "under color of law," are the grounds of the most frequent complaints filed against law enforcement officers. The Civil Rights Act of 1871 gives rise to these causes of action under Title 42 of the United States Code, Section 1983. Liability under this law does not necessarily have to be based on the intent to violate a person's constitutional rights, because liability is based on the theory that the officer's conduct had a natural and obvious consequence and that, without intent, the officer's conduct resulted in a denial or deprivation of the person's rights.

The Civil Rights Act of 1871 provides:

Every person who, under color of any statute, ordinance, regulation, custom, usage, of any state or territory, subjects or causes to be subjected, any citizen of the United States or any other person within the jurisdiction thereof to the deprivation of any rights, privileges, or immunities secured by the Constitution and laws, shall be liable to the party injured in an action at law, suit in equity, or other proper proceeding for redress.

The specific causes of action under this law include the following:

- False arrest and detention
- Excessive force and physical brutality

- Illegal search and seizure
- Denial of counsel and illegal interrogation
- Denial of First Amendment rights
- Denial of medical attention
- Discriminatory or retaliatory prosecution
- Use of perjured evidence
- Verbal abuse or harassment
- Failure to provide police protection
- Misconduct resulting in death through the use of deadly force

The vital points are: (1) that intention to deprive is not a necessary prerequisite to legal action, and (2) that an action can be brought for failure to prevent a violation (that is, when an officer knows that a violation or deprivation is taking place but takes no affirmative action to prevent the violation).

Negligence

To understand the basics of negligence, it is necessary to consider its four elements:

1. A duty owed
2. According to a standard of care
3. A failure to perform that duty according to that standard
4. A loss or injury resulting from that failure

The major areas in which actions can arise are as follows (American Bar Association, 1972):

Negligent Appointment. The plaintiff alleges that the officer who injured him or her was unfit for appointment and that the appointing official knew or should have known about this unfitness.

Negligent Retention. The plaintiff alleges that the officer who injured him or her was unfit to be retained as a police officer and that the retaining police manager knew or should have known of this unfitness.

Negligent Assignment. The plaintiff alleges that the police manager assigned an officer under his or her command to certain duties for which that officer lacked appropriate training and experience, or that the officer was unable to perform, and that the police manager knew or should have known about these deficiencies, but made the assignment anyway.

Negligent Supervision. The plaintiff alleges that the administrator was under an affirmative duty to supervise his or her subordinates and that, in failing to do so, caused the plaintiff to sustain injuries or loss.

Negligent Training. The plaintiff alleges that the police manager has not trained his or her officers—especially in highly critical areas such as firearms, driving, defensive tactics, and first aid—and that the plaintiff was injured as a result.

Negligent Direction. The plaintiff alleges that the police manager has failed to anticipate problems arising in the field, to minimize police discretion at the operational levels, and to promulgate comprehensive written directives guiding police actions and behavior. Failure to do this is equivalent to not assuming the duty to direct personnel, and the manager is responsible.

CITY OF CANTON V. HARRIS (1989)

Harris was stopped for speeding and was arrested after she became uncooperative with the officer. She was transported to the police station in a patrol wagon and upon arrival was found sitting on the floor. She was brought inside for processing where she collapsed to the floor two times. The officers left her on the floor for approximately one hour during processing and failed to summon medical attention. Court testimony revealed that the shift commander was responsible for determining the medical care of arrestees but did not receive training with which to make medical decisions. She was released into the care of her family whereupon she was taken to a hospital by an ambulance summoned by her family. She was diagnosed as suffering from emotional stress reaction, anxiety, and depression. She was hospitalized for a week and received outpatient medical care for about one year. She sued the city for a variety of claims, but most notable were the claim of denial of medical care while in custody, and training deficiencies of officers in medical care for arrestees. Harris prevailed and was awarded $200,000 in damages. The city appealed to the Sixth Circuit Court of Appeals, which ruled that a municipality could be held liable for failure to train when a plaintiff could prove intentional, reckless, or gross negligence on the part of the municipality. An error was made by the court in explaining jury instructions and a retrial was ordered. Prior to retrial, the city sought review by the Supreme Court and they granted *certiorari* to determine the issue of whether a municipality could be held deliberately indifferent to the training needs of its officers. The Court concluded that the standard with which to examine claims of failing to train is deliberate indifference. Deliberate indifference can mean a callous disregard of known risks and failing to take steps to abate it, or a conscious choice from among several alternatives. While the Court ruled that a municipality must provide ongoing training for recurring job tasks an officer encounters, the justices did not state how frequently training must be provided nor the duration of the training. On remand the appellate court reversed its former decision, based on deliberate indifference. This case is significant because the Court has expanded the standard of deliberate indifference to claims against administrators for failing to train their officers. Deliberate indifference is a higher standard for a plaintiff to prove in court. Officers must receive realistic ongoing training to "obvious" recurring job functions. The decision also applies to correctional officials.

Source: Ross, Darrell L. (2013). *Civil Liability in Criminal Justice*, 6th ed. Boston: Elsevier/Anderson Publishing.

Avoiding Liability through Selection and Training

One of the surest ways of reducing the potential for lawsuits is to staff the police department with the best people possible. A systematic approach to selection and training starts with the assumption that, for the most part, the selection and training process goes on at each of the following six steps or phases: *recruitment, initial selection, psychological evaluation, academy training, field training,* and *probation.*

Recruitment. The manager selects where he or she recruits, who he or she is recruiting, and by whom the recruiting is done. The chief actually filters people out by the way in which he or she goes about the recruitment process. In other words, the quality of the recruits may depend in large part on the design of the recruitment program.

Selection. At this point, the chief applies certain selection criteria, utilizing background checks, polygraph results, and whatever else he or she may want to use within legal and ethical guidelines.

Psychological Evaluation. The courts have recognized and accepted the use of psychological testing for police officer candidates. It is recommended that tests be administered to candidates, then scored and interpreted by a psychologist who will also interview each candidate and then make recommendations to the police chief. The psychologist should be familiar with the police profession and be able to defend his or her decisions in court, present findings logically and professionally, and be willing to recommend rejection of unqualified candidates. A final caution: psychological evaluation only gives an assessment at a particular point in a person's life. The chief cannot use the test to guarantee predictions of how a person is going to handle the job three years down the road or when unforeseen events (a broken marriage, financial problems, friction with a difficult supervisor) cause stress.

Academy Training. For many years, methods of training have not received a great deal of scrutiny, but they will in the immediate future. A proper training program for recruits is based on job task analysis and the subsequent validation of a curriculum that includes performance objectives for each block, a plan of instruction, and a training guide. Evaluation of both courses and instructors, along with simulation exercises and role-playing, should be considered essential.

Field Training. This innovation has, over the past 10 years, been one of the most beneficial ways of providing officers with both training and job-related evaluations. It does much to counterbalance the "street nullification" so common in the past, and it is the best preparation for solo assignments.

One problem encountered in field training is with development of supervisors. Supervisors are often trained by the supervisors they served under, who may, in some cases, be inadequate. The department may thus only perpetuate inadequacies and may not take the steps needed to improve the system. Supervisors are usually not trained prior to their promotion, and few are trained afterward. Field training programs for supervisors and managers could be very beneficial. Such programs can also reduce the effects of negligence.

Probation. This is a legal right that has seldom been employed properly, but it can challenge recruits to maintain their drive. It is during this period that the manager can make the most knowledgeable and intelligent choice of who has the potential to be the best officer in the organization. In most instances, the decision to allow officers to enter career status and achieve tenure is made when they graduate from the academy; at that time, much of the information and evaluative material that is almost strictly job-related has not yet been gathered. During this period, supervisors must be conscious of their responsibility to continue the training of the recruit officers in certain one-on-one situations by critiquing their performance and offering advice.

The components of this systematic approach are not new but, taken in combination, where each part complements the others, they can help to put better prepared officers into the system and into individual police departments.

The Protection Circle

The alarm has been sounded often enough to warn police managers about the imminent dangers of lawsuits and adverse judgments. What is now needed is a description of a comprehensive liability protection program. Regardless of the level at which the manager operates, given the vulnerable areas that have to be improved and protected, as well as the burden of responsibility on the manager's shoulders, these steps will provide a framework on which a **liability protection program** can be built. Simply put, the protection circle, as it applies to liability, consists of three equal parts or phases— *direction, maintenance,* and *assessment*—operating in three consecutive time frames (see Figure 16-1):

1. Proactive: policy and support from the executive
2. Active: training and supervision
3. Reactive: discipline and evaluation

There is no way that policy can be effective without training and discipline. Each function must flow from and be consistent with the one that precedes it, because the **protection**

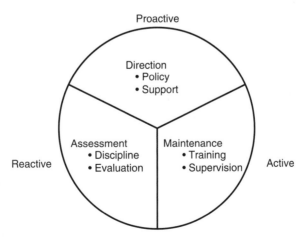

FIGURE 16-1 The protection circle.

circle is a combination of policies, training, and discipline integrated so that each follows, supports, and then improves the next while indicating changes necessary to improve the overall process.

To expand on the protection circle, and to lay out a series of steps that will, if followed, make it possible for concerned police managers to assess their danger and react accordingly, it is necessary to start with the chief, the top-level manager. The chief must:

1. Be knowledgeable, stay informed, keep abreast of trends and precedents, and read the literature. Identify agencies that are trendsetters and regularly ask for their policies, find out what they are changing, and start a dialogue with their chiefs.

2. Identify the areas of greatest concern for liability, preferably after completing a job task analysis of personnel. List the areas that produce the most lawsuits, both for the agency and for others in the area, and track the general trends around the country. These areas might include firearms training, supervision, medical assistance, defensive tactics, arrest procedures, and pursuit driving.

3. Make an annual review of policies, practices, and procedures with respect to these areas of liability. Simple changes in policy language may be enough to avoid a lawsuit—or at least eliminate the chief from it—if they are coupled with some training and appropriate discipline. Match the areas of greatest concern—the critical tasks—with policies, practices, and procedures and ask whether all these elements are articulated adequately (i.e., what personnel must do, whether the practices are described in the manner desired, and whether the procedures are the best that the state of the art can offer). If the chief is not completely satisfied, he or she can make changes where necessary.

4. Identify the standards of care with regard to these critical tasks. It is against these standards that actions will be judged by comparing them with recognized, accepted performance levels in both emergency and routine circumstances. Check state statutes to see what they require. Review the policies of other departments, literature, court cases, and reliable experts on these topics.

5. At this point, have the services of dependable legal counsel available—an attorney who is familiar with this topic—who can offer expert legal advice and will be able to look after the department's interests. It profits little to hire an attorney who is unfamiliar with this topic. Your attorney must work on your policies and must be familiar with the demands of your profession, your personnel, and current legal thinking.

6. Prepare written directives for the police department, using a format that includes definitions and states pertinent policy in the clearest, most direct language, making sure that related policies are reviewed and changed accordingly, where they are affected by these revisions.

7. Train personnel accordingly. Simultaneously with the training itself, document the qualifications of instructors. Do not allow someone to train just because he or she is

"available" or has "always done it." Be critical of training methods and require written lesson plans, which should follow training guides developed along with the new major policies on such matters as deadly force, high-speed chases, and medical attention for those taken into custody. Managers need to be careful that the right way of doing something is emphasized and that inappropriate or wrong methods are clearly indicated. They must be particularly careful about documenting everything pertaining to the training, such as reviewing attendance-taking procedures, whether by roll call, sign-in, or having the instructor take attendance. It is advisable to give tests (competency-based examinations) of one sort or another to ensure that the training is adequate.

8. Keep everything current—instructors' qualifications, lesson plans, and their contents, which can become outdated because of new state laws and new policies.

9. Conform discipline to policy and training. Make sure that it is consistent and progressive. The manager must be certain that records are kept of disciplinary actions for all policy violations. Checking disciplinary records can be used to review the effectiveness of policy and training. An increase in the number of disciplinary incidents might indicate the need for revision of the policy or for additional emphasis in training.

10. Keep in contact with professional groups by maintaining an active membership and demanding that they provide professional assistance. The police manager can also work closely with other police departments and exchange copies of policies and procedures, thereby producing model policies or adopting uniform policies. Regional or statewide policies are easier to defend, because they indicate a more general consensus of professional opinion on what should be required; on the other hand, it is more difficult to have expert witnesses develop standards and have them imposed by the courts. The manager must realize that police agencies can no longer afford the luxury of not cooperating. As in other things, there is strength in unity. All this can be done without sacrificing autonomy.

11. Make the next year one of consciousness raising on the subject of civil liability. Lay out a plan of attack—a training plan with goals and objectives for the whole department. The plan, for example, can provide for two days of **liability training** for everyone, with additional days in high-liability areas. Task forces and study groups can be formed to examine practices and procedures in the department on an ongoing basis. Incidents in the **high-liability areas** should be reviewed as training examples. Personnel can be debriefed on these incidents and the department can gain much value from them. Special attention can be paid to the supervisors, and it can be made undeniably clear that they have direct responsibility for the conduct of their subordinates.

Although these steps will not eliminate lawsuits, they may help to protect the police manager from liability.

Training in the Future

Two important trends will soon make greater demands on the law enforcement profession and its training system. Although tremendous progress has been made in the past 15 years in police officer training, too much emphasis has been placed on the quantitative process and not enough on the qualitative one. We are currently entering a time when, for a number of reasons (especially lawsuits and adverse judgments), much more emphasis will be placed on the qualitative side of training.

The courts themselves are giving the law enforcement profession credit for a higher quality of training than actually exists. In the immediate future, the courts may—in addition to a monetary damage award—order that the police agency submit a 40-hour training program that is acceptable to the court. They may further demand that all personnel go through this training within a certain period.

It is preferable that the police chief understand these developments and take action to improve the local training academies (by active participation on advisory boards, elimination of improper techniques, assignment of the best personnel to the training function, and elevating the status of training) than to have to live with the consequences of inaction. An action that agencies can take to help present the case that they have worked toward more professionalism, and can document high standards of professionalism, is to seek accreditation.

Accreditation

Accreditation is a process in which an institution or an organization is granted approval by a review board after specific requirements have been met. As with hospitals, colleges, law schools and medical schools, the law enforcement accreditation process was established to ensure the public that quality services are delivered by professionals meeting high standards.

Although the law enforcement accreditation process is voluntary, agencies involved in this process invite inspection, in which the organization and its programs are judged against a mandatory set of standards.

Compliance with these standards is verified by professionals in similar organizations, serving as a peer review. The accreditation process provides an evaluation of an agency and its programs, encouraging constant improvement.

Origins of the National Accreditation Process

In 1979, a seed was planted by four predominant groups in the law enforcement profession: The International Association of Chiefs of Police (IACP), The National Sheriffs Association (NSA), The National Organization of Black Law Enforcement Executives (NOBLE), and The Police Executive Research Forum (PERF). These groups facilitated the creation of the Commission for Accreditation of Law Enforcement Agencies, more commonly known as CALEA (1998).

Approximately 1,000 national accreditation standards presently exist as a challenge for contemporary agencies to meet and exceed. These performance standards were not created arbitrarily, but are the result of multi-year task force efforts from such significant research efforts as:

- The Challenge of Crime in a Free Society (Presidents Commission, 1967)
- "Police" (The National Advisory Commission on Criminal Justice Standards and Goals, 1973)
- Standards Relating to the Urban Police Function (American Bar Association, 1972)

These national standards focus on significant organizational areas such as:

- Law Enforcement Roles, Responsibilities and Relationships
- Organization, Management, and Administration
- The Personnel Structure
- The Personnel Process
- Law Enforcement Operations
- Operations Support
- Traffic Operations
- Prisoner and Court-Related Activities
- Auxiliary and Technical Services

Benefits of Accreditation

The accreditation process provides dynamic, recurring benefits. Beyond reduced liability from possible civil lawsuits, CALEA accreditation offers more inter-agency accountability, greater government official support and added community orientation (CALEA, 2012a).

Specifically, the accreditation process benefits the police manager in the following ways:

- Requiring an in-depth review of every aspect of the organization, management, operations and administration, to include:
  - Establishment of agency goals and objectives with provisions for periodic updating.
  - Re-evaluation of whether agency resources are directed toward accomplishment of the agency goals, objectives, and mission.
  - Re-evaluation of agency policies and procedures.
  - Correction of internal deficiencies and inefficiencies before they become public problems.
- The accreditation standards provide norms against which agency performance can be measured and monitored over time.
- Accreditation provides an organization with a source and flow of information about exemplary policies, procedures and projects.

- Accreditation standards provide neutral guidelines for developing strong budget justifications, especially for personnel and their allocation across functions and activities.

Officers in an accredited agency also benefit, because:

- Agency personnel benefit by having all policy and procedures available and in written form.
- Accreditation standards strive to insure that personnel systems are in accord with professional standards, and are both fair and equitable.
- Employee morale is positively affected by increased confidence in the effectiveness and efficiency of the agency.
- Accreditation policies address officer safety issues and provide for adequate training and equipment of the officers.
- The agency is compelled to operate within specific guidelines. It is accountable to the Commission. The agency must stay in compliance with the standards to retain its accreditation.
- Accreditation is a coveted award that symbolizes professionalism, excellence, and competence. Employees take pride in their agency.

A community served by an accredited agency benefits:

- By realizing the agency's commitment to professionalism by adherence to a body of standards.
- Community leaders and members are assured of a commitment to high-quality services facilitated by effective and responsive policies and procedures.
- An accredited agency proffers a commitment to the community by providing a broad range of programs, such as crime prevention and disaster preparedness.

Relationship to Liability

The benefits of seeking accreditation and adhering to a professional set of standards have a direct relationship to positively addressing the many significant areas of law enforcement liability. By voluntarily creating policies, procedures, and mechanisms addressing such high-risk and high liability areas as use of deadly and non-deadly force, vehicular pursuits, arrest, and search and seizure, the police manager is proactively affecting legal vulnerability.

Various standards relating to police pursuits mandate the creation and implementation of directives requiring personnel to evaluate pursuit circumstances, responsibilities of pursuing officers and supervisors, roadblocks, termination of pursuits and even after-action critiques.

National standards further require written directives that define the legally mandated authority of agency personnel, procedures for assuring compliance with all applicable constitutional requirements, procedures for search and seizure, use of lethal and less-than-lethal force, and demonstrated, documented proficiency in use of force applications.

National accreditation standards address not only operational areas of liability, but administrative and managerial areas as well. Various areas of vicarious liability, embracing negligent retention, failure to train, failure to supervise, and similar areas are addressed by accreditation standards. Mandatory standards requiring a codified disciplinary process, as well as stringent requirements for recruitment selection and training of personnel, further help to greatly diminish an agency's liability.

By voluntarily meeting the mandatory standards, an agency reduces the likelihood of vicarious liability suits, with some organizations actually realizing reduced liability insurance costs (CALEA, 2010a). Additionally, CALEA's website states, "(M)any agencies report a decline in legal actions against them, once they become accredited (CAELA, 2010a, para. 2).

Agency Participation

Even with the benefits to be realized from accreditation, including a proactive approach to diminishing agency liability, only a small percentage of departments nationwide have actively pursued national accreditation. With state and local agencies numbering more than 17,000, fewer than 1000 agencies, or less than six percent, have attained or are pursuing national accreditation (CALEA, 2011).

Some agencies elect to seek accreditation from state level commissions. Six states (Florida, New York, South Carolina, Pennsylvania, Virginia and Wisconsin) have state law enforcement accreditation processes (Law Enforcement Accreditation Consultants, 2011) However, the majority of accredited agencies receive national accreditation from CALEA. The CALEA client database reveals that the Midwest and Southeastern regions lead the nation in accredited agencies (CALEA, 2010b).

Why such a small number? Becoming accredited requires a sincere commitment by the police executive. It requires a commitment of staff resources to develop and codify policies and procedures over a multi-year period. It requires a budgetary commitment to procure the required equipment for personnel and the operations of all functional units of the organization. It requires a personal and professional commitment by the police manager to pursue excellence throughout the agency, by meeting and exceeding the national standards. Commitment must be obtained from governmental leaders to support the budgetary needs related to facilities, manpower allocation, and training.

The police manager must relinquish varying degrees of autonomy and power, especially as it relates to recruitment, selection and promotion of personnel, to strive for fair and equitable personnel and disciplinary systems.

Achieving accreditation is neither easy nor inexpensive. As case law relating to police liability continues to evolve, and governments strive to successfully address risk management issues, the number of agencies pursuing accreditation will increase.

Many law enforcement agencies have formed accreditation coalitions within their respective states, such as the Fla-PAC (Florida Police Accreditation Coalition, 1998). Fla-PAC is composed of agencies seeking either state or national law enforcement accreditation or correctional accreditation. Many agencies seek all three certifications. Members of these coalitions share in policy development, and stay informed of relevant case law that affects their operations and liability. Thirty states have established accreditation coalitions (Mitchell, 1995).

The Accreditation Process

The formal accreditation process consists of five phases:

- Application
- Self-Assessment

This is perhaps the most difficult phase. An agency may spend from one to three years preparing policies and procedures, completing facility modifications and construction, and general equipment acquisition to comply with accreditation standards and prepare for the formal inspection.

The police executive may take various approaches to completing the self-assessment process. Some agencies designate a small group or an individual with completing the entire process, including policy development, which is submitted to the CEO for final approval. A majority of agency personnel have minimal participation in, or familiarity with, the accreditation and policy process. Accreditation may represent only a word or an ambiguous process to them.

Some executives involve all levels of their organizations in the development of policies and procedures, and provide an educational opportunity to their personnel about how their components function in relation to the entire process.

- On-Site Assessment

When an organization completes its self-inspection, an inspection team consisting of professional peers, representing the accreditation commission, spends days reviewing the agency's compliance with mandated standards. The inspection team provides immediate feedback to the police executive, as well as written reports of its findings to the accreditation commission. The agency must correct any findings of non-compliance by this team in order to receive commission approval for the awarding of accreditation.

- Commission Review

The assessment team's final report is submitted to the commission when all applicable standards and required activities are in compliance. The commission then schedules a hearing during one of its quarterly meetings, at which an agency's CEO is invited to be present at the review of the final report. Testimony is given by agency personnel, assessors, commission staff, and others. If the commission decides that an agency is in compliance with the applicable standards, accredited status is awarded for a three-year period.

- Maintaining Compliance and Reaccreditation

To maintain its accredited status, the accredited agency must remain in compliance with the standards. Annual reports to the commission are required (CALEA, 2010c).

As an example of achieving and maintaining compliance with CALEA accreditation standards, agencies are required to accomplish a variety of time-sensitive activities, such as those noted in Figure 16-2.

Conclusion

The police manager's ability to manage liability is the direct result of his or her knowledge of the accepted standards and the initiation of liability protection programs in the police department. Nothing can prevent managers from being sued, but managers can take steps to protect themselves and their department from liability.

Liability can be seen as both an enemy and an ally. It can be a moving force for great change, which might not take place were there not the danger of liability. It can exert tremendous leverage on the system and, if properly countered, can be a force that helps to initiate needed change and increased professionalization of law enforcement. With the proper resources, it can be managed.

Responsibility	Activity/Purpose	Frequency/ Distribution	Reference
High-Risk Incident Commander	Review of hostage barricaded person plan	Annually, January	CALEA 46.1.5
Special Investigations Commander	Crime Analysis Analytical Reports	Weekly, Sheriff, Undersheriff, Sector Cmdrs	CALEA 15.1.1(e)
Fiscal Mgt., Division Mgr.	Independent audit of agency's fiscal activities	Annually, Sheriff, Undersheriff, Accreditation	CALEA 17.4.1.,
Criminal Investigations Commander	Inspection to insure adherence to control of procedures for property/evidence	Biennially Sheriff, Undersheriff, Accreditation	CALEA 84.1.6.
Professional Standards Division Commander	Analysis of use of force incidents to indicate training needs and/or policy modifications	Annually/Dec. Command Staff	CALEA 1.3.13

FIGURE 16-2 Example of accreditation time-sensitive activities. *From Orange County, Florida Sheriff's Office (1996). Time Sensitive Activities, General Order 208. Orlando, FL.*

Accreditation exists to make its standards available to the police agencies that want them. Furthermore, police managers should not confuse uniformity with lack or loss of autonomy. With lack of uniformity and subsequent imposition of standards from without, there is a loss of autonomy. Uniformity to a degree can lighten the burden of police managers, because they then will be able to rest assured that broad segments of the profession will have similar standards. Uniform policies, standards, and accreditation are ideas whose time has come, and they will go a long way toward helping police agencies in the courtroom.

References

American Bar Association Project on Standards for Criminal Justice. (1972). *Standards relating to the urban police function*. New York: Institute of Judicial Administration.

Avery, M., & Rudovsky, D. (1980). *Police misconduct: Law and litigation*. Chicago, IL: Clark Boardman Callaghan.

Commission on Accreditation for Law Enforcement Agencies. (2010a). Law Enforcement Program: The Benefits. Retrieved from http://www.calea.org/content/law-enforcement-program-benefits

Commission on Accreditation for Law Enforcement Agencies. (2010b). CALEA Client Database. Retrieved from http://www.calea.org/content/calea-client-database

Commission on Accreditation for Law Enforcement Agencies. (2010c) Law Enforcement Program: Process. Retrieved from http://www.calea.org/content/law-enforcement-program-process

Commission on Accreditation for Law Enforcement Agencies. (1998, February 7). *About CALEA*. http://www.calea.org Retrieved from CALEA Online.

Florida Police Accreditation Coalition. (1998, January 30). *Florida Police Accreditation Coalition Introduction*. www.fla-pac.org Retrieved from FLA-PAC Online.

Law Enforcement Accreditation Consultants, Inc. (2011). Frequently Asked Questions. Retrieved July 18, 2012. Available online at http://www.leac.net/faq.html

Mitchell, Stephen S. W (1995). *Accreditation Manager Training Manual*. Alexandria, VA: CALEA.

National Advisory Committee on Criminal Justice Standards and Goals. (1973). *Police*. Washington DC: USGPO.

Orange County, Florida, Sheriff's Office. (1993). *Reports Required by Accreditation, General Order 201*. Orlando, FL.

Orange County, Florida, Sheriff's Office. (1996). *Time Sensitive Activities, General Order 208*. Orlando, FL.

President's Commission on Law Enforcement and the Administration of Justice. (1967). *The challenge of crime in a free society*. Washington, DC: USGPO.

Ross, D. L. (2013). *Civil liability in criminal justice* (6th ed.). Boston: Elsevier/Anderson Publishing.

Discussion Questions

1. Why should the average police officer be aware of the rules of civil liability?
2. How can the protection circle best be applied to a small police department?
3. What can police departments do to avoid civil liability in the future?

4. Assuming you agree to seek accreditation, how would you go about meeting the standards?
5. Which are the most important standards?
6. Which are the least important standards?

17

Ethics for the 21st Century

LEARNING OBJECTIVES

1. The student will understand the different theories of ethical systems.
2. The student will be able to relate an ethical system to an effective leadership style.
3. The student will be able to develop a principle, define an action, and relate the answer to an ethical system.

Introduction

Police managers are drafters, designers, and implementers of the ethical standards of their departments. By their behavior, they establish norms that become standards within the department. Because other police managers throughout the profession are influenced, they are able to raise the ethical standards of the profession itself. These standards become the basis for making decisions, hiring personnel, judging daily actions, and demonstrating the police department's values, beliefs, and principles. High standards will continually raise the level of professionalization.

Ethics are defined as principles of correct or good behavior. They are the standards governing the conduct of the members of an agency, a profession, a community. They are, in essence, a contract between the police manager and personnel within the police department, the city government, and the community.

There are numerous purposes for developing strong ethical standards. High standards bring outcomes of credibility to the individual police agency. As a result, all members of the police department—sworn and non-sworn—are accepted by the community as helpers, protectors, and advisors. In many instances, people from the department become leaders within city government and the community. High standards produce social good for the community. By having a set of professional ethical standards, the police agency learns to be trusted and learns to trust.

As mentioned in Chapter 2, there is a difference between ethical and legal standards. **Legal standards** are those that are defined by the law. **Ethical standards** are those that are defined by a profession, a community, or an individual police manager in his or her leadership role. There are **moral standards** that are standards established on an individual basis, which may or may not have anything to do with the agency. Finally, there are **performance standards**. The police manager must prioritize these four sets of standards. In his or her role as a law enforcement official, implementation and adherence to legal standards always come first. Then there is the opportunity for the individual police manager to prioritize ethical, moral, and performance standards. This chapter explains the different theories of standards of ethics and the way in which each of these theories has an effect on the leadership role and how power is used to gain the specific outcomes desired by the police manager.

In the leadership role, the police manager is influenced in his or her ethical conduct by a series of factors. The behavior of his or her superiors plays an important role in determining the limitations of behavior that can be attached to any standard. In addition, in many instances the professional ethical standards of other department heads can play a role. For example, if the personnel department believes that people should be promoted with a strong emphasis on race or sex, and police executives believe that the best qualified people should be appointed to supervisory and management positions, a conflict arises as to which ethical standard should apply to the police department.

The practices of the law enforcement community in the police manager's region have a strong influence on the standards that the police chief may be able to establish. For example, if the police chief wants only college graduates as police officers and yet he or she is the first chief in that geographical area to impose such a standard, there will again be a conflict, especially if the department is not able to attract a sufficient number of qualified college graduates to meet its needs.

The **moral climate** of the community also affects the ethical conduct of the chief. For example, some communities believe that having police officers act as school crossing guards is important. However, the police department may find that such a standard is not cost-effective and is an inefficient use of personnel. The same might be true of walking beats in a downtown area. However, because of the influence of such groups as parents or business owners, the agency might be ordered to perform these tasks.

We now will examine five ethical systems: (1) utilitarian ethics, (2) rule ethics, (3) social contract ethics, (4) justice ethics, and (5) personalistic ethics. Figure 17-1 shows the relationship of these systems.

Ethical Systems

Utilitarian Ethics

The **utilitarian ethical theory** was developed by Jeremy Bentham in 1789. The rightness or authority that the police manager would use is to concentrate on the consequences of his or her behavior. Police managers who emphasize utilitarian ethics determine whether their action or another's action is right or wrong by concentrating on the consequences of the behavior. Any action taken by members of the department from this ethical point of view is valid if the sum total of its outcome is greater than the sum total of negative effects produced by the action itself. This ethical system emphasizes the role of happiness. In theory, if someone desires to do something that will bring happiness to him or herself as well as others, he or she is acting in an ethical manner.

Ethical Systems	Proponent	Rightness Is Determined By	Leadership	Power	Decision-Making Strategy
Utilitarian ethics	John Stuart Mill (1806-1873) Jeremy Bentham (1748-1832)	Considering its consequences	Manipulator	Coalitions through conning	Test for results
Rule ethics	Immanuel Kant (1724-1804) John Locke (1632-1704)	Laws and standards	Bureaucratic	Position in agency	Test for procedures
Social contract ethics	Jean-Jacques Rousseau (1712-1778)	Customs and norms of a particular community or group	Professional	Knowledge and experience	Test for organizational values
Justice ethics	Aristotle (384-322 B.C.) John Rawls (1921-)	Ensuring that all receive opportunities and fair share of output	Team	Coalition by groups, associations, employees	Test for agreement of others
Personalistic ethics	Martin Buber (1878-1965)	One's conscience	Transforming	Empowerment	Test for personal conviction

FIGURE 17-1 Ethical systems.

Rule Ethics

Rule ethics was developed by Immanuel Kant (1963) around 1800. The rightness of someone's behavior is determined entirely by laws and standards. For example, if there is a law demanding that the police department perform certain acts, then under rule ethics there is no room for compromise. In a larger legal, theoretical sense, industry is not necessarily governed nor does it need specific authority to bring about changes. Industry is free to undertake many endeavors unless it is in some way constrained by the law—for example, the need to be licensed or to be open to certain kinds of inspections. Government, on the other hand, can only operate when there are specific laws that grant authority to that facet of government. For example, the police department could not operate unless there were specific state statutes granting cities, towns, and counties the authority to form police departments, and each police agency must be formed by a specific law passed by the county commissioners, city council, or town board. Because of this philosophical approach to the need for laws and standards prior to the undertaking of any large government endeavor, such as police, fire, or public works, in government we find a heavier emphasis on rule ethics.

The negative feature of rule ethics is that too much emphasis can be placed on very definitive rules and, as a result, freedom of judgment is taken away from members of the police department. If the city council adopts a rule that says police officers are to work certain shifts, it has taken away from the discretion of the police manager the assignment of personnel to different shift schedules to meet the goals of the department. The same holds true if the chief of police designates that personnel within the agency must reach certain decisions such as shaking doors on the midnight shift or the manner in which equipment must be kept in the patrol units. This takes away the freedom of choice from the individual officers. Sometimes police chiefs correctly view the need to pass rules in order to provide for the ultimate goal of safety. An example would be mandating the wearing of bullet-proof vests by all department personnel whenever they are performing their assigned functions in the public arena. This would include not only sworn officers, but also commanders, investigators, and possibly even support personnel such as crime scene technicians.

Social Contract Ethics

Social contract ethics is based on the theory of Jean-Jacques Rousseau (1947), which he developed about 1760. According to social contract theory, the rightness of behavior in policing is determined by the customs and norms of the department, the city or government, and the community itself. In many instances, under social contract theory, guidelines are not in any written rule or procedure, but become custom, which may be an unwritten but strongly supported tradition. For the individual police manager, this may include such issues as which civic groups are important for the police leader to join and how to contribute in an effective manner. Under this theory of ethics, each person must act under the authority of the general will of all people. For example, if the agency has a strong tradition of police executives attending or not attending shift parties and a new chief or a newly promoted executive decides to attend the next shift party, his or her presence in one instance would be viewed as a positive act, but in the other he or she may be viewed as breaking the custom and therefore may be viewed as having negative intentions. The general will of people within the police department will serve as the ultimate standard for determining what actions the individual officers should take. Sometimes social contract ethics come into play when the question of responsibility of an individual officer to advise superiors of improper conduct by a fellow officer is raised.

Justice Ethics

Justice ethics was first taught as a theory of ethics by Aristotle in approximately 340 B.C.E. According to this theory, the rightness of any behavior is determined by ensuring that all persons receive opportunities and a fair share of whatever resources might be available. Police managers who espouse this theory of ethics may believe strongly in seeing to it that all people receive basically the same dollar amount in a specific pay raise or may demand that if certain personnel have special privileges, such as a take-home car, then all personnel within that class of employment (for example, sworn members of the department) would also be assigned a take-home vehicle. Justice ethics in many instances is defined as a democratic principle. That is, it is a responsibility of government to provide some kind of service to all persons within the community. As a result, police executives may find themselves having to allocate resources to geographical areas of their city or county even though there are very few calls for service or crime is very negligible in those areas. In some communities, police departments are obligated to have walking beats at each shopping mall solely because there is a crime problem at one mall and if something is done for one, it must also be done for all others.

Personalistic Ethics

Personalistic ethics was first espoused by Martin Buber (1955) in 1930. The rightness of any behavior under this ethical system is determined as adhering to one's conscience. This theory emphasizes the truth solely in the eyes of the beholder, and it is based on human existence, not necessarily on knowledge of what may be provided. Individual personal convictions serve as the ultimate standard for determining what the individual police manager should do. The police chief who strongly believes that it is a waste of taxpayers' dollars to put walking beats in the malls and downtown may be willing to be dismissed solely because of the principle of effective use of taxpayers' money. Police executives are faced with dealing with people who emphasize personalistic ethics over rule ethics. Police officials must protect abortion clinics regardless of what their personal feelings are concerning the issue of abortion; they must emphasize adherence to the law. The people who are demonstrating may be relying on personalistic ethics and place what they personally consider their conscience to be above the law. As a result, there is a confrontation and it is almost impossible to convince such people that the law is the guide that should be adhered to in such demonstrations. As a result, the police official must be aware that personalistic ethics may not only create a conflict, but also require the use of special resources and tactics to resolve the issue, as the demonstrators may have a strict reliance on their own individual conscience.

Leadership and Ethics

Leadership styles may be emphasized differently depending on the ethical system employed.

Utilitarian Ethics

Utilitarian ethics provide a leadership style consistent with the autocratic manager. This individual may use manipulation to achieve the results that he or she demands. Manipulation in and of itself is not always negative. It means the ability to influence someone else's behavior without disclosing the true intent. For example, the police executive may decide that certain officers should attend certain training programs. He or she then brings these people into the office and explains the benefit that could be achieved by attending such a program—for example, the first-line supervisory program at the local community college. However, one of the major intentions behind this executive's move is to see to it that certain personnel that he or she has selected in advance will do better in the promotional process and, as a result, he or she would be viewed as an effective leader.

Generally speaking, people who emphasize utilitarian ethics in their leadership role test for results and concentrate on such results. Therefore, the outcome that they achieve may be positive in one area but may hold numerous negative outcomes for which the police manager has not prepared. To the manipulator, the most important requirement for success in the police department is power. He believes that without power, there can be no authority, without authority there can be no discipline, and without discipline there is difficulty maintaining order, systems goals, and in making effective decisions on a daily basis. As a result, police managers who emphasize utilitarian ethics maintain this ethical stance by developing support prior to implementing a decision.

Another example of leadership in this ethical system is when an investigator decides that it is proper to give immunity to someone who has committed a breaking-and-entering offense so that the investigator may solve a robbery case. The investigator may believe that his or her superiors will not support the decision and therefore will manipulate the decision by going first to the people of higher command who would be responsible for assisting in such decisions later on. An example would be a discussion with the local district attorney or state attorney. As a result, the investigator presents the proposal to the police supervisor or manager with an emphasis on having already spoken to the prosecutor, who was solidly behind the proposal.

Rule Ethics

Police leaders who emphasize rule ethics relate very much to the **avoidance style of management**. Most of what they say or do depends on the principles of a good bureaucracy. They believe that the police department's organizational structure should emphasize control over coordination or communication. They rely heavily on the position that they hold within the police department to establish an ethical standard. Consider the police chief, who, working his or her way up through the department for many years, never said much about a dress code, yet on being promoted to the position of chief of police, immediately passed a general order establishing a strict dress code within the department. Police executives who follow this ethical system make decisions based on written procedures. If an officer behaves in a way that is inconsistent with the department's norms or customs, the officer is not disciplined, but instead, a new rule is written so that the next person who acts in the same way can be disciplined because a new rule has been established.

Police executives who support rule ethics usually emphasize a promotion system in which seniority and past achievement weigh heavily, and rewards such as salary are based on the position that the people hold within the hierarchy, not on the contribution they make to the overall goals of the police department. They would, for example, demand that salaries of non-sworn personnel never be higher than sworn personnel of equal status within the department, thereby always guaranteeing that sworn personnel are considered more important to the agency. The emphasis here is based on rules and regulations, not on the ability or contribution of the individual.

Social Contract Ethics

Police managers who emphasize social contract ethics are sometimes referred to as implementing a "professional" style of leadership. Many of the principles underlying this ethical approach were later espoused by Peter Drucker in his numerous texts on management. The principles that the professional police manager strives to achieve are the department's objectives and goals through the effective and efficient deployment of all resources, including money, people, and materials. Police managers who emphasize social contract ethics rely on knowledge and experience but do not limit this knowledge and experience to themselves. In fact, they have a tendency to seek additional knowledge and to emphasize other people's knowledge and experience in both the establishment of purposes and the action to be taken. There is a heavy emphasis on **department values** in such a police department and, as a result, the police executives, in deciding the evaluation of individual actions, will rely on the intent of the action as opposed to the rule that may have been violated. Police executives who follow this system would praise an officer who bypassed a rule to achieve a stated principle. An example would be an officer who orders the immediate replacement of the front door of a home that had accidentally or through error been served with a search warrant. As a result, the citizen feels good, and the department—although rules may have been bypassed—evaluates such an action based on the positive intent that the officer had in performing his or her duty.

In many instances, dress codes that exist within police departments arise out of social contract ethics. When personnel dress in a professional manner, even though a specific rule, such as the wearing of a hat, may be violated, the personnel are supported for their behavior, and in many instances the rule, which may have been unenforced over the years, is finally removed from the procedure manual. One of the features that police managers may find negative in following this system is how to deal with personnel within the department who believe that some of the rules and traditions should be changed. Obviously, when a police official believes strongly in the system, he or she will allow personnel to speak and to be supported in that right. In many instances, police officials who use this system emphasize a compromising leadership style.

Justice Ethics

Police managers who emphasize justice ethics rely heavily on **team management** practices. They acquire authority and power by involving numerous groups in the overall purpose of the department. This coalition, which is formed by integrating numerous purposes, can be an effective way of bringing about an improvement in the ethical standards of a police department. This democratic principle can be seen in many instances by the manner in which city councils designate their budget or in the way a department will be required or not required to emphasize an affirmative action program so that all minorities such as women, African-Americans, Hispanics, and Asians are included within the department. The negative feature of an emphasis on this ethical system is that sometimes pressure groups become powerful within the department itself. An example would be if the Police Benevolent Association or Fraternal Order of Police began to dictate what the overall policies or ethical standards of the department should be. Police managers, in implementing this ethical system, rely on testing for agreement from the groups who are responsible for implementing ethical standards.

Personalistic Ethics

The main principle behind this form of leadership is to allow people within the agency to become better human beings. They emphasize transforming themselves and others into better people than they originally thought they could be. Police managers who implement personalistic ethics rely on a relationship between themselves and others within the department. The personal contact and adherence to the leader's high standards for the department are strictly enforced. This leader receives great joy from the successes of others and takes every opportunity to praise the personnel of the police department. The police chief who is thinking of implementing a new personnel allocation system under personalistic ethics would involve the men and women of the department who must implement the process and be committed to its objectives. The negative feature is that the manager empowers other people, some of whom may not be able to respond effectively to the new degree of authority and responsibility placed on them; however, the police leader would give such people time to develop, provide them with the necessary knowledge, and be in tune with their specific desires for personal growth and how that personal growth affects the overall growth of the police department.

Managing Subordinates: Ethical Concerns

It is vital to a law enforcement agency's morale to have managers using ethical guidelines to influence their decision making, but it is just as important that managers be vigilant of unethical behavior among their subordinates. A police manager who tolerates unethical behavior among his or her officers risks an increase in this behavior.

Sherman's research (1982) concluded that police officers who became involved in serious deviance typically began with lower levels of deviance. He referred to this progression as an officer's **moral career**. The first consideration of this progression is referred to as contingencies. **Contingencies** are social pressures exerted on officers that influence their attitudes and behavior toward corruption. They do not dictate an officer's behaviors, but they can influence the behaviors. For example, if an officer sees her sergeant accepting gratuities, the ethical acceptability of that behavior is transmitted to the officer. The second step is the officer's **moral experience**. This can be compared to a sudden awakening to corruption or opportunities for corruption that can no longer be denied. This realization or opportunity forces the officer to decide what his or her **options** are. These range from not reacting at all, to escaping the ethical dilemma through a transfer or leaving law enforcement altogether, to blowing the whistle on the corruption. This final option would, of course, cause problems for the officer and potentially embarrass the entire department. Finally, those officers who become involved in corruption in the line of duty, form *apologia*. **Apologia** refers to the rationalization and justification that an officer makes to neutralize the cognitive dissonance that results from acting unethically. An example of this would be an officer deciding that accepting gratuities is tolerable because no one is harmed.

It is important to note that police officers do not enter their career fields to be corrupt, and most do not become unethical. Sherman's explanation demonstrates how the officers who do become corrupt do so gradually and incrementally. The first step into unethical behavior tends to be the easiest to resist. Each subsequent step becomes slightly easier to take because the line of unethical behavior has already been crossed. Therefore, it is important that police managers take steps to guide their officers' actions. Part of this is a clear and consistent intolerance for unethical behavior, but it can also consist of specific policies dealing with ethical quandaries that officers may face. This includes guidance on issues which young officers could face in their first ethical dilemmas.

Gratuities and Graft

Many of the most common types of unethical police behavior come from gratuities and graft. It is important for a police manager to be aware of these questionable behaviors so he or she can recognize them among subordinates.

Gratuities

Gratuities are low-level gifts that citizens give police officers. This can be as minor as free meals or coffee for police officers to giving holiday gifts. Gratuities create dilemmas for police because there is no way to determine whether the gift-giving civilians are trying to curry favors that they can exchange for police assistance later, or whether they genuinely just want to do something special for a given officer. Of course, if officers frequent a restaurant for the free meals, the owner is guaranteeing a degree of police coverage even if he or she never asks the police for a favor. This can create problems for police managers who may have to answer phone calls from other restaurant owners who complain about the officers providing extra coverage to their competitor's establishment.

Note that despite any overt nefarious intent, the acceptance of gratuities can create the impression of special treatment. This can erode public confidence in the police. This is not to say that gratuities are always bad. Kania (1988) notes the benefits of informal relationships resulting from conversations with shop owners over free cups of coffee. The important thing for police managers to remember is that there are complex layers of ethical issues that arise from something as simple as gratuities. If a department is going to allow gratuities, police managers must be prepared to watch their officers closely enough to make certain that the behavior does not lead to the next step of corruption. They must also be prepared to answer public concerns about such a practice.

Graft

Graft is a much more serious type of corruption that is typically broken into two layers of seriousness: clean graft and dirty graft. Graft refers to the acceptance of money by public officials to act or fail to act in specific situations. For police, this means officers accept money to enforce laws under specified circumstances, or fail to enforce the law under other circumstances. **Clean graft** refers to officers overlooking illegal behaviors in exchange for money. For example, a foot patrol officer may be asked to overlook gambling on his or her beat. In exchange for doing nothing, the officer receives bribes. **Dirty graft** occurs when police officers are more active in pursuit of bribe money. For example, extorting protection money from local criminals is dirty graft. Obviously, street level officers are not likely to share these types of corruption with their managers unless the managers have demonstrated a tolerance for such behavior. Still, being aware of potential graft can help a manager detect it if it does happen.

Duty Neglect

The nature of police work and its supervision allow subordinate officers many opportunities to engage in questionable practices. This includes variations of neglecting their duties. (See Figure 17-2.) Police discretion allows officers to work entire shifts, or multiple shifts, without showing tangible evidence of performance. If no tickets are written and no arrests made, there is little evidence that the officer was actively pursuing his or her duties. This does not mean that an officer did nothing; it just means documenting the

---

Both the law and ethical standards obligate those who hold public office to be faithful to their lawful duties. Three common failures are:

nonfeasance—the failure to perform one's duty by oversight or omission, usually inadvertent (willful nonfeasance typically will be considered malfeasance)

misfeasance—the wrongful performance of one's duties, usually in the form of making mistakes, not following procedures correctly, or other unintentional blunders

malfeasance—the intentional performance of an official act or use of one's official powers to achieve an end that is circumstantially illegal, harmful, and/or unjustified

FIGURE 17-2 **Neglect of one's duties.** *Source: Kania, R., & Davis, R. (2012). Managing criminal justice organizations. Boston: Elsevier / Anderson Publishing.*

officer's work can be difficult at times. The police manager needs to recognize that prolonged absence of productivity evidence may require further inquiry.

Policy versus Example

Making policies to eliminate unethical behavior among officers will never completely eliminate deviant acts by police. Unethical behavior cannot be legislated out of existence. However, policies and guidance concerning the moral dilemmas that officers will face can clarify behavioral expectations that new officers may be experiencing for the first time. For example, if a rookie officer has never been given a policy or any guidance on the subject, he or she may accept a gratuity without realizing it is an ethically questionable behavior. Therefore, it is important for police managers to prepare officers to act ethically in the line of duty.

WHY IT'S IMPORTANT

The issue of ethics is not always taken seriously, particularly in police work. Many police officers feel like they have to bend or break typical rules of acceptable behavior in dealing with the hardened criminals they face. Another consideration that shows up in policing, as well as in other occupations, is the belief that only token consideration of ethics is required. In general, we all tend to think of ourselves as ethical. As a result of this bias, we do not tend to think that we need to spend much time contemplating our own ethical place in the world. This kind of thinking can be dangerous because we may often justify our own actions even though others may find them unethical. Even Hitler believed his actions and values were morally acceptable while numerous other countries found them so reprehensible that they were willing to spend their soldiers' lives fighting against them.

This danger is particularly a concern for law enforcement personnel because of the added responsibilities that society grants them. Law enforcement personnel are the only members of society who are legally able to use force to gain compliance for verbal commands. They are the only people who can legally remove a person's liberty or search through a person's dwelling or belongings without the suspect's permission, albeit with other legal limitations.

Police managers should emphasize the importance of ethical self-examination among their officers as well as themselves. History has demonstrated that police managers who tolerate unethical practices among their subordinates will eventually find that various forms of corruption escalate to the point that they are hard to rein in. This often leads to agency-wide embarrassment and to the loss of jobs for a number of officers, including supervisors. Therefore, it is vital that police agencies emphasize ethical behavior at the officer selection stage of the hiring process, as well as throughout the careers of subordinate officers.

Conclusion

Each type of leader uses power differently. The manipulator develops coalitions that are not necessarily out in the open. The bureaucratic police chief relies on his or her position in the department. The professional police manager relies on knowledge and experience in the principles and methods of effective management. The team leader relies on his or her relationship with other groups that affect the ethical standards of the department. Finally, the transforming leader relies on the empowerment of others. Each of these styles makes a significant contribution to the overall development of ethical standards.

In some instances, the results are extremely important. In others, adherence to the laws and standards would tend to solidify the growth of the department. In yet other instances, customs and norms should be honored whenever possible and only changed on agreement with those affected. When all people receive opportunities and a fair share in how the department operates, they, too, raise their level of commitment. And finally, when individuals are able to go home at the end of each workday and be satisfied that their behavior is consistent with their individual conscience, you begin to have highly successful, happy, and productive police officers.

Sometimes people seek a simple set of guidelines in helping them to be considered ethical people or police managers. A simple set of guidelines has been developed and used by Lou Holtz (1999), who was University of Notre Dame's head football coach for many years. He has three very simple guidelines: (1) do what is right, (2) give it your best effort, and (3) treat others with dignity and respect. These three guidelines answer the three major questions that every police officer and employee will have of his or her manager. When you do what is right, you have answered the question, "Can I trust you?" When you do your best, you have answered the question, "Are you committed?" Finally, when you treat others with dignity and respect, you have answered the question, "Do you care for me?" Although these guidelines appear simplistic, in reality they work very effectively.

One way to help determine the ethical standards of the individual police manager, as well as the police department, is to see how he or she deals with some very specific issues. The issue of accountability is first. Are members of the agency held accountable for their behavior? Think about the police middle manager who has been ineffective in his or her position for years and yet no one holds this individual accountable for poor performance. The result is that the individual establishes a low standard that becomes the new standard for the police department. The second issue or question that is answered is, "How much public scrutiny are we willing to allow?" Police departments that emphasize an openness to the public are very rarely asked to provide or to support a civilian review board. On the other hand, when departments attempt to hide from public scrutiny, there seems to be a much stronger emphasis, especially from the news media, on getting the police department to be more open in every way. As a result, stronger influence is brought for the establishment of some form of civilian review.

The third issue deals with liability. Does the department support its personnel or does it automatically assume that there is liability just because someone has made an accusation against an officer or the department? How does the department deal with people who gripe, complain, and "blow the whistle"? If people bring forth ideas or a grievance that clearly shows that the department is operating in an inefficient or ineffective manner, is that individual chastised or praised?

The important answer to all these questions is that they allow any police department to be carefully evaluated as to its minimum and maximum ethical standards. We judge police leaders by their actions, not by their statements of intent. If their actions are unethical, they cannot withstand public scrutiny. By the same token, if they act consistently, with high ethical standards regardless of the system, they become leaders in the department, profession, and community.

References

Bentham, J. (1789). *An introduction to the principles of morals and legislation.* Oxford, England: Oxford Press.

Buber, M. (1955). *Between man and man.* Boston, MA: Beacon Press.

Holtz, L. (1999). *Winning every day: The game plan for success.* New York: HarperCollins.

Kania, R. (1988). Police acceptance of gratuities. *Criminal Justice Ethics, 7,* 37–49.

Kant, I. (1963). *Lectures on ethics.* New York: Harper and Row.

Rousseau, J.-J. (1947). *The social contract.* New York: Hafner Publishing Company.

Sherman, L. (1982). Learning police ethics. *Criminal Justice Ethics, 10,* 10–19.

Learning Exercise

Police managers have discovered that it is often easier to recruit and hire ethically minded officers than to try to train unethically minded officers into an ethical mindset.

- Develop an ethical scenario that could be included in the interview process for new police recruits.
- What other questions or probes would you ask to try to detect a potential recruit's ethical mindset?

Discussion Questions

For each of the following sets of facts, develop a principle (from Chapter 2), define the action to be taken, and identify the ethical system used in your answer.

1. People in your department are not allowed to exceed a certain number of overtime hours because of budget constraints. Your officers are so dedicated that they have been working more than the maximum but not submitting to be compensated for them.
2. You read in the paper that an officer in a neighboring community has been arrested and charged with showing pornographic literature to a minor. The arrested officer states that he has been having a homosexual affair with your Officer Jones. You ask Jones, and he admits that he is homosexual and intends to continue this behavior. You determine that Jones had nothing to do with the showing of pornographic literature to

the minor. You find that Jones's work is average to above average, he is never late, and he has never created any problems within your agency. About one-half of your officers come to you about Jones, 50 percent of those stating that they do not like the idea that they have to work with a homosexual, but the other 50 percent saying that it does not bother them at all.

3. Your captain, after securing your pledge of confidentiality, confides in you information that makes you realize that the city/county is violating its affirmative action responsibilities under the law. When you point out the problem, the captain says that, politically, you and he have no choice in the matter.

4. The established working hours are 8:30 A.M. to 5:15 P.M. with 45 minutes for lunch. You notice that people in one unit are leaving between 4:45 P.M. and 5:00 P.M. every day. You check on the work output of that unit and find that it is on schedule and of excellent quality. Other unit heads have mentioned the early departure pattern to you as an observation without saying whether they thought it was good or bad.

5. What ethical system primarily guides your ethical decisions? Why do you think that?

18 ⣿

The School Resource Officer Program: Establishing a Police Presence in Schools

LEARNING OBJECTIVES

1. The student will understand how to build a positive relationship with youths.
2. The student will understand the relationship of community relations and crime reduction to the mission of the school resource program.
3. The student will know how to implement a school resource officer program.
4. The student will know how to prepare for and investigate critical incidents.

Introduction

The law enforcement profession took a new turn at the close of the twentieth century that has continued into the new millennium. Police officers are now commonly deployed in public schools as part of *school resource officer* (SRO) programs. The National Association of School Resource Officers (as cited in Theriot, 2009) reports that this assignment became the fastest-growing type of law enforcement work during the 1990s and 2000s. This increase is largely attributable to a widespread belief that schools were becoming more violent. However, evidence from the University of Virginia's Youth Violence Project (2007) and the Department of Justice (Robers, Zhang & Truman, 2012) demonstrates that serious violent incidents have decreased since the mid- to early 1990s, with some occasional yearly fluctuations. Yet, as violent incidents at schools declined, high-profile shootings, such as the 1999 shooting at Columbine High School in Littleton, Colorado, which left 13 students and staff dead and 24 wounded, led to the popular belief that school crime rates were growing. As a result, more schools have deployed school resource officer programs. These programs are not in place solely to prevent critical incidents. They also allow law enforcement officers to be involved with children during the impressionable years when they are involved with academics and the school community.

There are multiple purposes or goals of the school resource officer program. Each is important but independent. Additionally, each facet serves different groups of the community, thus satisfying multiple entities. The main goals of the school resource officer program are:

1. to provide a safe learning environment for children
2. to build a positive relationship with youths
3. to provide an excellent community relations tool for the law enforcement agency
4. to provide crime prevention to youths by deterring them before they enter the age of criminal activity
5. to aid and protect the law enforcement agency from civil liability

Providing a Safe Learning Environment

Due to concerns over school violence and liability threats that accompany this concern, the safe school initiative must be a top priority of the school resource officer program. Initially, the establishment of a full-time police presence on campus assured that help was nearby in the event of an emergency. Additionally, there was a police presence to combat youth gang activity. At its inception, this mere police presence served its purpose. However, the rising public concern about school crime demands that the school resource officer make extra efforts to combat the threats that now exist on campuses.

The biggest threat to the safety of the children comes from those on the campus themselves. Students who have opened fire on other students regardless of the presence of police on campus have become a top priority for law enforcement agencies. The prevention, intervention, and response of law enforcement in the battle against school shooters must be aggressive and proactive. Police agencies can no longer assume that the presence of a school resource officer will prevent such a massacre. One successful protocol, that of the Orange County, Florida, Sheriff's Office, will be detailed later in this text. This protocol indicates an aggressive stance against school violence with a proven track record. This aggressive proactive mentality is now mandatory in the mission to ensure a safe learning environment for children.

Building a Positive Relationship with Youths

Part of the process of preventing children from starting a life of crime is building a trusting relationship between youths and law enforcement. Theoretically, if there is a positive law enforcement presence in the child's life, he or she will be less likely to turn to a life of crime. This objective is accomplished by the daily presence of law enforcement in the child's life at his or her school. Additionally, the presence of law enforcement at the school gives the child a place to turn with his or her problems. These problems could be personal, family, academic, or crime-related. By helping the child with his or her problems, the school resource officer becomes a trusted source for the child to turn to in a time of need. This personal relationship gives law enforcement the opportunity to affect impressionable youths during the maturation process, as well as showing children the personable or human side of the law enforcement officer. By constantly reinforcing to the child that a life of crime is taboo, the child will have a better chance of growing up and choosing to be crime- and drug-free.

The presence of a full-time law enforcement officer at a school meets these objectives and aids in building a relationship, or friendship, between children and law enforcement. This relationship begins at the elementary level and proceeds through high school graduation. It is also fostered by the school resource officer teaching various curriculums, including *DARE* (Drug and Alcohol Resistance Education) and *G.R.E.A.T.* (Gang Resistance Education and Training), as well as life skills and law awareness classes. By teaching the students these curriculums, the school resource officer has the opportunity to have a positive impact on children in the same manner as full-time teachers.

Community Relations Tool for the Agency

As a police administrator supports a school resource officer unit, he or she makes a statement that the service, protection, and development of our children are a top priority. Additionally, the position of school resource officer is rewarding to those who want to have an impact on children. This approach is different from the traditional police approach of responding to a problem. By having an impact through positive policing at the period prior to the initiation of criminal behavior, the school resource officer achieves a sense of accomplishment. The law enforcement agency can point to the program as an attempt to meet its objective of crime control and deterrence.

Another advantage of the school resource officer program is the public statement of support for a safe learning environment for children. This is different from the actual core belief stated above in that the program's mere existence speaks volumes about the law enforcement agency's commitment to the children of the community. This public statement carries on to extracurricular activities, including PTA meetings, social activities, and school athletics. When there is a law enforcement presence at these after-hours activities, it provides the community with the opportunity to view firsthand the commitment made by the law enforcement agency. This community contact frequently is the only contact many will ever have with their local police department. By making this initial, and sometimes only, contact a positive one, the community views the police department in a more positive light. This action also notifies the public that the law enforcement agency is committed to the safety and maturation process of the youths within its jurisdiction.

Provide Crime Reduction through Deterrence

Deterrence of youths from committing crimes is an essential goal for a law enforcement agency. If an agency wishes to combat crime, it must emphasize prevention as well as detection and apprehension. This mission is effectively accomplished by the existence of the school resource officer's involvement in the student's life. By seeing the students on a daily basis, the school resource officer is familiar with the child's positive or negative progression. The school resource officer has the opportunity to make contact with the child's parents by telephone or by meeting them at school. This consistent law enforcement presence and involvement serves as a deterrent for the child who may be contemplating, or exposed to, criminal behavior. It also gives law enforcement the opportunity to aid families of their community by providing a positive police influence on the child.

Protection from Civil Liability

While the above-listed reasons for the implementation of a school resource officer program may be considered immeasurable in specific and definable terms, effectiveness can be measured. Unfortunately, this measurement is often in the form of monetary damages as a result of a civil suit filed against an agency for its failure to protect children on campus. This measurement can be defined as millions of dollars in the event of such a suit. Without the presence of law enforcement, school administrators must conduct investigations involving rumored upcoming school shootings, weapons possession at school, and gang fights, just to name a few. School administrators are not adequately trained to investigate these types of cases. Furthermore, they are often reluctant to call law enforcement until the situation becomes more than they can handle. By this point, the responding officer is reacting to an ongoing event, not preventing it.

Evidence of the willingness to file suit against law enforcement is clearly present in the suits filed against the Jackson County Sheriff's Office as a result of the Columbine High School shooting, which occurred on April 20, 1999. Columbine High School had an assigned school resource officer who was conducting proactive police work at the time the shooting began. He was looking for students who were smoking and potentially truant at a nearby park (Ramey, J., August 10, 2001, personal communication). As the responding police personnel arrived at the school within minutes, a traditional perimeter was established around the school. This was the appropriate tactic per training, but it allowed Eric Harris and Dylan Klebold time to continue killing students and a teacher. In fact, the teacher that died bled to death as a result of delayed rescue efforts. According to the plaintiff's attorney, the traditional response by law enforcement was a contributing factor in the deaths of several innocent victims (Ramey, J., August 10, 2001, personal communication). Unfortunately, a textbook police response, such as the one at Columbine, will no longer satisfy the courts. For this reason, the implementation of a school resource officer program with training in additional response methods is the best defense against civil liability. The method of a tactical response titled "Move to Contact" will be addressed later in this chapter.

The Implementation of the School Resource Officer Program

The creation of a new unit in an existing law enforcement agency is always a challenge. This is especially true if a police administrator is attempting to sell the program to his or her chief or sheriff. Factors that include the size of the agency, its budget, and the number of schools within its jurisdiction make the task of implementing such a program challenging. The criteria below are viewed as essential in the process of establishing the program. This list highlights the essential steps involved in the formation period of a school resource officer program. It is not intended to be an all-inclusive list of steps to establishing the existence of the program.

Selling the Concept

The first and foremost element required in establishing a school resource officer program is the desire by the community and school board to have one. Without this public support, a police administrator is likely to encounter resistance in his or her quest. If this desire is not present, the benefits of the program must be explained to the community, the school board, and the police executives. Essentially, the concept of a law enforcement presence in schools must be sold to those who must approve it. The benefits of the program must be termed as reasons why a school resource officer unit is necessary. This may be titled as the law enforcement agency's expanding commitment to protect and influence youths, and another proven method of crime reduction.

Once backing is obtained from the entities who fiscally and politically support the idea, the administrator or individual assigned to coordinate the effort to begin the school resource officer program must meet with school board personnel to advise exactly what a school resource officer's duties would be while on campus. At this meeting, it would be beneficial to have an agency staff attorney present to clarify general legal obligations and limitations. When this meeting takes place, the school board's security department (if one exists) should be briefed on the agency's definition of what role the school resource officer will play regarding school security. It is suggested that a preliminary legal contract be drafted and presented to those who are affected by the existence of a school resource officer program. Appendix D provides an example. It is the contract between the Orange County, Florida, Sheriff's Office and the Orange County Public School Board. This contract has been in place for several years.

Assuming these entities support the implementation of such a program, the administrator who is piloting the program should next meet with those who will be most affected by the school resource officer. These would be the principals of the schools and their staff. Additionally, area superintendents (the persons to whom the principals report) should be present. At this meeting, the police administrator should emphasize the proposed relationship that would occur between the school resource officer and the school, which is outlined in the contract. School principals are often given free rein to run their schools as they see fit. They must be told that a police presence will have no effect on the academic procedures established at their individual campuses, as well as what the general obligations of the school resource officer will be. These obligations include increased school safety through a constant police presence, the investigation of all criminal matters that occur on campus, counseling assistance for students and parents, and a concerted effort to foster relationships between law enforcement and youths. If the school board desires a law enforcement presence in the classroom, specific curricula, such as DARE and G.R.E.A.T., should be presented for academic consideration. By doing this, the police administrator should not insult the educator. It is important to avoid giving the impression that law enforcement is "taking over" the school's curriculum. This should be left to the educating experts and the school board, and this fact should be clearly explained to those reviewing the proposal. Additionally, specific limitations on the officer should be addressed to avoid any confusion as to what will be accomplished by the police presence on their campus. The school board must understand that it is in charge of the campus, but the law enforcement agency is the entity that directs and supervises the school resource officer assigned to their campus. Additionally, any criminal matters arising on campus would be the responsibility of the law enforcement agency.

Funding

The issue of budgeting will also need to be addressed if the agency desires the school board to assist in funding. The **joint funding** of school resource officer programs is quite common. The concept of joint funding also gives the presenter the opportunity to offer full-time employees to the school board and the law enforcement agency at a substantially lower cost. An excellent example of a jointly funded school resource officer program is that of the Orange County, Florida, Sheriff's Office. Specifically, the Orange County School Board is responsible for the education of more than 175,000 students in kindergarten through grade 12. As of 2009, the school board was the twelfth largest in the country. The Orange County Sheriff's Office has jurisdiction of approximately 63 percent of these campuses (OCPS, 2009). The salary range for a deputy sheriff in Orange County is $38,000–52,000, excluding benefits (Orange County Sheriff's Office, 2012). Currently, there are 68 school resource officers with the Orange County Sheriff's Office. In addition, there are eight sergeants, two lieutenants, and one captain. The Sheriff has agreed to provide one full-time deputy sheriff for all middle schools, two for all high schools, and one for every four elementary schools. In exchange for this staffing, the school board compensates the Sheriff $22,500 per deputy per year. The $22,500 figure was reached by taking one-half of the average base salary (excluding benefits) of a deputy sheriff. This contract results in $1,413,500 annually being paid to the Sheriff from the Orange County School Board.

The selling point the police administrator may present is that the school board is getting a full-time police presence at approximately one-third the cost. The agency is manning schools (which they are already responsible for) at approximately one-half the cost. Combine this argument with the benefits or reasons for a school resource officer program, and one has a compelling argument for the creation of such a program.

At this stage, an agreement between the law enforcement agency and the school board may appear. If this occurs, and a general protocol is agreed upon, a final contract between the agency and the school board must be created. This contract should detail obligations, assignments, chain of command, teaching (if applicable), and funding. It should be drafted by the law enforcement legal staff and renewed annually.

Implementing the School Resource Officer Unit within the Agency

When both entities have agreed on the creation of a school resource officer program, it becomes the agency's responsibility to properly budget and select personnel for the position. The selection process for this position is critical to ensure its success. The success of any unit within a law enforcement agency depends on the caliber and dedication of those within the unit. Therefore, the agency must place only the most qualified personnel in this assignment. To ensure proper assignment within the new unit, the newly selected school resource officer must have experience, education, and the desire to be part of the building process of a challenging endeavor. He or she must also desire to work with youths in an effort to prevent future criminal activity, as opposed to the action-oriented response mode present in many younger law enforcement officers. To ensure that the agency assigns the proper personnel to this unit, standards consistent with the goals of the school resource officer program must dictate the type of officer selected. For example, requiring previous experience in dealing with juveniles would be more relevant than having served as a SWAT team member. This is not to say that SWAT team members would not make good school resource officers, only that their previous experiences are not as beneficial as that of officers who have experience dealing with juveniles. Additionally, the school resource officer who has earned a bachelor's degree would be better suited for work in an educational environment than the officer with no college education.

Most law enforcement agencies require significant experience with the agency before an officer will be considered to be a school resource officer. This experience is frequently reduced in years when the officer has a college degree. Additionally, law enforcement agencies look for officers who have had some experience in dealing with youths and crime prevention. These qualities show that the candidate is capable of the day-to-day tasks of a school resource officer. These experiences need not be in the realm of police work. Law enforcement officers with prior teaching experience in school systems make excellent school resource officers because of their desire to be around youths.

When the agency sets the standards for application to the school resource officer unit, an interview process will be established. During this interview, the agency should explain to the candidates the **objectives** of the school resource officer program and the expected duties of the individual. This will allow the agency to state clearly what it hopes to achieve through the school resource officer unit. With this added information, the candidate can assess whether this is an assignment he or she wants. Once these objectives are laid out and the candidate confirms his or her desire to work in the unit, certain questions should be asked. These questions serve as screens for those who may be unfit for the assignment. Examples of these screening questions include:

1. Why do you want to work in the school resource officer program? Officers should state that they enjoy working with juveniles and desire the opportunity to have a positive influence on children.

2. Can you work with minimal supervision? Officers should demonstrate that they have this capability because they see their supervisors less than do average officers. A typical school resource officer may see his or her sergeant once or twice a week because the sergeant has to visit several different campuses.
3. What experience do you have with working with juveniles? Officers should provide a detailed explanation of their work with juveniles and elaborate on what positive outcomes were developed.
4. Would you have a problem taking the life of a child if the situation called for such action on a school campus? Officers should indicate that they would treat youthful offenders the same as they would treat adults. If taking a life was called for, they should not hesitate. After all, they may be required to use deadly force on a child.

These questions are not intended to be an all-inclusive list for an interview, only essentials that serve as potential eliminators. If the candidate answers one of these in a manner inconsistent or contradictory to the answers noted above, the agency should reconsider whether the officer is a viable candidate for the position.

Once the officer is selected for the position of school resource officer, he or she should be given the standard **psychological screening** that is given to others in potentially high-stress assignments. Typical assignments requiring a psychological screening include vice and narcotics investigations, sex crimes, child abuse, and homicide investigations. While the officer may be well-suited for many positions within the agency, the psychological screen protects the agency from assigning an officer to a position that he or she might not be able to handle. This extra precautionary measure will also protect the agency in the event of a negligent assignment lawsuit resulting from an improper action committed by the school resource officer.

Training the School Resource Officer

Because the agency has implemented a new **specialized unit**, it will not be possible to train personnel with experienced school resource officers. The method of training new personnel must come from outside agencies that already have an existing school resource officer unit and are willing to assist, or from within through the creation of special orders or directives. Most agencies, whether they seek outside assistance or not, should create a written guideline of what is expected of the school resource officer. These written guidelines provide a clear method of operation for the officer and some liability protection for the agency. An example of a special order and written directives can be found in Appendix E. The special order pertains directly to the duties and responsibilities of the school resource officer as well as his or her supervisor. The **written directives** provide guidelines on how all agency members are to handle situations that deal with juveniles.

The written directives can be used to train the school resource officers on how to conduct daily operations at the school. Procedures in dealing with juveniles should not differ from one assignment to another. Consistency across all assignments of the agency is mandatory to ensure the same treatment of situations, regardless of assignments. These documents serve as the basis of knowledge expected of the newly assigned officer.

A second written procedure needs to be developed that serves as a **field training evaluation program** (FTEP). Specific expectations and job descriptions need to be explained and documented. An example of this type of FTEP is shown in Appendix F. This program, titled "D.A.R.E./S.R.O. Orientation Week," was implemented by the Orange County Sheriff's Office. Bear in mind that this agency has an existing school resource officer program and has senior deputies providing orientation to newly assigned deputies. However, in an agency where no unit exists, the supervisor could serve as the senior deputy and provide specifics of the new assignment. This FTEP also serves as documentation for the supervisor and the agency, should the officer not meet the minimum standards required by the agency for this specialized position. It is intended to mirror the field training program already established in most agencies—but it addresses specific standards that apply to the position of school resource officer.

THE EVOLVING ROLE OF TECHNOLOGY

Despite the controversy arising from policing schools, it is clear that many law enforcement agencies will have school resource officers in schools for the foreseeable future. There are a number of technological advances that can prove helpful for these officers. Furthermore, grants and divided costs between agencies and schools can make these devices a more affordable option.

Schools now have the option of video camera security systems that allow several locations to be simultaneously monitored. Centralized control centers can allow school resource officers to maintain visual contact on locations where offenses may take place. Additionally, the advent of digital cameras allows video images to be saved on computer hard drives to preserve as evidence without requiring the burdensome space requirements of videotapes. Of course, the cameras are installed in public areas so as to avoid any legal questions of student privacy. While controversial, metal detectors have now become part of school systems' equipment. These are primarily used for detecting weapons. Handheld metal detectors can be used easily in most any location.

The Department of Justice has funded the creation and implementation of software packages that SROs can use. The School COP software is a freely available software package that helps school staff and SROs track types of incidents, their locations, and the people involved in the incident. This software can be located online at www.schoolcopsoftware.com where instructional videos can be found.

The Investigation of and Preparation for Critical Incidents

Perhaps the most important and difficult task assigned to the school resource officer unit is the prevention of school shootings. The Centers for Disease Control and Prevention (CDC) summarizes the findings of long-term research titled the "School-Associated

Violent Death Study" (2010), which examined violent school victimizations from 1992 to 2006. The research concluded that violent deaths in schools made up less than one percent of suicides and homicides among children ages 5 to 18. Additionally, school-associated homicides decreased during that time frame. The rate of these homicides had begun leveling, and nearly two-thirds of the homicides resulted from gunshot wounds. Given the high-profile nature of school shootings, and the high percentage of school-related deaths resulting from shootings, preparation and prevention of this type of incident should be a paramount concern for school resource officers. To accomplish this enormous task, three equally important phases must be detailed and addressed. The phases are *prevention, intervention,* and *response.* Each phase leads to the next, yet all overlap.

Prevention

Prevention is synonymous with education. The school resource officer must also be familiar with his or her students and what type of behavior should be considered normal for each. When a child begins to act differently, someone will notice. This information should be forwarded to the school resource officer, who will then take note of the changed behavior. Specifically, the school resource officer looks for the presence of general **warning signs**. These general warning signs only indicate that the child may be experiencing some type of stress or personal problem. Multiple signs should be observed in order to avoid the "**false positives**"—situations in which a child is assumed to be a potential for violence when in fact he or she is not. False positives can also cause problems for a child who is presently free of stresses, creating a problem when one never existed.

When the school resource officer identifies multiple signs, he or she should give the child an opportunity to speak with a qualified and concerned adult. This adult could be a school counselor, teacher, or the school resource officer. There are multiple purposes for having this conversation. The primary purpose is to allow an inquiry to determine whether the child is experiencing a personal problem that has affected his or her behavior. Additionally, this proactive measure shows the child that there are adults that are concerned and it gives the child a place to turn for present and future problems, instead of handling them in a potentially violent manner. Another benefit of initiating a conversation is **intelligence gathering**. Personal intelligence as well as intelligence on potential violence can be gathered. Intelligence on potential violence includes issues at home, weapons at home, and how the child handles stress. The following is a list of general warning signs that have been compiled from various reputable studies:

- A fascination with violence and weapons
- Bullying (either physical or social, usually being the victim)
- Socially withdrawn ("loners" or their group is viewed as "outsiders")
- They have access to guns
- Openly speaking about revenge

- Verbal expressions of their inability to handle present stressors, including those at home and school
- Depression
- Has attempted suicide in the past
- Prefers TV shows, movies, video games, music, or other materials dealing with violent themes

This conversation will likely be different from the traditional fact-finding dialogue conducted by the school resource officer. The usual police interview consists of specific questions designed to determine whether certain laws were broken and, if so, by whom. This conversation will consist of **open-ended questions**, listening, and observing. The purpose of the conversation is not to seek an admission or uncover facts, but to learn personal details about an individual who may be experiencing problems consistent with grade school students. The school resource officer will likely hear that students are dealing with issues that seem relatively simple to them, but are devastating losses to the child. It is critical that the school resource officer see the issue through the eyes of the child, not through the officer's more experienced and mature view.

Intervention

The next step of involvement by the school resource officer is intervention. It is important to distinguish between *intervention* and *prevention*. In the prevention stage, the school resource officer takes an intervening role, but this role is assumed as part of his or her job description. This initiative is expected because youths often experience stress and personal problems. Intervention, conversely, requires an unanticipated or intervening action. Additionally, different levels of intervention on behalf of the school resource officer are possible.

Proactive measures may be prescribed at the intervention stage. A term used by Dr. John Nicoletti and Dr. Sally Spencer-Thomas (2001) to describe these measures is "**planting trees**." They define "trees" as barriers that are placed in the path of the child who is heading toward committing an act of violence. These "trees" come in various shapes and sizes. Some of these "trees" are easily averted, while others are so large that the child knows he or she will not be able to navigate around them. When this occurs, the child will stop his or her path toward violence. Specific examples of "trees" include questioning, confronting, or implementing consequences (Nicoletti & Spencer-Thomas, 2001).

The "tree" used initially and in less serious cases is direct questioning of the child. By conducting an investigation and asking the child direct questions about the school resource officer's suspicions, the child knows that he or she is being watched. This frequently serves the greater purpose and the child stops traveling down the path of violence.

The next level of "tree planting" is confronting. This is done by the school resource officer through a direct verbal warning or statement. These "trees" are prescribed when suspicions are confirmed or serious warning signs (which will be defined later) are displayed. Other confrontational "trees" include physical obstacles. Examples of these types of physical confrontational "trees" include security systems as well as vehicle and locker searches on campus.

The last level of "tree planting" is through the use of consequences. These actions range from **legal ramifications** (probation) to school **administrative sanctions** (suspension or expulsion). These "trees" should only be used when other, smaller obstacles have proven inadequate.

Bear in mind that "trees" must be the appropriate size for each situation. It would be inappropriate to plant a consequence "tree" in front of a child who may have displayed only one or two general warning signs. This would be considered overreacting and may cause more problems for a troubled youth, who may not even be considering an act of violence. On the other hand, merely questioning or warning a child who has provided specific details of a planned attack would be an example of planting too small of a "tree" in the path of a child who is a serious threat. This child would likely not even see this "tree"—in other words, the intervention would go completely unnoticed (Nicoletti & Spencer-Thomas, 2001).

School resource officers learn from experience that the most frequent initiator of intervention by the school resource officer is usually the result of a child who has displayed some general warning signs and the officer has talked with the child. As a result of this conversation, the school resource officer has become more concerned. At this point, the school resource officer will provide specific intervention, such as school counseling, advising the child's parents on general warning signs observed, psychological referrals, and a suggestion to the parents to secure all weapons in the home. Additionally, a team-oriented approach is formed with parents who share the school resource officer's concerns and show a desire to intervene. Specific information would be obtained from the parents, including: medications the troubled child may be taking and whether the child is taking the medications as directed, family problems the child may be experiencing, depression, and determining whether the child was expressing anger over a recent event such as humiliation, rejection, or discipline.

When the school resource officer has raised these concerns about the child, he or she should be open to the possibility that the child could be fantasizing about committing an act of school violence. At this point, a suggested course of action would be, at a minimum, to monitor the child's behavior at home and at school. This is done by constant contact with the child and parents, in a manner showing concern.

Specific examples of obstacles that have proven most useful at this point include home visits by the school resource officer with the purpose of looking for evidence of a planned act of school violence. During this home visit, the school resource officer should seek consent to examine the child's journal, bedroom, and computer, as well as other frequented areas of the home. This examination could yield information that could confirm the school resource officer's suspicions.

The most serious type of intervention is required when the child displays serious **warning signs**. Serious warning signs are indicators that the child may be motivated to plan an act of school violence or may have progressed to the planning stage. They should be viewed as real and imminent. These signs include:

- Bringing a gun to school
- Specific or direct threats to commit an act of school violence
- "Leakage"—telling others details of their planned attack
- A preference of violence in writings and drawings—this would include essays of committing mass violence, drawings of mass violence (these drawings or writings should be examined to determine if specific individuals are depicted. If so, a determination as to why those described could be targeted should be made.)

Response Plan— "Move to Contact"

The final element of preparation for critical incidents involves the assumption that all other tactics have failed. This stage of planning concludes that the agency has no other choice but to handle the situation proactively, forcefully, and at times lethally. This stage is a last resort, but must be sufficient to handle any situation that could arise. This response plan is used only when a critical incident involving an active shooter occurs on a school campus. This element, a response plan, must be developed, practiced, and strictly adhered to, ensuring consistency by those involved in its deployment.

As critical examinations and reviews of several school shootings began (specifically Columbine), law enforcement agencies realized that relying on a traditional SWAT response was not a sufficient response plan. The administration of the Orange County Sheriff's Office, under the direction of SWAT commanders Chief Matt Weathersby and Captain Butch Hummel, realized that in certain school situations, time was of the essence. They realized that the traditional police response of setting a perimeter and waiting 45 minutes for a SWAT response was not appropriate when a school shooter was actively killing children within earshot of officers surrounding the school. Additionally, they identified a potential civil liability in utilizing this traditional tactic. Instead, they formulated a plan designed to have on-scene personnel tactically and safely locate, isolate, and neutralize the threat, long before the SWAT team arrived, potentially saving dozens of children's lives. They titled this response plan "**Move to Contact.**" This plan is a tactic intended to stop the active commission of murder by an armed school shooter as soon as possible, ensuring that additional lives are not lost.

The principle behind the "Move to Contact" response plan is the same as any SWAT search tactic. It involves the first four law enforcement officers, regardless of assignment or agency, to enter the school in a four-person team. The team forms a diamond shape formation, thus visually covering 360 degrees. Each member of the team is responsible for certain areas of coverage as the team begins its search of the area for the suspect or suspects. This is done by the methodical search method when the whereabouts of the shooter is unknown. Should the shooter resume firing at innocent individuals, the team moves toward the sound of the shots being fired. At the point where the team locates the active shooter, the team neutralizes the shooter via whatever means necessary.

Certain principles are essential in making this tactic successful. The first principle is that the team is just that—a team. They move as one toward the threat. The formation is closely knit together, moving as one, fulfilling the purpose of locating and neutralizing the threat. The second principle is that each member carries a certain area of responsibility, which makes the team 100 percent effective. If a member of the team fails to meet his or her obligations or responsibilities, the team's effectiveness is sacrificed. Specifically, if the left guard's area of responsibility is hallways on the left and he or she fails to cover this area, all team members are exposed to potential hostile fire from this quadrant due to one member's failure to meet his or her obligation. Based on this philosophy, it is imperative that each team member be familiar with all positions of the team and trust the other team members to carry out their responsibilities. Different tactics are employed for different areas of the school. Open areas, corners, hallways, and room searches require certain tactics by each team member.

On March 10, 2000, it is believed this tactic was first used in a school shooting scenario. Charles "Andy" Williams entered Santana High School, just outside of San Diego, California. He began to open fire on students, eventually killing two and wounding 13. Coincidentally, in the school were off-duty and on-duty officers from various jurisdictions. Each heard the shots and began to react. None had been trained on "Move to Contact," but they were familiar with its concept. They formulated their own team and began to move toward Williams, who was in the restroom shooting at other students. When the team of officers arrived at the restroom, they confronted Williams, who was actively reloading his weapon. They secured the threat, and the situation ended without further incident (J. Cook, 2001, personal communication). What is important to note is that Williams had already shot and killed others. He was reloading and logically one could assume that he would have continued on his killing spree. By employing this tactic, lives were likely saved. Imagine if those officers had decided to set a perimeter and wait 45 minutes for a SWAT response. One could only imagine how many more innocent children might have died. Based on this incident and police response, one can conclude that the "Move to Contact" response has merit.

Training School Resource Officers in "Move to Contact"

Chief Weathersby and Captain Hummel agreed to train all sworn members, including all school resource officers, on the "Move to Contact" tactic. Behind this project was the belief in the likelihood that SWAT will not respond in time and on-scene personnel will be forced to handle the incident. SWAT teams initially trained approximately 1,400 deputies. This training consisted of classroom presentations, small group demonstrations on tactics, and practical, realistic scenarios. The classroom presentations included video examples of what the team's and each team member's responsibilities were. The entire class then went to a local high school and worked on specific tactics, including team progression through hallways, open areas, corners, and room searches. The SWAT team then provided deputies with realistic scenarios. These scenarios involved a SWAT team member at an unknown location in the school shooting loud blanks. The team had to progress toward the threat, passing through simulated injured and dead students, students running at them providing incorrect information, and unfamiliar surroundings until they reached the shooter. The team had to take appropriate action, including the use of deadly force. This training was beneficial and is provided by SWAT team members to school resource officers annually to keep them competent in this tactic. It is recommended that should an agency administrator seek to employ this tactic, he or she should consult with a law enforcement agency that provides this type of training.

Conclusion

Now that a general idea of how to create, select, implement, and train potential school resource officers is laid out, a police administrator has an outline of what steps to take. It should not be construed that the steps listed in this text must be followed exactly to create an effective school resource officer program. It has worked in one agency, and this agency has aided other agencies through the use of this guideline in establishing new school resource officer programs within law enforcement agencies nationwide.

Undoubtedly, the question "Do I really need such a unit?" will enter the police administrator's mind. In answering that question, one should ask other questions, such as: "What would I do in the event of a critical incident at a school within my agency's jurisdiction? Would the existence of a school resource officer program better enable my agency to meet the ever-changing demands placed on police? Would other methods of crime prevention, community service, and youth involvement better meet the objectives established by my agency?" The answer may or may not indicate the need for a school resource officer program. This is a decision that each police administrator must make on his or her own. In making this decision, one could also consider the five benefits of a school resource officer program outlined at the beginning of this text. Ask yourself, "could my agency better meet the needs of the community through the use of this tool?" If so, you may wish to follow the outline provided herein.

References

Centers for Disease Control and Prevention. (2010, July 20). Major findings. *School-associated violent death study.* Retrieved from http://www.cdc.gov/violenceprevention/youthviolence/school violence/SAVD.html.

Nicoletti, J., & Spencer-Thomas, S. (2001). *Violence goes to school.* Lakewood, CO: Solution Tree.

Orange County (Florida) Public Schools. (2012). Orange County Public Schools Annual Report. Retrieved from https://www.ocps.net/Documents/AnnualReport2012.pdf

Orange County (Florida) Sheriff's Office. (2012). Law Enforcement Positions. Retrieved from http:// www.ocso.com/EmploymentInfo/LawEnforcementPositions/tabid/97/Default.aspx

Robers, S., Zhang, J., & Truman, J. (2012). *Indicators of school crime and safety: 2011.* (NCES 2012-002/ NCJ 236021) Washington, DC: National Center for Education Statistics, U.S. Department of Education, and Bureau of Justice Statistics, Office of Justice Programs, U.S. Department of Justice.

Theriot, M. T. (2009). School resource officers and the criminalization of student behavior. *Journal of criminal justice, 37,* 280–287.

University of Virginia Youth Violence Project. (2007). *National statistics.* Retrieved April 16, 2012, from http://youthviolence.edschool.virginia.edu/violence-in-schools/national-statistics.html.

Discussion Questions

1. How can a school resource officer program be implemented?
2. List the steps needed to develop a school resource officer program.
3. Define the roles of different participants in the program.

19 ⠿

Assessment Center Process

LEARNING OBJECTIVES

1. The student will be able to recognize the advantages and disadvantages of using an assessment center in the promotional process.
2. The student will be able to recognize the eight steps to be included in the development of an assessment center.
3. The student will recognize and understand the most common exercises used in an assessment center.
4. The student will recognize and understand the use of different rating scales in an assessment center.

Overview

Through an assessment center, candidates for promotion can be observed and evaluated over a specific period, such as one or two days, during which they undergo a series of exercises designed to test specific characteristics. In some situations, assessment programs can be used to guide career development, to select new personnel, to determine supervisory and management candidates for the future, and to identify training needs. The assessment center process allows individual candidates to be evaluated on the basis of their observed capabilities and behaviors. Exercises are geared specifically toward real-life situations within the agency and the dimensions are related to the position being sought.

Assessment centers have proven to be effective for promotions to management positions. However, when numerous candidates seek first-line supervisory positions in medium to large police departments, assessment centers can become caught up in a cumbersome bureaucratic process, and this may fail to produce the desired results. They appear to be more effective in testing candidates for management positions. Overall, assessment programs can be useful in filling executive positions, but they become less practical as one moves down the organizational structure.

In running an assessment center, the police manager must be aware of the question of trust between agency personnel and the assessors. That is, it may be necessary to use outside assessors until such trust is developed. Usually, in the first few assessment centers, police managers tend to use a combination of **inside and outside assessors**. It is advisable to use at least one inside assessor on each exercise in order to deal with special policy questions, as well as to clarify the exact meaning of phrases that may be unique to the individual police agency. Prior to the implementation of an assessment center, it is important to train both assessors and candidates and to conduct a job analysis from which **criteria** can be established.

Many police departments use aspects of the assessment center approach for promotional testing to the first-line supervision position and full assessment centers for mid- and top-level management positions. The assessment center concept combines an array of performance tests, both written and oral, with evaluations by human observers. The center includes the observation of actual behavior and is considered more job-related than many traditional selection/assessment methods.

There are benefits to be derived both by the participants and by those conducting the evaluation. Normally, a promotion made on this basis—as opposed to the more traditional written test and oral interview—can be made with greater confidence.

One major issue to be overcome by large police agencies, especially in first-line supervision, is how to select the candidates for an assessment center. The issue is still open for debate, and many agencies are in the process of testing different devices. The most common method involves a written test, followed by a short oral interview by a board made up of personnel from within the department. These exercises are scored, and the top 12 to 15, depending on the number of open positions, are included in the assessment center itself. If this does not produce enough candidates for promotion, follow-up assessments are conducted.

In many instances, the assessment center approach benefits the assessors as much as or more than the candidates. Many corporations, such as General Electric, believe strongly that the benefits of assessor training are great; they therefore increase their assessor participant ratios in order to expose more personnel to the experience. Among the benefits to assessors are improved interviewing skills, broadened observation skills, increased appreciation of group dynamics and leadership styles, new insights into behavior, strengthened management skills through repeated exposure to case problems and situations, a broadened repertoire of responses to problems, the establishment of standards by which to evaluate performance, and the development of a more precise vocabulary with which to help describe behavior and feedback processes on a day-to-day basis.

Assessment centers offer benefits to all officers regardless of whether they are promoted. The two major benefits for a police department that develops an assessment center are: (1) the identification of management potential and (2) the development of the candidates' skills. Most assessment programs help the candidates—those who are promoted and those who are not—to recognize their individual strengths and weaknesses. This gives the candidates insight into how their management potential can be enhanced.

If the procedure is to aid the individual candidates significantly, they must behave in a certain way. For example, they need an opportunity to talk with those who evaluated their behavior. This is normally done in the feedback process. There is a need to be honest and candid when isolating weaknesses and strengths, and candidates need to seek ways in which to improve their conduct or behavior patterns.

In any promotional process, it is extremely rare to find a single individual who greatly surpasses all other candidates in every facet of an assignment. This is also true of the assessment center. Normally, candidates have a tendency to score well in some parts and poorly in others. The evaluation of an individual officer's strengths and weaknesses prior to promotion gives the police chief an opportunity to see which areas may require more intensive, personal attention. Thus, the chief can be more effective in helping a new commander to become an effective member of the management team.

Sometimes **consultants** work closely with an individual police department in helping it develop an assessment program. Usually the personnel department sits in on meetings in which the consultants play the role of facilitators. Questions are raised, examples of how to deal with issues are addressed, and eventually an assessment center is put together. The consultant plays an advisory role for the first assessment center, in many instances participating as an evaluator. Once the first assessment center has been completed, the consultant helps by evaluating the program itself—whether its purposes were met and how future programs might be made more effective. After the first couple of assessments, the police department usually conducts its own programs. Sometimes outside evaluators are called on to sit in as individual assessors, but normally they have little to do with the development of additional centers for the police agencies.

In many instances, police departments use psychological testing as part of their assessments. These tests are designed to assist the newly promoted candidate and the supervisors or managers to work better in the future. They carry no weight in terms of the assessment itself. The most common tests used are the Myers-Briggs Type Indicator, the Edwards Preference Test, and the Styles of Management Inventory. If these tests are used, the candidates are given either group or individual interpretations of the results.

Advantages of the Assessment Center

On the positive side, an assessment center approach is usually seen by police personnel as a "fair" system. Therefore, its results are more easily accepted, not only by those promoted and those who did not receive promotion, but also by other members of the agency. A second positive feature involves a process by which the officers receive feedback about their strengths and weaknesses. Just as important, top-level managers and the chief receive feedback concerning what might be serious issues that need immediate attention. For example, it may prove that some candidates for assessment resent the performance evaluation system more than the department's top managers had realized. Upon being informed of this, the police chief may be able to check out the process more thoroughly and make immediate changes, if necessary. Solutions offered during the exercises may produce useful ideas for the police department. In this way, even unpromoted candidates sometimes get to feel that they have a stake in the growth of the police department.

A third reason assessment centers are popular in government is that they are generally accepted by the courts as being fair (*Kirkland v. New York State Correctional Services*, 1988). This allows police chiefs to implement affirmative action programs and meet other legal requirements.

Disadvantages of the Assessment Center

Like any management tool, the assessment center has negative aspects. It is time-consuming. A promotional process that involves only a written examination can be conducted in a half-day to one full day; assessment programs may run anywhere from two to five days. This does not include the time necessary for preparation, training of assessors, or final evaluation and analysis.

A second problem is that of locating good assessors. Experienced assessors are not common because of the novelty of this approach. As more assessment centers are implemented, qualified assessors are becoming more and more common.

A third negative consideration is cost. Assessment centers can be expensive, especially when compared with more traditional methods. Usually the cost of the first assessment center includes that of the consultants who help to develop it. It may, in some instances, require a job analysis, which is used as a basis for the development of dimensions. In many areas, assessors are paid honorariums or at least are reimbursed for their expenses. As a result, the overall cost can rise. But when agencies in the same general area train assessors and share such personnel, the costs are reduced.

Experience shows that assessment centers normally provide highly detailed feedback to the police chief. This information is developed and presented in a few days, sometimes short-cutting years of informal feedback.

An assessment center approach may help avoid lawsuits that require a police department to defend its present practices. In essence, assessment centers are more likely to be realistic in demonstrating that they actually test for the abilities a candidate will need in his or her new position.

Assessment centers are used to help enforce departmental policy. For example, in agencies that believe in encouraging the personal growth of their employees, the assessment center can serve as a tool to test such growth. Individual plans for personal growth can be developed with the help of the assessment program. In one police department, the police chief recognized the strengths and weaknesses of each of the candidates after conducting an assessment center. The chief offered each candidate the opportunity to develop his or her strengths and overcome weaknesses.

Assessment centers tend to identify training needs, especially in the human systems approach to running the police department.

The personnel department should be involved in implementing and developing an assessment center by providing job analyses and developing adequate dimensions that are consistent with personnel practices. Personnel departments may bring about community involvement, either through input prior to the actual assessment center or by providing people from within the community to act as assessors.

Personnel departments can assist in the physical arrangement of an assessment center. They also play a key role in coordinating it, taking care of the numerous details, such as housing for assessors and outside candidates, providing meals, and, when necessary, providing role-players.

Although an assessment center approach might be expensive, it tends to reduce the chances of promoting people to positions for which they are not qualified. As a result, the cost of the assessment center tends to be far outweighed by the quality of personnel promoted.

Developing the Assessment Center

There are eight steps to be taken from early discussion to final completion. These include: (1) performing a job analysis, (2) developing dimensions, (3) creating a matrix, (4) developing guidelines, (5) developing exercises, (6) training assessors and candidates, (7) conducting the assessment center, and (8) ensuring feedback.

Performing a Job Analysis

In this first step, either a formal task analysis can be performed or personnel from within the agency can be called together to carefully discuss the behavior and traits required by the position. In general, agencies have a tendency to bring together personnel of the rank of captain or deputy chief to discuss what these people perceive to be the more important characteristics of their positions. These characteristics then become the job analysis. Consultants who have experience in developing **task analysis** studies for police departments are also available. The expense incurred, however, is sometimes prohibitive, especially for smaller agencies. In many of the larger police agencies, a continual job analysis is performed by the personnel department, and its findings often serve as a basis for the assessment center.

Developing Dimensions

In the second step, dimensions are developed. **Dimensions** are the behavior traits to be examined during the assessment center. These dimensions fall into four broad areas. General dimensions may encompass commitment to handling responsibility and authority as well as command presence. The second area includes technical skills such as work perspective, complaint handling, and career development. The third general area includes rational skills, including the ability to handle written communications, decision making, time management, planning, fact finding, and control. In the final area, human skills, the candidate is observed and examined for characteristics that are necessary for personal development as well as to foster growth in others. Human skills is usually the most important category. These include such dimensions as leadership, oral communication, interpersonal sensitivity, stress management, dealing with people, and team development. A sample list of dimensions is included in Figure 19-1.

Once dimensions are agreed on, they must be prioritized. It is impossible for an assessment center to test for all possible dimensions the candidate may need to perform his or her assigned job. Realistically, the dimensions that can be tested in an assessment

1. General
   a. Command presence
   b. Commitment to service
   c. Handling of responsibility
      and authority

2. Technical skills
   a. Work perspective
   b. Technical and professional
      knowledge
   c. Career development
   d. Handling of complaints
   e. Dealing with rumors

3. Rational skills
   a. Communication (written)
   b. Judgment
   c. Decision-making skills
   d. Management of time
   e. Planning and organizing
      skills
   f. Fact-finding skills
   g. Control skills
   h. Delegation skills
   i. Problem analysis
   j. Follow through

4. Human skills
   a. Leadership
   b. Emotional maturity
   c. Oral communications
   d. Interpersonal sensitivity
   e. Assertiveness skills
   f. Adaptability
   g. Fairness
   h. Flexibility
   i. Attitude toward development
      of personnel
   j. Stress management
   k. Attitude
   l. Handling of people
   m. Power
   n. Enthusiasm
   o. Patience
   p. Integrity
   q. Intuition
   r. Team development
   s. Stability
   t. Organizational climate

FIGURE 19-1 Assessment center dimensions.

center number between 12 and 15. Once the dimensions are prioritized and the most important ones are established, it is possible to move on to the next step.

Developing a Matrix and Exercises

In the third step, a matrix is drawn up that lists the dimensions on one side and the possible exercises across the top. Normally, each part of the assessment center will test for six or seven dimensions. It is possible for dimensions to be tested in more than one exercise. The more important dimensions are tested in three out of a possible four exercises. In some assessment centers, a dimension may be tested once; for example, command presence in the role-play situation.

Figure 19-2 shows an example of a typical evaluation matrix for an assessment center for a police department.

Developing Guidelines

Once the matrix and exercises are agreed on, **guidelines** are developed for each part of the assessment center. The guidelines include the purpose, a brief definition of the individual

	Project Development and Presentation	In-Basket Exercise	Leaderless Group Exercise	Oral Interview	
1. Work perspective		X	X		(2)
2. Command presence	X			X	(2)
3. Oral communication	X		X	X	(3)
4. Written communication	X	X			(2)
5. Interpersonal sensitivity	X		X	X	(3)
6. Decision-making skills		X	X		(2)
7. Stress management				X	(1)
8. Control skills	X	X			(2)
9. Emotional maturity				X	(1)
10. Delegation		X			(1)
11. Planning and organizing	X	X	X		(3)
12. Flexibility			X	X	(2)
	6	6	6	6	

FIGURE 19-2 Evaluation matrix for assistant chief.

dimensions, and examples of behaviors that should be considered positive and those that should be considered negative. In the guidelines, specific behavior patterns for the individual police department are given so that assessors can understand which behaviors should be rated high and which should be rated low. For example, in the dimension of written communication, high grades should be given for complete sentences, conciseness, and correct spelling. Low grades should be given for poor spelling, poor organization, or incomplete sentences.

Developing Exercises

In the fifth step, each exercise is developed in great detail. In the oral interview panel, the assessors are selected and questions that are common for all candidates are developed. In the **role-play situation**, a role-player is selected. Instructions for the role-player as well as the candidate are prepared. Whether to use audio or video equipment is also decided. Video can be used for two purposes. First, it can allow the command personnel of the police agency to identify the behavior patterns of each candidate after the completion of the assessment center. Second, and just as important, it is a way to give individual feedback to candidates on how they were graded and how they appeared during their assessment.

Special instructions for each exercise should contain as much detail for the assessors as possible. For example, in the in-basket exercise, instructions may include even the fact that the name should be placed on envelopes. Instructions should be read carefully, and if extra answer sheets are needed, assessors can provide them. For leaderless groups, the instructions might include the fact that the assessors should provide name tags and solicit questions prior to the beginning of the exercise.

Instructions are provided for each exercise. One set of instructions goes to the candidates. In a role-play situation, the instructions may designate the information to be provided to the candidate. They may say that the candidate is to role-play the position of captain and that he or she is going to interview a disgruntled employee who has received a performance evaluation report. In addition, instructions are provided for the assessors. These are usually one or two paragraphs in length and are concise, so that the assessors understand their role in the process.

Next, the problem is defined for each exercise. The written plan problem may be extensive in its detail. It may include pages of data from the department's annual and monthly reports. In another instance, it may contain information from other facets of the department, such as memoranda from the chief and policy statements. The last part is the scoring form, which is necessary to help assessors complete the scoring as consistently as possible and in the terms and manner in which the police department deems most effective.

Training

In the sixth step, assessors and candidates are trained. In assessor training, it is a common practice to hold a short meeting with the assessors for each exercise, usually the night before or a few hours prior to the beginning of the assessment center itself. In some areas of the country, a general pool of assessors is trained at a community college; they then are called on by individual agencies within a general area as they are needed. Usually this short-term training program is conducted by giving an overview of the assessment center and then going through the guidelines for the individual parts for the assessors in great detail. Emphasis is placed on the assessor's understanding of his or her role and of the definitions of each dimension as it applies to that individual agency. In most assessment centers, one assessor is assigned the responsibility of playing the lead role. Usually this is the more experienced assessor, especially for that individual exercise. In this step, some agencies have taken the opportunity to prepare individual candidates for an understanding of the assessment center approach. This training usually takes a maximum of five hours and involves explaining the meaning of the dimensions and how candidates will be graded.

Conducting the Center

In the seventh step, the assessment center is conducted. It takes place in a neutral locale and the **coordinator** does not take part in the exercises. The coordinator is responsible for seeing that candidates are on time and that assessors' questions are answered. One of the major tasks for the assessors is to get together at the completion of the center and meet with the police chief to give their personal views of each of the candidates. This kind of feedback is not designed to qualify any candidate but only to give to the police chief the personal impressions of the assessors. This feedback is given after the center has been completed and all scores have been tabulated. In this way, scores or rankings cannot be adjusted and the integrity of the assessment center approach is not compromised.

Ensuring Feedback

The eighth and final step involves giving feedback to the individual candidates. This is done within two weeks of the completion of the center. Each candidate must receive as much information as possible, avoiding comparisons, and simply helping candidates understand their performance and what steps they might take to improve it in the future.

A common approach of feedback is for a single assessor to receive comments from other assessors, study the individual scoring forms, and then hold a personal interview of about 30 minutes with each candidate. In some police agencies, candidates are required to appear before a departmental assessor from each exercise. In this manner, the candidate has four feedback sessions with separate assessors as opposed to one summation. Either method is satisfactory. The important factor is that the candidate is provided with feedback within a reasonable time.

Components of the Assessment Center

There are numerous exercises available to police chiefs who wish to implement an assessment center. The most common exercises include oral interviews, leaderless groups, in-basket problems, role-play situations, oral presentations, a written plan, and scheduling.

Oral Interviews

In the oral interview phase, there are three assessors, although many times a fourth is also included. Three is usually the most effective number, and two tend to make the interviews not inclusive enough. Four, on the other hand, can create a situation in which the issues are discussed only superficially. Three assessors, however, generally have enough time to let each one ask specific questions. Time frames are extended for top-level management positions. For example, for the position of police chief, the time might range from one and one-half hours up to as many as three hours. For positions such as first-line supervisors, for which there are many candidates, the times are shortened to 45 minutes. A minimum of 30 minutes for each interview is normally needed to obtain the necessary information.

An additional quarter-hour should be allowed to give the assessors a chance to score the candidate immediately after the interview. The interviewing process, although very common in police departments, is not necessarily the most effective measure of future behavior patterns. Usually the interviewing panel is made up of one member of the department, another member of city government, and a third member with a special skill, as in psychology or a technical area relevant to the specific position.

Each candidate must receive the same questions in oral interviews. Sometimes candidates are given as many as 10 to 15 questions, which is too large a number to permit answers of any depth. When the questions are restricted to four or five, they can be open-ended. An example of such a question would be the following: Assuming the police chief asks you your opinion on a certain issue, such as the color of vehicles, would you state your honest opinion? At this point the questions continue, regardless of what the answer might be, leading the candidate through his or her approach not only to the chief, but also to other managers, fellow supervisors, and subordinates. The real issue is at what point the candidate is able to distinguish the priority of two values—loyalty to the police department and honesty toward subordinates and superiors.

In the oral interview, it is advisable to develop specific questions to which the police agency requires answers. For example, if the police department is facing an affirmative action program, questions dealing with how such a program might be implemented would be important. If change or dealing with conflict are also important issues, then questions related to them should be developed. It is not advisable to have **stock questions** that have no clear-cut relevance to the examining police department. For example, a question such as "Do you believe in professionalization?" does not really help the assessors to discover how the candidate would behave in the new position.

Sometimes, questions asked in the oral interview have no special value to the grading process but are designed to provide feedback for the police chief. Such questions may focus on what the candidate may have done to prepare for the position, what he or she perceives the position to include, and how he or she would rank the individual candidates. This last question provides the police chief with feedback about how the candidates perceive one another and who they think is the best within their group.

Leaderless Groups

Leaderless groups are designed to test an individual's ability to work in a small group. The minimum number needed to make such an exercise effective is usually five. The maximum number is eight. There are two approaches to the kinds of questions to be asked within a leaderless group. The most common method is for the police department to develop one large issue or a series of small issues that are important to the present environment. For example, policies that are presently being studied can be presented for discussion by the leaderless group. Such policies might include off-duty work, the use of firearms, or reorganization. In some instances, more than one problem is given. For example, three small issues might be: (1) whether the department should accept gifts at Christmas; (2) whether the agency should issue press releases, and if so, on what incidents; and (3) whether cars should be assigned to personnel on a permanent basis.

Sometimes fixed problems that have nothing to do with the police agency are also used. Examples include group scenarios such as "Lost in the Desert," "Lost in the Arctic," or "Man on the Moon." In these exercises, some answers are recommended by experts; however, the purpose of this part of the assessment program is not to elicit the "correct answer," but to see how the candidates work together.

A third approach involves asking each member of the leaderless group to play a specific role. For example, candidates seeking the position of assistant chief of police may be asked to role-play other department heads, and the issue may be how to best reduce the citywide budget. This may give each person the opportunity to show some understanding of how other agencies deal with problems similar to those within the police department. Some departments restrict the role-playing to positions within their own agency. This seems to be the least effective, however, because it restricts the individuals involved. It therefore is not necessarily used when a large amount of information is to be analyzed during a leaderless group problem.

The leaderless group exercise usually lasts 45 minutes to one hour. To add stress, the assessors will sometimes collect the answer, have a short discussion among themselves, and then advise the group that the solution it has produced is inadequate. They then ask the group to continue to work on the exercise for an additional 15 minutes. Usually this additional time tends to place people under high stress, so that they begin to exhibit behavior patterns that may not have been evident before.

In-basket Problems

The in-basket exercise is considered especially effective, because it explores the candidates' abilities to set priorities and their understanding of departmental policies, rules, and standards.

In most police departments, a series of real-life memoranda are gathered approximately 60 to 90 days prior to the assessment center. Copies are made—changing names and dates—and most of the items in the exercise are then based on them.

The most common approach is to bring all the candidates together in a room and present the in-basket at that time. The answers are written on pieces of paper, and each candidate, upon completing them, places them in an envelope. The envelopes—one for each candidate—are then returned to the assessors. In some instances, names are excluded and candidates are judged only by assigned numbers. In this format, the only knowledge the assessors have is through the written documents provided by the candidates.

Another approach has the candidates complete the in-basket problem in 45 minutes. They are given the memoranda, asked to prioritize them, and required to briefly describe what they would do in each instance. Upon completion of this task, they present their written answers to three evaluators. The assessors read the answers and then take approximately 20 to 30 minutes to question each candidate concerning any issues they may feel are not totally resolved in the written responses. This allows a wider range of information to be evaluated.

In the in-basket exercise, the departments provide a priority list and model answers. Priorities are listed as those that should be handled within eight hours and those that could wait 24 to 48 hours. Model answers are usually one or two sentences at most, and these serve to guide the assessors as to the direction that the correct answers should take.

Role-play Situations

In these exercises, individuals are asked to play a specific part. The most common example involves the use of a disgruntled officer who objects to his or her performance evaluation report. In some instances, women play the role of complainants of sexual harassment or African-Americans complain about discrimination. Sometimes a combination is used to focus on more than just one issue. For example, an African-American sergeant might complain to the candidate, who is role-playing a captain. The sergeant complains that the performance evaluation report is not fair—that it is based predominantly on racially discriminatory attitudes on the part of his lieutenant. In such situations, the same role-player must be used in each instance.

A police department can use a role-player from within the agency. This individual may play the part of a captain with candidates seeking the position of assistant chief. The role-player may be accused of taking something from a crime scene, and it is up to the assistant chief to conduct an interview to determine whether the accusation has any merit. In some instances, two role-players, both of whom are professional actors, can be used. They role-play the parts of two employees, subordinates to the candidate, who are involved in a conflict concerning the best way to implement a certain project. They have opposite points of view and, during the role-play situation, both indicate severe stress by raising their voices, standing, and pacing about the room.

In another instance, the candidates seeking the position of police captain might be brought into a room and advised that they are to give a speech to the chamber of commerce within 10 minutes. A specific issue is presented—one on which the candidates already know the department's point of view. They will also already have the data they would need to deal with this issue as police captains. After 10 minutes of preparation, each candidate presents a 10-minute speech and role-plays the situation as if he or she were speaking to members of the chamber of commerce. The evaluation would include not only the role-play presentation but also the candidates' handwritten notes.

Usually the role-play situation is limited to 30 minutes. Assessors are given an additional 15 minutes to discuss their ratings.

Oral Presentations

In the oral presentation, the candidate is given a specific question and is asked to respond within a short period, such as five to 10 minutes. Oral presentations include such issues as "Why do you seek this position?" "What do you feel are your personal qualifications?" or "How do you view your strengths and your weaknesses?" The weight given to this part of an assessment program is usually small, as it does not require a tremendous amount of forethought on the part of the candidate. Because of the nature of the questions and the amount of time provided, an in-depth analysis is not required of the assessors.

Some police agencies include an oral presentation in conjunction with a specially developed personal qualifications appraisal task. A series of questions and tasks are given to prospective candidates at least 30 to 45 days in advance. For example, the candidates may be asked to interview people in their professional and personal life, summarize what they have learned from these people, and supplement such knowledge with their own perceptions of themselves. They may be asked to write a short scenario about where they would like to be in their personal lives in five years. This would include such issues as lifestyle, vocation, organizational life, family, and free time. They are also asked to write an outline of their expectations for the police department within the next five years. During the oral presentation, they are given 15 minutes to explain their written document and are granted an additional 30 minutes in which to expand on their plan on the basis of questions provided by the assessors.

Written Plan

In the **written plan exercise**, candidates are given from 90 minutes to three hours to prepare a written document concerning a specific issue within the police department. The problems are varied, depending on the nature of the position sought. For example, in one police department, because the position being sought was in management, the problem involved planning for a rock concert at the civic auditorium. Other written plans have included broad issues, such as: (1) what promotional system should be implemented within the police department, (2) how the department should go about recruiting additional women and African-Americans to meet the requirements of the city's affirmative action program, and (3) how to develop team management practices.

The police department may give candidates approximately 45 days in which to develop a five-year budget plan for the police department. The budget documents are submitted at the end of that time. The assessors are then given approximately two weeks to read through these documents. Each candidate is given 10 minutes to explain additional information and then an additional 30 minutes during which to answer questions from the assessors. Only after all of this information has been gathered is the written plan evaluated.

The police chief should recognize that a written plan is a good exercise only when the position being sought requires people to write such plans. For example, a police department that has a Research and Development Unit should not necessarily demand a long written plan from every candidate for a supervisory position. Only for those seeking posts in the Research and Development Unit would such an assignment be appropriate.

Scheduling

In the scheduling exercise, the candidate is given the personnel roster of a given unit and is asked to allocate the time of these people—that is, to develop a scheduling system—to achieve the overall goals of the police department. To create stress, the problem may be complicated by introducing additional information halfway through the 30-minute exercise. For example, individuals may resign, call in sick, or need to be scheduled for training programs. In this way, flexibility and the ability to make decisions under stress can also be analyzed.

Rating Scales

Numerical Scales

There are different ways in which scoring scales can be developed to evaluate the individual candidate during the assessment program. In most cities, a specific numerical value is assigned to each exercise. For example, an oral interview might be worth 40 points; an in-basket exercise, 30 points; a leaderless group, 20 points; and a role-play situation, 10 points. Each candidate, upon completion of the assigned exercise, is rated individually by each assessor. Once the individual ratings are completed, assessors discuss the ratings and come to a consensus as to the final numerical score. After all candidates have completed an exercise, the raters examine final consensus scores given to each and make any adjustments necessary to clearly show differences that may be greater than originally agreed upon. For example, suppose that candidate A received 28 out of 30 points, and candidate B received 26. The assessors may later agree that candidate B was not two points but three points behind. Thus, the candidate B's score might be changed to a 25.

In using numerical ratings, it becomes difficult to show large differences between the candidates, especially when the maximum score is below 20 on any exercise. When numerical ratings are used, each exercise should be graded on a score of at least 30. The total scores of all exercises can be computed to reflect an overall grade of 100 percent. For example, if there are four exercises, the first might contain 30 points, the second 40, the third 50, and the fourth 60, for a total of 180 points. This score can easily be computed to a scale of 100 percent. (Divide the applicant's score, for example 120, by the total of 180, for a final grade of 66.6.)

Strengths and Weaknesses

A second approach is to use a rating form that discusses the strengths and weaknesses of each candidate. Under this form of rating, however, no numerical grade is given, and the police chief receives feedback on the strengths and weaknesses of the individual candidates in each dimension of each exercise. The final judgment as to the value of strengths and weaknesses is left up to the person responsible for the final promotion.

Composite Graphs

The third method is to develop a composite graph. In this method, points are given to each dimension instead of each exercise. For example, if decision-making is examined in three of the four exercises, then the number of points given to decision-making is placed on a bar or line graph denoting the score for each exercise. In this way, the person responsible for the promotion has a composite graph from which to analyze individual scores on each dimension and where dimension scores may appear the strongest and the weakest. Again, using decision-making as an example, an individual may be an effective decision-maker in a one-to-one situation such as role-playing during an oral interview process, but he or she may not have exhibited strong decision-making skills in the leaderless group. Thus, the police chief has an understanding of how the candidate will behave in different situations.

Forced Choice

Another approach is to have assessors rate the candidates on a **forced-choice scale**. They have to rate candidates first, second, third, and fourth during each part of the assessment center without giving assigned weights. This system has not proved to be effective in giving an overview of the candidate's behavior during the total assessment center.

Consensus

In the rating process, individual assessors must rate the candidates prior to any discussions between themselves. Once they have completed their individual ratings, the assessors discuss them and come to an overall consensus. All the scoring is given to the candidate during the feedback process. In this way, the integrity of the assessment center is maintained and more data can be analyzed before the final consensus is reached.

Conclusion

In conclusion, police chiefs must recognize that assessment centers will not solve all promotional problems. They are designed to serve as a tool in police agencies where such tools may be useful. History has shown that the assessment center approach may help to pinpoint quality candidates and, more importantly, lend a sense of fairness to the promotional process. These are both important criteria, especially in government agencies. The assessment center must be recognized as only a tool; therefore the belief that this approach always produces "the best" is not necessarily justified. Police chiefs must recognize that they personally must be strongly committed to anyone who is promoted to a key management position. Assessment centers can help to develop that commitment by identifying the strengths and weaknesses of persons to be promoted. This tends to reduce the amount of time it takes a police manager to learn about key managerial personnel. Thus, conflicts are reduced and working relationships develop more quickly and effectively.

Although assessment centers may not be the final answer, they are certainly helpful in identifying the assets and liabilities that a candidate may bring to a new position.

Reference

Kirkland v. New York State Correctional Services, 711 F.2d 1117 (1st Cir. 1983).

Discussion Questions

1. Do you believe that an assessment center is the best approach for making promotions within a police department? If so, why?

2. What issues could be addressed in a typical assessment center?

3. Why do you believe assessment centers are perceived as fair by the candidates?

4. Is there a better and more effective way of promoting personnel in a police department than the assessment center approach?

20 ▦

Leading Small and Medium-Sized Law Enforcement Agencies[1]

LEARNING OBJECTIVES

1. The student will be able to understand the role of the chief in dealing with change.

2. The student will be able to understand the importance of interpersonal communication.

3. The student will be able to understand the effective tasks of leading.

Introduction

The majority of law enforcement agencies in the United States are small agencies with fewer than 25 officers (Hickman & Reaves, 2003). This means there is a great likelihood that many officers will, at some point in their careers, work for a small to medium-sized agency. Because of vast variations in agency sizes, it is difficult to generalize information that fits appropriately with all agency sizes. Nonetheless, an overview of issues that accompany managing smaller agencies can be helpful for potential supervisors in these agencies.

Leading—or working as a manager in—a small law enforcement agency offers a number of challenges that are different from that in larger agencies. For example, a large number of sheriff's departments are rural agencies. Sheriff's departments have responsibilities that police departments usually do not have, such as running the county jail and providing security in courtrooms. While sheriffs with large departments also have these responsibilities, small to medium-sized jurisdictions often have unique responsibilities, due to the specific issues that may exist.

Because there is a smaller tax base in small towns, jurisdiction size easily impacts budgetary issues, which can affect equipment, salaries, personnel, and even organizational structure. Small jurisdictions may have a chief and only two or three sergeants, each of whom supervises just a few officers. As a result, the command structure is flattened. Thus, the smaller department has some drawbacks, but it also offers some benefits. The shorter command structure ensures a greater **span of control** for managers. This refers to the number of subordinate officers that a manager supervises. Swanson, Territo, and Taylor (2001) state that seven is the upper limit of the number of officers a police manager can supervise most effectively. It is obviously more likely for managers in

---

[1]Chapter 20 is included with the permission of Edward Werder.

smaller jurisdictions to have such a number of subordinates, assuming that budgetary constraints don't keep sergeant numbers so low that they are all supervising more officers than would be considered effective.

A flattened command structure can also make **unity of command** easier to maintain. There are fewer opportunities for misunderstanding a chief's orders if they have gone through fewer people. This should help keep all the agency's officers with the same understanding of the chief's commands. Furthermore, in smaller agencies, first-line officers are more likely to know the chief on an individual basis, which can also be beneficial to employee morale. The officers can associate orders with a person they know. In larger agencies, the chief may not be able to know all the officers.

Capsambelis (2009) notes the importance—and occasional absence—of policy and **procedure manuals** in small rural agencies. Up-to-date policies need to be written for the sake of clearly communicating departmental expectations, but also to protect the agency in the event of a critical incident. Keeping the manual up to date may prove a challenge for understaffed small to medium-sized agencies. There may simply not be enough time to update the manual on a regular basis if the officers are all occupied with other important duties. Capsambelis (2009) documents one case in which a new chief in a small jurisdiction found that the only policy-and-procedures manual the agency had was a folder with papers kept inside it in no particular order. In other cases, some small agencies have no manual at all. Establishing the clarity and importance of a procedure manual should be one of the primary concerns for the chief of a small agency. When a culture of indifference to critical agency issues has long been established, especially in a small agency where many of the officers are friends with each other, a new chief should consider organizational modification.

Organizational Modification

There is no predetermined point at which an organization should be modified or replaced. Organizations wear out much like capital items or, in some cases, people. The key to leading a small organization may depend on the proactive recognition of when the organization requires enlightened leadership, management, communication, value system, or all of the above.

An important factor that may bear upon the recognition of the need for **organizational modification** or replacement has to do with how the leader has achieved his or her position. When speaking about the head of an agency, whether that person was appointed from outside the organization or from within can make an important difference in how that person proceeds. It is also important for the leader to know his or her mandate; that is, whether his or her role is to become a **change agent** or to maintain the status quo. An improper or incorrect analysis of the role that is to be played and the tools that are available for use can spell the difference between success and failure.

At times, an individual who has come from outside the organization has a more objective vision of both the organization's strengths and weaknesses. On the other hand, that same individual may misdiagnose the weaknesses and strengths of the agency and perhaps apply the wrong solution to the correct problem or, conversely, apply the right solution to the wrong problem.

For the individual who has been appointed to the leadership role from within the organization, he or she may find that problem recognition is difficult. The sources of information may be biased, and the objectivity of both problem recognition and solution identification may be myopic. In addition, the ability to implement effective solutions through the efforts of employees who have come to recognize the leader in a very different role may lead to less-than-optimal success.

The Need for Change

Clearly, the need for modernization and change is important to organizational vitality. The primary goal of the leader of a small to medium-sized law enforcement agency may well be the employee's acceptance of change. It seems that organizations that are composed of individuals who are not only capable of risk-taking, but feel comfortable in doing so, often have the greatest success in adapting to new situations or modifying old ones. Thus, establishing an environment within the organization clearly becomes one of the primary goals of a leader, regardless of how he or she attained the position.

One of the most interesting contradictions of human nature is its ambivalence toward things new and different. In many cases, those involved in law enforcement may be very adaptable to change in their personal lives, while continuing to focus on their reluctance to do so organizationally. It seems that while we seek changes for the better in our personal lives, we are equally content to resist organizational change. In some cases, the reasons for such resistance are well-founded; there may have been organizational conflicts, disciplinary action, or knowledge of, or involvement in, detrimental changes that have caused the reluctance to adapt to current or future ones.

Organizational change may also require realignment of personal relationships. This is probably more true for the leader who has assumed his or her position from within the agency, perhaps through a series of promotions and elevations, as opposed to the leader who is selected from outside the organization. It is quite difficult to have both friend and foe in an organization objectively consider the new role of the leader, much less adapt his or her behavior in such a way that it allows the new role to have a reasonable chance of success. Sometimes an individual leader may believe that the organization has been either under-led or over-managed. The inaccurate assumption, regardless of which is true, will have negative consequences for all. Thus, the leader is not always given a fair and equal chance at success based upon the experiential base of the workforce.

Historically, we have come to realize that changes will occur regardless of how strongly they are opposed. The result may be that changes will be ineffective and have no relationship to their intended outcome. The key may well be that the leader must consolidate differences and identify commonalities if there is to be any chance not only for success, but tremendous achievement.

Interpersonal Communication

The leader of a small to medium-sized police agency must realize prior to assuming command that the function of the patrol officer is just as important as that of the executive. While the tasks each must perform are decidedly different, the leader's role must be to enhance the role of the individuals who deliver the primary level of service to the community. The latest focus on community policing requires that an informed, well-trained, and energetic work force provides the basis upon which the agency will be judged. While the chief executive of the agency may have exposure to community groups, it is, in the final analysis, the quality of the service that is provided each and every day that determines community acceptance and overall agency effectiveness. Thus, a caste system cannot be arranged that establishes more into the rank structure than was ever intended. Each role in the agency must be identified for what its function is, what accountability standards will be applied, and what the timeline for achievement will be. Subsequently, the chief executive must affix accountability and get on with the job at hand. One assignment should be no more important than another and, if reviewed analytically, must in effect complement the work of other specific functions if the agency as a whole is to be deemed successful.

Perhaps the most important attribute in a well-run organization is an effective communications system. That does not speak to the technical requirements of dispatching and radio transmissions, but rather day-to-day **interpersonal communication** between and among ranks and between and among job classifications. The value of communication cannot be overestimated; it makes the difference between success and failure, between goal attainment and goal avoidance. It affects the standing of the law enforcement agency not only within its constituent community, but also among the law enforcement community within a radius of many miles.

The Leader

One of the other features that affects an organization and its leader is the background of the leader himself or herself. The potential executive in many cases gets his or her start in one specialty or another. That can form the basis for an **organizational bias** which, if not checked, can create the impression on the part of many that they are invisible and that their contributions are not important or valued. Thus, in order to be effective, a leader must ensure that everyone's contribution is valued, appreciated, and that the penalty for doing something wrong remains less than the penalty for doing nothing at all. In today's law enforcement agencies, that is not universally true, and it continues to confound organizational success.

Individuals are hired who have skills and abilities that were recognized by both the organization and the chief executive in their selection; yet within a certain time frame, they are sometimes viewed as incapable of making a significant contribution and ineffective at helping to achieve the organizational goals. This invalidates the need for a strong contribution from every employee, and actually enhances the cost of law enforcement operations. If an agency continues to give up on employees who, for one reason or another, have not reached their potential or, having reached it are contributing less, we add to the payroll those individuals who must pick up the slack and fulfill not only their own role but help compensate for the roles that are not being fulfilled by existing employees. In today's society, with concepts like cutback management, we can ill afford to fund duplicate positions to accomplish a singular task.

In distinguishing the similarities and differences between managers and leaders, both the managers' and leaders' abilities to develop empathy with their people and to acquire wisdom about them represents one of their heavy obligations. Whether leaders or managers, knowledge of their most expensive and valuable resources is essential if any semblance of organizational accomplishment is to occur. This reinforces the previous comments with regard to the experiential base of the leader; a narrowly focused career on his or her part can reinforce a narrowly confined view of organizational components' importance and perhaps undervalue those who are working in assignments that do not share the historical similarities of the leader.

Neither managers nor leaders can leave their ethical standards at the department or office door. To be effective, they must be seen as dedicated to values that are bigger than they are, and also willing to serve and sacrifice for them. The most significant conclusion about the motivation of subordinates is that it is not what you do, it is what you are that counts.

Thus, we see that the most important role of the leader is to provide the environment in which motivation can occur. It is, in most cases, left up to the individual employee to be motivated, but the leader's role must be to establish the environment. If the employees do not trust him or her, any method, including the best human relations techniques, are likely to fail. Many of today's organizations are seriously unbalanced in the type of values that have guided them at the top and throughout the various levels of the management hierarchy.

There is not a management style that has a single ideal approach. The key to success in management or leadership is for each manager to identify his or her own strengths and weaknesses and to lead from them and work on his or her weak areas. A second key factor in management success is putting together a team based on the principle of **complementarity** (should the team be all alike in their views) or differences.

It seems clear that if complementarity is not practiced, a leader can be blindsided by issues, problems, and concepts that are dissimilar from his or her previous experience. Thus, it will appear both from the outside and from within that the leader is biased by virtue of his or her single-purpose viewpoints and solutions. This is not only unhealthy but can increase the vulnerability and durability of the leader in that role. Leaders often have lost their job and have never seen it coming.

The widely held view of the American law enforcement agency is of a big agency in a large metropolis. However, the vast majority of law enforcement agencies in the United States are small agencies. More than half of the country's local departments have fewer than 10 sworn officers. Ninety percent of American agencies have less than 50 officers. In fact, about 5 percent of the country's agencies have no full-time sworn personnel. Obviously, these agencies are serving small populations; about 90 percent of local agencies serve jurisdictions with a population of less than 25,000 citizens. Even if officers are not currently working for small agencies, there is a chance that they eventually will. Understanding the social dynamics and implications of departmental policies may be different for agencies in these different settings.

Research indicates that rural police officers confront some of the same challenges as their urban counterparts, but they also have to deal with challenges that are unique to the rural environment. For example, small-town officers tend to have less anonymity, so they are more likely to deal with the challenges of being called on for matters that are barely police matters. Additionally, they have to deal with crimes that are specific to the rural landscape, such as agricultural and wildlife crimes. It is important for a police manager in a small community to be familiar with community norms. For example, it may be necessary for managers to remind their officers that driving some pieces of farm equipment on public roads may not be legal in the strict sense, but it will benefit the esidents, the department, and the officer to allow the equipment on the road for short distances.

Tasks of Leading

As we speak to the issue of leading a small to medium-sized law enforcement agency, there must be clear goals and a timetable for their accomplishment. That requires that the organization be accurately assessed in terms of its strengths, weaknesses, opportunities, and shortcomings. An inventory should be completed on its assets: primarily its human resources and not just those fixtures, appliances, and capital items that are adjunct to the most important resource.

When goals have been set, a clear agenda needs to be established in their accomplishment. Paralleling that agenda must be the intensive communication that comes with informing those who will be responsible for their accomplishment as to how the goals were arrived at, the process used in soliciting input throughout the agency and what role the employees can play. If the leader has arrived at the agency from outside, the goals and agenda are often set unilaterally. While not always true, if the agenda and goals were established by virtue of employment discussions with the hiring authority, there may be a little latitude in at least some of them. But the wise leader will not set the goals nor establish an agenda that is assumed to be complete. However, some initial topics should be identified and the timetable set for their success. Internal communication and staff meetings should be arranged subsequently in order to add more goals, enhance that agenda, or improve the organization through such concepts as quality circles early in his or her administration.

It is important to set high standards. It is generally true that people will not perform above expectations, so therefore it is important to have high expectations. Laying out concepts and identifying programs is important, but it is more important to let subordinates execute them.

Credibility of action is the single most important determinant of whether a leader will be followed over time. Leadership is not a place, it is a process. In essence, leadership begins where management ends, where the systems of rewards and punishments, control and scrutiny, give way to innovation, individual character, and the courage of convictions. When we think of leaders, we recall times of turbulence, conflict, innovation, and change. When we think of managers, we recall times of stability, harmony, maintenance, and constancy. In essence, leaders tend to shake things up. That does not mean that managers cannot be leaders but it does describe a style which some individuals who prefer to exclusively manage do not subscribe to.

Roles that were common in decades past from the 1950s through the millennium are now disappearing at an alarming rate. In 1980, there was one job for every nine candidates in middle management; in 1995, there were 47 candidates for every job. Organizations continue to downsize, lay off employees, contract for services, or otherwise look for ways to improve the bottom line. The private sector has been involved in this process for some time, while government is a more recent player in retrenchment management.

Thus, to remain viable as a law enforcement agency, we must work smarter, not necessarily harder. In reality, the best organizations work both smarter *and* harder. Leading a small to medium-sized law enforcement agency is really about leading people. People in important management positions should not only be enthusiastic themselves, they should be selected for their ability to engender enthusiasm among their associates and subordinates. Nothing more effectively involves people, sustains credibility, or generates enthusiasm than face-to-face communication.

Many small to medium-sized agencies are in rural areas. If a newly hired manager comes from a more urban background, there may be some difficulties learning the rural culture. However, it is vital that the manager strive to understand the citizens he or she is serving as well as the subordinate officers. Because **population densities** are lower in rural areas, word can spread quickly in the community and within the agency. Face-to-face communication can go a long way in establishing good working relationships with both groups.

There is a formula that seems to hold true in managing any size agency: P = A+M. The formula stands for "productivity = ability + motivation." The leader of a small to medium-sized law enforcement agency often inherits individuals with whom he or she is unfamiliar. An assumption can be made that most individuals who make up the staff of an organization are capable, qualified, and competitive or they would not have been selected. However, what happens to individuals is a product of the organization itself. In essence, sometimes an organization that does not enhance the ability of its employees removes the environment in which motivation can occur. In addition, when leading a small to medium-sized law enforcement agency, one must remember that

empowerment is not the things you do *to* or *for* people, it is the impediments you take away, leaving space for people to empower themselves.

Change is a door that can only be opened from the inside. As a result, in leading a small to medium-sized agency, individuals who may have lost initiative, competence, or even hope, must be given an appropriate environment in which change can take place, and the time to change. For some, particularly those who have been anxiously awaiting an opportunity for change, it will come easily and quickly. For others, who may have lost faith in their profession, their organization, or their leadership, it may take more time. There may be impediments to achieving their overall metamorphosis quickly. In a world where success depends on brainpower and curiosity, the self-managed growth of the individual becomes paramount.

It is clear that in the leadership positions within an organization, the goals, objectives, values, and mission of the organization must be laid out in such a form that all can and will embrace them. For some it will be an easy process, while others will have some or even great difficulty. But if the organization is to be successful, it is important to bring along as many as possible, if not everyone, with the leader toward the achievement of that goal. It is an amazing phenomenon to witness an organization that has been valued little by its community and whose internal values have also been compromised, achieve great things without changing one employee; the only thing that has changed is the will to succeed in an environment where they know that it is possible and likely.

It is important that the leader be able to evaluate the difference between motion and direction. In the leadership roles, it may be that people are very busy with activity. But that is not the same as moving toward a given goal or objective. There is an adage that busy people get things done, but "busy" must be defined as at least incrementally moving closer to the overall objectives of the organization *with the same ethic* the leadership has embraced.

Activity and accomplishment are quite different, because many individuals in organizations continue to remain busy but at the end of their shifts they may not have moved the organization toward any of its goals. And it is important to remember that a goal is a dream with a deadline. To say an organization has goals, particularly a small to medium-sized agency, is not to define how those goals will be accomplished and over what period of time. To establish an objective without a level of accountability for the time it will take to accomplish it is a whimsical thought rather than a statement of intended reality. There is an expression that suggests that work will expand with the time available to do it; that is true in both large and small organizations. The problem is that smaller to medium-sized organizations cannot afford to waste any time, for they generally do not have a high level of specialization or the support personnel to add to the complement of people who will help the agency along its way.

It is also important for the leader to focus on opportunities, not problems. In many cases of assuming command of a small to medium-sized agency, the leader will be overwhelmed with individuals who outline problems, with only a few outlining its strengths and opportunities. If one begins with a belief that employees did not arrive at their present state of competence by themselves, and that the organization had much to do with the level of leadership within and was in some part responsible for the level of commitment and competence of its employees, then a place to start is not far behind. To assume that individuals are not immediately competent, committed, or capable is to shortchange not only the task at hand but also the individuals who must in some way accomplish the organizational goals. With rare exception, most individuals are salvageable and can assume greater responsibilities than even *they* imagined if the leadership of a small organization will but attempt **employee development programs** and training.

Employee development in some cases involves communication, in others training, and in others reassignment. But it must be remembered that one cannot trade on yesterday's training to achieve tomorrow's results. Training may consist of a few words from the chief executive to develop a clear vision of the future, or it may involve intensive classroom settings or actual performance opportunities in the field. But whichever is the course for each employee, it is clear that all employees cannot be treated the same and achieve the same results. Fair and **equitable treatment** is not the same as **equal treatment**. Neither will the results be equal if the same standard measuring stick and level of interest is applied to each employee, rather than finding key development criteria for each employee regardless of which level he or she holds within the organization.

Sometimes encouragement may come from allowing the employee to "try easier," not harder. Some employees become so frustrated and concerned about their tenure that their effort is so narrowly focused that they will achieve very little, if anything. It is quite possible that encouraging an employee to relieve the cycle of pressure, to find enjoyment in the tasks at hand, and to try to develop an eye for detail and a sense of urgency will spur major accomplishments. Success often breeds success. An individual who has tasted not only success, but the recognition for it, will try again and again to improve not only his or her future opportunities but also future recognition and compensation.

In leading a small to medium-sized law enforcement agency, some words come to mind that may be missing from management today: *pride, enthusiasm, caring, commitment, responsibility, trust, love* and *fun.* People do not always care what you know unless they know that you care. An analysis of the organization may find that many are not doing things right and some are not even doing the right things. Therefore, establishing an agenda, a focus, and a time period for benchmarks will allow everyone to recognize that success is not only an ongoing process but also an ultimate destination. That will encourage more and more individuals to be successful. Whether we refer to the leadership of an organization or to each and every employee, it is clear that success is not what you achieve, but rather what you become. Most employees will find that if, in fact, there has been an interest in their development and a sincere effort on the part of the organization to enhance their abilities, widespread consensus in embracing the organizational objectives cannot be far behind.

It is also clear that many chief executives of law enforcement agencies will attempt to restructure an organization by appearing at various community functions and joining a rather large number of outside organizations. But to lead a small to medium-sized law enforcement agency, one must spend as much or more time restructuring the role of the police executive *inside* the organization. In order to sell a product or service properly, one must have the assurance that the product is sound and will accomplish what it has been represented to accomplish. Law enforcement organizations are similar. If an agency represents that it has a certain capacity or that its employees are approachable and competent, and the public finds out later that that is clearly not the case, it not only undermines the acceptance of the organization but clearly represents that the leadership of the organization is not in touch with reality.

How do we know when we are making progress? Sometimes the indicators are obvious; other times they are not. Some of the signs may have to do with the amount and severity of discipline necessary, the overall morale of the organization, the openness of communication, and the actual change in the community, not only in terms of the reduction of crime and the increased clearances, but also the approachability of the department from the community standpoint.

As Pat Riley (1994) wrote in *The Winner Within,* a leader creates an empowering relationship. Regardless of the level within the organization or the job description, individuals come together with the sense that they can accomplish a great deal more because it is not only expected, it is also appreciated. One will find in such an organization that there is a sense of both **interdependence** and independence. This can replace total reliance upon subordination and allow both job enrichment and job enlargement. Decision making becomes the responsibility of everyone. Standards are upheld, not by one individual, but rather upheld by all. Development of a team approach to problem solving and decision making creates a system of checks and balances. This allows calculated yet effective risk taking, with the accomplishment of the agency's agenda as the primary focus. A small to medium-sized law enforcement agency should value adaptability, the quality that encourages the breaking of molds and the expansion of ideas and skills. Flexibility becomes part of the makeup of every member of the department's "team," with inflexibility tolerated only during the learning process.

The effectively led organization also creates a sense of duty. The striving for and the attainment of ethical and effective performance is an uncompromising standard that everyone recognizes and is compelled to attain; compromise is neither desirable nor acceptable. The small to medium-sized law enforcement agency should be an environment where coming to work is fun. Enjoyable, yes; challenging, yes; a learning experience, yes; but also fun. The enjoyment of one's work, even under circumstances that are sometimes uncertain and even dangerous, can be enhanced by the skillful leader who knows how to balance priorities with needs. A small to medium-sized law enforcement agency is similar to conducting a small orchestra. It is not only a matter of whether the instruments can be played, but also how well they are played and the harmony they produce. The great organization, one that has achieved both internal and external success, is capable of achieving orchestrations that others cannot. Even though each employee may be different, and the notes on the sheets of music may be different, the instruments will of necessity be coordinated, and the melody that results functions as one song, played well and with the listener and not the musician in mind. The small to medium-sized law enforcement agency that has achieved this understands the need for the community to hear the sound of excellent orchestration played by artisans who are skilled, balanced, and dedicated to playing the right notes at the right time.

In such an organization, there is a sense of equity where people aren't always treated equally, just fairly. The balancing of the contributions of each employee remains vital to the successful outcome of the team.

Finally, attitude is everything. The leader of a small to medium-sized agency is trying to become a better person in addition to being a better police officer. Imperfections exist, as they do in all human beings, but those who show the signs of greatness are neither ashamed of their weaknesses nor are they afraid to accept them. Thus, in such an organization, self-improvement of the leader as well as those who respond to him or her will simultaneously improve, and the team will be substantially enhanced.

Learning Exercise

"Nearly a year." Nathan was talking quietly to himself about his first post-college job as he settled into his patrol car. He could barely believe that he had been working for this rural sheriff's department for the last 10 and a half months. When he first started, he barely knew his way around the area. Nathan had grown up in the suburbs of Nashville, Tennessee, before going to college in a town that was more sparsely populated than he was accustomed to. When he graduated a semester early, he began working for this sheriff's department. It was not the kind of place he had anticipated working, but it was the only opportunity he had in law enforcement and he was glad to have it. But he had struggled to learn the various coves and roads in the county and the bigger challenge had been learning the culture of the clannish rural residents.

As Nathan turned on to a road on a particularly sparse end of the county, he was impressed with how much he had learned. Apparently, his supervisor was as well. This was the first time Nathan's sergeant was willing to let him take a shift alone. The department was so small that they would often keep a single officer on patrol through the overnight shift. Sergeant Sawyer had told Nathan that she thought the typically slow night shift was a good way to let Nathan get his first try at solo patrolling. For the first three hours of the shift the sergeant had been correct. Then the radio crackled to life as the department dispatcher sent Nathan to answer a call. Nathan acknowledged receiving the call, then twisted his lip in slight consternation. He tested himself to see if he knew how to get near the address. Finally, he admitted to himself that he didn't know where it was. He typed the address into his GPS receiver and began following the instructions.

When Nathan arrived at the complainant's house, he found an angry-looking man standing in overalls on the steps of a weathered wood house at the end of a gravel driveway deep in the woods. Nathan stepped out and introduced himself. Without introducing himself, the man began pointing into the night's darkness and voicing his complaint. "I heard some son'bitch shooting over here on my property. Let's go get 'im."

Nathan stopped the man from walking into the dark forest so he could collect more information. The complainant told stories of a neighbor boy and how he had often found old camp sites at various spots on his land. Nathan finally got the man to tell him about a road that bordered his property in the direction of the gunfire. Nathan said, "Well sir, how about you go inside your house and let me see if I can find anything on the road. I'll either come back or have the dispatcher call you." The man wanted to be more proactive in defending his property, but he finally relented and agreed to Nathan's plan.

While driving on the dark road, Nathan felt uneasy. He was not familiar with this end of the county or any of the people in the area. He had also never dealt with a search for an unseen suspect in a dark forest. He drove back and forth on the road four times before spotting something that looked out of place. There seemed to be a break in the weeds from the complainant's property onto the road. Nathan stopped the vehicle and walked over to it with his flashlight in his left hand and his right hand on his sidearm. Then he saw a drag path with blood spatters leading from the woods up to large tire tracks. He shined his light into the forest and followed the path. It was only a short distance before he came to a gut pile from a deer that had apparently been shot. The complainant was right. Someone had been shooting on his property. But Nathan was flummoxed. He was a deputy sheriff, not a game warden. He did not know any of the game laws. He didn't even know who the local game warden was. After a few moments of uncertainty, Nathan radioed dispatch. "Can you contact the local game warden and have him meet me out here?"

- Note the unique challenges that this small, rural department faces. The deputies are often without immediate backup. Not being from the local area, Nathan was often lost geographically, but also socially. He was struggling to learn the social customs of the area. What can a police manager do to help a new officer get indoctrinated to the rural culture?
- Also note that there are types of crime that only occur in rural areas. How can a police manager of a small, rural agency help his or her officers prepare for these types of challenges?

References

Capsambaelis, C. (2009). *Policing in Rural America*, Durham, N.C.: Carolina Academic Press.

Hickman,, M. J., & Reaves, B. A. (2003). *Local police departments, 2000* (NCJ Publication no 106534) Washington, D.C.: U.S. Department of Justice.

Keegan, W. J. (1984). How to cultivate your management style. *Office Administration and Automation, 30.*

Peters, T. (1994). The pursuit of wow. *The Police Manager.* New York: Vintage Press. p. 66.

Riley, P. (1994). *The Winner Within: A Life Plan for Team Players.* New York: Berkley Books.

Schwarzkopf, N. (1992). Schwarzkopf on leadership. *Teleconnect, 44.*

Swanson, M. J., Territo, L., & Taylor, R. W. (2001). *Police administration: Structures, Processes, and Behavior.* Upper Saddle River, N.J: Prentice Hall.

Werder, E. J. (1996). The great sergeant. *Beretta USA Leadership Bulletin, 2*(1), 5–6.

Discussion Questions

1. Why is dealing with change such an important function for a chief of police?
2. Which size agency is best to lead—small, medium, or large?
3. Assuming you are a new chief in a small-sized agency, what would you emphasize in the first 30 days?
4. Assuming that you take over a medium-sized agency, discuss what you would want to accomplish in the first 30 days.

Afterword

The Future

The future cannot be predicted precisely, but without an anticipatory vision, it may seem frightening and unmanageable. The future belongs to those who have the foresight to plan, the intelligence to implement their plans, and the courage to take personal risks in order to improve the present.

The police leader of the future will deal with critical choices on a daily basis. His or her decisions will be basically positive but will also have negative potential. In short, every leader must have the capacity to apply the lessons of the past to the problems that are yet to be faced.

A major issue for the police leader of the future will be the amount of control required to operate the individual agency. There are two areas in which, if a police leader loses control, he or she will no longer be able to direct departmental operations: finance and personnel. It is therefore incumbent on the leader of the future to attempt in all ethical, legal, and moral ways to gain control over the financial resources of the department and over its personnel practices. In bureaucratic situations, trade-offs that call for compromise may be required, as when the demands of law enforcement must bow to a level of equality with other agencies of city or county government. If law enforcement is really to reach its highest level of effectiveness, this must be done in ways other than by attempting to place law enforcement agencies on a par with all others. The law itself has recognized that law enforcement officers are required to operate at a higher legal standard than other government employees. This is because of the ultimate responsibility and trust placed in each officer. If officers are to be accountable and if chiefs are to be accountable for officers' behavior, then they must be able to implement the high standards required to bring about what is considered to be truly professional law enforcement.

Successful Police Agencies

In their book *In Search of Excellence,* Thomas J. Peters and Robert H. Waterman Jr. studied a series of successful American companies and found that certain common factors tended to create an effective organizational culture and allowed the company to achieve its goals. These same criteria can generally be applied to a police department.

Typical Factors

For years, theorists have stated that the critical success factors include zero-base budgeting, management by objectives, matrix organization, the use of computers, strategic planning, and management science techniques. After looking at law enforcement agencies throughout the country, one of the authors has concluded that poor police departments use all of these strategies. However, good police departments also use these strategies. They are basically techniques that can be purchased or installed, much as a tire can be placed on a car or a stereo system in a home, without necessarily providing all the requisites for departmental effectiveness.

Effective Factors

The following factors seem to be characteristic of police departments that are successful in reaching their goals and in developing a climate in which people are committed to their work. The first and most important factor is a bias on the part of the police chief toward some form of action. Phrases such as "we must delay" or "it may not be the right time" are not used in these departments. Instead, the emphasis is on performing now and being willing to take risks to achieve the department's important goals. Police leaders in the future, therefore, should have a bias toward action.

The second factor is that effective police departments usually have a simple organizational structure. They have a lean staff—that is, a small ratio of staff to line personnel—which requires line-assignment members such as patrol and investigations to make many decisions that affect the activities of the entire department. Personnel within the department are keenly aware of the leader's role, personality, and goals.

A third factor is that such departments are oriented toward productivity, and such productivity depends on the improvement of the people within the agency—not just on mechanical devices such as computers or equipment. This is not to say that computers and other equipment are not important, but only to say that they do not determine the level of productivity. Only when each individual within the department develops the highest possible capability does productivity reach great heights. In such departments, people are treated as individuals, regardless of whether they act in an individual or team capacity. In such departments, commanders of units are not told how to do their jobs, but rather what they are expected to achieve. For example, a patrol shift may be told to reduce the number of armed robberies being committed in a certain area of the community during a certain period against a certain target, such as convenience stores. The manner in which this goal is reached is left up to the people who are responsible for the actual implementation. Thus, they become autonomous and accountable. Individual officers know where they stand and also how well they are doing with the ideas that they have generated and put together as a group.

There is also a fourth factor. The police leader emphasizes a few key goals and does not burden the department with so many rules and regulations that the big picture is lost. Instead, three to five goals are defined, such as reduction of the crime rate, quicker response time, and development of department personnel. The role of the leader is to see that these purposes are achieved. Almost every action that follows—whether initiated by police officers, supervisors, or middle managers—is geared toward the achievement of the three major goals. An example is the McDonald's Corporation, which stresses that: (1) its stores are to be kept clean, (2) people are to be kept moving in and out, and (3) each outlet is to sell its food at prices equal to or lower than those of other fast-food chains in the area. These three basic guidelines have helped to make an idea grow into a multi-billion-dollar business.

In a similar way, a highly effective police department might stress that: (1) requests from the public are to receive the fastest possible response, (2) all police officers are to do their utmost always to be courteous, and (3) the law is to be justly enforced.

Finally, although the police leader should have controls to see that work is completed, he or she should also be willing to loosen these controls when possible and to spend extra time attempting to coordinate activities and communicate purposes. "Loose but tight" controls include the ability to allow personnel and the department to make judgments at any time to do whatever is best in a given situation. Rules therefore are viewed not as rigid controls, but rather as guidelines. They may be observed most of the time, but people can still feel free to come up with new solutions to special problems so as to do whatever is best for the department and the community. This requires a police leader who can be both flexible and consistent—flexible in day-to-day operations but consistent in the overall direction of the department.

What, then, does all this suggest about the police leaders of the future? It would seem that police leaders will not be able to hide behind traditional practices. They will not be able to find easy acceptance by defining activities, such as the number of arrests or miles driven. These leaders may have to play a much stronger role, having to take and defend strong stands. They will have to build imaginative police departments that can continue to grow, develop, and help bring about a better life for all.

Personal Characteristics

Police leaders of the future must realize that they do not necessarily have any special insight—no special credentials that will guarantee their total success. Instead, they must possess certain characteristics. In examining law enforcement agencies for more than 20 years, one of the authors has come to the conclusion that effective leaders implement three major characteristics on a daily basis: attitude, courage, and enthusiasm.

Attitude

Attitude is defined as a position assumed for a specific purpose. The police leader of the future must assume the position of being a winner for the purpose of achieving. A winner is one who shapes the world; nonwinners are those who accept the world as it is; and losers are those who proceed to set impossible goals or no goals at all, thereby depriving themselves of success and guaranteeing failure. To develop this kind of attitude, police leaders must constantly seek the truth and must have the skill to use this truth. Their attitude should include the strong commitment to implementing the truth, thereby guaranteeing the success they seek. Police leaders of the future need to recognize that they are whatever they think they are. If they firmly believe they can win, they will. If they believe that they are going to lose, they will lose.

Police leaders of the future can test their attitude, especially when they come face to face with an obstacle. If they stop behind the obstacle and stay there, committing all their energies only to complaining about the presence of such an obstacle, they will probably lose. If, on the other hand, they have a winning attitude—the ability to go through the obstacle, around it, over it, and in some instances even under it—they will win. A winning attitude defines the purposes of the department as more important than its rules. If rules present an obstacle to the achievement of these purposes, rules can be changed.

Leaders with positive and winning attitudes do not say things like "They made me do it" or "We can't make it." They never use the words "I can't," because this can bring about failure in the present and in the future. Police leaders recognize that a positive idea is unbeatable. Their attitude is one of accepting responsibility and being accountable for their individual behavior and the decisions necessary to run the agency.

Courage

The second important characteristic, courage, is defined as the inner strength to preserve one's legal, ethical, and moral values. These values must first be established, and then their importance must be prioritized. For example, will it be more important to be honest with people or to be tactful? Will it be more important to be honest and admit one's mistakes or to try to avoid criticism? Effective leaders have the ability to be honest, to trust others and themselves, to implement their attitudes with courage, and to practice self-discipline. Self-discipline is the ability to eliminate the parts of one's behavior that serve no useful purpose. The police leader who can speak to large groups and does so in an effective manner is not necessarily practicing self-discipline. However, such discipline is shown by the police leader who may feel uncomfortable in such situations but is still willing to take part in them, practices, and does a good job.

A police leader who achieves courage has the ability to believe in the personnel of the department. The leader will have the courage to share ideas, set goals, and produce loose but necessary controls to see to it that ideas are realized effectively. He or she also has the ability to be open and honest with all people. Courage is the ingredient that allows the leader and others to be accountable for their individual behavior.

Police leaders recognize that they have three separate aspects: goals, joy, and individual behavior patterns. There is what they want to be, their potential for the future, and what others think they are. This latter part is nothing more than an approximation of the truth. Effective police leaders do not waste time and energy trying to impress people, but rather press forward to achieve their potential. They are willing to be what they really are.

It takes courage to deal with others in a police department. Police leaders of the future must express such courage. They must attempt to praise people in the department and not spend time criticizing. Leaders will walk the halls and speak both to people who report directly to them and to anyone else in the agency. Leaders will take a few minutes each day to develop others' self-esteem. They must be willing to be honest and recognize that personnel of the department hunger for the truth and for the opportunity to tell the truth. They will want to share their opinions, their judgment, their feelings, and their knowledge. Such steps demonstrate that they are satisfied with the present but are looking forward to a more productive future.

It takes courage, but police leaders of the future will recognize that, in dealing with people, their true impressions must be reflected in their actual responses—otherwise they will come across as insincere.

Enthusiasm

Enthusiasm is defined as a strong, positive sense of excitement and anticipation. It allows us to grow. It is the leadership quality on which all others depend. With it, the police leader has everything; without it, he or she has very little. People with enthusiasm demonstrate it by the sparkle in their eyes, the swing in their walk, and the energy with which they implement their plans. Police leaders who develop alibis and excuses are usually dooming themselves to a life that lacks enthusiasm and to an eventual loss of respect and trust.

To possess and demonstrate enthusiasm, the leader must try to do things differently than they may have been done in the past. For example, when a person feels down or depressed, he or she acts in a way that then makes himself or herself even more depressed. However, effective leaders begin to act enthusiastically about any project, about the work environment, about the people they work with, and about the opportunity to spread ideas and see people and projects grow. Once one begins to act in an enthusiastic manner and to feel that way, one continues to do so. The loser has a tendency to place actions on top of feelings; the winner has a tendency to place the feelings on top of the actions.

Effective police leaders are winners when they practice attitude, courage, and enthusiasm. It is rare to find an effective leader who was ever an enthusiastic loser. Instead, enthusiasm gives one the ability to win.

Effective law enforcement did not really begin until people possessed the kind of enthusiasm that grew and made their departments the realities of their dreams. An enthusiastic police leader is possessed with a spirit that allows him or her to go further than others. He or she is a driving force that no power can overcome. It is the choice of the leader of the future to accept life enthusiastically, enjoy it, and change it for the better or to accept the world and follow the direction of others.

Police Chief, City Manager, and Council

Police Chief to City Manager

Every police chief who reports to a city manager will eventually become aware of the role that he or she must play with the city manager. The police chief, therefore, must understand the city manager's point of view—that is, what the city manager may expect from the police chief, what the city manager may expect from the council or commission and, finally, what commissions or councils usually expect from their city manager.

In the first instance, the city manager has certain expectations of the chief of police. The chief must recognize that he or she is but one department head and in many instances can only spend a few hours on a weekly basis dealing with the city manager. In some instances, such as in large communities, this contact may consist only of formal staff meetings and informal sessions over lunch. What, then, does the city manager really expect from the chief of police?

The average city manager expects the police chief to give professional advice and to know law enforcement. Although the city manager might not expect the chief individually to be able to answer all questions, he or she expects the police department to provide the office of the manager with a solution and other alternatives as well. The chief of police therefore must be able to communicate effectively to a non-police person, the city manager, in language that the city manager can understand.

A city manager expects the chief of police to present the police department's point of view. It is incumbent on the police chief to know the department and the views of the police officers. The police chief is not expected to play games with his or her manager, or to use highly technical arguments, when the real problem may be nothing more than a difference in points of view or an understanding of differences of opinion. Police chiefs should attempt to make themselves understood and, whenever possible, not become involved in highly emotional discussions, thereby creating feelings of anger on the part of one or the other.

The manager expects the police chief to understand the broader point of view. The manager will expect the police chief not only to recognize the need for budget restrictions within the police department, but also to understand and analyze the budgetary problems that face the city as a whole. It is incumbent on the police chief to learn something from other department heads concerning their priorities and—just as important—what they consider necessary to serve the citizens of the community effectively.

The city manager expects the police chief to be a manager and to assume the necessary responsibility to take initiative and be accountable. Normally, a city manager would expect the police chief to make recommendations and not continually ask the city manager what the manager wants done. The police chief should, therefore, have his or her information carefully analyzed before discussing any serious issue with the city manager. The police chief is expected to be candid with the city manager about what the manager needs to hear in order to pass information to other department heads, administrative personnel, and the council or commission. The police chief must keep the city manager advised of serious issues, such as high absenteeism or the effect of poor equipment, before the city manager finds out about such issues by reading about them in the newspaper or listening to criticism from the council. It is usually better for a police chief to provide more information than less. When important facts are left out, these facts may come back to haunt both parties, not only in dealing with that issue but, more importantly, in dealing with the long-term issue of a relationship of trust.

The chief of police must attempt to be as understanding as possible about disagreements. The chief of police should not attempt to place a city manager in a corner so that he or she has only one alternative. Under all circumstances, the police chief should share the information so that there are no big surprises for the city manager that could make him or her feel locked in a corner.

In summary then, it is incumbent on the city manager and chief of police, through day-to-day contacts, to develop a relationship of earned respect and trust in which honesty plays an important role.

City Manager to City Council

A city manager has expectations of the council or commission. He or she normally expects the council to advise him or her of what it expects the manager to accomplish. The manager expects the council or commission to give the city manager feedback, especially when problems exist. The city manager expects the council to observe behaviors within city government, including those of police officers, and report on those observations. The manager further expects that when such issues arise, they will be brought to the city manager's attention rather than directly to department heads.

The city manager expects the council to bring employee issues such as tardiness, sloppiness, or ineffective work habits to him or her for possible action. The city manager expects that the council will support the manager in increasing service levels, in reducing costs, and in improving the image of city government in general. Overall, the city manager expects the council to be supportive and positive not only in the program area, but also in helping to develop new directions, so that the major purposes of city government can eventually be achieved.

City Council to City Manager

The police chief must also be aware that the typical city council or commission has certain expectations of the city manager. In many instances these expectations can only be fulfilled by a close working relationship between the city manager and the police chief.

Most councils expect their city managers to keep them as informed as possible as to what is happening. They expect their manager to be abreast of problems, especially those that become public. For example, if there were a series of newspaper articles concerning the promotional process within the police department, they would expect the city manager to be aware of how the police department was dealing with these issues.

Councils expect the city manager to explain to them what the manager needs to perform his or her duties effectively. They expect the manager to make specific recommendations as to how an issue—such as the image of a department or the reduction of employee dissatisfaction—can be resolved.

City councils expect to evaluate the important key positions within city government. Normally this includes the position of chief of police. Therefore, the chief of police, in sharing as much as possible, is able to guarantee that the council itself will gain further knowledge of the performance of the police chief. A council expects the city manager to keep it abreast of any legal actions that may be brought against the city. For example, if a police union refuses to accept the promotional testing process and intends to file a lawsuit, it is incumbent on the city manager to keep the council advised from the moment of possible rumors until the conclusion of any lawsuit.

In general, the city council expects the city manager to perform in a timely fashion, at a low cost, and without disrupting service to the citizens. Obviously this is a very difficult task. However, the police chief can help the city manager to achieve a high degree of success. Finally, the city council expects the manager to be in good health. Therefore, the police chief must share the workload, not only running the police department but also helping to run the entire city government. Otherwise, the city manager's job may become one in which burnout is prevalent and the manager becomes ineffective after a short time on the job, thereby adding to the problems of the chief of police.

Final Thought

What, then, can the police chief of the future do first as a leader? As a department head, he or she can strive to develop individual responsibility and accountability in every member of the police department and as much as possible in every member of the community. He or she can see to it that the police department provides a positive role model for the entire community. This applies to the areas of honesty, service, and commitment. The police leader can develop feelings of self-esteem, self-worth, and confidence in his or her subordinates to the point at which they will have freedom and at the same time be responsible. The police leader can develop the rational and human skills needed to implement these standards.

The police leader can also lead the community. He or she can help develop opportunities for the enrichment of citizens' lives by letting the department participate in cultural, recreational, and developmental programs that will help make the community the best place to live. Through leadership, the police chief can foster strength, spirit, and community involvement in the law enforcement endeavor. This can be done through openness with the news media, special community work projects, and public appreciation days.

The police leader can help the community by making a determined effort to bring together those who need help and those who can help. A police department can develop volunteers and services that will help young people in times of stress. One of the greatest positive role models for youth is an effective police officer. Walking the beat, although not popular, is effective because the individual officer gets to know the individual citizens and each plays a role in making the other feel important.

The police chief can further provide citizens and groups of citizens with easy access to information about how the department operates and how the resources at the police department can be utilized. The development of a simple hotline to answer questions and offer help can go a long way toward meeting this overall purpose. In the area of crime reduction, the police chief can attempt to make citizens aware of their roles in crime prevention through school programs and encouragement on the part of all citizens to report anything suspicious, especially any time they become the victims of crime. The leader can further encourage the public to utilize the crime-prevention programs generated by the department.

Both police and fire personnel can assist architects and builders in planning and designing structures so as to discourage crime and increase public safety. By making crime prevention a strong consideration in the designing of buildings, cars, and public areas such as airports, the leader of the future can affect the entire community.

In the future, the police leader may need to involve the courts and correctional agencies in crime prevention. The police leader can take the attitude that everyone within the criminal justice system plays a role in the prevention and reduction of crime.

The role of the leader in the future may appear complicated, but it is challenging and rewarding.

The future belongs to those who are willing to accept its challenges.

Appendix A
Orange County Sheriff's Office General Order

Effective Date: November 5, 1993	☒ **Rescinds** General Order 1.0 (4/1/93) ☐ **Amends**	**Number:** 200.0
SUBJECT: PHILOSOPHY		
Distribution: ALL PERSONNEL	**Related CALEA Standards:**	

This order consists of the following numbered sections:

1. Purpose
2. Vision
3. Values
4. Beliefs
5. Principles
6. Expectations

1. Purpose

The purpose of this order is to express the agency's values, beliefs and principles to guide all agency functions, and provide general guidance for Sheriff's Office personnel in all their activities.

2. Vision

The purpose of a vision is to give direction for all members of the Orange County Sheriff's Office, and provide understanding for our community. Our vision of the future for the Orange County Sheriff's Office is extremely positive.

We envision a law enforcement agency highly professional in all its actions, an agency that is considered both a leader in law enforcement and a showcase of our profession.

We envision an agency cooperating closely with all levels of law enforcement agencies, and all entities of County and other governments, by sharing our talents, listening and understanding their needs.

We envision the Orange County Sheriff's Office as being staffed by highly competent, motivated, trained, educated members, equipped to meet the goals and objectives of our agency and needs of our community.

3. Values

The purpose of values is to provide a basis for our philosophy. Values are defined as our assumptions about the ends we believe are worth striving for, and are reflected in our everyday decisions.

The Orange County Sheriff's Office holds forth professional integrity as our overriding value.

Integrity includes:

HONESTY
Being truthful, sincere and straightforward
COMMITMENT
Being reliable, involved and law-abiding
SENSITIVITY TO OTHERS
Being compassionate, sharing and kind
LOYALTY
Being principled, accountable and supportive

4. Beliefs

The purpose of beliefs is to demonstrate what assumptions we think are true. The major beliefs of the Orange County Sheriff's Office include the following:

We believe that ...

Orange County Sheriff's Office personnel are committed to make Orange County a better place to live, to unselfishly serve its citizens and guests, and pursue excellence.

Our personnel develop commitment to excellence when they participate in decisions about the management of their areas of responsibility.

The best method to provide efficient and effective service to the citizens of Orange County is to hire talented people, and give them the opportunities for training and education that they need to develop their talents and initiative in the fullest.

In fostering an environment that promotes creativity and encourages positive thinking throughout the Orange County Sheriff's Office, personnel will be effective and take intelligent risks without fear of failure.

Victims of crime and their families need special consideration in coping with the traumatic experiences of suffering a violation of their personal rights, losing a beloved one, or loss of their personal possessions.

The Orange County Sheriff's Office is responsible for treating victims of crime, and their families, in a manner which assures their dignity, self esteem and constitutional rights.

5. Principles

Principles are derived from our values, beliefs and vision of the future. Principles provide guidance in the exercise of judgment by members of the Orange County Sheriff's Office. Our basic principles are as follows:

We shall …

Do everything within our power and authority to prevent criminal behavior from occurring in Orange County.

Protect the constitutional rights of all persons.

Treat all persons with dignity, respect, courtesy and compassion.

Always tell the truth.

Neither shirk from our sworn duty, nor use our power for personal gain.

Promote an open and trusting flow of information within our organization.

Make decisions consistent with high legal, ethical and performance standards to guarantee justice to all.

Hold all persons accountable for the reasonable consequences of their behavior.

Sustain an organizational climate within the Orange County Sheriff's Office in which our people can succeed.

6. Expectations

We all have expectations that we want to meet as a result of our actions. This is the basis for all motivation.

The purpose of an expectation agreement is to provide guidance to employees for making effective decisions, for establishing priorities and for assistance in evaluating our behavior.

Sheriff's Office members can expect the Executive Team to:

Adhere to our stated visions, values, beliefs and principles.
Adhere to high legal, ethical and performance standards.

Provide you support.
Make timely decisions.

The Executives expect Sheriff's Office personnel to:

Do what is right. Always give the best you have.
Treat others with dignity, respect and compassion.
Support the Orange County Sheriff's Office vision, values, beliefs, principles and decisions.

_____

Sheriff

Cooper City Police Department Leadership Plan for 1997–1998

Vision

We want Cooper City to have the most professional law enforcement services available, equal to or better than the best communities in the country. We will continue to accomplish this by providing responsive, quality service.

Values

We Will Honor the Public Trust Through:

- Respect and dignity for those with whom we deal.
- Respect and care for the environment.
- Equal opportunity.
- A work force selected with care, treated with respect and rewarded for performance.
- Open, honest communication.
- Positive action and innovation.
- Teamwork.
- Responsible use of public resources.

Mission

The Cooper City Police Department pledges to protect life and property and maintain order through a continuing commitment to service, integrity, the highest standards of ethics and respect for individual rights in a diverse population.

Goals

We Will Focus on Community Service By:

- Supporting the priorities of this community for 1997-1998.

- Listening and responding to our citizens/residents/visitors.
- Cutting red tape.
- Improving public awareness of Police Department services.
- Improving effectiveness of internal support service.
- Implementing a goal-setting and ongoing improvement process through **Total Quality Management** through the efforts and involvement of all employees.
- Planning, initiating, implementing and evaluating office programs and projects thoroughly.
- Improving our interaction with various segments of the community to promote greater understanding.
- Providing Law Enforcement services that meet or exceed national standards as established by the Commission on Accreditation for Law Enforcement Agencies (CALEA).

Appendix B
Orange County Sheriff's Office General Order

Effective Date: November 9, 1994

☐ **Rescinds**
☐ **Amends**

Number: 204.0

Re-Evaluation Date:

SUBJECT: TOTAL QUALITY MANAGEMENT
Distribution: ALL PERSONNEL

Related CALEA Standards:

This order consists of the following numbered sections:

1. Purpose
2. Policy
3. Procedures

1. Purpose

The purpose of this policy is to produce quality results, be cost-effective, promote professionalism, and encourage the involvement of personnel in the process of achieving the goals and objectives of the Orange County Sheriff's Office.

2. Policy

The Orange County Sheriff's Office is committed to protecting and providing quality service to our citizens.

3. Procedures

  A. The following are three (3) major functions that assure Total Quality Management (TQM) is implemented throughout the Sheriff's Office:

    1. Accreditation
Law enforcement accreditation ensures the agency meets an established set of nationally recognized professional standards.

    2. Training
Training prepares employees to implement programs as directed by the Sheriff, Undersheriff, and Command Staff.

    3. Quality Assurance
Establishes a review of the quality of service provided by the agency.

  B. The following procedures, though not all inclusive, shall be used to implement Total Quality Management (TQM):

    1. Surveys of citizens, employees and other governmental agencies.

2. Review and input from supervisory personnel.
3. Employee meetings and input.
4. Encourage supervisors to explain the purpose of directives.
5. Elicit advice from within and outside the agency for continued improvement.
6. Adhere to the Philosophy General Order 200.0.
7. Evaluate compliments and complaints involving Sheriff's Office personnel.
8. Conduct command staff, general staff, division staff, and employee committee meetings.
9. Encourage walk-throughs by command staff of agency components.

_____

Sheriff

Appendix C
Status Report Required Documents

REVISED:

Chapters Or Document:	Behind Schedule	Due Date	Received	Returned	W/Policy Committee	AT R&D For Printing	Distributed	Div Commander	Comments
CHAPTERS									
1:LE ROLES AUTHORITY		9/30/93	X				X		
2:JURISDICTION, MUTUAL AID, REGIONAL SERVICES		9/30/93	X				X		
3:CONTRACTUAL AGREEMENTS		10/1/93	X				X		Contracts on file as "Proof of Com"
4:AGENCY RELATIONSHIPS		10/1/93	X				X		
5:CRIM JUST SYS IMPROVMNTS		9/30/94							Being developed
11:ORGANIZATION		9/30/93	X				X		
12:DIRECTION		9/30/93	X				X		
13:GENERAL MANAGEMENT		10/1/93	X				X		
14:PLANNING & RESEARCH		11/1/93	X				X		
15:CRIME ANALYSIS		3/30/94	X				X		
16:MANPOWER ALLOCATION		3/30/94	X			X			
17:FISCAL MANAGEMENT		3/30/94	X			X			
21:CLASSIFICATION		9/30/94	X			X			
22:COMPENSATION/BENEFITS		6/30/94							
23:CAREER DEVELOPMENT		6/30/94	X		X		X		
24:COLLECTIVE BARGAINING		00/00/94							NA'd by Function
25:GRIEVANCE PROCEDURES		3/30/94	X				X		
26:DISCIPLINARY PROCEDURES		3/30/94	X				X		
31:RECRUITMENT		9/30/94	X			X			
32:SELECTION		9/30/94				X			
33:TRAINING		3/30/94	X				X		Need FTO docs for compliance
34:PROMOTION		9/30/94	X		X				
35:PERFORMANCE EVALUATION		6/30/94	X				X		Signed G.O.
41:PATROL		3/30/94	X			X			
42:CRIMINAL INVESTIGATION		6/30/94	X			X			Sgt. Eastern making revisions
43:ORGANIZED CRIME/VICE		6/30/94	X			X			Still need select Special Orders
44:JUVENILE OPERATIONS		6/30/94	X		X				Pending Review
45:CRIME PREVENTION		6/30/94	X		X				Needs Revisions
46:UNUSUAL OCCURRENCES		6/30/94	X		X				Pending Review
47:SPECIAL OPERATIONS		6/30/94	X						Pending Review
51:CRIMINAL INTELLIGENCE		6/30/94	X				X		Signed G.O.
52:INTERNAL AFFAIRS		3/30/94	X				X		
53:INSPECTIONAL SERVICES		3/30/94	X				X		

Function / Document	C1	C2	Insp	Date/Freq	Cmpl	Comments
54:PUBLIC INFORMATION				3/30/94	X	
54:COMMUNITY AFFAIRS	X	X		6/30/94		
55:VICTIM/WITNESSES ASSISTANCE	X			6/30/94		
61:TRAFFIC ADMINISTRATION	X	X		6/30/94		
62:TRAFFIC LAW ENFORCEMENT	X	X		6/30/94		
63:TRAFFIC ACCIDENT INVES.				6/30/94		NA'd by Function
64:TRAFFIC DIRECTION/CONTROL	X			6/30/94		
65:TRAFFIC ENGINEERING			X	9/30/94		
66:TRAFFIC ANCILLARY SVCS	X			6/30/94		Pending Review
71:PRISONER TRANSPORT	X	X		6/30/94		
72:HOLDING FACILITY	X	X		9/30/94		Pending Review
73:COURT SECURITY	X			3/30/94		Pending Review
74:LEGAL PROCESS	X			6/30/94	X	
81:COMMUNICATIONS	X	X		9/30/94		Pending Review
82:RECORDS	X	X		6/30/94		Pending Review
83:EVIDENCE:COLLECTION/PRE	X			9/30/94	X	Pending Review
84:PROPERTY MANAGEMENT	X			6/30/94	X	Awaiting CID Components
DOCUMENTS/REPORTS						
REVISED GOALS/OBJECTIVES	X			Qrtly		3rd Quarter Report filed as Proof
GOALS/OBJ PROGRESS RPTS	X			Qrtly		3rd Quarter Report filed as Proof
ASSIGNMENT AVAIL FACTOR			X	2/28/94		Limited Réponse
DISTRIBUTION BY WRKLOAD			X	Qrtly		Need proofs of compliance
INDEPENDENT AUDIT REPORT	X			1/30/94		Filed as Proof of Compliance
CAREER DEV RESOURCES INV	X			1/30/94		93 Proofs of Compliance filed
ANALYSIS OF GRIEVANCES	X			1/30/94		93 Proofs filed
TRAINING PROGRAM EVALS	X			1/30/94		
PROMOTIONAL SYS EVAL	X			1/30/94		Filed as Proof of Compliance
YRLY PERFORMANCE EVAL						
PERFORM EVAL INSPECTION	X		X	1/30/94		

(continued on next page)

—cont'd

Chapters Or Document:	Behind Schedule	Due Date	Received	Returned	W/Policy Committee	AT R&D For Printing	Distributed	Div Commander	Comments
JUVENILE PRGM EVALUATIONS	X	1/30/94							
REVIEW/UPDATE UNUSUAL OCCURRENCE PLAN	X	2/28/94							Work In progress
UPDATE EMERGENCY OPS		3/30/94	X						Filed as Proof of Compliance
TRAFF ENF PRGM EVALS	X	12/31/93							
FIRE EQUIP TEST/INSPECTNS Dir's		12/31/93	X						Rec'vd Insps: still need Written
COURTHOUSE SEC SURVEY	X	1/30/94							
COMPLAINT CONTROL/FIELD REPORTING EVALS		11/30/93	X						
SO STAFF INSPECTIONS		MO	X						Need copies of Staff Inspections
EVALUATION OF COMMUNITY RELATIONS PROGRAMS		Semi-Ann	X						Filed as Proof of Compliance
REPORT OF COMMUNITY CONCERNS, PROBLEMS AND RECOMMENDATIONS		MO	X						Need Proof of Compliance
CITIZEN OPINION SURVEY	X	12/31/93							Need Proof of Compliance
VICTIM/WIT NEEDS ANALYSIS	X	BI-YRLY							
SCHOOL CROSSING SURVEY		7/31/94	X						Filed as Proof of Compliance
OC & VICE STATUS REPORT		QRTLY	X						Filed as Proof of Compliance
CRTHOUSE: FIRE ALARM TST		MO	X						Filed as Proof of Compliance

	Frequency		Notes
HOLDING CELL, SANITATION INSPECTION	WEEKLY	X	Filed as Proof of Compliance
HOLDING CELL SECURITY INSPECTION	WEEKLY	X	Filed as Proof of Compliance
FIRST AID KIT INSPECTIONS	WEEKLY	X	Filed as Proof of Compliance / Need Proof from F.D. Staff
COMM POWER TESTING	WEEKLY	X	
PROPERTY CONTROL	MO	X	Memo to OA directing same
PROCEDURES INSPECTION			
UNANNOUNCED PROPERTY INVENTORY	YRLY	X	Memo to OA directing same
UNANNOUNCED PROPERTY STORAGE INSPECTION	SEMI-ANNUAL	X	Memo to OA directing same

Orange County Sheriff's Office Reports Required By Accreditation

Report Title or Documentation Subject	Frequency	Y1	Y2	Y3	Assigned To
Revised, Written Goals and Objectives	Annual-March				All Div. & Sec. Cmdrs.
Progress Toward Written Goals and Objectives	Quarterly				All Div. & Sec. Cmdrs.
Weapons Use Report	As Required				All
Organizational Structure/Chart	Annual-Feb.				All Div. Cmdrs.
Agency Report of Activities	Daily Monthly, Annually				All Components
Allocation and Distribution of Patrol Manpower	Annual-Feb.				Field Serv. Div.
Reassessment of Personnel Allocation	Annual-Feb.				All Div. & Sec. Cmdrs.
Reassessment of Personnel Distribution by Workload Comparison of Each Division	Annual-Feb.				All Div. & Sec. Cmdrs.
Review of Specialized Assignment	Annual-March				All Div. & Sec. Cmdrs.
Agency's Accounting Status Report	Monthly				Fiscal Mgmt.
Agency's Independent Audit Report	Annual-Dec.				Fiscal Mgmt.
Review & Revision of Classification Plan	Annual-Oct.				HRD Staff
Inventory of Resources Used for Career Development Program	Annual-Jan.				HRD Staff
Analysis of Grievances	Annual-Jan.				HRD Staff
Evaluation of Training Programs	Annual-Dec.				Prof. Dev. Cmd.
Evaluation of Promotional Process	Annual-Jan.				Cmd. Staff
Performance Evaluation of Each Employee	Annual-Eval. Date				Appropriate Supervisor
Inspection of Performance Evaluation System	Annual-Jan.				Quality Assurance
Performance Evaluation of Sworn Probationary Employees	Bimonthly				Appropriate Supervisor
Expenditures of Investigative/ Confidential Funds	Quarterly				MBI Dir, CID
Status Report of Vice & Organized Crime Control	Quarterly				MBI, CID Cmdr. Intelligence
Evaluation of Programs Relating to Juveniles	Annual-Jan.				COP & CID Cmdrs.
Evaluation of All Crime Prevention Programs	Annual-Dec.				COP Div. Cmdr.

Report Title or Documentation Subject	Frequency	Y1	Y2	Y3	Assigned To
Review and Update of Unusual Occurrence Plan	Annual-Feb.				Field Svcs. Div. Cmdr.
Review and Update of Emergency Operations Manual	Annual-March				Field Svcs. Div. Cmdr.
Statistical Summary of Internal Affairs Investigations	Annual-Dec.				Prof. Stnds Div. Cmdr.
Staff Inspections of Organizational Components	Ongoing-Mo. Reports				Quality Assurance
Report of Community Concerns, Problems and Recommendations	Monthly				COP Div. Cmdr.
Evaluation of Community Relations Programs	Semi-Annual				Quality Assurance
Survey of Citizens' Attitudes and Opinions	Annual-Dec.				Quality Assurance
Analysis of Victim/Witness Needs & Services	Biennial				CID Cmdr.
Evaluation of Selective Traffic Law Enforcement Program	Annual-Dec.				Special Ops. Div. Cmdr.
Survey to Identify the Locations in Need of School Crossing Supervision	Annual-Jul.				School Guard
Documented Inspection of Fire Equipment	Weekly				Court Security Sec. Cmdr.
Documented Testing of Fire Equipment	Weekly				Court Security Sec. Cmdr.
Document Testing of Facility's Auto Fire Detection Devices & Alarm System	Monthly				Court Security Sec. Cmdr.
Documented Sanitation of Holding Facility	Weekly				Court Security Sec. Cmdr.
Documented Security Inspection of Holding Facility	Weekly				Court Security Sec. Cmdr.
Documented Inspection of First Aid Kits	Weekly				Court Security Sec. Cmdr.
Security Survey of Courthouse	Annual-Jan.				Court Security Sec. Cmdr.
Dissemination of Stolen Vehicle Information	Daily				Comm. Sec. Cmdr.
Documented Testing of Alternate Sources of Electric Power	Weekly				Comm. Sec. Cmdr.
Evaluation of Complaint Control Recording & Field Reporting Processes	Annual-Nov.				Quality Assurance
Inspection of Property Control Procedures	Monthly				Quality Assurance

Report Title or Documentation Subject	Frequency	Y1	Y2	Y3	Assigned To
Inventory of Property Unannounced	Annual				Quality Assurance
Inspection of Property Storage Areas-Unannounced	Semi-Annual				Quality Assurance

Appendix D
Agreement between the School Board of Orange County, Florida and the Orange County, Florida, Sheriffs Office for the School Resource Officer Program

This agreement is entered into by and between the School Board of Orange County, Florida, a public body corporate organized and existing under the Constitution and laws of the State of Florida, hereinafter referred to as the "School Board," and the Sheriffs Office of Orange County, Florida, hereinafter referred to as the "Sheriffs Office" and shall take effect as stipulated herein.

Witnesseth

NOW, THEREFORE, in mutual consideration of the covenants herein, the Sheriffs Office and School Board agree as follows:

1. This Agreement shall be in effect from July 1, 2003 through June 30, 2004, unless otherwise terminated as provided herein.
2. The Sheriffs Office shall assign 56.75 deputies to be school resource officers ("SROs") for public schools in the Orange County school district. All SROs shall meet or exceed the following qualifications.
   A. Minimum of two years of college and two years experience in law enforcement operations, or four years of experience in law enforcement operations. Preferably, at least one year of the officer's experience in law enforcement operations occurred in Orange County, Florida. This requirement may be modified by mutual agreement of the Sheriffs Office and the associate superintendent, education services, for the School Board.
   B. Certified by the State of Florida as a law enforcement officer.

3. Each SRO's work year will follow that established by the School Board for 10-month teachers. The parties may agree to summer school assignments for SROs.

4. SROs assigned to elementary schools shall teach the DARE (Drug Abuse Resistance Education) curriculum as guest presenters in fifth grade classes. They shall also teach DARE in other grades, as agreed between the parties. A school resource officer assigned to an elementary school shall be called a "DARE Deputy."

5. SROs assigned to middle schools may teach one of the following curriculums: (1) DARE; (2) GREAT (Gang Resistance Education and Training); (3) "Law Awareness," or (4) a combination of the first three programs. The "Law Awareness" program includes topics such as (1) the justification for rules and law; (2) the consequences of crime; (3) juvenile and adult criminal justice systems; (4) career opportunities in law enforcement; (5) substance abuse prevention; and (6) crime and fire prevention.

6. SROs assigned to high schools may instruct specialized short-term programs by invitation of the principal or a member of the faculty.

7. Any exceptions to the instructional responsibilities outlined herein must be mutually agreed upon by the School Board's associate superintendent, education services, the applicable schools' principals, and an authorized representative of the Sheriffs Office.

8. SROs shall be responsible for the following additional duties:
   A. Encouraging individual and small group discussion with students, faculty, and parents about matters related to law enforcement.
   B. Making referrals to community agencies offering assistance to juveniles and their families, such as mental health clinics, drug treatment centers, etc. when the deputy deems appropriate.
   C. Informing principals, as soon as practicable, about law enforcement activity undertaken on school grounds, as allowed by the State law.
   D. Assisting other law enforcement officers in matters relating to the SROs' school assignments.
   E. Completing student and program records requested by the School Board.

9. Each SRO will reaffirm his or her role as a law enforcement officer by wearing a uniform at least one day a week, unless doing so would be inappropriate for scheduled school activities. The uniform will also be worn at school events, where it will enhance the image of the deputy and his or her ability to perform applicable duties.

10. SROs are under the direct supervision and control of the Sheriffs Office. They remain employees of the Sheriffs Office and are responsive to the Sheriffs Office chain of command. SROs will coordinate their activities with the principals and other appropriate staff members of their assigned schools. They will seek permission, advice, and guidance prior to enacting any programs within the schools.

11. SROs shall not be assigned any duties regularly given to school personnel, such as lunchroom or hall duty. Nothing herein is intended to preclude the deputy from being available in areas where interaction with students is expected.

12. SROs are not school disciplinarians. If the principal of a school believes that a violation of law has taken place relating to a school, he or she shall contact the SRO assigned to that school, who shall assess the situation and take whatever action he or she deems appropriate. The SRO may only transport suspended or disruptive students with the approval of his or her supervisor.

13. Should it become necessary to conduct formal law enforcement interviews on school grounds with students or staff, Sheriffs Office personnel shall abide by applicable State law and Sheriffs Office policy and procedure. School Board personnel shall cooperate with those efforts.

14. Principals shall inform and update SROs about situations arising on campus that may involve criminal activity.

15. Nothing herein shall be construed as imposing a legal duty for school and/or student security upon the Sheriffs Office. This Agreement shall not be construed as creating a special relationship between the Sheriffs Office and any person or entity.

16. The School Board shall pay the Sheriffs Office an amount not to exceed $1,135,000. for the services described herein. Payment shall be made in two equal installments with the first payment due on or before December 31, 2003, and the second installment due on or before June 30, 2004.

17. Either party may terminate this Agreement without cause upon 30 days written notice to the other party. In the event of such a termination, the Sheriffs Office shall be paid on a pro rata basis for services rendered to the date of termination. Further, either party may immediately terminate this Agreement for cause upon giving written notice to the other party and a 30-day opportunity to cure any material default.

18. Neither party may assign this Agreement.

19. The terms and provisions of this Agreement constitute the entire contract between the parties with respect to the subject matter hereof and shall supersede all previous communications, representations, or agreements, either verbal or written, between the parties. No change, alteration, or modification of this Agreement shall be effective unless in writing and signed by both parties hereto.

20. This Agreement shall be governed by and construed in accordance with the laws of the State of Florida. The venue of any litigation arising hereunder shall be Orange County, Florida.

21. It is understood and agreed to by the parties that at no time shall a law enforcement officer acting pursuant to this Agreement be an employee or agent of the School Board. The law enforcement officer shall always be and remain an employee of the Law Enforcement Agency when performing their function herein.

22. SROs are required to be absent from campus from time to time to attend training, to appear in court and to perform certain administrative functions required by their position with the Orange County Sheriffs Office. The deputy's Sergeant will approve all such absences and ensure that the site administrator is informed, in advance.

IN WITNESS WHEREOF, the parties have caused this Agreement to be executed by the undersigned persons as duly authorized.

SHERIFFS OFFICE OF ORANGE COUNTY, FLORIDA
BY:_____

Kevin Beary as Sheriff of Orange County, Florida
DATE: _____

THE SCHOOL BOARD OF ORANGE COUNTY, FLORIDA
BY:_____
as its Chairman

(Corporate Seal)
By: _____
Ronald Blocker Superintendent
DATE: _____
(Corporate Seal)

Approved as to form and legality for the reliance of the Sheriff of Orange County, Florida, only, this _____ day _____ 2003.
BY: _____

This document has been reviewed by the School Board Attorney on behalf of the School Board, this _____ day of _____ 2003.
BY: _____
General ***

Appendix E
Orange County Sheriff's Office
Special Order

Effective Date: May 18, 2001   ☒ Rescinds - S.O. 16.0 (July 7, 2000)   Number: 16.0
                                      ☐ Amends

SUBJECT: DA.R.E./S.R.O. UNIT   Print Date:
Distribution: DARE/SRO   CALEA Standards: 44.2.1, 82.2.1
PERSONNEL   CFA Standards: 19.01

This order consists of the following:

1. Purpose
2. Procedures

1. **Purpose**

   The purpose of this policy is to establish guidelines and procedures for all D.A.R.E./ S.R.O. program personnel.

2. **Procedures**

   A. Position/Training Requirements

   D.A.R.E./S.R.O. requirements are established in General Order 271.0.

   B. Specialized Training

   Whenever possible, supervisors shall ensure that D.A.R.E./S.R.O. deputies participate in special training seminars during teacher workdays, holidays, summer sessions, and upon supervisors and/or the agency's request.

   C. Leave Time

   1. In accordance with General Order 305.0(H)(1), notification of illness must be made to your immediate supervisor. D.A.R.E./S.R.O. deputies shall also notify the principal or désignée of any absence.

   2. Annual Leave

   Annual leave for D.A.R.E./S.R.O. deputies shall be scheduled when schools are not in session.

   D. Assignments

   1. Tour of Duty

      a. The duty day for D.A.R.E./S.R.O. deputies shall be eight (8) hours. Duty hours shall correspond to the school day in assigned schools and will be adjusted as needed to accommodate after school activities.

b. D.A.R.E./S.R.O. deputies shall minimize time off campus. Personnel shall not leave the school grounds without permission of their assigned supervisor. In all cases the principal or désignée shall be notified.

2. Directed Patrol

When school is not in session, D.A.R.E./S.R.O. deputies shall participate in directed patrol or other duties assigned by his/her supervisor. At the discretion of the Division Commander or désignée, when workload permits, deputies assigned to the D.A.R.E./S.R.O. program shall work 36 hours per calendar year with a Patrol Squad to maintain their proficiency in report writing, complaint handling and other patrol procedures. Supervision discretion will allow D.A.R.E/S.R.O to ride with a patrol FTO when applicable.

3. School Assignment

S.R.O. deputies shall be assigned to one middle or high school, unless circumstances dictate a more flexible assignment of resources. D.A.R.E. deputies shall be assigned to multiple elementary schools as determined by their unit supervisor.

4. Monthly Activity Form

D.A.R.E./S.R.O. deputies shall complete the Monthly Activity Form which shall be submitted to his/her supervisor.

E. Supervisor's Responsibilities

1. D.A.R.E./S.R.O. Unit supervisors shall direct deputies who are assigned to the elementary, middle and high schools of the School Resource Section, and help personnel develop a positive relationship with the students, faculty and administration within the Orange County Public School System. D.A.R.E./S.R.O. Unit supervisors shall:

   a. Maintain a liaison with the principals and administrators at each school where personnel are assigned.

   b. Monitor D.A.R.E./S.R.O. deputy's activities on a daily basis including statistics, payroll, reports and other documents.

   c. Resolve problems with parents, school administrators, students and citizens.

   d. Perform other administrative duties (e.g., evaluations, counsels).

   e. Inspect equipment and personnel on a regular basis.

   f. Perform other job duties as required.

F. Attire

D.A.R.E./S.R.O. deputies shall wear uniforms daily unless otherwise directed by a unit supervisor. Uniformed D.A.R.E./S.R.O. deputies must wear his/her issued duty belt at all times while on campus.

SHERIFF KEVIN BEARY

Appendix F
Orange County Sheriff's Office
D.A.R.E./S.R.O./Orientation Week

Kevin Beary Sheriff

DARE/SRO Orientation Week

Purpose: The purpose of the "Orientation Week" is to familiarize the newly assigned Deputy Sheriff to the DARE/SRO Section. There are many additional procedures that Deputies need to be aware of. Many of these procedures apply only to the DARE/SRO Section.

Day 1

Purpose: The newly assigned DARE/SRO will be advised of his/her expectations. They will be orientated to administrative requirements of the assignment.

The newly assigned DARE/SRO Deputy will meet with his/her Sergeant.

The Sergeant will discuss squad, sectional, and divisional mandates. The Sergeant will provide the Deputy with a DARE/SRO handbook and go through all applicable material. This includes, but not limited to:

*DARE/SRO Special Order
*General Order #271 (Juvenile Operations)
*Agency/Orange County School Board contract
*SRT (School Response Team)
*Critical Incident Response Plan
*Search Policies of School Board Members vs. Sheriff's Office
*Student Code of Conduct

Days 2, 3, 4, and 5

Purpose: The newly assigned DARE/SRO Deputy will be exposed to the daily activities and functions of his/her new assignment.

The new DARE/SRO Deputy will be assigned with a senior Deputy at the Sergeant's discretion. The newly assigned Deputy will observe the daily actions of the senior Deputy and assist in routine duties encountered by the senior Deputy (report writing, assisting with traffic control). Additionally, the senior Deputy will discuss the below listed check-off items with the new Deputy.

Note: ALL check-off items should be "Explained" to the new DARE/SRO Deputy by the end of week 1. When this is done, the senior Deputy and/or Sergeant should initial and date in the appropriate location.

Training Check-off List (Please initial)

	Explained	Practiced
1. Introduction & personnel		
2. Chain of Command		
3. Work Schedule/hours		
4. Supervisory Notification		
5. Dress Code		
6. Alpha Pagers		
7. AT&T Phone		
8. Activity/Stats		
9. Notifying Administrators		
10. Checking of Mailboxes		
11. Subpoena Process		
12. Gang Unit/Meetings & Responsibilities of SRO's assigned to schools)		
14. Report Review (Juvenile cases)		
15. On-campus Interviews/interview requests		
16. OCSO policy on obtaining Comm. Ctr. Tapes		
17. Faxing Time Sheets		
18. Email (proper vs. improper items to send)		
19. Divisional Goals & Objectives		
20. Radio procedures		
21. Alcohol Stings		
22. Use of Force (Documentation)		
23. Interviewing Juveniles on Campus (OCSO policy/school board rep present on behalf of juvenile)		
24. Transporting Non-Arrested Juveniles		
25. VOCC arrest procedure		
26. Speakout Hotline (AT&T)		
27. Truancy/Truancy sweeps		
28. Extracurricular Functions		
56. No authority in school discipline (Deputies CANNOT enforce some student code of conduct violations-dress, hats, etc.)		
57. Hands on → 10-15 (General rule of thumb)		
58. Parental Notification (agency policy)		
59. S.A.D.D. Groups		
60. Metallic Wands		
61. Field Trips (Permission Slips required)		
62. Coaching or Paid Position		
63. Patrol of campus and surrounding community of school		
64. Communicating with students/parents via morning announcements schools TV monitors/school newspaper.		
65. Classroom presentations (GREAT, DARE, Law Awareness)		

	Explained	Practiced
66. Security for after school events		
67. Student/Parent consultations		

New DARE/SRO			
	(Print)	(Signature)	(Date)
Senior DARE/SRO			
	(Print)	(Signature)	(Date)
DARE/SRO Sergeant			
	(Print)	(Signature)	(Date)
Lieutenant/Commander			
	(Print)	(Signature)	(Date)

At the conclusion of the Orientation week, the check-off list will be forwarded to the new SRO's sergeant for inclusion in the supervisory level file.

Extension of Orientation Week

In the event that the senior SRO and his/her sergeant feel that the new SRO's orientation week should be extended, this input along with **supporting documentation** will be presented to the lieutenant for consideration. This request must contain the following:

1. The identification of a specific identifiable problem.
2. A specific documented remedial training plan that is designed to correct the identified problem (developed by the Sergeant and senior SRO).
3. Is it the belief of the senior SRO and his/her supervisor that the remedial training will correct the identifiable problem?

The lieutenant will review the plan and approve or disapprove the request. If the lieutenant denies the extension request, a memo to the DARE/SRO Captain must be executed, stating the reason(s) why the request was denied and a recommendation to resolve the deficiency.

In the event the request is approved, the orientation period will extend up to one (1) week. When the senior SRO and his/her sergeant feel the deficiency is resolved, the lieutenant will be advised. If the lieutenant agrees the deficiency is resolved, the new SRO will be assigned to a school. If however, at the conclusion of the one (1) week extension the new SRO has not corrected the deficiency, the senior SRO and his/her sergeant will meet with the lieutenant. The three will review all related documentation and jointly make a recommendation to the DARE/SRO Captain concerning the approval or disapproval of the new SRO's transfer to the DARE/SRO Unit. The lieutenant will then present the recommendation to the DARE/SRO Captain. The DARE/SRO Captain will have final authority to deny the transfer, continue remedial training, or approve the transfer.

Index

Note: Page numbers with "f" denote figures; "t" tables; "b" boxes.